The frothy edge of the alkaline lake is bordered with elephant grass and acacia trees. In the right foreground, the ropy, sinuous mound is a dome of solidified lava which flowed upward through a crack in the overlying rock layers and cooled upon reaching the surface. It makes a good promontory for pelicans and cormorants. An African fish eagle perches in a drowned snag of acacia, while a small flock of flamingos passes overhead. In the background, the volcano Lemagrut rises over all, five thousand feet higher than it is today.

LUCY'S
CHILD

LUCY'S CHILD

The Discovery of a Human Ancestor

Donald
Johanson
and
James Shreeve

WILLIAM MORROW
AND COMPANY, INC.
NEW YORK

Library of Congress Cataloging-in-Publication Data

Johanson, Donald C.
   Lucy's child: the discovery of a human ancestor / by Donald Johanson
and James Shreeve.
       p.   cm.
   Bibliography: p.
   Includes index.
   ISBN 0-688-06492-2
   1. Johanson, Donald C.   2. Anthropologists—United States—
Biography.   3. Australopithecus afarensis.   4. Fossil man—Africa,
East.   I. Shreeve, James.   II. Title.
GN50.6.J64A3   1989
569'.9—dc20   89-9461
                                                            CIP

Printed in the United States of America

BOOK DESIGN BY NICOLA MAZZELLA

To my wife, Lenora,
for
the magic she has brought into my life
—DJ

To Chris, Marah, Luke, and
Lilah, each one and together
—JS

Acknowledgments

I wish to extend my sincerest appreciation first to my Tanzanian colleagues Mr. Prosper Ndessokia, Mr. Paul Manega, and Mr. Pelagi Kyauka; Dr. Simon Waane, Mr. Amini Mturi, Dr. Abel Nkini, Mrs. Jane Kessy, Mr. Omari Minazi, Mr. Harubu, Mrs. Digna Tilly, and Mr. Shadrack Kamenya in the Tanzanian Department of Antiquities; in the Tanzania National Museums, Dr. Fidelis Masao, co-leader of the Olduvai Research Project and coordinator of the archeological research, and Mzee Mrisho; Dr. Peter Schmidt (now at the University of Florida), Mr. Jonathan Karoma, Professor James Mainoya, and Professor Aswathanaratana at the University of Dar es Salaam; and Professor A. Msangi, Mrs. Lyaruu, Dr. Bitanyi, and Dr. Hirji of the Tanzania Commission for Science and Technology (formerly the National Scientific Research Council). I am deeply indebted to the above-named organizations and to the Tanzanian government generally for constant encouragement, support, and permission to undertake research at Olduvai Gorge and Laetoli.

Thanks are due to the members of the Olduvai project and visiting scientists: Lew Binford and Nancy Stone, George and June Frison, Alberto Angela, Michael Black, Hilary Wright, Jeremy Paul, Robert Drake, Robert Walter, Berhane Asfaw, Gen Suwa, William Kimbel, Carl Swisher, Robert Blumenschine, David Basiji, Stewart Patrick, Walter Hartwig, and Tim White. Thanks to the camp staff at Olduvai who kept us well fed and saw that the camp ran smoothly and to our drivers who could always be counted on to keep us supplied. For logistic assistance in the field I want to thank Sandy Evans and Annie Vincent of Abercrombie and Kent, and Hans Schneider for his aerial acrobatics. The smooth running of the Olduvai Museum and the excellent standard of lectures and guided tours of Olduvai are a result of the dedication of Peter Lauwo and his team, including Lucas Tarimo, John Pareso, Godfrey Olemoita, and Miss Dina.

I have had the delight of working with my close friend and colleague Gerald Eck in the laboratory and in Africa for nearly twenty years, and it is with sincere appreciation that I thank him for his dedication to excellence.

My appreciation also to Ian Tattersall, Fred Grine, Fidelis Masao, Prosper Ndessokia, and Tim White for their careful reading of the completed manuscript and their constructive suggestions. "Biblio Bill" Kimbel was especially helpful for his critical reading of the manuscript at various stages, his invaluable comments, and his considerable bibliographic help.

I am extremely grateful to the National Science Foundation, Gordon Getty, David H. Koch, the Ligabue Research and Study Center, and to Agip Petroleum (ENI) in Rome for their generous financial support. Gordon Hanes provided the necessary funding and expertise to upgrade the windmills and electrical system at the Olduvai Camp.

To Don Cutler and Maria Guarnaschelli for guidance in the stormy world of publishing.

Without the understanding and support of everyone at the Institute of Human Origins, it would have been impossible for this project to have been completed, many thanks to all of my colleagues there. For all of her administrative assistance and her special talent to keep track of my hectic schedule, I want to thank Larissa Smith.

Analysis and comparative study of the OH62 specimen was conducted in Cleveland and I want to especially thank Dr. C. Owen Lovejoy, Mr. Scott Simpson, and Mr. Richard Sherwood at Kent State University for stimulating discussions and assistance in the laboratory. Dr. Bruce Latimer and Mr. Lyman Jellema of the Cleveland Museum of Natural History offered critical help in our comparative studies with the Hamann-Todd Collection. Special gratitude is expressed to Jim Ohman and Picker X-Ray for the generosity and guidance in utilizing Cat-Scan equipment at their plant.

—DONALD JOHANSON

I would like to express my thanks first to the investigators whose generous gift of time and insight made the writing of this book possible. These include Richard Alexander, Lewis Binford, Robert Blumenschine, Henry Bunn, Garniss Curtis, Robert Drake, Gerry Eck, Robert Foley, Clark Howell, Nicholas Humphrey, Bruce Latimer, Owen Lovejoy, Henry McHenry, Todd Olson, Yoel Rak, Peter Rodman, Meredith Small, Randy Susman, Elisabeth Vrba, Bob Walter, and Sherwood Washburn. There are others, equally generous, who deserve thanks, though the book eventually veered away from "the Miocene mess" that drew me to them. These include Peter Andrews, David Frayer, Leonard Greenfield, Terry Harrison, Misha Landau, Lawrence Martin, David Pilbeam, Martin Pickford, Elwyn Simons, Milford Wolpoff, and especially Vincent Sarich.

At Olduvai, I would like to express my gratitude to my hosts Prosper Ndessokia and Gerry Eck; to Berhane Asfaw and Gen Suwa for sharing their floor and passing the time (as well as the bottlecap); to Dr. Bob Walter, bane of dik-diks, and to Jim O'Connell and Kristen Hawkes for bringing some fresh perspective into camp.

In addition to the readers named above, Lew Binford, Robert Foley, John Pfeiffer, Nancy Stone, and Elisabeth Vrba all read chapters of the manuscript and provided many suggestions. I would like to especially thank Tim White for the clarity of his explanations and the rigor and thoroughness of his readings, and express my deep appreciation to my friend Bill Kimbel. These two went far beyond what could be expected of them to help bring this book into being. Victoria Pryor of Arcadia Ltd. is a writer's kind of agent, and I thank her for her part in keeping a sometimes difficult project on course. Maria Guarnaschelli at William Morrow, to my mind the best editor in New York, gave the book her intelligence, her enthusiasm, and the strength of her conviction, and I am very glad to have wandered into her domain.

My affection and gratitude to John Pfeiffer, for the inspiration he exudes and the example he sets as a writer and a friend. Finally, my loving thanks to my wife, Chris, who listened, read, edited, reshuffled, brainstormed, and then patiently listened some more. So selfless and constant was her contribution that it was sometimes all too easy to take it for granted.

—JAMES SHREEVE

OLDUVA

Serengeti

Naisiusiu   MAIN GORGE

FLK-NN

0   500 m

Camp   FLK

Dik-dik Hill   MAIN GORGE

SIDE GORGE

MNK   HWK

The Castle

Museum

THE   JUNCTION

0   1   2   3 km

Fifth Fault

SIDE GORGE

Kelogi

D. Beckner

GORGE

N

Naibor Soit

Second Fault

Junction

ongoro

SERENGETI PLAIN

OLDUVAI
GORGE

Lake
Ndutu

LAETOLI

Lemagrut

0   20 km

Lake Eyasi

Olbalbal

RIFT ESCARPMENT

Lake Natron

Oldoinyo
Lengai

Olmoti

Ngorongoro Crater

Oldeani

EASTERN RIFT VALLEY

Lake
Manyara

Timeline of Hominid Evolution

arboreal ape-like ancestor

terrestrial ape-like ancestor

7

6

5

Australopithecus
afarensis

A. africanus

A. robustus

4

A. boisei

A. aethiopicus

3

Homo habilis

H. neanderthalensis

2

H. erectus

early H. sapiens

1

Millions
of
years
ago

modern H. sapiens

PRESENT

In this rendition of the fossil record for the human family, the known duration of each species is represented by the shadows cast by the figures. The exact relationship between extinct hominid species is a matter of interpretation, and their placement here is not meant to suggest a particular phylogeny. DESIGN AND GRAPHIC BY DOUGLAS BECKNER. AFTER RICHARD HAY, *GEOLOGY OF OLDUVAI GORGE*, UC PRESS, 1976.

Contents

PART I:

Back to Africa

CHAPTER ONE:

Cold Reflections

Once more on my adventure brave and new.
—Robert Browning

AS SOON AS MY EYES opened I reached for my watch on the bed table. I knew already it was close to 3:30 A.M. Over months of restless sleep I'd developed an ability to sense what time it was the moment I found myself awake, as if every minute through the long night had its own familiar scent that I could instantly recognize. Guessing the time had become a sort of grim pleasure, a little bit of consolation for being awake in the first place. It didn't matter whether I was sleeping at home in Berkeley, in a hotel room in Ames, Iowa, or in Addis Ababa, Ethiopia. It made no difference when I went to bed, or what seemed to have brought me out of sleep in the first place— a shout outside the window, a nervous dream, a knotted back muscle. I nearly always guessed within ten minutes of the clock.

I wonder if all insomniacs share this useless expertise.

On this night I was in a room on the second floor of a hotel in Dar es Salaam, Tanzania. In a few days I would join up with colleagues for a field expedition I was leading to Olduvai Gorge, some four-hundred miles to the northwest. I am a paleoanthropologist. I have spent the last twenty years trying to understand the origins of our earliest ancestors—how they evolved from apelike predecessors, what they looked like, how they moved and what they ate, and ultimately, what novelties of behavior led them to become the most powerful beings the world has ever seen. To answer these questions, I look at the evidence they have left behind—primarily fossilized bones. Ironically, most of what we think about these ancient ancestors comes from fossils uncovered only during the past half a century. Olduvai Gorge had played a big part in that new influx of knowledge—so big that anyone about to lead an expedition there should have been able to excuse himself for not being able to sleep. Especially if he had hardly worked in the field for nearly a decade. Especially if it seemed his whole reputation and future in science had come down to what he might find when he got there.

In the dim glow from the window I could just read the watch face: 3:28. Not bad. With a piercing brightness I suddenly remembered the dream that I had been having just before I awoke. I was standing on the edge of a deep, cool lake bordered with palm trees. The surface of the lake was mottled with a shifting swirl of color, as if someone had poured rich pigments into the water and let the currents take them away. People—friends of mine, mostly, fellow anthropologists—emerged from behind the palms, speaking in hushed tones about something of obvious import. In pairs and small groups they approached the lake, and then one by one they dove from the bank, turning somersaults as they fell. Each disappeared into the water without a splash. Suddenly I saw myself running along the bank, waving and shouting. I wanted to dive too, but something kept pulling me back from the edge. I was all alone, but around me the air was filled with a bustling murmur, a sound like that of a hundred whispered conversations taking place all at once. It began to grow cold. I hugged my shoulders and shivered.

Now awake, it struck me that I was in fact shaking with cold. Beneath the window an air-conditioning unit gave forth a pulsating hum, blowing frigid air toward me across the empty twin bed between. I got up to examine the unit, dragging the bedspread along with me. The air conditioner was housed in a long, vented metal box painted the same dingy beige as the walls of the room. Underneath a panel on the top there was a knob. I tried to turn the machine off with my fingers, but the knob refused to budge. The rushing of cold air from the vent below seemed to shoot out and grab hold of my ankles. I hopped up and down on the bare linoleum floor, wrapping the bedspread tighter around me.

On field expeditions I always carry with me an all-purpose tool, one of those ingenious devices that you can transform into a knife, a pair of wire cutters, or fifteen other implements by flipping open the right sequence of hinges. At this moment I desperately needed the thing to become a pair of pliers. I found the tool in the bottom of my duffel bag, and with a little fiddling it assumed its plier persona. The air conditioner hummed and snorted, louder than ever. I grabbed hold of the knob with the pliers and turned it full to the left. Nothing happened. I gave it a full twist to the right. Nothing still.

I yanked off the covers on the unused twin bed and spread them out on my own bed, together with a surprisingly thick blanket I found in the closet. Crawling in, I pulled the covers up to my chin and stared up at the ceiling. Only then did it strike me how strange it was to be lying awake in a hotel room on the tropical African coast, huddled up with cold.

People say I am a lucky man. From 1973 to 1977 I co-led a series of expeditions to Hadar, part of a remote and desolate region of Ethiopia called the Afar Triangle, two hundred miles northeast of Addis Ababa. We returned from these expeditions with fossil specimens beyond our wildest hopes. In 1973, when I was barely out of graduate school, I found a humanlike knee joint that proved beyond doubt that our ancestors walked erect close to three and a half million years ago—long before they developed the big brains that had once been thought to be the hallmark of humanity. The next year, while a colleague and I were looking for fossils on the slope of a gully, just before lunchtime, I looked down and noticed a piece of an elbow joint lying on the ground. A few feet away I spotted the back of a skull. A thighbone turned up next, then some vertebrae, a part of a pelvis, ribs . . . suddenly it dawned on us that we might be standing among the remains of a single humanlike individual, a skeleton more complete and millions of years older than anything like it yet known. That was a lucky prize indeed.

In three weeks' time the expedition team had collected and pieced together nearly half the skeleton, with no duplication of parts that would suggest there was more than one individual. Without question it was a hominid—a member of the family of erect-walking primates to which we, *Homo sapiens,* belong and of which we are the sole surviving representatives. Because of its small size and pelvic structure we could tell that the specimen was female. We named her

"Lucy," after the Beatles song "Lucy in the Sky with Diamonds" that was playing in camp on the day she was lifted from the obscurity of that little gully. It was largely on account of Lucy that our work became known to an audience beyond the scientific community. But my luck did not run out with that find. The next year we returned to Ethiopia and uncovered an even more exciting treasure—a collection of more than two hundred hominid bones from a single site, representing at least thirteen separate individuals, perhaps all struck down in a single event three million years ago. These fossils came to be known as "The First Family." With the consent of the Ethiopian government, we borrowed the whole Hadar collection and took it back to the Cleveland Museum of Natural History, where I was curator, to begin the long process of analysis.

Yes, I have been lucky. The Hadar finds in fact turned out to be a gold mine for all of us who study human origins. Paleoanthropology is a science that is forever rooted in chance. But the luck that nourishes its progress has little to do with the kind that wins a hand of blackjack or finds a parking space at midmorning in downtown San Francisco. Consider what it means to find a hominid skeleton. When an animal—any animal—dies on the savanna, the scent of its decay immediately attracts scavengers of all kinds. They tear apart the hide, devour the soft tissue, crush the bones in their jaws. Very little remains uneaten. The few bone fragments and teeth left behind will be bleached white by the sun, and in three or four years disintegrate into dust. They will leave no trace of their existence.

A very few animal carcasses, however, suffer a different fate. Their scattered remains sink slowly into river silt or lake mud, where they lie hidden from the sun. If the soil is too acidic, the bones will disintegrate after all. With the right chemical balance, however, the process of fossilization begins. It is a slow metamorphosis, still little understood by chemists, of bone tissue into stone. Meanwhile, the centuries pass, piling hundreds of feet of earth between the fossils and the open sky. Of course, not all the fossilized bones will be hominids. Even when two or three hominid species shared the savanna habitat two million years ago, they accounted for a tiny percentage of the mammals found there. And even among the hominid remains that are turned to stone, all but a handful remain deep in the earth, buried forever.

Millions of years after their burial, and only in certain parts of the world, violent shifts of the earth's crust deliver a few bones near to the surface again. Ten thousand more years of rain and wind claw at the ground, and then one day a spring storm flushes the last bit of dirt away: A fossil lies exposed again on a rocky slope. Even then, the chances are fantastically remote that a trained fossil hunter will come snooping around in just the right place. More likely, the bones will just be washed away, or splintered into fragments by years of fluctuating moisture and temperature, or trampled to dust by generations of wildebeest moving across the savanna.

But let's say the fossil hunter does arrive in time. Let's say too that he happens to take precisely the right pattern of footsteps as he edges across the slope. If the sun is slanting down at just the right angle to catch the luster of bone against the muted dust, and if at that moment he should look down and see a fragment of his ancestry gleaming at his feet, then yes, I would say that he is a very lucky person indeed. *Every* fossil find is miraculous. Luck, of course, is not the only advantage one needs to bring into the field; most discoveries have been made by skilled collectors who through years of experience have developed the ability to spot fossils virtually invisible to the untrained eye. Nevertheless, any field-worker who has succeeded against such overwhelming odds acknowledges in his heart the debt he owes to luck—if such an uncanny conspiracy of volcano, earthquake, rain, wind, and time can be distilled into such a paltry word.

In all, the Hadar site yielded up some 6,000 fossils, of which 250 proved to be hominid—jawbones, teeth, skull fragments, limb bones, toes, fingers. In a matter of a few seasons we had multiplied by many times the record available from a crucial and dimly understood period in human evolution, three to three and a half million years ago. Eventually each fossil would play its part in the unfolding of a whole new story of the origin of the human lineage. My colleagues and I proposed a new ancestral species for mankind. Together with one of those colleagues—Tim White of the University of California at Berkeley—I used this new species to construct a new human family tree. Because of Lucy and the other Hadar finds, I would be asked to lecture across the country, appear on television, be host to a popular nature program. With science writer Maitland Edey, I would write a book about the Hadar discoveries and what they tell us of the human career. The book was a best seller, translated into Russian, Dutch, Japanese, and half a dozen other languages. Later I moved to Berkeley to establish a new institution for the study of early man. More interviews would follow, more requests

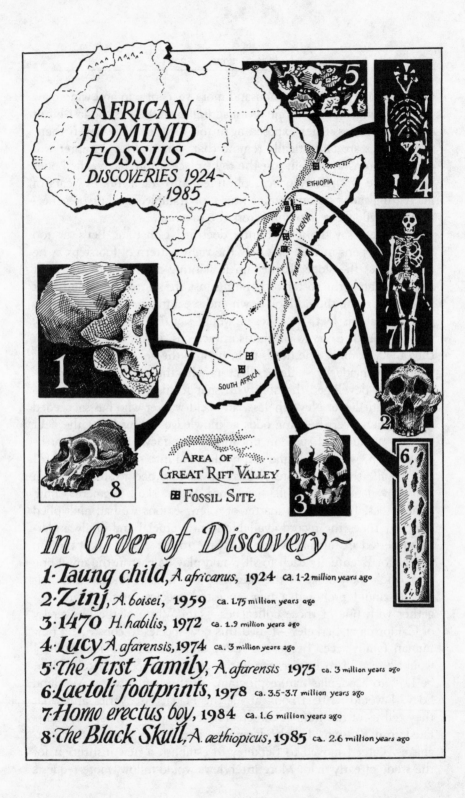

AFRICAN
HOMINID
FOSSILS ~
DISCOVERIES 1924 –
1985

ETHIOPIA

KENYA

TANZANIA

SOUTH AFRICA

AREA OF
GREAT RIFT VALLEY
⊞ FOSSIL SITE

In Order of Discovery ~

1·Taung child, A. africanus, 1924 ca. 1-2 million years ago

2·Zinj, A. boisei, 1959 ca. 1.75 million years ago

3·1470 H. habilis, 1972 ca. 1.9 million years ago

4·Lucy A. afarensis, 1974 ca. 3 million years ago

5·The First Family, A. afarensis 1975 ca. 3 million years ago

6·Laetoli footprints, 1978 ca. 3.5-3.7 million years ago

7·Homo erectus boy, 1984 ca. 1.6 million years ago

8·The Black Skull, A. æthiopicus, 1985 ca. 2.6 million years ago for lectures and appearances. I was introduced to royalty, given awards, and came to be regarded as a public spokesman for American anthropology.

But the celebrity Lucy brought me had a bitter side as well. Along the way, I would also be called a prima donna, a slick operator, a publicity hound. I lost friends, including some of my closest colleagues in the field, whose interpretations of humanity's origins were thrown into serious doubt by Lucy and her Hadar companions. My hopes for a return to Ethiopia to complete the work we had started there would be frustrated again and again. Other field expeditions yielded nothing. Slowly I would come to doubt my famous luck. Eventually I would find myself alone in a hotel room in Dar es Salaam, shivering the night through and wondering whether I was finished as a practicing scientist.

I was pulled from my thoughts by the air conditioner. Suddenly its throaty hum modulated upward to a hysterical whining pitch, shaking its side panels with a sound like the rattling of chains. I was beginning to begrudge it a will of its own, a single-mindedness of purpose that commanded respect. The temperature continued to fall. I pictured myself frozen where I lay, discovered in the morning by a maid. I imagined her standing in the subtropical hallway wearing a light cotton dress with short sleeves: She knocks and enters, letting out a grasp as the arctic air hits her solar plexus. She marvels at the icicles hanging from the lampshades, the walls caked with layers of hoar. Then her eyes reach the bed, and there she finds a man dressed in his socks, underwear and turtleneck, encased in a clear block of ice.

Alarmed by my own imagining, I considered getting up to alert the night manager. But then I remembered a conversation at the hotel front desk, soon after I'd arrived. I'd been traveling for over thirty-six hours and was in need of a shower.

"There doesn't seem to be any hot water in my room," I told the clerk at the desk.

"We're sorry, sir, but the water heater is temporarily out of order," she said.

"How long has it been broken?"

"Just over a year," she said.

I thanked her and went back to my room, reminding myself on the way to take such inconveniences in stride. Westerners have an overblown sense of authority over their environment. We fully *expect* hot water to pour from every faucet, effortlessly and on demand—as if heated water running through a system of metal pipes were part of the natural order, like gravity or sunshine. Each time I come to Africa, I rediscover how much we live at the mercy of our own contrivances. It's not so much that things fail to work; it's that they don't always work according to our expectations of how, when, and in what fashion they *should* work. Once, for example, I found that the phone lines in the city where I was staying were down and it was impossible to call across the street. But the next minute the hotel switchboard put me through on a call to my mother in California, and she sounded as clear as if she had been speaking from the next room.

As if to confirm my thoughts, the air conditioner suddenly gave out a series of bone-jarring thumps and turned itself off, leaving behind a self-satisfied silence, as if it were confident that there was enough cold air stockpiled in the corners to last till morning. But after a few minutes I could sense the warmth begin to creep palpably back into the room, first along the walls and then edging toward the bed in luscious, swirling drafts. I got out of bed, still wrapped in the bedspread, and walked over to the window. Dawn had just touched the tops of the buildings, a soft, pearly light sketching in the outlines of the streetscape—the rambling market buildings and in the near distance the bulky facade of an old office building. Across the road I could just read the CAL TEX sign above a gas station. Not a soul moved. Dar es Salaam in Arabic means "haven of peace," but this was the first time I'd seen it living up to the name. By day it is a bustling metropolis, the sidewalks crowded with people and merchants' stands, the streets laden with overstuffed buses riding low on their suspensions, leaning precariously into every turn.

I worried about what the day would bring. When I'd arrived the morning before, I had been met at the airport by Dr. Fidelis Masao, an archeologist and director of the National Museum of Tanzania. Masao had been instrumental in arranging the Tanzanian side of the expedition to Olduvai. A handsome, athletic man of inexhaustible good spirits, Masao nevertheless had a worried look on his face when he shook my hand.

"We've had a little trouble securing permits for all the visitors to Olduvai," he explained. "The permit to survey at Laetoli has yet to be approved as well."

"Who's not been approved to go yet?" I asked. I tried to sound casual, but was aware of an abrupt sinking sensation, giddily unpleasant.

"Binford and Frison and their wives. Perhaps some others."

This was distressing news. Lewis Binford and George Frison were archeologists we were relying on to bring a fresh perspective to the famous Olduvai excavations of early human-occupation sites. A problem with access to Laetoli, twenty miles to the south, could be even worse. The fossil-bearing deposits at Olduvai end abruptly in a bedrock of basalt 2 million years old; Laetoli's sediments extend backward in time almost twice as far. Already they had yielded a fine collection of hominid teeth and jaws, at 3.5 million years among the oldest indisputable hominids in the world. And it was at Laetoli ten years before that a member of Mary Leakey's team had made the sensational discovery of a trail of footprints, left behind in wet volcanic ash by some ancestors to the human species, 3.5 million years ago. Olduvai was to be our base of operations, but secretly I was pinning my hopes on what we might find at Laetoli.

"How serious a problem is this?" I asked, throwing my suitcase in the trunk of Masao's car. He shrugged.

"I think not very serious. Most everyone is excited about getting things under way."

As we drove into Dar, Masao brought me up to date on the status of preparations, going over arrangements and acquainting me with officials we would need to meet with the next day to secure final permissions for the field. What he said was reassuring. He had scheduled a meeting for me with the Principal Secretary for the Ministry of Community Development Culture, Youth and Sports, responsible for overseeing the joint expedition. Masao believed I would find her wholeheartedly behind the joint Tanzanian-American expedition. Indeed, the permit delays seemed to be simply a matter of bureaucratic tangles. But I still could not get over that sinking feeling—it was all simply too familiar.

In 1982, I had flown into Addis Ababa, Ethiopia, overjoyed to be on the brink, finally, of a return to Hadar. The expedition had been long in coming. Following our successes in the mid-1970s, it was predictable that a certain amount of competition would develop among anthropological teams trying to gain a foothold in the vast, unexplored deposits of the Afar Triangle. Anthropologists tend to be a competitive lot under the best of circumstances. In this case, at stake was nothing less than a share of the richest fossil deposits ever discovered. I was still surprised, however, when rumors began to circulate in Addis that I and my colleagues were incompetent, or that we were intentionally trying to shut others out. There was no truth in any of this. Nevertheless, the government stopped issuing permits to work in the Afar. All we could do was be patient and wait.

By 1982 the situation appeared to be brightening. In the previous fall a team of anthropologists led by Berkeley archeologist Desmond Clark had been granted permission to explore a region in the Afar called the Middle Awash. The team unearthed precious finds in the field, including some four-million-year-old hominid fragments. But the expedition's greatest significance lay in its long-range hopes. Among the members were some young Ethiopians, including Berhane Asfaw, a graduate student in anthropology at Berkeley. He had come to the Afar to accumulate field experience that would serve him well later on. Rather than simply play host to foreign investigators, Ethiopians like Berhane would eventually earn their doctorates and assume responsibility themselves for coordinating the development of their country's spectacular paleoanthropological resources. Meanwhile, through the effort of Desmond and other Berkeley scientists like Tim White, Clark Howell, and myself, a new laboratory and storage facility for collected material had been built at the National Museum—another step toward establishing a nationally based science of anthropology in Ethiopia.

The success of the Middle Awash expedition in 1981 had kindled great hopes for the 1982 trip back to the Afar. But when I had flown into Addis and met Tim at the airport, he had looked nervous and tired.

"Don't rush to unpack," he told me. "We've got trouble, and it looks bad. The government has declared a moratorium on all foreign research into prehistory."

"A ban? Now? How could this happen?"

"That's what we've spent the last week and a half trying to figure out," Tim said. "In a nutshell, until they've got formal guidelines written up for coordinating research, they don't want foreigners in here. To tell you the truth, I can't really argue with that. It's just been too haphazard in the past. Somebody gets a permit, excavates, finds a fossil. Then off it goes on loan, to be studied in some other country, written up in a foreign journal by authors with foreign names.

These are Ethiopian national treasures—you can't blame the people here for wanting to take control of them."

"But that's precisely what you've been trying to accomplish by establishing the center at the National Museum," I said. "Good storage facilities, controlled access to the collection . . ."

"The problem is not what we're doing or not doing. The problem is what some of our so-called colleagues *say* we are doing. There are rumors going around that the new lab is for *our* exclusive use. I've even heard we've begun training Ethiopian students only recently, to make things look good. That really burns me up. Desmond has been training local students and academics in his expeditions for decades."

"So what do we do now?"

"I don't think there's anything we can do to salvage this season's work," Tim said.

He was right. After meeting with officials the next day, it was clear that we would get no closer to Hadar that season. They could give us no guarantee for field research the following year either, or at least until the new regulations could be written and put into effect.

In a profession crowded with *if*'s, it pays to develop a thick-skinned optimism and be prepared for anything. We agreed that we should assemble all the equipment for a field season in 1983, to be ready in case the ban was lifted. Once those details were taken care of I flew home, hoping once again for a chance to be back the following year. But there was not to be any expedition to the Afar in 1983, nor in 1984, nor the year after.

It was easy, under the circumstances, to feel frustrated by all that had happened. A few years earlier, Tim and I had proposed one of the most controversial theories of human evolution in the last fifty years. In a nutshell, we suggested that Lucy's species, which we called *Australopithecus afarensis*, was the common ancestor of all subsequent hominids, including *Homo*. If we were right, then everyone who believed that *Homo* was much older than Lucy's three million years was wrong—including Mary Leakey and her son Richard, who upon the death of his father Louis had assumed his place as the most famous living paleoanthropologist. The evidence Tim and I needed to further test our theory could be found only in the rich deposits of the Great Rift Valley, a Y-shaped scar in the earth's crust that runs north through Tanzania, Kenya, and Ethiopia. This gigantic continental seam has been pulling apart for millions of years, to the accompaniment of volcanoes and earthquakes. The violent geological history of the Rift Valley, delivering long-buried strata to the surface, has been an enormous boon to fossil hunters, including myself.

But Tim and I were affected by rifting of another sort. Ten years earlier, we could regard Mary and Richard Leakey as our friends and collaborators. Since then both of us had feuded openly with the Leakeys, who controlled the principal research sites in Kenya and Tanzania. The likelihood that we would ever be welcomed to work in those countries was extremely remote—and now Ethiopia was indefinitely closed as well. Thus, through a strange mating of ancient geology and modern politics, we were effectively shut out of East Africa, with no access to the fossils that could prove us right or wrong.

As it was, I had little enough time to spend brooding over lost opportunities. In 1981 I had left my position at the Cleveland Museum of Natural History to establish the Institute of Human Origins in Berkeley. For years it had been my dream to create a research institution devoted solely to the study of prehistory—a think tank that would bring together scholars from all over the world, sponsor field expeditions, and serve in training scientists and technicians from the United States and from the countries where the fossils were to be found. Berkeley was a perfect location for such a resource. Though the Institute would not be affiliated with the university, it could work in collaboration with members of the anthropology, earth sciences, and paleontology faculties—people like Clark Howell, Tim White, Desmond Clark, Garniss Curtis, and the others who made Berkeley the leading center for paleoanthropology in the world.

With the help of some interested supporters, IHO began operations in a small basement room just off the Berkeley campus. All we had were some surplus desks, chairs, bookcases, and a rented IBM typewriter. It was a modest beginning, but given time I imagined the Institute maturing into a real force in the field. In my mind's eye I saw shelves upon shelves of fossils and casts accessible to all who would come and take advantage of them. I imagined the most up-to-date radiometric dating labs, where geologists could verify the ages of the latest fossil discoveries. I envisioned casting and molding labs, journal collections, film libraries, publishing enterprises, conferences, symposia—and most of all I imagined IHO field expeditions in operation in East Africa and beyond.

Dreams like that get a hold on you and won't let go. They also take a lot of money to keep alive, much less to mature. We needed two hundred thousand dollars just to start, and another half a million to staff and supply the Institute for the first two years. Far more would have to be raised for the endowment we would eventually require. On our side we had people like Gordon Getty, Diana Holt, Hubert Hudson, David Koch, Arnold and Joan Travis—all of them passionately dedicated supporters who dove headfirst into the challenge of keeping the fledgling Institute on its feet. But I knew that its ultimate survival would depend on my success at raising more funds, more interest, more support. I devoted myself to appearances and lectures, channeling all the honoraria I received back into the Institute. I was learning a lesson from the Louis Leakey School of Anthropology: To keep yourself in the field 10 percent of the time, keep yourself on the stump the other 90 percent.

As a student I had listened enraptured to the famous Dr. Leakey's lectures, and I knew what made them such a success. In spite of how much he privately griped about the demands made upon him, Leakey did not lecture simply to raise money. He lectured because he loved to talk about his work. The huge auditoriums crowded with the curious worked on him like a drug; he inhaled the public's fascination with human beginnings and boomed it back at them a hundredfold. I too counted on the eagerness and expectation of the audiences to inspire me, and they rarely let me down. Wherever I went, people turned out to hear the man who had found Lucy, the man who could tell them more about their origins. I lectured in great halls in New York, Chicago, and Los Angeles. I lectured in college classrooms in Palo Alto and Boston, in high school auditoriums in Salem, Massachusetts, and Bozeman, Montana. The reception was no less energetic overseas. Desmond Clark and I once lectured together in a little town west of Venice called Rovigo, where they packed a thousand people into a tiny amphitheater and turned away hundreds more.

The public interest in human origins is itself a phenomenon to be reckoned with. Ever since Darwin proposed that we were not always as we are now, people have been consumed with an urge to know what we were before. Thomas Huxley, Darwin's champion on the lecture circuit, talked to houses packed with scientists and laypeople alike. When in 1925 an obscure anatomist named Raymond Dart announced that he had identified the skull of a man-ape found in a South African lime quarry, the headlines ran in banners around the world. Louis Leakey never spoke of his discoveries in a lecture hall that wasn't mobbed with people squatting in the aisles and practically hanging from the light fixtures. His son Richard is no less popular today.

Without diminishing the contributions of these investigators, I think that Lucy appeals to the public imagination in a special sense. Part of her attraction is her great age. Lucy burst into the twentieth century straight from the remotest beginnings of our past. Before she was found, paleontologists had only a handful of older specimens presumed to be hominid. A piece of an arm bone believed to be 4 million years old. A shard of lower jaw dated at 5.5 million years. A single molar, half a million years older still.

All of these fossils are weatherbeaten, anonymous fragments. Lucy is not a piece of bone. She is a *skeleton*, a work of organic architecture much like ourselves. We found 40 percent of her on that hillside in Hadar. But because we had pieces from both sides of her body, and because the two sides of a skeleton are mirror images, we were later able to accurately reconstruct over 70 percent of her. There is immense scientific value in a specimen so complete, but Lucy's substantiality excites more than our intellects. Enough of her has been recovered from the past for our imaginations to fix upon and fill in the rest, the way we can gather the gist of a conversation just by listening to stolen snatches of it. Only in this case, it is a conversation taking place three million years in the past.

There is something else that draws us to Lucy, beyond her age and completeness. I know this is a provocative thing to say, but I think Lucy's popularity has a lot to do with her sex. A piece of jaw or a fractured skullcap has no gender, and if we endow them with one, it will tend automatically to be male. In our society male is still the undifferentiated standard, the "generic brand." Lucy becomes all the more recognizable for being female. Whether or not one believes, as I do, that her species was a direct ancestor of humankind, her sex grants her the rudiments of a human identity. And I think it also taps a very deep well in our collective imaginations. In an elusive but powerful sense she represents the Mother, Gaea, Isis—or whatever history has called the fertility that lingers at the beginnings of our conciousness.

As a scientist, I am treading dangerous ground by speaking of Lucy in "mythic" terms. Lucy's real significance, of course, is not to

Ato Woldesembet Abom-isa, storekeeper of the National Museum of Ethiopia, with skeleton of Lucy
DONALD JOHANSON

be found in symbol; it rests in whatever empirical evidence she provides for the understanding of the process of evolution, specifically the evolutionary origins of the human species. Nevertheless, it is important to acknowledge that for many people, the search for those beginnings excites the same regions of the mind once served by the sustaining myths of religion. This places a heavy responsibility on those of us engaged in prehistorical research. When Louis Leakey toured the United States twenty years ago, he told of ancient men at Olduvai building stone dwellings, slaughtering herds of giant buffalo, or tripping up game with rounded stones tied together with thongs. Leakey was speaking the truth as well as he knew it at the time, but much of what he said has since been disputed. In the last decade especially, paleoanthropology has hardened itself as a science, developing ever-more-precise methods and greatly expanding the mass of evidence that lies at its roots.

In the process, a rigorous skepticism has put into shadow the liberally subjective methods that once epitomized the field. The more we know about our origins, the more we must question assumptions long regarded as fact. This critical caution has sometimes been misinterpreted by the so-called "creation scientists" to be a sign of weakening of conviction among paleoanthropologists in the conclusions of evolution science. Just the opposite is the case. It is a sign that paleoanthropology is at last coming of age.

I had an obligation to my field to get that point across to the public—an obligation that seemed on a collision course with the public's expectations of what I had to say. As I lectured around the country, I began to be bothered by the feeling that my words were being interpreted as having some special authority. I looked into the faces in the audience—businessmen stiff in their chairs, undergraduates scribbling wildly in notebooks, elderly people smiling encouragement—and I could see myself mirrored in their eyes as the representative of my own ineffable truth, as if I'd been to the Mount and brought back a crisp, spanking-new version of the Beginning, this one etched in logic and the solemn surety of science. I could see the hunger for that truth in their faces, and hear it repeated in the scratching of the pens in the notebooks. And I could hear its echo in the questions people would ask after the lecture. What makes us human? When did mankind develop a moral sense? What is the future of our species?

Rather than inspire me with self-importance, the questions only filled me with a nagging sense that something was going wrong. I am an anthropologist, not a priest. Donald Johanson's opinions on the future of mankind have no more intrinsic worth than those of any other reasonably informed individual. More to the point, even my views on human origins—including my firmly held interpretation that Lucy's species was the direct ancestor to the human line—are necessarily tentative. I would be the first to reject that hypothesis if new evidence proved it false. But it didn't seem to matter how many qualifiers I put in my talks, how many *maybe*'s and *in my opinion*'s I laced into the text. I stared out at the people and could feel, like a weight, their ready concurrence: *Johanson said it; that's the way it is.*

There was another, more fretful reason for that sense of things-gone-amiss. I knew of course that the people in that auditorium had come to hear me because of what I had already accomplished in the Afar. But how long could I use the past for my platform? Ever since the opening of the Institute in 1981 I had been spending more and more time keeping up with its demands—fund-raising, lecturing, hiring staff, administering. It was not simply the lack of a place to do field research. Less time than I liked to think was going toward the nitty-gritty stuff of the science, the analysis of specimens and the writing of interpretive papers. It was all I could do to keep up with reading the journals in the field. From what I read and through discussions with colleagues, I was well aware of the advances that were taking place. But what part would I play in them? Serving the role of a public spokesman for paleoanthropology suited me well—but did that mean that I could not be a paleoanthropologist at the same time? And if I was no longer a working paleoanthropologist, what right did I have to speak for those who were?

Meanwhile, the Institute was growing toward my original vision. In 1983 we moved into larger quarters, sharing a building, quite amiably, with the Church Divinity School of the Pacific, an Episcopalian seminary. A highly sophisticated laboratory for dating fossil deposits, headed by Garniss Curtis and Bob Drake, was set up in the basement. Upstairs a staff was busily working up ideas, writing grants, drafting papers. Already we had hosted conferences and participated in several expeditions overseas. The paleoanthropological lab downstairs was nearly in place. The chemicals used in casting and molding lay in boxes on the floor. In one corner, a cast of Lucy was spread out on a table among the newly installed fixtures and apparatus. But the blue, felt-topped workbenches were clean, the cabinets uncluttered. With no route back to Africa, it all seemed a magnificent creation waiting for a purpose, like a thoroughbred horse with no track to run upon.

The promise of an end to the frustration came unexpectedly. One day in the spring of 1985 I was dictating some correspondence when Gerry Eck walked into my office. Eck is an old friend and colleague, an expert on fossil monkeys who also happens to be brilliant at managing field expeditions. My first expeditions to Africa had been in the Omo of Ethiopia, and it was "Field Marshal" Eck who had kept the Omo teams fed, supplied, and moving forward on four wheels—a monumental task, given the isolation of the region and the extremities of the climate. Since 1974 he had been teaching at the University of Washington in Seattle.

Eck is never wholly calm—he always seems charged up and ready to do battle with some nagging problem that only he fully appreciates. On that day he was almost twitching with excitement.

"I've got something for you," he said. "It might be nothing, or it might be something very big."

"Let me guess. Richard Leakey's decided to let us have five minutes alone with the Kenya National Museum specimen of our choice."

"This is serious. What do you know about Prosper Ndessokia?"

"He's a Tanzanian student working in the Berkeley paleontology department. He was with Glynn Isaac on the Lake Natron expedition in 1982. Nice guy. Working on baboon skulls."

"Which is why I went over to see him in the first place. But not why I'm here."

"So what's the point?"

"Ndessokia is a paleontologist in the Tanzanian Antiquities Department. According to him, an application from us for a permit to work in Tanzania would be a good idea. It might even get us into Olduvai Gorge."

"Forget it, Gerry. Mary Leakey would never give us permission to work at Olduvai," I said. Mary had retired the previous year and moved to Nairobi to finish writing up a monograph on her most recent excavations at the Gorge. She would still have an interest in what went on there. And though Richard Leakey's authority over research sites ended at the Kenya border, I felt he might have something to say about who worked the Gorge as well.

"That's just what I told Prosper. He was shocked that I thought Mary had any authority over issuing permits for research in Tanzania. That's the Tanzanians' prerogative alone. And that applies to Olduvai, Laetoli, the whole shebang."

"Wait a minute. Are you saying we could work at Olduvai Gorge without Mary's consent?" I asked.

I must admit that at first the notion seemed oddly unsettling. For anyone with an interest in human origins, the name *Olduvai Gorge* is indelibly intertwined with the name *Leakey*. Mary and her husband, Louis, had put Olduvai at the very center of the paleontological map in East Africa with a series of brilliant discoveries beginning in the 1950s. While Louis had subsequently gone off to spend more of his time elsewhere, Mary stayed on at the Gorge, painstakingly excavating the archeological remains. Her monograph on the stone-tool industries at Olduvai is a classic in the field. Laetoli was less well known, but the footprints Mary had found there in 1978 ranked with the greatest discoveries ever made.

"I'm just passing on what Prosper told me," Gerry replied. "According to him, the Tanzanian National Scientific Research Council would be annoyed at the suggestion that we had to get clearance from an Englishwoman or a Kenyan national in order to work their sites, no matter what their last names happen to be. Not to take anything away from Mary Leakey, but she's not going to do more work in Tanzania, living in retirement in Nairobi."

"I think we'd better have a talk with Ndessokia," I said. "Soon."

Temperamentally, Prosper Ndessokia turned out to be as cool and unflappable as Gerry is nervous. His countenance suggested that no matter how chaotic life seemed to be on the outside, matters were slowly moving toward balance and resolution underneath. When we met with him the next day, Prosper bore out everything Gerry had told me, and more. The Tanzanian Department of Antiquities already had formulated ambitious, long-range plans for developing its country's rich prehistorical sites, including the training of Tanzanian scholars. The National Museum had decided to establish a natural-history museum in the regional capital of Arusha, a hundred miles east of Olduvai. But while the future seemed promising, the present was stalled for lack of expertise and funding. Save for the small staff who operated the little museum on the rim of the Gorge, the permanent camp at Olduvai had been vacant since Mary's retirement.

With Prosper's encouragement we applied to the National Scientific Research Council, or Utafiti, for a permit to conduct fieldwork in collaboration with Tanzanian scientists and students for a period of three years. On a morning in early May, my colleague Bill Kimbel greeted me at the door of the Institute, his dark, bearded face lit up by an irrepressible grin. He handed me a telegram from Mrs. A. E. Lyaruu, an official of the Utafiti. APPROVAL HAS BEEN GRANTED TO ENABLE YOU AND YOUR ASSOCIATES UNDERTAKE STUDIES FOR YOUR PROPOSED PROJECT RENEWED PALEOANTHROPOLOGICAL RESEARCH AT OLDUVAI GORGE. . . .

When I read those words my heart soared. Good news had been a long time coming.

"We're *in*, Bill," I yelled, "we're in the Gorge!"

Kimbel frowned. By nature he is cautious and methodical. Over the decade we've spent working together Bill has become accustomed to dampening my outbursts; we joke that he keeps a pitcher of cold water in his desk drawer for just such emergencies.

"Hold on to the hysterics," he answered. "We're not anywhere yet. That piece of paper means nothing until we've got the funding to put us in the field. God knows how we're going to work it out in time for a field season this year. . . ."

"So what's your prognosis, Dr. Killjoy?"

"Get Eck on the phone. I'll call Tim and tell him to get his butt over here. We've got some thinking to do."

Over the next couple of days, Tim, Bill, Prosper, Gerry, and I—along with geologist Bob Drake in the dating lab downstairs—took stock of what had to be done. It was patently clear to us that there was little hope of a full-scale expedition that year. Just to prepare the grant proposals for funding would require a review of all that had already been accomplished at Olduvai Gorge, which was after all the most thoroughly scrutinized piece of anthropological real estate in the world. Next, we would have to mount a convincing argument for why the Gorge deserved more study, not only for the possibilities it held for further hominid discoveries, but for the understanding of its geology, paleontology, archeology, and ancient environments. None of this would be difficult, we thought, but it would be time-consuming. The deadlines for most grant agencies had already passed.

In the end, we decided our best strategy was to take things one at a time. First, conduct a brief survey trip to Olduvai, financed by the Institute, to assess what Olduvai really had to offer. On the way, firm up relationships with the Tanzanians, get to know their priorities. Finally, draft proposals to finance full-scale operations in the summer of 1986. We had decided that Tim, Gerry, Prosper, Bob, and I would make the initial journey to Tanzania in July; Bill would stay behind to keep the Institute running.

Before leaving there was one more matter to attend to. Since our first discussions with Prosper Ndessokia, I had not communicated to Mary Leakey our hopes to renew research at Olduvai Gorge. For reasons I will go into later, my relationship with Mary had collapsed precipitously in 1978, and we had not spoken to each other since. I knew, of course, that she would not be exactly overjoyed to hear that I was going to be leading a research expedition at the site that for so long had been her workplace and her home.

Until we were sure we were going to Olduvai, I saw no reason to upset her by parading our hopes. If I had learned anything about the business of anthropology over the years, it was to resist the temptation to count unhatched chickens. More important, since Olduvai was a Tanzanian site, it was up to the Tanzanians to contact Mary. For us to tacitly seek someone else's blessing on the proposed research seemed to me at the very least inappropriate, and possibly insulting to our hosts.

In June, soon after we had received the telegram from the Utafiti, I sent a letter off to Mary letting her know we had been issued a permit to conduct research in northern Tanzania, specifically at Olduvai Gorge and Laetoli. I also promised to keep her informed of any developments. She wrote me back in July, expressing considerable alarm at our intentions and suggesting that I was "ignorant of the normal scientific procedures under such circumstances."

I have tremendous respect for all that Mary has accomplished at

Dar es Salaam, capital of Tanzania DONALD JOHANSON

Olduvai. But if I had violated any procedures at all, they were the unwritten customs of the "old boy" brand of anthropology that had held sway in East Africa since colonial times: The Leakeys had long held a claim to develop the Gorge, so they were entitled to some influence in deciding who would move in after they were gone. In my mind, however, it was time to stop thinking of the Gorge as the Leakeys' living room. It deserved a future as well as a past, and clearly that future was in the hands of the Tanzanians themselves. I even hoped that once she was over the initial shock, Mary would realize it was better that Olduvai should continue to contribute to paleoanthropology rather than lie fallow while potentially valuable fossils washed away in the seasonal rains.

In early August of 1985 we flew to Dar es Salaam and got down to serious discussions with officials in the Department of Antiquities, the Utafiti, and the University of Dar es Salaam. Our mutual strategies would focus on three areas—research, site management, and education. Well-known areas like Olduvai and Laetoli would be the immediate focus of research, opening up the famous Leakey sites to fresh approaches. Later, Olduvai's extensive facilities could also serve as a launching pad to explore new sites to the south. Plans would be developed to protect Olduvai's fossil deposits, both from the hooves of Maasai cattle and from the hands of the tourists who might unwittingly remove irreplaceable material from the site. A program of teaching and field training would be outlined for Tanzanian students, beginning with Prosper Ndessokia and his counterpart in geology,

Paul Manega. Recommendations would be made on how best to deal with the famous footprints of Laetoli. Several years before, Mary had reburied the footprints in an effort to protect them from the elements. It was a reasonable stopgap measure, but buried footprints were of little use to the science. More important, they were not immune from damage just because they were underground—water could seep down through the soil; acacia roots could burrow down and split them apart. How could the footprints be permanently preserved? Could they be excavated and transported to the proposed new museum in Arusha?

All of this would take years of effort and considerable funding. To start, we would have to convince granting agencies that the primary sites of Olduvai and Laetoli held as much promise as we thought they might. Olduvai does not contain vast, unexplored horizons, as do Hadar or the Omo. Generations of fossil hunters have left their footprints on its slopes; hundreds of pairs of eyes have peered into every little curve and recess in its fabric. Geologists have walked out, labeled, analyzed, and dated its deposits. Archeologists have excavated key sites of hominid activity. Paleontologists have labored over the meaning of its faunal remains, scrapped all their conclusions and worked them through again.

We knew that some observers might see Olduvai as a poor prospect, rather like a bargain bin in a department store that had already been picked through for months by keen-eyed shoppers. But in our calculations, those hundreds of eyes from the past would give scientists studying the Gorge a tremendous advantage over those working newer sites. To anthropologists, Olduvai connotes far more than a site for research. It has come to mean an incomparable body of knowledge, a well of information unmatched in its richness and depth. If there were new clues yet to be squeezed from its horizons, they would lock readily into place amid a complex, highly ordered system of data—rather like new pieces in a jigsaw puzzle that already has its borders complete.

Ten days were all we could afford in the field in 1985, just enough time to sweep quickly through the Gorge and take stock of what it had left to offer. As we climbed over its slopes and gullies, we weren't fooling ourselves about our prospects of making a sensational find. But we could be assured that whatever scraps of wisdom it still had to divulge would be doubly illuminated by all that had gone before.

What we found in those brief few days was more than enough to convince us that the famous old site was far from exhausted. The rains the spring before had been particularly heavy, and everywhere fossil bones and ancient stone tools were eroding from the slopes. In the bottom of one gully Gerry found a partial elephant jaw. A few days later, Bob Drake came upon a complete fossil cranium of a rhino. As a test of one particularly rich slope, four of us cleared every bone fragment and stone tool from a five-by-five-meter square. In thirty minutes of hard work we had recovered over seven hundred bits of bone, eighty-eight tooth fragments, one snake vertebra, and over two-hundred pieces of stone that we could see had been fashioned into crude tools by hominids millions of years in the past. We hoped that the evidence for the sheer density of fossil accumulations would help impress granting agencies of the need to carefully survey the rest of the Gorge the next year. When we returned, the cleaned patch of slope would also show us how much new material had been flushed out by a year of continued erosion. A side trip to Laetoli also revealed rapid erosion of the fossil beds. Numerous mammalian bones, three and a half million years old, dotted the landscape.

Having accomplished as much as we could, we packed up and headed home. Through the fall we worked on grant proposals to the National Science Foundation and the National Geographic Society, outlining an ambitious plan to survey the Gorge over three years and explore Laetoli's bush-covered deposits as well. We invited Lewis Binford and George Frison to join us for a few weeks of the field season. I was particularly interested in what Binford would have to say. A sharp-witted, often caustic iconoclast, Binford had already published a volume highly critical of the Leakeys' interpretations of Olduvai's ancient past, and I knew he would welcome a chance to study the sites firsthand. Meanwhile Bob Walter, a geologist who had helped establish the stratigraphy and dating of the Hadar deposits ten years before, offered ideas for expanding the absolute dating framework of Olduvai's deposits. For the first time in years, I felt charged up and on top of something new, heading a team of professionals with a promising site and an ambitious mission.

Then one day in May, Bill Kimbel came into my office with bad news. Our final proposal to the National Science Foundation had been turned down. The National Geographic Society, which had funded the Leakeys at Olduvai for a quarter of a century, had rejected another proposal a few days before. We called Tim over from his lab on the Berkeley campus, and the three of us grimly shuffled through the stack of grant reviews, trying to understand where we had come up short.

In academic science, grants are awarded or turned down by the "peer review system." Copies of proposals are sent out by the granting agency to other professionals in the field who have the expertise to judge their relative merit. After writing up a critique of the grant, each reviewer summarizes his or her evaluations in a rating, ranging from excellent to poor. After all the reviews are in, the ratings are averaged and the grant is given a rank in relation to all the others being considered. Awards are then made according to how much money is available to each field in that particular granting period— perhaps all of those rated "very good" will be funded, but if money is tight, only those with consistently excellent ratings may be supported. Peer review is by no means a perfect system, but it is one way to ensure that in a highly competitive environment, the best projects have the best chances of being funded.

The anonymous reviews of our proposal were decidedly mixed— not surprising, perhaps, in a field distinguished by some bitter sparring between competing camps.

"With the access, facilities and support of Tanzanian government and researchers, Olduvai should be the big news of the next decade," wrote one reviewer, rating the proposal excellent.

"Not systematic," wrote another, suggesting that the NSF would be paying for scientists simply "to clamber around looking for hominid fossils with absolutely no guarantees." He or she checked the box marked "fair."

"For whatever reasons," noted a third, "neither Olduvai nor Laetoli have been fully tapped for their treasures . . . It is thus rather exciting to see some promise of 'more to come' from a group of experts with extensive field experience, cross-disciplinary ties, and the apparently active support of Tanzanian authorities."

But the next one I turned up in the pile believed just the opposite: "Given the number of years of research at the site, it is not too likely that the team will find much more hominid material." That reviewer also gave us only a fair rating.

"This one says it's 'a huge gamble,' " Bill said, handing me a white sheet. "But it still rates the project 'very good.' What do you make of that?"

"Get a load of this one," Tim grumbled, " 'The dice are heavily loaded against the discovery of significant quantities of good new hominid material.' What is this, a crap shoot?"

" '. . . somewhat improbable that marked new quantities of new hominid specimens will be located,' " I read. "Are you beginning to detect a theme here?"

"Yeah," Tim answered, "Nobody believes Olduvai has anything left to give. Or at least that's what they *say*."

"What do you mean?" Bill asked. "What aren't they saying?"

"I'll paraphrase it for you: 'If you guys think you can go out and raid the Leakeys' garden, go ahead and find your own dough,' " Tim replied.

"I don't hear that," Bill said.

"Then listen to this one," said Tim. " 'Omission of any mention of the Kenya National Museum is so striking that it might be interpreted as deliberate and could suggest that there are political undercurrents in the proposal.' Since when is a proposal for research in Tanzania obligated to mention a museum in a neighboring country, just because its director is Richard Leakey? Forget the undercurrents—the politics in that review are pretty obvious."

Then Tim turned to me with one of his wide, lopsided grins.

"So how about it, Johanson? Don't you think it's time to put on one of your pinstripe suits? There must be some people out there who still think good paleoanthropology is worth supporting."

"We don't have much time," I said. Nobody had an answer to that.

Later that week I was scheduled to participate in a "Celebrity Chef" contest in San Francisco to benefit the March of Dimes. I was looking forward to the event as a break from Institute anxieties. The judges for the contest included some very big names in cuisine—Jeremiah Tower from the Santa Fe Bar and Grill, Wolfgang Puck from Spago's in L.A., and Craig Claiborne, among others. I'm a decent amateur cook, good enough to know that any razzle-dazzle concoctions would not impress chefs of that caliber. Better to keep things simple. I chose a recipe that Gerry Eck had made for me once, chicken thighs prepared in an orange cream sauce.

For a *sous-chef*, I'd drawn Gordon Getty's wife, Ann. We set up our booth at the formal evening gathering and put on aprons. Gordon appointed himself our official cheerleader, and the three of us unwrapped the ingredients and set them out on a board. I browned the chicken in some foaming butter, slapped a cover on, and let it cook for half an hour. Meanwhile, friends drifted by and kibitized. When the thighs were almost done I put them aside, grated some orange and lemon rind into the pan, splashed it with some wine and sherry, and stirred in a half pint of heavy cream. When the sauce was well thickened I eased the chicken thighs back in and let them bathe until they were done. Late in the evening, the prizes were announced by Beverly Sills. The winner for entrée—Chicken Thighs in Orange Cream Sauce. We collected an ice bucket for our efforts.

It was all just a lot of fun, and toward a good cause. But in the back of my mind I couldn't stop worrying about Olduvai. Maybe some of that worry showed on my face.

"Bill Kimbel told me about the grant problems," Gordon said to me when we finally sat down.

"They don't think there's anything left to find," I said.

"So what do you think?"

"Maybe there is, maybe not. But it's wrong to think of the Gorge as some overfarmed piece of bottomland with nothing left to give. Those slopes are steep. One heavy rain could change the whole complexion of the place, I'm sure of it."

"It seems to me that it's worth the gamble," said Gordon. "I'd like to help get you there, this season."

Gordon was a generous benefactor, but he was also a friend. If I were to approach him for funding, it should be under different circumstances.

"You've done a lot for the Institute already," I said, and meant it.

"Then think of me as just another fan of IHO cuisine," Gordon laughed. "I've been swept off my feet by Chicken Thighs à la Eck."

Gordon's "chicken grant" was the beginning of a hectic few days. By the end of the week we had received limited support from two other sources—David Koch and the Ligabue Research and Study Center in Italy. The expedition would not be the full-scale effort we had hoped for, but at least we would be in the field for a couple of months.

On July 12, 1986—two days before my cold encounter with the hotel air conditioner—I had flown to London to catch a KLM flight to Tanzania. We landed at Kilimanjaro International Airport just after midnight, well ahead of schedule. Inside the terminal I drank a cup of coffee and waited to embark on the last leg of the journey to Dar es Salaam. I looked out the observation window at the huge DC-

10 parked on the tarmac, its loading bays flung open, fuel trucks and baggage carts bustling around beneath the plane's enormous silver belly. The flight crew descended the gangway, looking worn out. On the far edge of the circle of light and activity, the eye of an African hare shone briefly, and I could just make out the animal's form as it skipped off down the runway and into the blackness. Finally, we reboarded the plane and took off for Dar. I watched the sun rise from thirty thousand feet.

Fidel Masao was at the airport to meet me, bringing with him the report of possible permit problems. By then I was exhausted, my anxiety caused as much by jet lag as it was by the disconcerting echo, in his news, of Tim's somber greeting at the airport in Addis, four years before.

"There's something else you should know," Masao said as we drove toward Dar. "It seems Mary Leakey has hired a lorry to drive out to Olduvai. From what I hear she's removed everything that wasn't nailed down—tables, chairs, mattresses, beds, stoves, casts, books, perhaps even the windmills and generator. It's hard to know exactly what's going on."

"Wonderful. What's Eck done about it?" I asked. Gerry was scheduled to have arrived in Dar ahead of the rest of us to purchase equipment and supplies. Then he was supposed to move on to Arusha, where we would all rendezvous on the seventeenth.

"What do you think Gerry would do?" Masao grinned. "He's spent the last two weeks putting furniture together, whenever he wasn't searching the bazaars for pots and pans. When he finally had everything packed and ready to go in the Antiquities Department lorry, it blew a cylinder liner. That took two more days to replace."

"Good old Eck. Maybe we'll have edible food out at the camp, maybe not. But he'll make damn sure we have a place to sit and eat it."

Masao dropped me off at my hotel, with a promise to come by after breakfast the next day. I had been traveling for thirty-six hours straight. I discovered the lack of hot water, and after my fruitless inquiry at the desk, settled for a cold sponge bath over the sink. I went to bed with my mind in two worlds. In a few days' time—if all went well—we would be descending the Ngorongoro Crater onto the famous Serengeti Plain, Olduvai Gorge a dark furrow in the near distance. Over and over again my thoughts rehearsed the moment when the camp gate would appear around a bend in the road, the sun drenching the dusty grass in the yard, people moving about, establishing camp, *working* again, at last. I imagined what it would be like if, while "clambering around looking for hominid fossils," we actually found something of value. But I still could not turn off the part of me fretting over details of business back home—phone calls at the Institute I'd left unreturned, budgets and proposals to complete, lectures to prepare. And then there were the permit problems to face in the morning. Through the wall came voices and muted music from a portable tape player. I fell asleep to the sound of a reedy saxophone playing "New York, New York" over the indifferent rhythm of an electric band.

As things turned out, Olduvai Gorge did have another secret to reveal that summer. True to its African nature, the discovery would frustrate all our expectations, cause us grief and confusion, and still leave us utterly enchanted. But I am getting ahead of my story. Like every hominid fossil, the new discovery takes on meaning only in the context of all the discoveries that have come before it. In 1859, in a quiet little cadence to *The Origin of Species*, Charles Darwin hinted that his theory of evolution by natural selection might throw light on the true beginnings of mankind. Ever since, people have been worrying the earth for traces of our ancient ancestors. But the past is very deep, and the clues to its meanings are few and fantastically subtle.

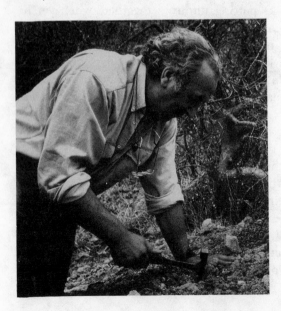

Dr. Giancarlo Ligabue examines fossil-bearing sediments at Olduvai Gorge. The Ligabue Study and Research Center has collaborated with the Olduvai Project since 1986.

CHAPTER TWO:

The Antiquity of Man

*That then this Beginning WAS, is a matter of faith, and so infallible.
WHEN it was, is matter of REASON, and therefore various and
perplex'd.*

—John Donne

"DESCENDED FROM THE APES!" EXCLAIMED the bishop's wife to her
husband. "My dear, let us hope that it is not true, but if it is let us
pray that it will not become generally known."

Her prayers notwithstanding, knowledge of Darwin's theories
spread like a fire through all strata of Victorian society; the first printing
of *The Origin of Species* sold out in one day. The idea of evolution
itself—the development of new species out of older, more primitive
forms—was not original with Darwin, and not everyone in late nine-
teenth-century England found it as unpalatable as the bishop's wife.
There was even something decidedly attractive about the idea. Evolution could be thought of as the biological equivalent of the Victorian faith in progress—a gradual, ladderlike progression of experiments,
each one slightly "more fit" than the last, leading ultimately and
ineluctably to life's supreme refinement, man himself. For a society
bursting with the self-congratulatory fervor of a colonial power and
the potency of an industrial revolution, it took very little effort to
prop this biological premise under a social construct and extend the

ladder just a bit to justify the white man's inherent superiority over the "lesser" peoples of the earth.

Thus evolution was a tolerable concept, even a jolly good idea. What rankled was the mechanism Darwin had proposed as the force driving it forward. According to his theory of natural selection—Darwin's *real* heresy—the physical and biological environment that a species inhabits determines which of its members will survive and reproduce the most offspring. The traits that adapted the surviving individuals to their environment will be more prevalent in the next generation, and the species will evolve accordingly. Thus all species—including our own—are not the end product of some process of internal refinement; they are simply the material result of environmental pressures acting upon random variations in the traits represented in each generation of individuals. This apparent lack of design, divine or otherwise, was distasteful even to many of Darwin's supporters, and his detractors found it completely indigestable. "A law of higgeldy-piggeldy," sneered one eminent scientist, while another cast it as "a moral outrage." No wonder: Through the lenses of Darwinian selection, man was no more the apotheosis of creation than was the mosquito who sucked his blood, or the microbes that lived on his excrement.

Darwinism's strongest opponents were in fact not bishops and their wives, but other scientists. Leading the attack in England was the famous anatomist Richard Owen. Owen attempted to squelch the notion of man's descent from the apes on the basis of explicit anatomical evidence. While he acknowledged some similarities between *Homo sapiens* and the great apes (chimpanzees, gorillas, and orangutans), Owen labored to impress upon his fellow scientists that there were irreconcilable differences as well. He focused in particular on differences in structure that would not be influenced by environmental pressures, and therefore could be counted on to remain the same through unending generations. For example, Owen offered, consider the prominent brow ridges featured on the skulls of gorillas. Since no muscles attach to these ridges, it is hard to envision what behavioral role they might play in the animal's relationship to its environment, and thus they must have remained unchanged through the gorilla's ancestry. Human skulls, on the other hand, do not have prominent brow ridges, and their *absence* would be a human trait no matter how far back in time one wishes to press the mater. Ergo, gorillas and humans can never have been related.

Neandertal skeleton found near La Chapelle-aux-Saints, France, in 1908. The curvatures in the limb bones, and other deformities, led scientists to believe that Neandertal walked with a stooped, bent-kneed gait. Decades later, it was shown that these were in fact the remains of an old individual crippled with arthritis.
JOHN READER/SCIENCE
PHOTO LIBRARY

In 1856—still three years before the publication of Darwin's great work—some strange bones were found by workmen in a quarry cave in the Neander Valley near Düsseldorf, Germany. The bones appeared to be human, but weren't like those of any normal human alive: The leg bones were bowed, the limbs exceptionally robust, with pronounced muscle attachments suggesting enormous strength. The flattened skull of the specimen seemed to have housed a brain just as large as that of a modern human, but Richard Owen notwithstanding, the skull's eye sockets were shaded above by very prominent brow ridges. Whatever Neandertal Man was—and the attempts to answer that question gave vent to some of the most imaginative thinking in the history of science—it could be ignored neither by the evolutionists nor by their opponents.

Like it or not, Darwinian evolution was at least a workable scientific hypothesis. It could make predictions that could then be tested with evidence. Darwin assumed that proof of his theories, including testimony to our common ancestry with the apes, would be borne out from the accumulating fossil record. But two decades after he published *The Descent of Man* in 1871, the evidence for that relationship was still meager. Neandertal Man was about the only material on which to base any judgment. Naturally, the bones drew the intense scrutiny of scientists on both sides. If the pro-Darwinists could prove that they indeed represented some earlier step in the ladder leading to man, then mankind had evolved from a more primitive condition. If the anti-evolutionists could somehow explain them away, then the paleontological evidence for man's more primitive past would be reduced to zero.

From the quarry cave near Düsseldorf the odd bones first made their way to the laboratory of a German anatomist named Hermann Schaaffhausen. After careful study he concluded that they were indeed ancient in origin, belonging to a member of the wild, barbarous races encountered by the Roman armies. Schaaffhausen's paper began to draw fire from the anti-Darwinists when it was translated in England. The German was wrong, they declared—the Neandertal bones were thoroughly modern. The bowlegs and low-slung skull were merely the remains of a mental idiot who had suffered from rickets as a child. The poor wretch had spent his life with his brow furrowed against the pain of the disease—hence the protruberant brow ridges. Another critic named Mayer concluded that the so-called Neandertal Man was in fact a Mongolian Cossack who had deserted from the Russian army chasing Napoleon in 1814. The horseman had apparently taken ill and crawled into the cave to die. As "Darwin's bulldog" Thomas Huxley pointed out, however, Mayer's theory failed to account for how or why the dying Cossack would have climbed sixty feet up a vertical cliff and buried his own bones under two feet of loam.

Even when another Neandertal skull was discovered in a small museum on Gibraltar, the anti-Darwinists proceeded undaunted. One of the most eminent scientists in Europe at the time was the German pathologist Rudolf Virchow, and it was he who offered the final word from the generation of scientists who had been trained before Darwin. Ignoring the Gibraltar skull, Virchow scrutinized the disturbing anomalies of the original Neandertal Man and concluded that the specimen was indeed the remains of a man who had contracted rickets as a child—but he had later been subjected to traumatic blows to the head, finally to be victimized by crippling arthritis as an old man! That such a sorry case should survive into old age, Virchow pronounced, was further proof of its recent origin. Only a civilized, agricultural, *modern* society would care for and protect its weaker members to such an extent.

It was easy for the Darwinists to scoff at such desperate explanations—but they were having their own troubles with Neandertal Man. Early in the debate Huxley published a detailed description of the bones. Although they were certainly more apelike in some respects than anything else known, the fossils failed to prove the direct link he sought between the apes and man. From a collection of modern human skulls Huxley was able to select a series with features leading "by insensible gradations" from an average modern specimen to the Neandertal skull. In other words, it wasn't qualitatively different from present-day *Homo sapiens*. Most important, the cranial capacity was every bit as large as that of modern humans—larger, in fact, than those of many living people. Huxley was forced to conclude that Neandertal was old, but fully human. In so doing, he set a standard for judgment—braininess equals humanness—that would have profound implications for the entire subsequent history of human evolutionary studies.

The generation of anatomists inspired by Darwin and Huxley thus had a firm platform of theory to work upon, as well as the obvious anatomical similarities between humans and apes. But for thirty years they had very little fossil material to support their claim of a biological link. Paleontological digs sprouted up in England, Germany, and France. These efforts provided much-needed refinement in methods for dating fossils, but in spite of fervent nationalistic hopes, they failed to reveal the remains of the first Englishman, German, or Frenchman. Then in the early 1890s, a young eccentric Dutchman named Eugène Dubois made a series of discoveries on the distant island of Java. One of Dubois's finds was a skullcap of what appeared to be a manlike chimpanzee; another was a fossilized femur, or thighbone, of an individual that had clearly walked upright. Dubois decided that both specimens belonged to the same individual: an erect-postured, apelike man he dubbed *Pithecanthropus erectus*. In triumph he proclaimed to colleagues in Europe that the missing link had been found.

After the long drought of fossils, it was inevitable that the arrival of Dubois's collection of bones from Asia should trigger enormous excitement. Wherever he lectured he was honored and applauded for his accomplishment. His interpretations, on the other hand, met with more ambivalence. The femur was clearly manlike, but the skullcap was too thick and primitively featured to satisfy the expectations many scientists had for an ancestor of man. Virchow, for instance, dismissed the skull as belonging to that of a gigantic gibbon. Dubois stuck to his guns nonetheless, carting his box of bones to England to be assessed by Arthur Keith, who was beginning to emerge as one of the prominent anatomists of the time.

Keith agreed with Dubois that the specimens could all be the remains of a single individual, but surprised him by concluding that the skullcap should be classified not as an ape, nor as a transitional form between apes and humans, but as yet another primitive human. Echoing Huxley's belief that big brains meant human beings, Keith maintained that the key question was whether or not the specimen had crossed what he called "the cerebral Rubicon." With a cranial capacity of 860 cubic centimeters, *Pithecanthropus* was certainly no mental giant, but its brain was still twice that of some living human beings—microcephalics—who walked upright and could perform simple tasks. Deeply disappointed by Keith, deprived of the confirmation of his "missing link" by nearly all the authorities of Europe, Dubois grew increasingly bitter and vindictive. Legend has it that he finally buried his precious fossils under the floorboards of his dining room. Certainly he restricted access to them.

Before *Pithecanthropus* was whisked out of sight, the view of it enjoyed by Keith and others was enough to convince them that the bones from Java fitted neatly into a ladderlike progression in the human line. First came *Pithecanthropus*, very old and comparatively small-brained, followed by Neandertal Man with his bigger brain but brutal aspects. Finally came true man. Appealing as it was, that simple scenario was about to fall apart, with Keith an instrumental part of its demise. In 1911 he turned his attention to a skeleton found some years before in a place east of London called Galley Hill. This specimen had always posed a problem: It was discovered in deposits which, by the look of the crude tools and extinct fauna found in them, could be dated with some certainty back to the early Pleistocene age. This meant they were much older than Neandertal, perhaps hundreds of thousands of years old. Yet their anatomy suggested a remarkably modern individual. Most authorities before Keith had concluded that the skeleton was the remains of a modern human who had been buried in ancient earth. But Keith decided that "Galley Hill Man" was in fact an ancient progenitor of modern *Homo*.

If the ancient but big-brained man from Galley Hill was our ancestor, where did that leave the more primitive but *younger Pithecanthropus* and Neandertal specimens? Evolution is usually a one-way street; natural selection would not start with something advanced like a big brain, render it more primitive, and then change it back to an advanced form again. Keith's explanation: The human family tree resembled a bush rather than a ladder.

"In the distant past there was not one kind but a number of very different kinds of men in existence," he told a meeting of the British Association in 1912, "all of which have become extinct except that branch which had given origin to modern man." In other words, his (thoroughly British) Galley Hill Man was the true ancestor; the Neandertal and Java specimens were merely the remains of "degenerate cousins."

Belief in man's antiquity was about to gain considerable new vigor—only this time the evidence was to be literally handcrafted. In November of 1912 the *Manchester Guardian* heralded the discovery of an ancient, large-brained protohuman with the jaw of an ape. From what could be understood from the geological context of the fossil, it was hundreds of thousands of years old. Even more exciting, the specimen had arisen not from some Teuton cave or in far-off Java, but right at home in England, in a gravel pit on a farm near Piltdown Common, Sussex.

Three weeks later the discoverers of the fragments—Charles Dawson, a solicitor and amateur fossil hunter, and Arthur Smith Woodward, a leading British paleontologist—presented their evidence to a packed, expectant meeting of the Geological Society. Arthur Keith was there, and so was Grafton Elliot Smith, another of Britain's anatomical bright lights. Both heralded Piltdown Man as perhaps the most important discovery of fossil human remains ever made. But Keith was skeptical about the "apeness" of the skull. Smith Woodward had pieced together the cranium so that the reconstruction had a brain capacity of only 1,070 cubic centimeters—beneath the range of most modern humans. When Keith performed his own reconstruction from casts of the fragments, *his* Piltdown brain turned out to be almost 50 percent larger. Smith Woodward had botched the reconstruction, said Keith—Piltdown clearly represented a much more modern-looking form than its finders had suggested. Nonsense, countered his opponent, who in any case had always thought Keith's insistence on man's antiquity to be "an amusing evolutionary heresy." In the debate Elliot Smith sided firmly with Smith Woodward, elaborating with crisp authority on the unmistakably apelike characteristics of the skull.

That Elliot Smith, probably the greatest neuroanatomist alive, should subject the Piltdown skull to thorough scrutiny and pronounce it apelike is truly astonishing. The skull was merely that of a modern human being. The jaw, on the other hand, was not merely ape-*like:* It was *ape* (an orangutan, to be precise), carefully stained to look old, its teeth filed down to resemble the flat pattern of wear seen in human teeth. The bones had been deliberately placed together in the gravel pit by human hands, so that they could later be "discovered" by a credulous world. Not just Smith Woodward, Elliot Smith, and Keith were fooled by the deception, but the entire British scientific establishment as well.

It would be over forty years before Piltdown was revealed to be a complete fraud. The identity and motivation of the deceiver still remain a complete mystery—Dawson, Smith Woodward, and Elliot Smith are among those who have been suspected of the crime. Most recently, a case has even been put forth to implicate Sir Arthur Conan Doyle, Sherlock Holmes's creator. Living only a few miles away, this master of mystery was fascinated by the Piltdown dig, possessed the chemical and medical talent needed to doctor the bones, and had a grudge of his own against the British scientific establishment. Who knows?

Most accounts of Piltdown leave that question hanging, and quickly move on to what is assumed to be the realy mystery: *How could so many trained scientists be so utterly and shamefully fooled?* But it's too easy to look down on the British evolutionists' gullibility. Consider how little they had to work with. No reliable dating methods. A bare handful of European finds. Some promising Asian material, locked up out of sight by their embittered proprietor. And then along come these sensational new bones, straight out of the British backyard. Of course the English experts would ponder and poke and wrangle over their meaning, little knowing that their very attention to it confirmed the specimen's legitimacy. And of course they would find in the fossil a fulfillment of their preconceived notions: Preconceptions were all they had. Outside of England, especially in America, Piltdown Man caused a great deal more head scratching, and within a couple of decades, enough new evidence would accumulate to reduce the fossil's status from that of a driving force in human paleontology to that of an annoying conundrum. But in the second decade of the century, England was the hub of paleoanthropology, and Piltdown was the evidence. Any new fossil on the block would have to reckon with its implications.

* * *

The fossil whose discovery marks the beginning of modern paleoanthropology came from an unlikely source. Through his mentor
Elliot Smith, the young Raymond Dart had obtained an appointment
as professor of anatomy at the University of Witwatersrand Medical
School in Johannesburg. In spite of its impressive title, the job was
no plum. In 1922 the university was barely three years old, located
in a glorified gold-mining town composed of little more than tin
shacks. It was a very long way, both geographically and intellec-
tually, from the world center of anatomy and medicine that London
had become.

Dart felt as if he were being sent into exile. When he and his
wife, Dora, arrived at the university medical school, they found the
walls of the vast dissecting room pockmarked by tennis balls—a sign
of its extracurricular use by the students—and the tables littered with
dried-up pieces of corpses. The mind-set of the university authorities
appeared to be equally dessicated; Dart's predecessor had been forced
to resign in disgrace for having committed the crime of divorce, while
Dart himself was regarded as an unfortunate choice as a replacement,
simply because he was an Australian.

For eighteen months the couple struggled to keep their spirits
up and improve upon the abysmal conditions at the school. Then
one day a pupil of Dart's, Josephine Salmons, showed her professor
the fossilized skull of a baboon that she had seen on the mantle of a
friend, a man who directed a limestone-mining operation at Taung
in the Bechuanaland Protectorate. Dart immediately arranged to have
any other fossils uncovered by the mining operation sent to him in
Johannesburg.

According to his own account, the first shipment of fossils arrived at his house on the very day he and Dora were to host a friend's
wedding; Dart himself was to be best man. He postponed dressing
for the occasion and ran out to take delivery of two large wooden
boxes. The first proved to hold nothing of value, but when he ripped
the lid off the second box, he was greeted with the thrill of his life.
On the very top was an endocranial cast, the rough impression of a
brain that sometimes forms when a fossil skull fills up with debris
that later becomes fossilized itself. The rounded stone that Dart held
in his hands showed the bumps and crevices of a living brain, forever
frozen in time. The cast was clearly from the skull of a primate larger
than a baboon.

Dart's neuroanatomical training with Elliot Smith enabled him to recongize immediately a startling feature. Toward the rear of primate brains there are two fissures formed by convolutions in the brain. Elliot Smith had noted that in apes these fissures are close together, while in man they are much farther apart, an indication of the evolutionary expansion of the cerebrum. In this endocast, the fissures were three times as far apart as in any chimpanzee or gorilla Dart had ever seen. Deeper down in the box, he found a large stone with a depression matching the endocast: Faintly visible in the stone were the outlines of the skull and face of the creature.

"Darwin's largely discredited theory that man's early progenitors probably lived in Africa came back to me," he later wrote. "Was I to be the instrument by which his 'missing link' was found?"

While Dart was occupied with thoughts of his place in history, his friend the bridegroom was pounding on the door in impatience. Dart closed up the box, hurriedly affixed his collar and tie, and joined the party just in time to see the wedding come off. As soon as the last guest had left, he returned to the crate. Clearly the next step was to remove the hard limestone matrix, or "breccia," that shrouded the fossil's face. That task would take Dart almost a month. Two days before Christmas of 1924, the rock broke free from the left side, exposing the face of a juvenile individual with a full set of deciduous teeth in place and with the first permanent molars beginning to erupt.

Dart spent the first two weeks of 1925 feverishly writing a report on the find to *Nature,* the prestigious British journal of science. In what has become something of a classic piece of scientific literature, he outlined his reasons for supposing his "Taung child" to represent "an extinct race of apes intermediate between living anthropoids and man." In addition to the position of the brain fissures, the endocast clearly indicated a high, rounded brain quite unlike the flat brains of apes. The forehead rose vertically from the eye orbits without any hint of simian brow ridges. The detentition—though only baby teeth, to be sure—revealed surprisingly humanlike characteristics as well. Perhaps most important for his argument was the position of the foramen magnum, the large hole in the bottom of a skull through which the spinal cord connects with the brain. In apes, which walk on four legs, this hole is located toward the back of the skull. In humans—and in this child from Taung—the foramen magnum is positioned closer to the front, so that the spinal column aligns vertically. This seemed to indicate that the creature had walked erect.

Professor Raymond Dart displays the Taung skull he found in 1924. F. HERHOLDT

Dart proposed for his fossil the ungainly name *Australopithecus afri-canus,* meaning "southern ape of Africa."

It is not too hard to imagine the shock of the editor of *Nature* when he received this astounding document from a practically un-known anatomy professor, writing from a colonial burg on the other edge of the earth. He responded, like a good editor should, by seek-ing commentary from the experts in the field—our old friends Ar-thur Keith, Arthur Smith Woodward, and Grafton Elliot Smith, plus Dr. W. L. H. Duckworth. While the news was filtering through the proper scientific channels in London, however, a reporter in Johan-nesburg had gotten hold of the story. Dart's "missing link" hit the international press on February 4, 1925. Three days before his *Nature* article was even published, Dart had already received two book offers and congratulations telegraphed from all over the world. The com-ments of the four English experts were published only a week later, but by this time their measured scientific opinions were muffled in the popular uproar. APE MAN HAD COMMON SENSE! ran the headlines. MISSING LINK THAT COULD SPEAK!

I wonder sometimes how much the instant removal of the Taung fossil to a public arena may have added to its increasingly chilly reception in scientific circles. Certainly Dart's overenthusiasm for speculation did not set the Great Minds at ease about his reliability as a scientist. Keith, Elliot Smith, and Duckworth all published cautious preliminary opinions congratulating Dart, but emphasized the ape characteristics of the fossil over those hinting at humanity. Smith Woodward's review was the most critical, though he joined the others in reserving final judgment until more evidence was forthcoming. In fairness, Dart *had* presented his evidence a little hastily, and with little background information to draw upon in Johannesburg. Moreover, his specimen was a juvenile—and hence did not carry the same weight of telltale characteristics as a mature individual would.

In the critical few weeks that followed, the experts only hardened in their rejection of Dart's claims. Arthur Keith viewed a plaster cast of the fossil. By this time the evidence had reached the public arena in a literal sense, the cast being placed on display at the Wembley exhibition hall. Keith—Sir Arthur, by this time—was obliged to view the cast along with curious members of the public, a circumstance he found extremely irritating. His final judgment?

"[Dart's] claim is preposterous," Keith wrote in *Nature.* "The skull is that of a young anthropoid ape . . . and showing so many points of affinity with the two living Africa anthropoids, the gorilla and chimpanzee, that there cannot be a moment's hesitation in placing the fossil form in this living group."

I am always willing to forgive judgments based on preconceptions when there is little else to go on—but in this case Keith was granted a look at a most compelling bit of evidence for human evolution, and he *still* managed to miss the point. Obviously his condemnation of *Australopithecus* was based on more than an annoyance at having to rub shoulders with the hoi polloi at Wembley. The real problem was that the Taung fossil posed a formidable challenge to Keith's own belief in the antiquity of man. For Keith, Galley Hill Man was still the perfect fossil. (Alas, it later proved to be nothing more than a modern *Homo sapiens* buried in exposed ancient deposits.) Piltdown, with the brain of a man but the jaws of an ape, was at least an acceptable cousin. But Dart's animal showed just the opposite pattern: the brain of an ape but the jaws and teeth of a human. Sir Arthur had only two choices: reject his own carefully evolved theory or pronounce Dart's preposterous.

Dart had shown the further bad sense to have found his fossil in quite the wrong place. By this time Darwin's prediction of an African origin for mankind was obsolete. Darwinism in general had in fact suffered from a sort of ideological atrophy. The tenets of natural selection had been indsicriminately applied in the interests of racism, eugenics, and laissez-faire capitalism. John Scopes was on trial for teaching evolution in Tennessee, and nobody was particularly anxious to find a resemblance between themselves and a chimpanzee. As the birthplace of mankind, Africa—tropical home of dark-skinned degenerates and uncouth apes—was *out*. Asia, cradle of ancient civilizations, was *in*. The influential American paleontologist Henry Fairfield Osborn, for instance, envisioned an Asian backdrop to man's origin as nobly tempered as a Constable landscape. Far from being suited to hairy apes, Osborn wrote, the ancient Asian environment was "a country of meandering streams, sparse forests, intervening plains and meadowlands. Here alone are rapidly moving quadrupedal and bipedal types evolved; here alone is there a premium on rapid observation, on alert and skillful avoidance of enemies; here alone could the ancestors of man find materials and early acquire the art of fashioning flint and other tools."

Through the late 1920s Osborn and others launched expensive fossil-hunting expeditions to China. These American "Missing Link Expeditions" yielded a great number of dinosaur bones, but no missing links. * Raymond Dart, meanwhile, had not followed up on his

---

*One much more modest Asian expedition did produce a "missing link," of sorts. In 1932, a Yale University graduate student named Edward Lewis returned from the Himalayan foothills with a scrap of fossil jawbone he called *Ramapithecus*. Lewis's claim that his discovery was a hominid was quickly shouted down by far more powerful voices in the science. Discouraged and disgusted, Lewis abandoned paleoanthropology altogether. But thirty years later, his late Miocene jawbone was rediscovered in a drawer by Yale paleontologist Elwyn Simons. Together with his colleague David Pilbeam, Simons convinced most investigators in the 1960s that this species was nothing less than the First Hominid. At the height of its popularity, *Ramapithecus* paraded through a series of Time-Life books as an erect-walking, social, big brained toolmaker—in other words, the quintessential early man. Simons and Pilbeam offered further evidence from the fossil record that the hominid line had diverged from the ape lineage at least fifteen million years ago, and possibly much more.

The legitimacy of *Ramapithecus*'s claim to hominid status was subsequently disputed by biochemists Vincent Sarich and Alan Wilson at Berkeley. They claimed that the very close similarities in some proteins from apes and humans indicated that the hominid line could not have diverged from that of the apes more than five million years ago. If that was true, then *Ramapithecus*, by this time believed to be as old as twelve million years, could not possibly be a hominid. New fossil evidence from the field, as well as subsequent studies showing the near identity in DNA structure between apes and humans, have largely borne them out. *Ramapithecus* is now believed to be an ancestor of the orangutan, and though the accuracy of the so-called "molecular clock" is still under dispute, molecular biology has come to play a critical new role in understanding the human past.

own field with more fossil hunting in South Africa, preferring instead to spend his time developing the neurological and anatomy programs at the medical school. In 1930 he finally got around to completing a detailed monograph on *Australopithecus* and sent it off to the Royal Society in London. The next year he followed up with a visit to London himself, fossil in tow, feeling "confident enough to tackle anything," and sure that in his spiritual home, he could convince his detractors of the significance of Taung.

His timing could not have been worse. Elliot Smith and Keith greeted him warmly, but they were not much interested in hearing his latest thoughts on Taung. Both men were bubbling over with excitement about the recent discovery of Peking Man. After nearly a decade of promise, a quarry in Choukoutien near Peking had finally yielded a magnificent trove of fossils believed to be closely related to Eugène Dubois's *Pithecanthropus erectus*. (The Java and Peking finds were later grouped within the human genus and given the name *Homo erectus*.) The expectations of an Asian origin of man had apparently been fulfilled. In a few days Elliot Smith would be presenting the new finds to the Zoological Society, and he invited Dart along to exhibit his *Australopithecus* skull as well.

At the meeting Elliot Smith launched into a masterful exposition of the significance of Peking Man, replete with projection slides and casts for the audience to handle as he dazzled them with evidence of Peking Man's upright stature, fire-making abilities, and propensity toward cannibalism. It was a tough act to follow. After the applause had subsided Dart was introduced. He appeared at the lectern with only his Taung skull cupped in his hands, and with very little to say that the audience had not already read in print. By the time he was halfway through his presentation, the politely indifferent expressions on the faces before him had shriveled his confidence. His talk trailed off toward its well-known conclusions, and a few days later he left London. Nobody's mind had been changed.

Dart's monograph on *Australopithecus africanus* was never published, and Taung faded out of the public eye. There was no mention of Raymond Dart nor of his find in the most widely read textbook of the time, E. A. Hooton's *Up from the Ape*. Nor did the young Louis Leakey devote a word to Taung in his popular book *Adam's Ancestors*, published in 1934.

Ironically, Leakey himself would be instrumental in bringing the focus on human origins back to Africa. But he too would have his early struggles.

* * *

Louis Leakey's name will forever be linked with Olduvai Gorge, but he was not the first scientist to discover its riches. According to a long-standing legend, on the high plains of the German colony of Tanganyika in 1911, a lepidoperist named Kattwinkel was chasing after a rare butterfly with such rapt attention that he accidentally discovered Olduvai Gorge instead, nearly plunging to his death when the butterfly led him to the brink of the three-hundred-foot drop. Whether or not that story is true, Kattwinkel did bring some mammal fossils back to Germany with him—enough to inspire a legitimate paleontological expedition in 1913 led by Dr. Hans Reck. The enterprise was phenomenally successful. Reck returned with some seventeen hundred fossils, a great deal of information on the geology of the Gorge, and another human fossil to add to the ranks of purported ancestors.

If Reck was right in his assessment, "Oldoway Man" was indeed a prize: a skull and skeleton of an amazingly modern-looking individual, found in deposits he believed to be at least a million years old. But many experts were skeptical, contending that Oldoway Man—like Galley Hill Man—was nothing more than a recent *Homo sapiens* buried by his companions in ancient deposits. To back up his claim, Reck planned another expedition to Olduvai the following year. Then war was declared between Germany and Great Britain, the conflict quickly spreading to their respective colonies in East Africa. The expedition never reached Olduvai, and its exposures lay untouched for over a decade.

Hans Reck would have another shot at defending his Oldoway Man in 1931, thanks to a tirelessly ambitious young man named Louis Leakey. The Kenyan-born son of a missionary, Leakey had formed an early interest in African prehistory and had set his sights on proving that Darwin was right in his prediction of an African origin for man. Though only twenty-eight years old, Leakey had already led two archeological expeditions in Kenya, uncovering some human fossils which he felt bore some powerful resemblances to Oldoway Man. Leakey believed his finds, however, had come from deposits much younger than the ancient sediments Reck claimed to have found at Olduvai. He was all but certain that Reck had been wrong in his assessment of the skeleton's age. And why hadn't Reck found any stone tools on his expedition? Leakey had collected a plethora of stone artifacts from Kenyan sites that he was sure were as old as Olduvai—but Reck insisted there were no tools to be seen at the Gorge. An expedition would clear up these questions, and Leakey invited him along. He even bet the German ten pounds that he could find a stone tool in the Gorge within twenty-four hours of their arrival.

Such spirited self-confidence was typical of Louis Leakey throughout his career. Born in 1903 in a mud house, Leakey grew up among the Kikuyu people that his father sought to convert to Christianity, learning their language before he could speak English and reveling in a boyhood notably free of restrictions. When he was sent away to prep school he found the conventions of polite society almost too much too bear. It was the same at Cambridge University, where Leakey continued to alienate his classmates and scandalize the authorities with his aggressive, boastful manner. He nevertheless graduated with highest honors and greatly impressed his teachers— one of whom was Arthur Keith.

Keith is often credited for planting in Leakey his unwavering conviction in the antiquity of man—a belief that Leakey himself would carry to inspiring heights. But the seed may already have been sown. Deeply religious by nature and training, Louis was still considering following his father's path into the ministry as late as 1925. Leakey was no creationist. But Christianity, unlike many other religions, teaches that man alone is endowed with a soul, and that his dominance over the rest of creation is part of the divine order. It is hard to imagine how Leakey's thinking could *not* have been influenced by a belief in this special relationship between man and the Creator. Such a faith does not easily accommodate the notion of a recent derivation of humanity from a chimpanzee look-alike.

Whatever its roots, Leakey's single-minded quest to prove an early origin for man led him to reject all the candidates that other people had proposed as ancestors. In this he never wavered throughout his long career. Piltdown Man, Neandertal, Java Man, Peking Man, the Taung child—*all* were "aberrant offshoots" to Leakey, the remnants of failed species that probably died out through their inability to compete with "true" *Homo*. The strength of that conviction, fueled by his inexhaustible energy, eventually yielded discoveries that would make Leakey an international celebrity, dragging paleoanthropology into the limelight on the sleeve of his familiar coveralls. But there were decades of frustration first.

The 1931 expedition started off with a bang. The party arrived at the Gorge at 10 A.M. on September 26, and by the next morning

Leakey had found his stone tool, a perfectly shaped hand ax from a period in prehistory called the Acheulean. (Thus in one stroke heralding a magnificent half century of Olduvai archeology, and relieving Hans Reck of ten pounds sterling.) Knowing the Gorge as I do, it is hard to fathom how Reck could have missed finding stone implements on his 1913 excursion—they are lying about all over the place. But it was simply another case of preconception determining the evidence. Reck had been trained in Europe to look for *flint* tools. There is no flint in Olduvai—hence no tools registered in the German's eyes. Leakey, on the other hand, had grown up in Africa and knew what to look for: crude implements made out of quartz, chert, and volcanic rock.

The next round went to Reck. Louis had come to Olduvai almost convinced that Oldoway Man was the product of an intrusive burial. Within four days he had changed his mind, and taken up Reck's position that the skeleton was indeed ancient. Ostensibly it was the presence of very old mammal fossils in the same geological layer where the skeleton had been found that convinced him. But he had been aware of that evidence before he ever arrived. More likely his discovery of an early stone culture tipped the scale in Leakey's mind, never far anyway from coming down on the side of ancient man. In *The Times* of London, Leakey reported that the expedition had established "almost beyond question that the skeleton of a human being found by Professor Reck in 1913 is the oldest known authentic skeleton of *Homo sapiens.*"

Not quite. Within a few months further study of the Olduvai geology and examination of the fossil confirmed that Leakey's first hunch had been right: The skeleton was indeed *Homo sapiens,* but clearly a modern human who had been buried only some twenty thousand years ago in older deposits exposed by faulting. After he had stuck his neck out so far, this could have been a career-crippling revelation for Leakey. But somehow the young Kenyan managed to sidestep the gaff and reemerged with another triumph instead. When Reck left Olduvai to return to Europe, Leakey had continued west to explore some deposits near a place called Kanjera close to Lake Victoria. There he found fragments of two skulls, in sediments containing both hand axes and the remains of a long-extinct species of elephant. Next, at nearby Kanam, a piece of human jaw turned up in what seemed to be even older deposits. Impetuous as ever, Louis concluded that he had found something still older than Reck's Oldoway Man, but with none of the primitive features that damned Piltdown and the Asian finds to dead limbs on the human family tree. He named his discoveries *Homo*.

A few months later, a special conference of learned scientists led by Sir Arthur Smith Woodward—knighted now, like Keith—was convened in London solely to satisfy the experts of the validity of Leakey's claims. On the first day Louis paraded his evidence, and after a second day of laborious discussion, the assembly agreed to his interpretation, congratulating him on what appeared to be a history-making find. But one scientist left the conference harboring some doubts. Percy Boswell, a geologist from the Imperial College in England, was a supporter of Piltdown Man and had been among those who had put the matter of Oldoway Man to rest, so perhaps he was predisposed to look coldly on the claims of "oldest men" from Africa. Whatever his reasons, Boswell picked away at Leakey's evidence with such nagging insistence that Leakey finally requested that the Royal Society provide funds for the geologist to travel down to Lake Victoria and evaluate the sites for himself.

It was an ill-fated trip. When Boswell arrived at Kanjera, Leakey found he could be certain only to within ten yards of the place where he had found the skulls. Kanam was worse. Local fishermen had made off with the iron pegs he had used to mark the fossil's location. A photograph of the site that he had passed around at the London conference proved to be a shot of a place hundreds of yards away. Boswell left the next day, "in a bad humour." Upon his return to England he published in *Nature* a devastating attack on Leakey's claims, concluding that the geological age of the bone fragments from both sites was entirely uncertain.

Nobody was particularly happy about having been misled at the London conference, however unintentionally. Leakey's standing in Cambridge took a further plunge in 1936, when he committed the arch social sin of divorce. He and his wife, Frida, had been spending most of their time apart for two years, and Louis had already begun his relationship with Mary Nicol. They were married soon after the divorce was final. With these two black marks on his record, Leakey would be regarded by much of Cambridge society as persona non grata for the rest of his life.

In the matter of the divorce Louis was right to flout convention: In Mary he had found an entirely more suitable companion than Frida, who much preferred the domesticities of Cambridge to life in the African bush. Leakey's conclusions about the fossils, on the other

Louis Leakey at Olduvai
Gorge holding fragments of
fossil elephant molars
MELVILLE BELL
GROSVENOR/NATIONAL
GEOGRAPHIC SOCIETY

hand, were wrong. The Kanjera and Kanam fossils were merely *Homo sapiens*. Leakey himself never accepted this. His entire subsequent career was in a sense a struggle to shore up respect for his Kanam Man with another sensational discovery. Only the next time he would be sure he had covered his bases.

With the Kanam fiasco, Louis Leakey earned in England the same reputation that had shadowed Raymond Dart when he left for Africa ten years before: that of a headstrong junior scientist too caught up in his own ideas to see straight, and too eager to rush to unfounded conclusions. After his own disastrous trip to London in 1931, Dart had returned to South Africa more inclined than ever to devote himself to the medical school and forget about human fossils. Were it not for the tenacious interest of the famous paleontologist Robert Broom, *Australopithecus*, the fruit of Dart's earlier work, would have died on the vine.

Like Dart and Leakey, Broom was brilliant, unorthodox, and unpredictable. In sheer eccentricity he outdid them both. On fossil-hunting expeditions he always wore an impeccable dark suit and starched collar and tie. By the 1920s he had earned an international reputation for his work illuminating the evolution of reptiles into mammals. At the same time, certain lapses and idiosyncrasies—such as his alleged habit of selling national fossils to foreign museums for personal gain—had provoked the wrath of South African authorities. While undoubtedly the most famous scientist in the country, he was nevertheless refused access to its national museum.

Two weeks after Dart had announced the discovery of the Taung child, Broom burst into the young professor's office. Ignoring Dart, he strode over to a table where the fossil lay and flung himself down on his knees "in adoration of our ancestor." By this time Broom was almost seventy years old and had little expreience in human prehistory. Never mind, he later said—he considered himself the best paleontologist who had ever lived, and was determined to become the best anthropologist as well.

It would be twelve years before Broom could act to support his belief in the Taung child's claim to human ancestry. In 1936 Broom got wind that a general store near the quarry of Sterkfontein was selling fossils as souvenirs. He contacted the man in charge of the mining operation, and nine days after visiting the site for the first time, found a skull embedded in rock-hard breccia. Unlike Dart's find, this skull was that of a mature individual. Thus many of the objections raised to the Taung child simply did not apply. Broom recognized the similarities between his fossil and Dart's but chose to call this one *Plesianthropus transvaalensis*—"near man of the Transvaal." Like Leakey, he was a wanton creator of new names. (We call such liberal taxonomists "splitters"; those who take the opposite tack and group as many fossils as possible under one taxon are called "lumpers.") The specimen was later put into the same taxon as Taung, *Australopithecus africanus*.

Broom's next find clearly deserved a taxonomic niche of its own. With the help of a local schoolboy, he located another hominid skull in the nearby quarry of Kromdraai. There was no doubt that it was an australopithecine, but Broom was amazed by the great thickness of the jaw and the massiveness of its teeth. The specimen was overall larger and more robust than either his first find or Dart's Taung skuil. Broom gave it the name *Paranthropus robustus*, meaning "robust relation of man." Most scientists now consider it to be a different species of the Taung genus: *Australopithecus robustus*.

With its bulky, overblown features, the new fossil did not appear to Broom to be a direct ancestor to man. But he had no doubt that such an ancestor would be found among the *family* of australopithecines that he had done so much to define—small-brained, erect-walking hominids with humanish teeth. The establishment perked up its collective ear, but remained unconvinced. There was still no indisputable evidence that the australopithecines had walked upright, and the line between them and the apes remained indistinct.

Another problem surrounded the question of age. Before 1960, dating hominid remains anywhere in the world was a chancy business, involving a painstaking analysis of the geology and the fauna found associated with the specimen. In places like Olduvai, the millennia had conveniently constructed "layer cakes" of volcanic ash and sediments, which made it simple enough to establish at least *relative* ages. If you found a fossil in an undisturbed layer of gray ash, for example, you could be sure that it was younger than the fossils in the red layer below, and older than those in the brown layer above. But there were no such guidelines to make sense of the South African caves. They were originally formed when surface water trickling down through the porous limestone dissolved minerals underground, leaving hollow spaces in the earth. As the subterranean caves enlarged, the rainwater might eventually open a channel to the surface, allowing bones and debris to fall in or be dragged in by animals. But when? For how long? It is impossible to say exactly, even today. Dart believed his Taung cave deposits were one million years old, but that was only a hunch. Current estimates put it closer to two million.

By the mid-forties—and with considerable help from Broom and the australopithecine remains he continued to uncover—opposition to Dart's original belief in the hominid status of his Taung skull was crumbling. Even Sir Arthur Keith had to admit there were manlike features in the fossils emerging from South Africa. In 1947, the great Oxford anatomist Sir Wilfred Le Gros Clark swooped down on Broom in Pretoria and submitted all the fossils to his own careful analysis. Le Gros Clark was thoroughly won over. From South Africa he traveled to Nairobi, where he was to be a featured participant at the First Pan-African Congress on Prehistory. The Oxford anatomist used the occasion to put his considerable weight behind the australopithecine claim to human ancestry. With that, the issue was all but settled.

Raymond Dart was at the Nairobi meeting to see his twenty-two-year-old claim vindicated at last. So was Robert Broom, then over eighty years old, but with further discoveries still ahead of him. Sir Arthur Keith, Taung's nemesis, was back in England. When he saw the report in *Nature* he retired to his study and drafted a letter to the journal. "I was one of those who took the point of view that when the adult form [of the Taung child] was discovered it would prove to be near akin to the living African anthropoids—the gorilla and chimpanzee," he wrote. "I am now convinced that Professor Dart was right and that I was wrong."

• • •

The organizer behind that landmark congress in Nairobi had been none other than the indefatigable Louis Leakey. The Kanam debacle long since behind him, Leakey had been working at a furious pace through the thirties and forties, opening up archeological sites all over Kenya and Tanzania. Mary Leakey too threw herself into the work, becoming expert on the stone-tool culture of the early humans of East Africa. Louis preferred looking for bones, but it was Mary who in 1948 spotted their most important fossil up to that point, a skull of an early ancestral ape called *Proconsul*. It was Mary who would make the next big find too, something far more intriguing than *Proconsul*.

The Leakeys had resumed intensive research at Olduvai early in the 1950s. They had uncovered tremendous numbers of mammal bones, including baboons the size of gorillas, and pigs as large as modern hippos. A giant buffalo they uncovered sported horns spanning seven feet. All over the Gorge they saw evidence of early human habitation too—stone tools, assemblages of broken mammal bones that seemed to be the remnants of hominid meals, even an ancient bog filled with the bones of giant herbivores believed to be driven to their deaths by ancient hunters. But the piece that would make the whole picture make sense—not man's leavings, but man himself—continued to elude them.

When the Leakeys finally found what they had been searching for over so many years, it was not at all what they had expected. One July morning in 1959, while Louis lay in bed fighting a bout of flu, Mary took her dogs and walked out to a gully, *korongo* in Swahili, that they suspected held evidence of a habitation by ancient humans. Called FLK, the site had been named years before after Louis's first wife: "Frida Leakey Korongo." Mary noticed a skull eroding out of the slope. Brushing away the dirt, she saw what appeared to be some hominid molars poking out of a jaw. She rushed back to camp to tell Louis, who forgot about his fever and followed her back to the site. What he hoped to find, of course, was a vindication of his Kanam Man—a primitive *Homo* who would account for the crudest of the stone tools of Olduvai. But a look at the teeth left him cold.

"Oh, dear," he reportedly said to Mary, "I think it's an australopithecine."

Leakey's initial disappointment must have been sharp. Through the years he had never accepted Dart and Broom's claim that their small-brained primitives were human ancestors. The fact that his opposition was a voice crying in an increasingly lonely wilderness fazed him not one bit. He was convinced the australopithecines were distant cousins, not nearly human enough to have made the tools found at Olduvai. And yet here one of them appeared to be emerging from the earth only a few feet from a scattering of the very same tools. To make things even more bewildering, when Louis and Mary dug out around the specimen they were amazed to find that the teeth Mary had believed to be molars were in fact premolars. The molars themselves proved to be immense, their chewing surfaces as large around as nickels. Indeed, everything about this skull *except* its brain and front teeth was oversized. Its huge face dwarfed even those found on Broom's "robust" skulls, and a massive bony ridge like that of a gorilla rose from the middle of the cranium to provide extra space for the attachment of the huge chewing muscles powering the animal's jaws.

With this astonishing fossil in hand, Leakey found himself on the horns of a dilemma as wide and unwieldy as those of his giant buffalo. If he called the skull *Homo*, he would have to ignore its obviously robust—indeed *hyper*-robust characteristics. His critics would never let him get away with it. But if he called it *Australopithecus*, then he would have to concede that the South African "near men" were toolmakers, and thus on the line to *Homo sapiens* after all. This would tear apart his whole notion of human evolution. There was a way out that he had used before, but he chose not to take it. Much earlier, Leakey had dismissed the specimens of Peking Man found at Choukoutien as not Man but "relics of his meat feast." Perhaps this creature too was simply an australopithecine who had been eaten by whatever true man was making the tools. But he rejected that idea. The skull had been fossilized while still virtually intact, and there were no tool marks anywhere on it. Besides, this skull was a *Leakey* find. He would never have admitted it, but that fact alone made it a little more human.

Leakey's field notes, which I came across when I was in Nairobi in 1980, bear witness to his consternation. In his journal, he made a list of the robustlike characteristics of the fossil, and another list of those traits that aligned it with *Homo*. The robust list was far longer than the *Homo* one. Nevertheless, in the journal he identified the fossil as *Titanohomo mirabilis*, or "miraculous giant man."

"He is a fabulous creation," Leakey wrote, just below a rough sketch of a top view of the FLK skull. "*Titanhomo mirabilis* would be a good name. People will say he is *NOT* human but he is."

A page from Louis Leakey's field diary after the discovery of "Zinjanthropus" in 1959. "He is a fabulous creation," Leakey wrote. "'Titanohomo mirabilis' would be a good name." DONALD JOHANSON

When it came time to publish, however, Leakey dodged the dilemma rather than resolve it. Rejecting both *Homo* and *Australopithecus,* he chose instead an entirely new name for the fossil, *Zinjanthropus boisei.* The genus name meant "East African Man," while the species designation honored Charles Boise, a generous donor. For a nickname Louis and Mary called it "Dear Boy," and another scientist gave it the sobriquet "Nutcracker Man," because of its powerful jaws. But the nickname that stuck was simply "Zinj."

Whatever he called the thing, Leakey was explicit about what it was. In his report to *Nature* he quickly acknowledged the many characteristics it shared with the australopithecines, even placing it within the same subfamily. But then he began to pull *Homo*-like traits from the skull too. His conclusion was that Zinj and the toolmaker were one and the same. After a quarter of a century, Kanam Man had at last found an ally.

Zinjanthropus made the Leakeys' name virtually a household word around the world. It also brought them the support of the National Geographic Society, and an end to the constant financial worries hounding their research. But the notion of a relatively small-brained hominid with millstone molars and the bony crest like that of a gorilla atop its skull did not sit well with many scientists. Leakey had another problem. Estimates of the fossil's age put it at about 600,000 years. According to his own notions on the speed of evolution, this did not allow nearly enough time for this primitive East African Man to develop the anatomical refinements of *Homo sapiens.* Louis explained away this dilemma with typical aplomb: Everybody knows that domesticated animals evolve faster than animals in natural habitats. By developing a tool culture, wasn't man in a sense hurrying up his own evolution by *domesticating himself*?

Possibly—but you can never really put such a subjective idea to the test. Leakey had a knack for weaving arguments together that could make far more preposterous notions ring with truth. In this case, however, his rhetorical skill would not be needed. Almost immediately after the discovery of *Zinjanthropus*, a new chemical method of dating volcanic deposits such as those at Olduvai came up with an objective, verifiable age of 1.75 million years for the FLK site.

Known as potassium-argon dating, the technique was to revolutionize the science of paleoanthropology. It took advantage of the fact that radioactive isotopes in volcanic rock—in this case potassium-40—"decay" into stable compounds—argon gas, in this case—at a steady rate over millions of years. By taking a sample of volcanic crystals and measuring the proportions of radioactive potassium to trapped argon gas, geologists Garniss Curtis and Jack Evernden at Berkeley were able to come up with absolute ages for the volcanic samples. The technique required incredibly sensitive instrumentation, and especially in its early forms, it was very sensitive to error by contamination from rock crystals that might have become mixed into a tuff from other geological strata. It could never be applied, furthermore, to date fossils directly—only the deposits that surrounded them. In spite of these limitations, however, potassium-argon dating provided a longed-for objectivity to a science overloaded with subjective interpretation. In time, the technique would prove to be a more priceless discovery than Zinj himself.

Leakey, of course, embraced the new age of FLK wholeheartedly. Why not? In one stroke his East African Man had been given more than a million extra years in which to evolve. With his customary flourish, Leakey told the readers of *National Geographic* that he had finally uncovered his first true man, the maker of the tools at FLK, "a state of evolution nearer to man as we know him today than to the near-men [i.e., *Australopithecus*] of South Africa." Most of his colleagues, however, were inclined to believe that his first impressions of the skull's identity had been right: It was another, hyper-robust type of australopithecine. Zinj eventually wound up in the same genus, with the formal name *Australopithecus boisei*.

Within a couple of years, news began to trickle in that Leakey had turned up something else at Olduvai, practically right under Zinj's feet. In November 1960, just two months after publication of the

National Geographic article, Louis and Mary's oldest son, Jonathan, was excavating the find of a saber-toothed cat near the FLK site when he uncovered a piece of lower jaw, or mandible, and some cranial fragments belonging to a juvenile hominid. Found in deposits the same age as those surrounding Zinj, the skull bones and teeth of "Johnny's Child" showed none of the merely near-mannish qualities of the previous find. Most important, it bore every sign of a big brain.

Johnny's Child or OH (Olduvai Hominid) 7 as it is officially called, was in fact far more like the true *Homo* Louis had been searching for all his life. But this time Louis swallowed his usual impatience and withheld announcement until the evidence could be studied in depth. With astounding good fortune, the Leakeys' survey team at Olduvai meanwhile found two more skulls bearing similar traits. The first was OH13, an upper and lower jawbone and some cranial fragments. This specimen was given the name Cinderella, or Cindy for short. Soon afterward OH16 was discovered—a trampled cranium and some teeth—near FLK. This one they dubbed George. These skulls echoed the humanlike traits of Johnny's Child. The cranial capacities were large. The cheek teeth—molars and premolars—were narrow, and small relative to the canines. Some hand, foot, and other postcranial bones had also been found at the OH7 site. The hand bones showed a finely developed precision grip, such as a tool user might possess. And the bones of the foot showed evidence of a full bipedal gait.

These traits were more than enough to convince Louis that the new hominids were unqualifiedly *Homo*. But before he could announce a new species, Leakey had another obstacle to overcome. Oddly enough, the genus *Homo* had never been clearly defined in the first place. Most investigators judged the humanness of a fossil skull on the basis of whether it had crossed Arthus Keith's "cerebral Rubicon." Just how big a brain had to be to pass over this famous threshold varied from between 700 and 800 cubic centimeters, depending on who was doing the judging. According to Leakey's colleague Phillip Tobias, the cranial capacity of the new Olduvai specimens averaged around 650 ccs. If they wanted to call them *Homo*, they would have no choice but to declare that the cerebral Rubicon was lower than anyone thought. They nudged it down to 600 ccs, which put their new fossils on the human side. Joined by John Napier, Leakey and Tobias announced their new species in a landmark paper in *Nature* in 1964. Here they said, was the *real* toolmaker of

Olduvai Gorge, *Homo habilis,* or "Handy Man," a name suggested by Raymond Dart. *Zinjanthropus,* never a very convincing human ancestor in the first place, fell in Leakey's estimation to become "an intruder (or a victim) on a *Homo habilis* living site."

In spite of Leakey's careful preparation this time, the announcement of his new *Homo* received a cold reception. On this occasion even the great Wilfred Le Gros Clark, long a Leakey friend and champion, deserted him. In essence, the paleoanthropological community had heard Louis cry "Man!" one time too often. Some scientists were uncomfortable with the fiddling necessary to squeeze *habilis* across Keith's cerebral Rubicon. To make matters worse, the specimens that Tobias had measured were incomplete and badly broken, and some of his colleagues questioned the accuracy of his measurements. On the basis of the teeth, Leakey and his two co-authors were on firmer ground. Using Le Gros Clark's own distinctions between *Homo* and *Australopithecus* teeth, the *habilis* dentitions fell into the former genus.

But it was not enough to win over many converts. Taxonomic "splitting" was out of fashion in the 1960s; most investigators were looking for ways to *reduce* the number of players on the hominid scorecard, not add new ones. Le Gros Clark summed it up for the opposition: All the new specimens from Olduvai Gorge could just as easily be accommodated into Dart's species *Australopithecus africanus.*

"One is led to hope that 'Homo habilis' will disappear as rapidly as he came," he wrote. "It certainly does not appear to merit prolonged controversy."

The most damning element in that response is the quotation marks around the name of the new taxon—little whisk brooms to brush aside its claims to the legitimacy conferred by italics. But in fact *Homo habilis* sparked one of the longest and most prickly controversies in the history of the field—one that would outlive Louis himself and is still very much unresolved. But I'll save that one for later. "Handy Man" was Leakey's final great find; he spent the last decade of his life involved mostly in lecturing and raising funds. He and Mary grew further apart. While Louis was regaling audiences around the world, Mary dug in at Olduvai Gorge. Eventually she would make it her permanent home, coaxing from its karongos an astonishing wealth of information on the stone culture of early man. Meanwhile, the paleoanthropological spotlight shifted its focus north, to fall upon Richard Leakey's finds near Lake Rudolf in Kenya and upon our own discoveries in the Afar of Ethiopia.

PART II:

The Road
to Olduvai

Science must begin with myths, and with the criticism of myths.
—Sir Karl Popper

DAR ES SALAAM IS NOT a beautiful city, but I still enjoy walking its streets. The town has a well-used, frayed look to it, rather like an old pair of shoes that you keep around out of habit and obstinate affection. Built by a sultan of Zanzibar in the 1850s, Dar's fortunes have been scoured by tides of occupation by Arabs, Portuguese, Germans, and finally the British. After independence was declared in 1961, the city blossomed as the capital of the new country of Tanzania, which combined the former colonies of Tanganyika and Zanzibar off its coast. Colonial buildings were converted to civic use, highrises and factories sprouted up, new warehouses and docks cluttered the shore to service trade in the port. But in the 1970s, the development began to lose momentum. In 1985, when I had passed through on our brief excursion to Olduvai, there were signs all around of improving conditions. By the following summer, the capital seemed even more invigorated. Whatever its economic fortunes, Dar never seems dreary or depressed—it is too full of bustling life. I've grown fond of its people, its crowded sidewalks and quirky shops, and the way the city seems to shake the dust off its streets every morning and start over.

For three days following my sleepless night in Dar, I shuttled back and forth between government offices and the National Museum, sometimes alone, sometimes with Fidelis Masao. For the most part the Tanzanian scientists and officials reaffirmed their enthusiastic support for the Olduvai project. Clearance for Lewis Binford and George Frison proved to be merely a matter of writing a letter. On the fifteenth of July I met with Zahra Nuru, the Principal Secretary of the Ministry of Culture, who also turned out to be a linguistic scholar. She asked me many questions about anthropology, while I plumbed her knowledge about the origins of Kiswahili and its spread to become the lingua franca through much of East Africa.

On Thursday the seventeenth I left Dar for the regional capital of Arusha, the research permit for Olduvai tucked safely in my pocket, along with clearances for all scientists and visitors. I had assurances from officials in the Department of Antiquities that the permit to excavate in Laetoli would soon follow. But I was still nagged by doubts. Earlier, I had learned that Richard Leakey had passed on to an official in the department a rumor that we had found two hominid skulls at Olduvai on the scouting expedition the summer before, and had taken them out of the country.

I had heard that Leakey was very angry about our "claim jumping" into his mother's territory, but I was still puzzled and dismayed by this report. It seemed impossible that Richard, with all his experience, would lend credence to such a notion. In all of its glorious history, Olduvai had produced only one complete skull—Zinj—along with a handful of crania like Cindy and Poor George. How could we have located two skulls in a period of ten days? And even if we had made such astounding finds, why in heaven would we try to smuggle them out of Tanzania? Anthropological contraband is useless. You cannot publish anything about it without exposing your theft, but if you don't publish, the material cannot be considered evidence—in effect, it does not exist. Whoever was responsible for the rumor, it indicated that there was still some suspicion of our motives. I would not feel wholly comfortable until all permits were secure.

I checked into the New Arusha Hotel in the early afternoon and called Sandy Evans, the local representative for Abercrombie and Kent, a prestigious outfitter for tourist safaris in East Africa. Through my friendship with Geoffrey and Jorie Kent, I had been able to contract with A&K to provide transportation and a supply line to the Gorge. Sandy told me that Gerry Eck, Lew Binford, and several other members of the expedition had decided not to wait for us and had departed for Olduvai that morning. I couldn't blame them.

Reaching the field becomes an overwhelming urge even for seasoned investigators, growing harder to resist the closer one gets to the destination. I only hoped that Gerry had loaded up on supplies before leaving. The A&K vehicles that would be ferrying us in and out could easily handle the rough road up the Ngorongoro Crater, but Sandy Evans could give me no assurance that supplies of vegetables, flour, and other basics would be routinely available.

Through the afternoon the remaining members of the team gathered at the hotel. Tim White and Berhane Asfaw flew in from Addis Ababa. Gen Suwa, a Japanese graduate student working with Tim, had come in by way of Nairobi. Unfortunately, Gen's luggage did not arrive with him, and he was still out at the airport trying to track it down. Tim and I walked over to the uncompleted National Natural History Museum, housed in what had been the German administrative headquarters for the region before Great Britain took control of the colony after World War I. We hoped that Pelaji Kyauka, the museum's Principal Curator, would be able to join the expedition for a few days; his Land-Rover would be especially useful in transporting the group to Laetoli. Kyauka was eager to go but had too many commitments to leave immediately; if all went well he would follow us out on Monday. When we got back to the New Arusha, Gen Suwa had checked in, looking very ragged and still without his luggage. We were all bushed and retired early.

At seven o'clock the next morning a sleek beige passenger van was waiting for us at the door of the hotel, ABERCROMBIE AND KENT painted in swirling chocolate-colored script across its sides. There was still no sign of Gen's bag; all he had with him was a toothbrush, a camera, a couple of books, and the clothes on his back. It looked as if he would have to stay behind in Arusha, then hitch a ride out with Kyauka on Monday.

"If you leave that suitcase at the mercy of the system, you might never see it again," Tim said over breakfast. "Wait here and get it cleared up. You'll be out in the field soon enough."

Tim has a way of putting things that make it difficult to contradict him, especially if he is your graduate-thesis adviser. But Gen looked ready to burst. After six years of study, poring over specimens in museums, reading paper after paper, the thought of three days cooling his heels in Arusha while the rest of us were trudging over the slopes of the most famous fossil site in the world was obviously a crushing prospect.

"There's nothing in that bag I can't get along without," he muttered into his plate. Tim shook his head and laughed.

"Okay, you win," he said. "Now does anybody want to lend Mr. Suwa a pair of socks and some underwear so we can get out of here and go find some damn hominids?"

We all pitched in some spare clothes to the "Gen Fund" and left his suitcase to its fate. Outside we piled into the waiting van—one of those eight-passenger affairs called "combis" that have been specially customized for wildlife sightseeing. With our blue jeans, T-shirts, and cameras we could easily have been taken for a rather motley group of tourists headed out on safari. Each of us sank into a plush swiveling bucket seat. We made a few stops for bread and other perishables, and then we were finally on the road, heading west out of town. The storefronts soon gave way to a messier conglomeration of long, low industrial buildings, junkyards, and dusty lots, interspersed with greener patches of vegetables. Gradually the green took over. Along both sides of the road groups of women in bright-colored tunics walked in toward town, chatting to each other. Beyond, rows of coffee bushes and banana trees marched away from the road. We passed over several streams, their banks crowded with women washing clothes and children splashing in the water.

The combi purred along, bouncing gently on cushioned shocks. It was an absurdly stylish way to travel to a dig, but before long I decided to stop feeling silly and just enjoy the ride. Out the window, the cultivated greenery gave way to a plain of low yellow grass, pockmarked here and there by isolated rounded hills—the eroded remnants of volcanic cinder cones. As quickly as signs of water disappeared, the human population thinned as well. Soon we were passing only an occasional pedestrian or bicyclist. In the distance I could see a line of cattle moving across the plain, Maasai herdboys lingering by their flanks. For the first time I felt wholly in Africa again, a moving point in an open plain studded with termite mounds and flat-topped acacia trees. Above, the blue vault of the sky straddled the horizons, the entire continent held in its grasp.

When I first set foot in Africa it was under much different circumstances. I was twenty-six at the time, just another graduate student in Clark Howell's lab at the University of Chicago, with nothing more substantial to offer than a little training in archeology and a growing familiarity with the arcana of ape teeth. Having received a small travel grant to Europe to gather data for my doctoral dissertation on chimpanzee dentition, I asked Clark if he would let me extend the trip and join his field expedition in East Africa. To my everlasting joy he agreed.

For three years Howell had been looking for hominid fossils in the Omo of Ethiopia, a one-hundred-square-mile, fossil-rich region named after the river that meanders through it before spilling into Lake Turkana, just over the border in Kenya. The hominid specimens Clark had discovered in the Omo before I arrived were themselves not exceptional, comprised mainly of teeth, jaws, and bone fragments whose telltale surface features had been "rolled"—worn smooth by fast-moving water. In fact, Clark would never make the big find that he hoped for in the region. What the Omo did provide was a uniquely legible record of mammalian evolution over a period from four to one million years ago. Ancient pigs, antelopes, elephants, giraffe—all evolving from the forms found in the older horizons to the forms present in younger one.

These mammal fossils, especially the pigs, proved to be the Omo's ace in the hole. By cataloguing the morphological changes in the pigs found through successive strata, paleontologists could trace the appearance and disappearance of pig species as they flouished and died out through the millennia—in effect, watch evolution proceed. Then, by correlating the species' times of origin and extinction with absolute ages provided by the potassium-argon dating technique, the evolving family lines of pigs themselves became a measure of the passing of time—not just in the Omo, but wherever those pigs could be found, the great gift of the Omo was thus a second yardstick, a way to assign ages to deposits that did not contain volcanic ash and were therefore beyond the reach of the potassium-argon technique. In one case, the Omo's "ace in the hole" would trump a claim for the oldest man ever found.

For me the Omo was a glorious, if sometimes painful, awakening. Like every rookie in the field, I harbored a secret conviction that I would be graced by an impressive find of some sort. Out there was a hominid jaw or skullcap lying in the dust, waiting for Johanson alone to come and complete its destiny. On the flight from Nairobi to the Omo expedition landing strip, I rehearsed the scene over and over in my mind—I saw myself rushing on ahead of the other surveyors, drawn by some magical affinity to the spot where a row of shining teeth was just beginning to erode out of the soil. "Over here! I think I've got something!" I'd shout. Clark Howell and the rest would come running over, flushed and out of breath—"*Good God, the kid's found a perfect mandible. . . .*"

What I really discovered in the Omo was my own ignorance. For my dissertation I had already amassed data on every nook and cranny of a chimpanzee's every tooth, and along the way had devised a new system for comparing dental characteristics of all the apes, including the extinct hominids. But I was pretty naïve about doing paleoanthropology in Africa. Minutes after the plane set down on the expedition landing strip, I was unpacked and out in the field, looking for fossils. That part of my daydream, at least, was coming true. Just as I'd imagined, the ground was practically littered with bone. The problem was that I had no idea what many of the bones were—which were antelope, which were pig, much less which were possible hominid. I also found myself stupified by the heat, on the verge of passing out. Far from bounding on ahead of the group, I was struggling to keep up.

At Clark's suggestion, the next day I stayed in camp in the afternoon, helping him sort through the bags of bones that had been collected from the morning's work. Over the next few weeks I gradually learned to recognize identifying features of the specimens. I also learned how to make myself useful at the routine, apparently trivial tasks essential to keeping an expedition alive. I mapped sites, sorted supplies, fixed vehicles, and helped keep the camp well-fed and happy. In short, I was learning what it takes to organize a field expedition, and after two more seasons in the Omo, I'd become fairly good at it.

In the early 1970s, research in the Omo was mounted jointly by French and American teams, their camps separated by about one mile. The two teams had different research approaches, and the relationship between them was sometimes rather distant and cold. I grew curious, however, about these other scientists living parallel lives so close to our own base of operations, and after a while I took to visiting the French camp, eventually making friends among the staff. That little bit of sociality turned out to have enormous consequence. The connections I made in the French camp led me to a young geologist named Maurice Taieb. Taieb had begun a study of a part of the Awash River valley in the Afar Triangle, a region northeast of Addis Ababa named for the Afar tribe indigenous to the area. He claimed that the deposits looked to be three million years old, and there were fossils lying about all over the place.

"Why don't you come out next year and see for youself?" he said. He made it sound so simple.

I took Taieb up on his invitation, but it was far from simple. Clark Howell objected that I still hadn't finished my doctoral dissertation, and that I had just accepted a teaching position at Case Western Reserve University in Cleveland, and had no business gallivanting around looking for new field sites. And where was I to raise the money for such an expedition? I knew Clark was right, but I still couldn't resist the itch to explore unknown territory. I was eager to get out on my own, and the Afar sounded like the right place to go. I was encouraged in my boldness, moreover, by a clear precedent: Several years earlier, when only twenty-three, Richard Leakey had himself left the Omo expedition and taken off on his own. Richard set up camp at Koobi Fora, a promontory on the eastern shore of Lake Rudolf (now Lake Turkana). When I first met him in Nairobi in 1971, he was already well-known for the fossils he had uncovered at Koobi Fora, in particular a beautifully complete *Australopithecus boisei* skull much like the Zinj fossil his parents had found at Olduvai ten years earlier. If the Afar held anything half so valuable, I wasn't going to wait around for someone else to find it. I managed to scrape together a little grant money; combined with my savings, it would be enough to finance a short exploratory mission to the Afar with Taieb.

In the spring of 1972, before the Omo season was to begin, Taieb and I met in Addis, where we were joined by geologist Jon Kalb. When we reached Hadar, I could see immediately that the gamble had paid off. Just as Taieb had promised, the Hadar deposits were riddled with bone, beautifully preserved mammal fossils dating—from the look of the pigs—from about three million years ago. After three months in the Omo, I flew back to the United States and took up my teaching job, working feverishly through the nights to complete my dissertation. Once I was over that hurdle, I applied to the National Science Foundation for funds to support an expedition to Hadar in 1973. The NSF awarded me $43,000. I wasn't a proven investigator yet, but I was no rookie anymore either.

Fourteen years had passed since then—the most tumultuous period of discovery in the history of my science. Now I was back in Africa once more, the sun-drenched grasslands speeding by on both sides as the combi rolled down the tarmac. I had first traveled that road on my way to visit Olduvai Gorge in 1972 as a guest of Mary Leakey's. I knew Mary only slightly, and I was nervous. She had a reputation for being difficult to get along with; one scientist I had talked to claimed she had thrown him out of camp for having "insulted" one of her dogs by helping it get into the back of a truck. But whatever her reputation, she proved to be invariably friendly toward me in those early days. She liked having someone around who made her feel comfortable, and she seemed to respect the risks I was taking to explore unknown Hadar.

"You were right to get out of the Omo," she told me one evening while we watched the twilight arrive over the Serengeti. "Louis and I told Clark Howell that the Omo was no good, but he wouldn't listen. But you'll find something. You're like a Leakey."

In the fall of 1973 the International Afar Research Expedition established its first camp on a level bluff overlooking the Awash River—a location that provided both water and a little relief from the furnacelike heat of the canyons and gullies where the surveying would actually take place. Taieb plunged headfirst into the task of figuring out the complicated Hadar stratigraphy. The rest of us followed suit. Day after day I scrambled around in the stifling heat. But if there were hominids to be found, they were keeping themselves well hidden. After several weeks of exploring, I had exhausted most of a grant that was supposed to have lasted two years, and had nothing to show for it. I wondered how I was going to explain that to the NSF.

Then, near the limit of our time in the field, Hadar suddenly fulfilled its promise. While surveying late one afternoon with a colleague named Tom Gray, I uncovered what looked to be a monkey's proximal tibia—the top end of a shinbone. A few yards away I noticed a distal femur—the lower end of a thighbone—lying in two pieces on the ground. I put the two pieces of femur together, and then carefully fit them against the tibia. That they matched perfectly was not surprising, since they were the same color, lay next to each other, and thus might be expected to form the knee joint of a single individual. What was surprising—astonishing, in fact—was the *way* they fit together. The thigh and shin bones of monkeys join to form a straight line. These two bones met at an angle, the femur slanting outward. There was only one living primate endowed with such a knee joint. Human femurs angle outward in order to give balance for walking on two legs. I could scarcely believe the evidence in my hands. If our preliminary dating of the Hadar deposits was correct, I was holding the knee joint of a hominid over three million years old: the earliest record of a bipedal ancestor yet discovered.

What *sort* of hominid I had found was anybody's guess. It was impossible to declare an isolated knee joint *Homo, Australopithecus,* or anything else; all I could say for sure was that the creature had been bipedal and surprisingly small. Most of the features on a skeleton that can pin down its identity are found from the neck up. Australopithecine faces, for example, project forward more than human faces do, and their jaws are generally more robustly constructed— presumably better suited to grinding up a diet of tough vegetable matter. Their molars are correspondingly larger, while *Homo*'s back teeth are small relative to their front teeth. And then there is the question of brain size. In the mid 1970s, a large brain was still considered such a hallmark of humanity that for many scientists, a specimen exhibiting that one feature alone would be pronounced human— regardless of less portentous traits that might argue otherwise. What I hoped to find when I returned the next year was a skull to go along with my knee joint, or at least enough of one to tell me what I was dealing with.

The year before, one of Richard Leakey's skilled team of fossil finders had come across just such a find at Koobi Fora. After Richard's wife, Meave, and anatomist Alan Walker had painstakingly reconstructed the skull from hundreds of fragments, it proved to be that of a hominid with a cranial capacity of 775 cubic centimeters— certainly larger than any australopithecine known. But what was most remarkable about the skull was its apparent age. On the basis of a potassium-argon date given to a volcanic tuff above the deposit where the skull had been found, Richard believed it to be 2.9 million years old. Such a date had stunning implications. The oldest known australopithecine was nearly half a million years *younger*. If the skull was *Homo*—and Richard emphatically believed that it was—then Taung and the other australopithecines could be dismissed from the human line after all. Richard had found the Oldest Man. Apparently, Louis Leakey's claims for the antiquity of our ancestry had been vindicated by his son.

By this time, Louis had been in bad health for several years, battling arthritis and a heart condition, refusing to relinquish responsibilities and curtail his schedule of public lectures. His relationship with his second son had long been strained, particularly since Richard's early successes. But when in September Richard brought the new skull from Koobi Fora to show his father, Louis was overjoyed. He believed the fossil—known to the world as KNM 1470, its acces-

Louis Leakey and his son Richard study a fossil cranium together at Koobi Fora, shortly before the elder Leakey's death. Richard's discovery of the Homo habilis skull 1470, which he believed to be close to three million years old, appeared to vindicate his father's belief in the antiquity of Homo. GORDON W. GRAHAM/NATIONAL GEOGRAPHIC SOCIETY

sion number in the Kenya National Museum—to be the final confirmation of *Homo habilis*, the embattled species he had named almost a decade before. With 1470 in hand, Louis's lifelong search for the true early *Homo* had ended. That same evening, Richard drove his father to the airport to catch a plane to London, the first leg of yet another grueling lecture tour of the United States. A few days later, Louis died of a heart attack in a friend's apartment in London.

The 1974 expedition to Hadar would yield its own share of discoveries. First came a series of remarkable finds by Alemayehu Asfaw, an Ethiopian member of the team: three beautifully preserved hominid jaws, two of them found within an hour of each other. One of the local Afar workers turned up a fourth jaw only a few days later. Now we had something more to go on, something with diagnostic possibilities. That the jaws were hominid and not ape was certain—their canines, to take just one example, were much less pronounced than those of gorillas or chimpanzees. But deciding whether the jaws were *Australopithecus* or *Homo* was much harder. Some of their characteristics were clearly primitive. One, for instance, showed a gap between the upper canine teeth and the incisor teeth immediately adjacent—an accommodation for projecting canines in the lower jaw. On the other hand, their molars were smaller than any I'd seen on the robust australopithecines from South Africa, and in general their jaws possessed *Homo*-like proportions. One of the jaws seemed as if it would fit very nicely onto Richard's 1470 skull. But were they really *Homo*? A reliable judgment, if one was there to be made, would require careful study back home in the lab.

In the meantime, it wouldn't hurt to have some other experts take a look at the jaws. I was itching to show them off, hear some opinions. Not everyone works this way. Some of my colleagues like nothing better than to hunker down over an enigmatic bone in solitude, absorbing its every detail before discussing it with other scientists. I am a throw-it-on-the-table type. My best insights are inspired when fossils are passed hand to hand, turned to catch the light, compared, argued over. I decided to write Richard and invite him up to camp.

Richard and his wife, Meave, flew in from Nairobi on November 28, together with Mary and paleontologist John Harris. To my delight, the Leakeys agreed with my suspicions that the jaws might be *Homo*. Richard and Mary were not only my friends, they were also the most famous investigators working in East Africa. Their opinion carried a lot of weight with me. If the jaws were indeed *Homo*, then I had found in the Afar no less than the oldest trace of man's tenure on the earth. That is a seductive idea for any physical anthropologist. For someone as young and ambitious as I was, it was almost irresistible.

After seeing my visitors off on the morning of November 30, I decided to remain in camp and begin planning a paper that would describe the jaws and tentatively assign them to the genus *Homo*. That was the morning that Tom Gray came into my tent and asked if I could show him a section of the site named Locality 162. A few hours later Lucy arrived in my life.

Before leaving camp that morning I'd sensed that we might find something significant. I seldom get that feeling, and when I do it usually pans out. But after surveying for several hours at Locality 162, we had uncovered no more than some horse and antelope teeth, a fragment of a pig skull, and a piece of monkey jaw. None of this added anything new to our overflowing mammal collection. It was close to noon and there was not much point in continuing. Most fossils are discovered in the early morning or late afternoon, when the oblique rays of the sun lend shadow and definition to objects on the ground. As the sun climbs higher in the sky, the gravel and rocks and bone all seem to fade into each other. At midday you could be staring right at a perfect arcade of teeth and not see a thing.

We headed back to the Land-Rover through a little gully on the other side of a rise. As always, I kept my eyes moving along the ground with every step. I knew that the gully had been worked over a couple of times before, so I wasn't surprised when it appeared to be empty of bones. But just as I turned to leave, I saw what appeared to be a fragment of an elbow joint lying at the bottom of the slope above. Tom and I knelt down to examine the thing. It was small, very small, but unquestionably a hominid. Then I spotted a piece of skull next to Tom's hand, and suddenly we seemed to be surrounded by hominid bones—a femur, a piece of pelvis, ribs, some vertebrae. For a while we just groped around from one bone to the next, too stunned to speak. It occurred to me right away that perhaps all these bones might belong to a single individual. But I was afraid to speak that thought out loud, as if by doing so I would break the spell, and we would once again find ourselves standing in an unremarkable, boneless little gully in the middle of nowhere. Tom, on the other hand, could not hold in his excitement. He let out a yell, and then I heard myself yelling too, and we were hugging each other and dancing up and down in the heat.

As we brought the fragments of her skeleton back to camp over the next few weeks, we laid them out as they would have been in life—vertebrae in line, rib fragments branching out in parallel arcs, the top of the thighbone firmly nestled in its pelvic socket. The effect was uncanny. We all shared the feeling that this ancient creature was being re-created, coming to life before our eyes. I knew as well that as Lucy emerged, my own life was irrevocably changing. Whatever she turned out to be, Lucy was sure to be one of the biggest finds of the century. To point to another skeleton in anywhere near the same state of preservation, one would have to advance in time all the way to the Neandertal fossils from the middle Paleolithic period in Europe, 75,000 years ago. This one was easily forty times as old. If I had made a significant find with the knee joint the year before, with Lucy I had made a reputation.

She did nothing, however, to clarify the identity of the existing Hadar collection. I had been leaning toward calling the jaws *Homo*, but the new skeleton brought me up short. The pieces of mandible recovered from the Lucy site told us that her lower jaw was V-shaped, a decidedly more primitive condition than anything associated with *Homo*. Her first premolars, the teeth directly behind the canines, had only one cusp as opposed to the two found in *Homo*—another primitive trait. The cranial fragments meanwhile suggested a very small brain, not much larger than that of a chimpanzee; indeed, at three and a half feet tall, Lucy was about the size of a chimp. Much as I wanted to believe that Lucy was human, I couldn't bring myself to accept anything so small and apparently primitive as *Homo.* Either I was wrong on my judgment about Alemayehu's jaws, or else we had in fact discovered *two* species in Hadar, both of which had lived approximately three million years ago. I was pretty sure I knew which alternative was right, but I needed more time to study the collection before committing myself in print.

Even more than time, I desperately needed additional evidence. The Hadar deposits did not disappoint us. The field season the following year yielded up a discovery surpassing even Lucy: a superb trove of almost two hundred hominid fossils from a location called Site 333, including more jaws, leg bones, teeth, foot and hand bones, ribs, vertebrae, cranial fragments, even a part of an infant skull. Oddly, there were very few other animals represented at the site— nothing but hominids littering a steep hillside, and even more when we began systematically to sift through the eroded deposits.

The Site 333 specimens came to be known as "the first family." Whether they were really the remains of a hominid family group is impossible to say, but they were certainly all members of one species. What that gave us was a glimpse through a rarely opened window— a healthy sample of *variation* among individuals of an ancestral population. That is what makes them priceless. It would be very convenient for paleoanthropologists if all the scattered individuals in an extinct species looked just like each other and nothing like the individuals of any other species—but evolution doesn't box life into neat compartments like that. By definition, two closely related species will have a good many traits in common, many of which will show up in the fossil record, while important differences between the species do not. With fossils so scarce and widely distributed, how can one tell which traits are unique to a single species, and which ones are shared?

Compounding this problem is its opposite: Individuals of the *same* species can exhibit a remarkable degree of variation among themselves. A million years from now, if the proverbial anthropologist from Mars comes across the skeleton of a female pygmy in central Africa and then finds another skeleton—this one a male Eskimo— in Alaska, will he know enough to assign both to the species *Homo sapiens*? Maybe not. Even within single populations our species shows marked differences in brain size, facial characteristics, jaw shape, and countless other traits. But if this same alien bone hunter found thirteen perfect skulls together in one place, all of them very much alike, he would probably make the logical assumption that they were members of the same species, even though they were all a little different from each other.

We did not find thirteen perfect skulls at Site 333, but we found the next best thing—fragments of at least thirteen individuals, including nine adults showing considerable variation in size. A cursory study of the new bones led me to suspect that they must belong to the same early *Homo* species as the jaws we'd found the year before. At the end of the season I stopped in Nairobi to show the new collection of fossils to the Leakeys. A number of other scientists were gathered in the National Museum, mostly those working with Richard at Koobi Fora and with Mary at her site of Laetoli in Tanzania. I knew that the fossils would cause a lot of stir. We laid them out on a table and set to talking, everyone picking up bones, rotating them this way and that to catch the light, asking questions, arguing and exclaiming. With the "first family" specimens before them, Richard and Mary were satisfied that *Homo* was indeed present in the Afar three million years ago, though it was obviously a very primitive type. They were convinced, however, that little Lucy was something else entirely.

I left believing they were right—enough at least to present the fossils in print for the first time. In March of 1976 Taieb and I published an article in *Nature* on the Hadar fossils, tentatively suggesting that some of the fossils from the first two seasons showed affinities with *Australopithecus*, while others resembled *Homo*. The 1976–77 field season only produced more evidence to strengthen my conviction. Meanwhile, one of Taieb's colleagues discovered some very primitive stone tools in a gully about three miles from camp. The ability to manufacture implements, no matter how crude, is still taken by most anthropologists to represent the beginnings of human culture. Judging from the potassium-argon dates from a nearby site, these tools were perhaps 2.6 million years old—the most ancient known signature of man's technological ability.

Though the evidence in Ethiopia was still circumstantial, it all pointed to one thing: As long as three million years ago, *Homo* had dwelt in Hadar side by side with *Australopithecus*. The Leakeys had already declared the same to be true at Koobi Fora between three and two million, and at Olduvai between two and one million. All along the Rift Valley, a simple, coherent pattern in time was taking shape. Etched into the center of that pattern—clear, distinct, and very old indeed—was humankind, just as Louis Leakey had predicted. No evidence existed that *Australopithecus* was anything more than the "aberrant offshoot" that the Leakeys had long maintained.

The trouble with simple, coherent patterns is that they tend to obscure messier truths. The evidence from Hadar, Laetoli, and Koobi Fora were about to be marshaled to tell a quite different story, one that would seriously cast doubt upon the Leakeys' familial claim for the antiquity of man. Ironically, the two scientists who would challenge that theory were both present at that meeting in Richard's lab in 1975, when I spread the Hadar specimens around for all to see. One of those scientists was a wiry, long-haired paleoanthropologist named Tim White. I would never have believed it at the time, but the other challenger would be myself.

Fifty miles southwest of Arusha, a dirt road branches off the main route and heads west toward the highlands. As the combi planed over potholes and "washboard" ridges, the landscape grew rockier, the road gouged periodically by old stream beds. Tim peered out of the window, scanning the countryside for exposures. Somebody had told him they had flown over some promising outcrops in the area. It was unlikely that we would pass anything worth investigating right alongside the road, which after all had been used by fossil hunters traveling to and from the Gorge for decades. Tim's vigilance was extreme, and not in the least bit out of character. At the same time he threw questions over his shoulder at Gen, debriefing his student on a cast of an enigmatic skull Gen had examined in Nairobi—the latest hominid emerging from Richard Leakey's dig west of Lake Turkana in Kenya.

After another hour I could just make out the highlands in the haze. Since my first trip to Olduvai in 1972 I had traveled this route many times, but for Gen and Berhane it was all fresh. We spent the time going over surveying strategies, catching up on news, joking nervously about the food we'd be eating for the next several weeks at the Olduvai camp. During field expeditions, Gerry Eck's culinary standards have been known to retreat somewhat from the heights reached by his Chicken Thighs in Orange Cream Sauce. On the scouting expedition the summer before, an endless succession of meals of goat meat and cabbage soup had left us—inexplicably—with a collective longing for peanut butter. There are plenty of peanuts in Tanzania, but I had never seen a single jar of peanut butter. Now I had a surprise for everybody. I reached under my seat and pulled out of my bag a small Waring blender I had packed along with the rest of my gear.

"What the hell is that?" Gen asked.

"Our salvation," I said. "Put peanuts in here, turn it on, and what have you got? Goat antidote."

"You're a clever son of a bitch, Johanson," Tim laughed. "But Mary's got your number. What if she's dismantled the windmills? No windmills, no electricity—no peanut butter. Foiled by the Leakeys again!"

Tim jokes a lot about the Leakeys. It would be safer for everyone to say that it's all meant in good fun, but in fact Tim's battles with Richard and Mary in the past have scarred him deeper than that. Behind his jibes are the memories of the mutual respect and affection he once shared with them both—emotions long since eroded. Tim is too much of a professional to let hard feelings hamper his work. On the contrary, I'd say they push him forward. Whether it stems from his relationship with the Leakeys or from some more distant hurt, there is a driving anger inside him that he harnesses to serve a frighteningly acute, unsparing intellect. I'll admit it makes him difficult to work with for a lot of people. It also makes him a terrific paleoanthropologist, possibly the best. "A damn magician with a bone," as one colleague put it.

When I met him in Richard's lab in 1975, Tim was a promising graduate student: very much a "member of the firm," as those who worked under Leakey's direction were called. Unlike the fractious expeditions that I'd often been associated with, Leakey's field programs were (and still are) models of teamwork. The scientists were bound together by an explicit code of loyalty to the expedition's goals and to those of its leader. This unusual commitment helped to make the Koobi Fora Research Project among the most productive paleoanthropological enterprises in history. But it also tended to blunt expressions of independence. I remembered listening to one of Richard's closest colleagues give a talk at a meeting in London the previous February. The speaker was occasionally prefixing his sentences with the phrase "I believe . . ." Then Richard caught his attention and shoved a piece of paper under his nose. The colleague quickly read the note and then went on with his talk—emphasizing each point thereafter with the phrase "*We* believe . . ." Richard was leaning back in his seat, the edges of a grin showing around his curve-stemmed pipe.

Leakey is known to return such loyalty in kind. He is also a shrewd judge of talent. The year before, Tim had been invited to work under John Harris, the Koobi Fora expedition's paleontologist. Tim's work had already kindled Leakey's interest and respect. He was also appreciated for how well he got along with the "Hominid Gang," the team of expert African fossil hunters that had found most of the Koobi Fora treasures. Whatever bitterness lay ahead in their relationship, in 1975 Tim White was Richard's man. Very soon, however, he would find himself deeply embroiled in the most troubling affair Richard had encountered in his brilliant young career. On the surface, the trouble amounted to nothing more than a disagreement about two different techniques for dating a particular layer of volcanic ash. But resting in the balance was the status of Richard's most treasured find to date: the 1470 skull that had vindicated his father's beliefs and made Richard famous practically overnight.

The terrain of Koobi Fora—or East Rudolf, as it was known in those days—is a baffling moonscape of rocky, gully-pocked undulations, a difficult challenge for any geologist to puzzle out. Volcanic deposits had been hopelessly shuffled about by erosion, as well as by the shifting level of the lake. Ash that had originally fallen elsewhere had also been brought in by rivers and streams that had themselves long since disappeared. Correlating tuffs to make sense of the many square miles embraced by the expedition's three research areas was a daunting prospect.

One of the Koobi Fora geologists was a Harvard graduate student named Kay Behrensmeyer. One day back in 1969, Behrensmeyer had discovered some crude stone tools in a grayish layer of volcanic ash, very much like the early artifacts found at Olduvai Gorge. This discovery was important for two reasons. Richard had already found his first *Australopithecus boisei* skull in another area to the north, in what was believed to be the same "horizon," or geological slice of time. Australopithecines were not thought capable of manufacturing even the simplest stone tools; hence the artifacts in the ash were the first hint that some species of *Homo* might have inhabited the site. Adding to the intrigue was the nature of the ash itself: The layer contained exactly the kind of crystals that lent themselves to dating by the potassium-argon method. Here then was an opportunity to assign a date to the tools embedded in the ash. Anything subsequently found in the deposits *below* the "Kay Behrensmeyer Site"—or KBS for short—would have to be older still.

Richard quickly sent off samples of the crystals to two British geochronologists named Frank Fitch and Jack Miller. Miller had run potassium-argon dates for Richard's father at Olduvai Gorge, but since that time the pair had been instrumental in developing considerably more sophisticated techniques. Their first response came back with a date for the tuff of 221 million years: clearly a false reading, unless one wants to believe that dinosaurs made stone tools. It turned out that the deposits from which Leakey and Behrensmeyer had collected the samples were contaminated by much older volcanic material brought down from higher elevations by rivers and streams.

Leakey went back to the KBS Tuff and collected what he hoped were purer samples and sent them off to Fitch and Miller. This time they came up with more gratifying results. The crystals were first dated at 2.4 million years; a further test pushed the date back to 2.6 million. That meant that the tools Behrensmeyer had found were the oldest indication of human habitation on earth, almost a million years older than anything found at Olduvai Gorge. Three years later, along came 1470—found well *below* the KBS Tuff. That was how Richard could announce with confidence that the new skull was at least 2.6 million years old, and probably closer to 3 million. With his "Oldest Man" securely in hand, funding for the Koobi Fora Research Project poured in. More fossils were found in 1973, including dozens of new hominid specimens. Meanwhile, geologist Ian Findlater completed a stratigraphic map correlating the complex volcanic tuffs at the three Koobi Fora research areas into a simplified, workable scheme.

Things were looking very sunny in Leakey's camp. Only one nagging doubt still needed to be put to rest, a little cloud on the horizon that took the shape of a pig. At first the threat it embodied could easily be shrugged off. But before Richard was through on the eastern shore of Lake Turkana, the shadow of the pig would spread to cast a pall over the entire enterprise.

As part of his site development, Leakey had very early on invited palentologist Basil Cooke to conduct an analysis of the rich collection of suids—members of the pig family—emerging from Koobi Fora. Cooke was the biostratigrapher who had used the evolving changes in extinct pigs to develop the Omo's "yardstick" of evolutionary time. He had also worked with Louis Leakey to develop a similar time scheme for the pigs of Olduvai Gorge. If the Koobi Fora suids could be sorted out and compared to those from the Omo and Olduvai sites, Richard thought, the biostratigraphy would bolster confidence in the radiometric date given by Fitch and Miller for the KBS Tuff. Simultaneously studies were under way with yet another dating system, one that uses regular, periodic reversals in the earth's magnetic field to determine the age of rocks that can be magnetized. This paleomagnetic study was producing a reassuring match with the 2.6-million-year potassium-argon date. Confirmation with biostratigraphic evidence would all but clinch the matter.

Unfortunately, Cooke's study did just the opposite. After months spent trying to make sense of the suids, he concluded that they indicated the 2.6 radiometric date was wrong. The fossils Cooke examined from the KBS Tuff matched instead the pigs in the Omo from much farther up in the succession, closer to 2 million years. Leakey and his colleagues were disappointed, perhaps, but not too bothered by Cooke's initial results. There had been some mistakes in the collection techniques early on, and who knows, maybe the real error was to be found in the Omo and Olduvai dates. They adopted a wait-and-see attitude. In the meantime, Richard stuck firm behind the radiometric study, declaring when 1470 was announced that the KBS Tuff had been "securely dated" at 2.6 million years.

Outside the Leakey camp, however, Cooke's pigs raised a few eyebrows—especially across the river in the Omo, only fifty miles north from Koobi Fora. Earlier, Clark Howell had expressed some skepticism about the Fitch-Miller radiometric date. For one thing, the doubtful pigs were supported by biostratigraphic studies on extinct elephants, antelopes, and other mammals. For another, Fitch and Miller's own study had never seemed rock solid to begin with. Two out of three of the reviewers of a subsequent paper had recommended that it be rejected; one commented that it "did not even approach the standards required of a scientific journal." That paper defending the 2.6-million-year date for the KBS Tuff was published nevertheless, virtually unchanged. Finally, results of an independent potassium-argon analysis conducted on KBS crystals by Garniss Curtis were indicating pig-ish dates of 1.8 and 1.6 million years.

By 1975 clear sides had formed on the issue. The Koobi Fora camp—mostly British scientists in Nairobi—rallied around the 2.6-

If enough is known about a species' lineage, the appearance and disappearance of particular forms can be used as a measure of the passage of time. In this illustration, changes in the chewing surface of the teeth of the pig genus Metridiochoerus *are placed in the context of potassium-argon (K/Ar) dates. The teeth can then be used to help determine the age of fossil deposits that may be undatable by the potassium-argon technique.* ILLUSTRATION BY DOUGLAS BECKNER. AFTER PHOTOS FROM T. D. WHITE AND J. M. HARRIS, *SCIENCE,* OCTOBER 7, 1977.

million-year KBS Tuff date reached by the apparently objective sophistication of Fitch and Miller's radiometric analysis. Howell's Omo group, comprised primarily of American scientists working out of Berkeley, threw their weight behind Basil Cooke's 2.0-million-year date, arrived at through tried-and-true biostratigraphic analysis. This tug-of-war was not some idle academic recreation: The rope stretched between the two camps was the human family line itself. If Cooke was right, then Leakey's 1470 was really no older than the *Homo habilis* specimens at Olduvai Gorge, and his argument for dismissing *Australopithecus* from the human lineage would fall apart.

In spite of its seriousness, the KBS controversy generated some of the great light moments in modern paleoanthropology. At one meeting held in an old castle in Austria, two scientists on opposite sides of the issue suddenly grabbed swords hanging on the castle walls, leaped up on a table and began to duel. (They had planned and practiced the melodrama the night before.) Koobi Fora archeologist Glynn Isaac once showed up at another conference wearing a "pig proof helmet." At a subsequent meeting in London in February 1975, Basil Cooke appeared sporting a novelty necktie with the letters MCP woven into it, standing for "Male Chauvinist Pig." By this time Cooke had amassed much better data on the Koobi Fora suids, particularly on a species called *Mesochoerus* that lived throughout East Africa about two million years ago; everywhere, that is, except Koobi Fora, where—if you believed the Fitch-Miller date for the KBS Tuff—it inexplicably appeared over half a million years earlier. At one point in the meeting Cooke stood up and pointed to his necktie. "You might think you know what MCP stand for, but you don't," he said. "It really stands for '*Mesochoerus* correlates properly.' "

Leakey was not amused.

"I was prickly and upset," he recalled later.[*] "I felt that Basil, as a member of 'my' team, should not have used the Koobi Fora data in the way he did without giving me a full report before the meeting." Cooke was mystified by this; his views on the pigs had not changed since the last time he had aired them, so he had seen no reason to solicit Richard's approval before presenting his work.

Equally mystifying to those of us who attended that London meeting was the "ecological hypothesis" that Leakey, Isaac, and John Harris were proposing to account for the 600,000-year difference in the faunal record between their site and the Omo. Their idea was that in environments separated by a geographic barrier—in this case, the wide Omo River—populations of animals might have evolved at different rates. The precocious pigs of Koobi Fora therefore only *appeared* to be half a million years younger than their counterparts across the river, because they had been evolving at a faster rate. Charles Darwin himself had deduced from his studies of finches in the Galápagos Islands that populations isolated from one another would take unique evolutionary paths. Most evolutionists believe, in fact, that geographical isolation is necessary for new species to evolve. But the geographical barriers Darwin was talking about were ocean expanses, not rivers. More important, such barriers would affect the *direction* of change, not the pace. It seemed to me that Richard's people were stretching a bit to justify their belief in the Fitch-Miller date. Elephants and other migrating browsers cross the Omo occasionally even today. It's hard to imagine them meeting their own evolutionary grandfathers on the other side.

If few people were impressed with the ecological hypothesis,

---

[*] As reported in Roger Lewin's book *Bones of Contention*, which contains an excellent, detailed account of the KBS Tuff controversy.

Leakey still had good reasons to remain committed to his 2.6-million-year date. Preliminary results on the KBS Tuff using another radiometric technique, called fission-track dating, were coming in very close to the potassium-argon results. By this time Richard also had an inkling that Basil Cooke's pig dates were questionable—thanks in part to Tim White. After collecting various fauna with John Harris in the field, Tim had gone back to Nairobi the year before and photographed some of the pigs previously collected by Cooke. He hadn't done any analysis yet, but what Tim and John had seen caused them to wonder out loud to Richard about Cooke's sorting methods. Perhaps further fieldwork would resolve the discrepancies.

Meanwhile, Richard still had another card up his sleeve at the London conference. He played it at a small party he gave after dinner one evening. Glynn Isaac was there, along with Kay Behrensmeyer and physical anthropologists Bernard Wood and Michael Day—all staunch "members of the firm" at Koobi Fora. But Richard had also invited Clark Howell, geologist Frank Brown, and some of their colleagues on the other side of the issue. The talk kept coming back to the KBS date, the pigs, the crystals, the geology, eventually descending into a shouting match over who was right and who was wrong. Richard just sat there, listening. Suddenly he got up, walked to another room and returned with a cast of a beautiful hominid hipbone—a big thing, *Homo erectus* by the look of it. Everybody was quiet.

"Here's a little something one of my Hominid Gang picked up during the off-season," he said. "It came from below the Tulu Bor Tuff at Koobi Fora." He settled back in his chair and smiled. We all knew that the Tulu Bor Tuff was *below* the KBS Tuff. Meaning that this amazingly humanlike pelvis was at least three million years old.

"That's impossible," Howell said.

"There it is," Richard replied, sucking on his pipe. "Let the fossil speak for itself." That started up a whole new argument.

Leakey was sure enough about the Tulu Bor pelvis to write a draft of a paper on the find for *Nature*. But what he'd heard from Howell and others convinced him that he'd better make doubly sure. In the summer of 1975 he sent Harris, White, and the Hominid Gang out to Koobi Fora alone to verify the provenance of the fossil—in other words, to check that the pelvis had been placed in the proper geological and paleontological context.

"We went out to the place where the pelvis had come from and did some collecting," Tim remembers. "The pigs we found were nothing like the ones below Tulu Bor—it wasn't the same tuff at all. That was the first hint we had that the Koobi Fora stratigraphy was all screwed up."

Quickly Tim and Harris reported back that the pelvis had really come from much higher up in the succession, and could not be older than 1.9 million years. The *Nature* paper was withdrawn, saving Richard considerable embarrassment. Ian Findlater was called down from London, where he was working on his dissertation, to take another look at the strata. He admitted there was the possibility of a mistake.

If the news on Tulu Bor was bad, Richard still had high hopes for what Harris and White would find out about the pigs. Basil Cooke was still expecting to spend the 1975 field season at Koobi Fora and continue his own analysis of the suids. Leakey discouraged him from coming. Instead he urged Harris and White to write their own monograph on the suids of Koobi Fora.

"The chronology that Basil had put together relied on only one evolutionary line of pigs, which is what he'd based his time correlations on between Koobi Fora and the other East African sites," Tim later told me. "But John and I were having trouble making sense of that scheme. We saw evidence of change in three separate pig lines, not one. When Richard heard that, he thought, 'Hey, if Cooke's pig family tree is screwed up, probably his dates are too.' That's what he wanted us to prove in the field. So he could keep his ancient *Homo* alive. But you can't always get what you want."

By the end of the summer the two young paleontologists had gathered enough new material to know that Leakey's 2.6-million-year date for the KBS Tuff was in trouble. Cooke's time correlations looked pretty good after all. There was still one slim hope: Though the sub-KBS pigs were correlating very closely with the Omo pigs dated at 2.0 million, perhaps the *Omo* date was misleading. To follow that angle, Tim would have to wait until early the following year, when he could return to the States and study the part of the Omo paleontological collection housed in Berkeley. What Tim found there only strengthened his suspicions. At the end of March 1976, Richard flew out to the West Coast himself to give a seminar. Tim picked him up at the Oakland airport.

"On the way back I told him everything," he remembers. "We went over the metrics, the geology, the stratigraphy, the whole damn analysis. The only thing he was displeased with was the dating on my chart. He was worried about the conflict with the potassium-argon results."

The last step in the analysis was to take another look at the rest of the Omo pigs, stored in a laboratory outside Paris. Harris joined Tim there in May, and after a week of study they had eliminated all doubt. They flew on to Nairobi in June and gave Richard the news. He offered no comment. John and Tim set to work writing up their monograph.

It looked to be a blockbuster. First, they would greatly expand on Cooke's original biostratigraphic work on the Plio-Pleistocene suids. Included for the first time were the species found in South Africa: an extremely important addition, since in the absence of the kind of volcanic material needed for potassium-argon dating, biostratigraphy remained the only reliable means of estimating the ages of the South African hominids found by Dart and Broom. Second, the pig data they presented would by its very nature trigger a complete reappraisal of the Koobi Fora geology and the tuff-numbering system in use there. Third, the pigs would prove that the radiometric date of 2.6 million for the KBS Tuff was skewed, for whatever reason. With the fall of that date, Leakey's Oldest Man would topple too.

"From the standpoint of the science, that last point was by far the least important," Tim says. "But that's what got everyone bent out of shape."

Richard had heard enough from different points of reference to know that the stratigraphy of his site was in serious trouble. In August he called a "summit meeting" in the field of everyone involved, including Glynn Isaac, Kay Behrensmeyer, and Meave. Ian Findlater flew down again from London. John Harris and Tim came up from Nairobi, bringing a draft of their pig monograph with them. The group drove from site to site, John and Tim pointing out the problems they saw with the tuff correlations on paleontological grounds, while Ian and Kay defended their original geological interpretations. After several such outings everybody could see that what had once seemed like a well-integrated scheme was now full of holes. Then Isaac proposed a temporary resolution: Instead of attempting to trace the volcanic tuffs *between* the research areas, each of the three areas would be mapped out with its own complex tuff-numbering system. Under Isaac's scheme, it would be very cumbersome, if not impossible, to pin *any* date of the fossils found between the tuffs. It was a compromise that pleased no one, but John and Tim reluctantly agreed to go along. They let everyone know they were planning to abstract from their monograph an article for *Nature* on the implications of their pig work. Isaac began drafting a manuscript to accompany it, explaining the new tuff-numbering system.

If Richard was upset by the direction in which his two paleontologists were leading him, he didn't show it. Meanwhile, there was better news from other fronts of the battle. Tony Hurford and Andrew Gleadow, the two geochronologists who were pursuing a fission-track date for the KBS Tuff, had refined their technique and could confidently report the KBS Tuff clocked in at 2.44 million years, give or take 80,000 years. This was a little younger than the Fitch-Miller date of 2.6 million, but even that trifling discrepancy quickly melted away: In the same issue of *Nature* that presented the fission-track study, Fitch and Miller revised their date upward to 2.42 million years. Some colleagues found this seamless agreement between the two radiometric methods almost too good to be true, but it certainly bolstered Leakey's position. Add to that the revelation that Garniss Curtis's reading of 1.6 million years had proved to be flawed by an improperly adjusted weighing balance, and it is perhaps no wonder Richard remained loyal to his geochronologists, pigs or no pigs.

Tim and John Harris finished their own paper to *Nature* early in September, including a discussion on the implication of the work for the hominids. Both men are convinced that Leakey, Isaac, and the other members of the Koobi Fora team were well aware of the conclusion they would present: The KBS Tuff was 2 million years old, not 2.6, and the famous 1470 skull and other hominids found below it were also much younger than claimed. John gave the draft to Leakey in his office in Nairobi. On September 7 Tim had a hurried meeting with Richard, who told him he didn't agree with the conclusions of the paper, but gave no indication that he was seriously displeased. The same day, Tim was scheduled to leave to attend an international meeting in Nice. But before leaving the museum, he stopped in at John Harris's office. What he learned there appalled him.

"John told me that Leakey was furious about our *Nature* paper," Tim recalls. "He had complained to John that we had not consulted him properly, which was nonsense—we'd spent the last two weeks of August outlining our intentions to everybody at Koobi Fora. Richard objected to our referring in the paper to hominid fossils that he claimed had not been published. Supposedly this was against a long-standing policy in the East Rudolf Research Project. I lost my temper over that. *All* the hominids we cited had been published by Richard himself in *Nature* and *The American Scientist*. He just didn't want us to present our evidence because it wasn't what he wanted to hear."

Reportedly, Leakey himself remembers the incident quite differently. Roger Lewin quotes him as saying that he told Tim about his objections directly, reminding him that the group's policy forbade any group member to mention fossils in print until the fossils had been formally described in *The American Journal of Physical Anthropology*. The rule, Richard explained, was meant to protect whoever was doing the nuts-and-bolts work on the material from being internally scooped by other members of the team. According to Leakey, Tim then exploded in rage, announced his resignation from the Koobi Fora project and stormed out of the office, slamming the door.

"That makes an interesting story, but it never happened," Tim tells me, and his journal entries from the time bear him out. "Furthermore, we didn't say anything about the hominids in that manuscript that a reader of *Nature* couldn't have said. We followed group protocol by giving Leakey a presubmission copy of our paper. It was insulting to be told secondhand that this was somehow wrong."

Badly shaken up, Tim left for the airport. If the *Nature* paper was to be emasculated by removing all reference to the implications for the hominids, then Tim wanted no part of it. John Harris, a better diplomat than his co-author (as well as Richard Leakey's brother-in-law), prevailed upon Tim to allow the paper to be rewritten with the implications for dating couched in ambiguous, less offensive wording. Harris then submitted the manuscript to *Nature* as planned—only to have it rejected. The editors claimed that it did not add significantly to what Basil Cooke had already published about the pigs.

Tim scoffs at that explanation, and it is in fact hard to justify. Whatever else the manuscript had in its favor, it revealed the time correlations for the South African pigs—information that had never been published and that would later prove absolutely essential to the reconstruction of the human family tree brought about by my discoveries in Ethiopia. Tim still suspects the *Nature* editors or reviewers had been influenced to reject the manuscript, but there is no way of proving that. Meanwhile, he and Harris submitted it unchanged to *Science,* where it appeared in October 1977. Thereafter, Cooke brought his own pig phylogeny into line with theirs. Tim made an attempt at patching things up with Richard, but their relationship cooled, eventually reaching absolute zero.

"You have to understand that the 2.6-million-year date was like a religion at Koobi Fora," Tim remembers. "My research reached a different conclusion, and Richard did his best to suppress it. No personal friendship, no political consideration, makes that acceptable to me. I was revolted by the whole thing."

As things turned out, the Fitch-Miller date for the KBS Tuff was proved to have been in error after all. A study conducted by a third, impartial geochronologist confirmed Garniss Curtis's date of 1.8 million. Further fission-track studies by Hurford and Gleadow came up with the same number. Richard abandoned his defense of the older date. The whole bitter episode had taxed his health, which was already seriously threatened by kidney failure. In 1979 a kidney transplant from his brother Philip was required to save his life.

Meanwhile, Tim White went on to work on the remarkable collection of hominid jaws that Mary Leakey had found at Laetoli, south of Olduvai. If Tim had played the devil's advocate at Koobi Fora, at Laetoli he'd prove to be the devil himself.

CHAPTER FOUR:

Breaking Ranks

It's not just what we inherit from our mothers and fathers that haunts us. It's all kinds of old defunct theories, all sorts of old defunct beliefs, and things like that. It's not that they actually live on in us; they are simply lodged there, and we cannot get rid of them.
—Henrik Ibsen, *Ghosts*

ON THE WAY TO OLDUVAI, shortly before the road begins to wind up the steep ascent to Ngorongoro Crater, there is a village called Mto Wa Mbu, which in English means "River of the Mosquitoes." It is a busy little town, with cattle, goats, and chickens in the streets and a constant traffic of buses and trucks. Mto Wa Mbu was our last opportunity to stock up on fresh fruit and vegetables.

As we fanned out through the network of stalls in the market, we soon found ourselves tailed by a group of young boys. Much to Gen Suwa's embarrassment, the boys decided to pretend he was Bruce Lee. Wherever poor Gen turned he was confronted by a flurry of martial arts gestures and unbridled giggling. Tim's wide-brimmed hat with its rattlesnake band was the next most popular attraction. Tim was comfortable with the kids. He would pretend not to notice them, and then suddenly he would whip around and chase them, waving his arms and charging into the group with a snarling grin. This display brought almost as many squeals of delight as the spectacle of a Kung Fu warrior wearing thick glasses and a blue UC Berkeley windbreaker.

The market at Mto Wa Mbu, on the road to Olduvai Gorge DONALD JOHANSON

We bought some oranges, green bananas, jackfruit, cabbage, and tomatoes. Back in the combi, we cut open a jackfruit for lunch and passed pieces around stripping the delicious, fragrant fruit off its skin with our teeth. Pretty soon the road began to climb the escarpment above Lake Manyara National Park. Near the top we pulled off to the side of the road and walked over to the edge of the cliff. In the valley below, Lake Manyara looked like a silver plate set out on a mottled green cloth. The green was darkest along the west shore of the lake, with another swatch of forest lining both sides of the snaking river that fed the lake from the north. On the far side, a cooler jade outlined the salt flats, infused in one place with a faint pinkish blush. While I watched, a ripple moved through the pink patch. Momentarily the color dispersed, then coalesced in another place. It suddenly dawned on me that something down there had startled a flock of flamingos. On our side of the lake, I could just make out a family of elephants browsing in a gallery of fever trees, flickering in and out of view like stones glimpsed through the water of a running brook. An eagle slowly circled above them, riding the updraft against the escarpment.

"Gen, Berhane—take a look at this," Tim said, pointing down into the valley. "Freshwater streams running into a wide, shallow alkaline lake. Gallery forests, marsh flats. This is the best modern analog for what Olduvai was like when Zinj was running around about two million years ago."

Good point. In the early Pleistocene, Olduvai wasn't a gorge at all, but rather an open plain surrounding just such a lake as this. It would be a busy spot, a place flickering with elephants and a menagerie of other herbivores attracted by the swampy richness; a place, like Manyara today, populated as well by lions, hyenas, and other carnivores. They all left their bones by the Olduvai lake millions of years before there was such a thing as the Serengeti Plain. Hominids too. We looked down in silence. As if we were all thinking the same thing, the four of us turned and walked quickly back to the van. If we pressed on we could still make the Gorge in time for a little poking around in its famous gullies before dinner.

Back in 1975, when Tim was still a valued "member of the firm," Richard Leakey had recommended him for a tremendously important assignment. Under Mary Leakey's direction, research expeditions to the Tanzanian site of Laetoli near Olduvai Gorge had collected some promising new hominid jaws and teeth from deposits believed to be over three and a half million years in age—older even than my Hadar finds. In all there were thirteen specimens in the collection, very primitive, but also showing some curiously *Homo*-like features. The best of the lot was a well-preserved mandible with nine teeth in place, labeled L.H.-4. Tim was given the job of describing the jaws for publication. He was twenty-five years old at the time and still two years shy of his Ph.D. To be invited to formally describe the hominids of Laetoli was a fantastic opportunity.

Tim was well into the work when I met him that day in Richard's lab. I had learned a little bit about the Laetoli hominids from Mary, and Tim had of course heard about Lucy and the other fossils emerging from Hadar. He had also heard something about me.

"Richard had warned me about this hotshot up in the Afar who didn't know what he was doing," Tim joked to me months later. "But I was waiting to make up my own mind. You turned out to be not half as dumb as Richard made out."

If Richard had any real doubts about my expertise he certainly was hiding it well. And I was placing great faith in his. I was all but convinced that we had discovered at least two species in the Afar: The larger jaws represented a very primitive species of *Homo*, while little Lucy and her ilk were something quite different, probably a primitive, though gracile (slenderly built), australopithecine. This arrangement was of course very much to Richard and Mary's liking. In those years they agreed on very little, but both were equally—and utterly—committed to Louis's faith in ancient *Homo*. I was taking my cues from them—not to curry favor, though being friends with Richard was unquestionably an advantage for any young paleoanthropologist working in East Africa—but because the Leakeys' scheme seemed the best way to accommodate the perplexing variation evident throughout the Hadar collection. I was also very much aware of the kind of attention that would follow anyone who spoke the words "I have found the oldest man." The hubbub around the Hadar fossils strewn about that lab table was just the beginning.

Tim's first words to me went right to the point. When the others had left the room, he emerged from a corner and approached the fossils. After he'd examined them for a few minutes he turned to me and said, "I think your fossils from Hadar and Mary's fossils from Laetoli may be the same." That startled me. Laetoli and Hadar were more than a thousand miles apart, and their hominids separated in time by at least half a million years. It seemed very unlikely. Then Tim showed me a couple for comparison. They were nearly identical.

"One species?" I said.

"One species."

"What about Lucy?"

"Lucy too."

"No way," I said. "She's much too small and primitive. Jaw shape, teeth, brain size—none of her makes sense with the others." I mentioned half a dozen other primitive traits. "Come to Cleveland and I'll show you."

"Lucy too."

"Come to Cleveland."

I wasn't buying Tim's idea, but his forthrightness and his obvious command of hominid morphology impressed me. We agreed to keep each other up to date on our work.

In March of 1976 my *Nature* article with Maurice Taieb appeared as planned, strongly hinting that there were at least two species represented in the Hadar, and possibly three: gracile and robust forms of *Australopithecus*, side by side with primitive *Homo*. I would meet Tim occasionally at meetings over the next year, and he would rarely fail to bring the subject up again. I listened with interest, but having committed myself in print, I was more inclined to find reasons to dismiss new points of view than I was to reexamine my own conclusions.

I didn't have to look far for an explanation for Tim's assessment. As a student of Milford Wolpoff and Loring Brace at the

University of Michigan, he had been trained in a tradition of "super-lumpers." By emphasizing the similarities among the various known hominid specimens over their apparent differences, the Michigan school had once trimmed the human family tree down to a simple trunk: At any time in the past, they maintained, there was only one kind of hominid living, just as there is only one today. The discoveries of the 1970s had rendered the "single species hypothesis" virtually indefensible; even Loring Brace had difficulty placing a relatively brainy skull like 1470 in the same species with the robust australopithecines, with brains the size of grapefruits, found in the same time period at the same site. But Brace and his colleagues at Michigan still looked unsparingly at any attempt to create rigid species distinctions on the basis of what they thought of as minor morphological differences.

"Of course Tim White sees only one species at Hadar," I thought to myself. "His eyes are trained to look for the sameness among things." I didn't know at the time that he had already quarreled with his teachers.

Even so, Tim's insinuations made me uneasy. At the time, I was struggling with a burden that most paleoanthropologists gladly would have shared: I was finding hominid fossils at a much faster rate than I could analyze them. Had I published too soon after all? I was almost relieved when the revolution in Ethiopia put off hope of a field season for 1977—at last I would have a chance to catch my breath and sit down to evaluate the collection in earnest. I had no inkling, of course, that I would not be allowed to return to the Hadar for many years to come.

Tim too found himself with some time on his hands in the summer of 1977. After the KBS dating debacle blew up in his face, he had not been asked back to work at Koobi Fora. The previous fall he had instead returned to Nairobi to continue work on the Laetoli descriptions and finish his thesis. He spent a lot of time working with Mary Leakey. Tim was alone when Christmas rolled around, and Mary invited him to celebrate the holidays at the Olduvai camp. She seemed to take to him, and Tim returned her friendship in kind.

"I felt quite a bit of sympathy for her," he remembers. "It went beyond the image of this tough, crusty lady living out in the middle of nowhere. Her husband had died. He hadn't been such a great husband in the first place. Her sons Richard and Philip hated each other. But she stuck with it, down there at Olduvai year after year with just her animals. I had a lot of respect for that dedication."

His work with Mary concluded, Tim came back to the States and visited me in Cleveland, bringing casts of the Laetoli fossils with him. We were anxious to have another look at them side by side with the much more extensive Hadar collection. We laid the fossils out on the counter in my lab and went to work. One thing was abundantly clear: The larger jaws from Hadar looked astonishingly like those from Laetoli. Knowing that superficial resemblances can be misleading, we worked over the specimens for days, one jaw, one palate, one tooth at a time, measuring distances and angles and examining the morphology of every cusp, trying to prove that our first impression was wrong. It wasn't. The teeth and jaws were virtually identical; it would be hard to find a single morphologist in the world who would dispute that. But I doubt that you could find two who would readily agree on what exactly they were.

Originally, both of us were inclined to see the big jaws as *Homo*. They did not have the large molars and heavy buttressing characteristic of australopithecine jaws. But then they also exhibited a puzzling array of very primitive, almost apelike features. Their arcade of teeth, for instance, resembled the boxlike ape pattern rather than the parabolic shape characteristic of hominids. The more we analyzed the teeth and jaws, the more they seemed to occupy some intermediate zone between apes and all other known hominids. But if they were *Homo*, how could they be more primitive than their own australopithecine ancestors?

And then there was Lucy. Her jaw was very different. First of all it was clearly smaller, Second, the dental arcade was V-shaped. What pieces we had recovered of her cranium, meanwhile, showed that Lucy's brain was much too little to qualify as *Homo* by any conventional standard; as a matter of fact, it wasn't much bigger than that of a chimp. Halfway through the analysis I was more convinced than ever that she was a different species from the bigger jaws at Hadar, including some from the First Family site. On the other hand, some of the First Family jaws were small and Lucy-like.

"How are you going to fit *that* problem into your notion of two species?" Tim taunted. It was 3:00 A.M. and we'd been working and arguing since the previous morning. "Or do you have two species represented in one family?"

"Don't be silly."

"It's the logical conclusion of *your* argument. Not mine."

"So how would *you* explain it?"

"I told you before. Sexual dimorphism. Combined with al-lometry."

Tim had been pushing these Michigan-influenced arguments from the beginning to explain Lucy's anomalies. Sexual dimorphism refers to the general morphological differences apparent between the two sexes of a species. These can include dissimilarities in canine-tooth size, cranial capacity, pelvic measurements, limb-bone dimensions, and a host of other features. Body size is a common example. The males of a pronounced sexually dimorphic species like the gorilla outweigh the females by as much as two to one. The sexes of less sexually dimorphic primates, including ourselves, are more similarly proportioned.

Allometry is a related phenomenon. Basically, it means that differences in anatomical *size* will lead to predictable changes in *shape* as well. You cannot "grow" a male gorilla just by expanding the dimensions of a female gorilla's anatomy. His canines are not just larger than hers, they are *proportionately* larger as well, and their shape is different. Similarly, a female amounts to more than a scaled-down model of the male. This was the argument that Tim was using to explain Lucy's oddly shaped jaw. Her front teeth were not only smaller than those of her male counterparts—they were proportionately smaller too. Since her jaw did not have to accommodate fuller front teeth, it could narrow toward the front into that distinctly V shape.

Allometry or not, I still could not accept Tim's argument. Lucy's jaw was simply *too* different from the rest. This kept leading me back to her other points of difference—her small stature for in-stance—even though I'd already conceded to Tim that Lucy's size could be accommodated with the others in a sexually dimorphic spe-cies. In the back of my mind too was that little brain. I kept think-ing how neatly one of my larger Hadar mandibles would fit on to Richard's 1470 skull, so much more advanced than Lucy's, and what *good sense* that would make out of the whole human evolutionary puzzle. Primitive *Homo,* walking erect three million years ago, brain enlarging—beautiful. I didn't need Tim to tell me there was little substance to this argument: From what we had recovered of their crania, we had no reason to believe that the larger Hadar hominids had brains any bigger than Lucy's. So I didn't talk about brain size— I merely *thought* it. What I talked about was jaw size and shape.

"Sure, Lucy's jaw is different, if you look at her up against the other extreme," Tim said to me one day. To demonstrate he placed Lucy's jaw on the counter next to the largest one from the First Family site. "But take your Leakey lenses off for a minute and look at *this*."

Putting those two fossils on either end of the long counter, Tim walked over to the shelf where we kept the other jaws in the collection. One by one he laid them down between the two extremes, so they formed a graduated series from largest to smallest. Suddenly Lucy didn't look so strange after all. The difference in size was quantitative, not qualitative; up against the jaws in the middle, for instance, Lucy's jaw didn't seem so unusual.

"All right, I'll concede that we can't argue for two species on the basis of size. But what about the jaw shape? You say allometry. If you can prove that, you win."

"You're on."

That took some time and a lot of patience. But when we had finished scaling down all the jaws in the collection to Lucy's size, the differences in shape all but disappeared. The last obstacle to Tim's claim for one species had been removed. The analysis had taken all summer and covered a lot more technical ground than I've described here. But in the end, I had to concede that all the fossils of Hadar and Laetoli comprised only one species. The next challenge was to figure out what it was.

Tim left at the end of the summer and I settled down to more routine tasks at the museum. Having worked around to accepting the plausibility of Tim's hypothesis, I gradually began to see how well it accounted for what I had once seen as unresolvable ambiguities. Topping the list was that vein of primitiveness running through the Hadar and Laetoli collections, combined with what were unmistakably *Homo*-like traits. I had been arguing from the preconception that *Homo* equaled advanced. Tim's line of reasoning demanded a mental flip-flop: Look on the *Homo* pattern as the primitive one, with the big-molared australopithecine pattern arising *later*. My two-species bias had pushed me to draw clear lines between categories that simply did not apply: human versus australopithecine, gracile versus robust, advanced versus primitive. Only after I'd pried myself free from the safety and convenience of those distinctions could I see what we *really* had: a single, very old, very primitive hominid species that was ancestral to *both Homo* and *Australopithecus*. The implica-

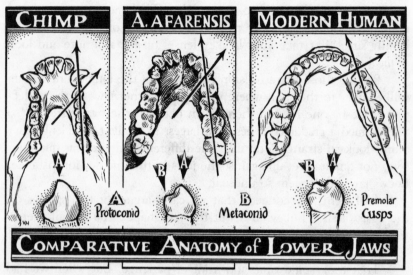

CHIMP | A. AFARENSIS | MODERN HUMAN

A. Protoconid

B. Metaconid

Premolar Cusps

COMPARATIVE ANATOMY of LOWER JAWS

The primitive characteristics of jaws and teeth led Johanson and White to conclude that A. afarensis was the ancestor of all later hominids. This illustration shows that the premolar of afarensis no longer has the cutting edge of a chimpanzee's premolar, but neither has it yet evolved into the true two-cusped form present in later hominids. Its crown is also set at a sharper angle to the tooth row, like a chimp's.

tions of that were flabbergasting. What we had in hand was the common ancestor to all other known hominids.

In November I wrote to Mary Leakey and told her that contrary to what I'd already published, I was now almost certain that my Hadar finds and her Laetoli ones represented a single species. ("Johanson's been '*white*washed!' " she joked to a colleague.) Though Tim and I had undertaken the interpretive analysis of the fossils, we considered that Mary, as the finder of the Laetoli hominids, fully deserved to be one of the authors of the paper we would eventually publish. (According to the terms of a formal agreement of the Afar Research Expedition, Yves Coppens, the director of the French team in the Afar, had the option to co-author the paper as well.) In my letter to Mary I suggested that we consider proposing a new *Homo* species, more primitive even than *Homo habilis*. She replied that it was too early to assign a species name—better to wait until we had some better cranial material in hand. But that reasoning could hang us up forever. Meanwhile, I suspected that Coppens was planning to use the Hadar specimens soon to name his own new species. After the summer spent day and night with those bones, I felt that Tim and I knew their import better than Yves, Mary, or anyone else. We couldn't waste time waiting for skulls to push out of the ground. We already had plenty to go on.

Early in December Tim returned to Cleveland for another, we hoped final, confrontation. We were very much aware that whatever we decided to call the species would raise a storm. Proposing a new species means much more than sticking a label on some bones so everybody knows what to call them. The creation of a taxon is a formal recognition that this creature *existed*—distinct, viable, reproducing with only its own kind, embodying an evolutionary past and future all its own. A species name defines its relation to all previously known species in its family tree. Unless the new evidence exactly matches what could have been predicted from the old, it will cause some changes in the tree that are bound to upset people. We were young, and had done nothing yet that would prompt unqualified respect. By opting for a single species at Hadar, I was in effect conceding that I had already made one serious mistake. Tim was developing a reputation as an able morphologist, but his brittleness wasn't making him many friends along the way. Why should anyone believe us? We had to be sure there was no reasonable argument against us that we hadn't already thought of ourselves.

The first thing we did was place the new, still unnamed species in a chronological context. The ages of most of the East African hominids were pretty well known through potassium-argon dating. To date Leakey's 1470 skull, the first known evidence of *Homo*, we used Garniss Curtis's radiometric date of 1.8 million for the KBS Tuff above it in the sequence. The hyper-robust Zinj (*Australopithecus boisei*) was contemporary with *Homo habilis* at Koobi Fora and Olduvai, so these two lines were clearly separate. The robust australopithecines disappeared from the fossil record just before one million years ago. *Habilis*, meanwhile, continued on to *Homo erectus* and eventually *Homo sapiens*. We drew a tree with two branches, the *Homo* line and the robust australopithecine line, with the latter branch lopped off by extinction at 1 million years. At the base we place the unnamed Hadar Laetoli hominid, dated between 3 and 3.5 million years old.

That left only the gracile A. *africanus* form to fit in. For the South African australopithecines, we relied on an age estimate between 2.7 and 2.1 million years, developed through biostratigraphic studies by Elisabeth Vrba, a South African paleontologist, as well as through Tim's correlations from his African pig study with John Harris. Raymond Dart had believed his species was ancestral to *Homo*—so did everyone else who believed that the human line arose from an australopithecine. But that no longer seemed to make such good sense. *Africanus* had clearly begun the pattern of large back molars, strongly buttressed jaws, and other adaptations for heavy chewing that reached their fullest expression in the later robust australopithecines. In light of the evidence, the simplest explanation was that *africanus* belonged at the foot of the branch leading to the later robust forms, and eventually to extinction. What we ended up with then was a simple two-pronged fork, with the Hadar-Laetoli species falling just before the branches diverged. (See illustration on page 116.)

The phylogeny complete, Tim and I had left the ticklish task of naming our common ancestor's genus and species. The genus is the more meaningful part of a new species binomen, since it links the newcomer with similarly adapted beings. For a genus designation we had three choices: *Homo, Australopithecus,* or "something else." Quickly we eliminated the last option; there weren't that many unique features about the new species, and a new genus name would completely obscure all the similarities that it shared with all the later hominids but not with the apes. For a while I pressed for *Homo,* once again on the basis of that small-toothed dental pattern. But I began to see more and more how odd that would seem, to admit into the human genus a species with a small brain capacity, a face that projected forward in an apelike manner, and a host of other primitive traits. So we were left with *Australopithecus.* Neither of us was delighted with the name, but it was the inevitable conclusion of our reasoning, the "least wrong" of three uncomfortable choices.

I knew that Mary Leakey would like it even less. She'd never cared for the term in the first place, believing that it was unwise of Dart to have named a genus on the basis of a juvenile skull. Much more to the point, by calling the common ancestor *Australopithecus,* we were declaring that the human line had to be younger than Lucy. Essentially, that would extinguish the notion of ancient *Homo* that had been passed like a torch from Arthur Keith to Mary's husband, Louis, and on to her son Richard. Unwelcome as that news would be, we hoped she would see that there was no logical alternative. For a species name, we came up with *afarensis,* acknowledging the geographical region of the Afar Triangle. We also found a way to pay respect to Mary Leakey's Laetoli site, and underscore the important connection between it and Hadar. According the International Code of Zoological Nomenclature, when naming a new species, one fossil must be chosen as a "type specimen," a sort of flagship fossil that formally represents the entire collection. As type specimen we chose L.H.-4, the fairly complete mandible from Laetoli that had already been published and that exhibited the features diagnostic of the species.

After two grinding weeks, Tim and I emerged with the bulk of our work finally behind us. We presented its outlines in a letter to Mary. She wrote back in January: Encouragingly, she conceded that it was perhaps time to name a new species, but as I had expected, she flinched at the name *Australopithecus.* By this time we knew there was no alternative, but we still felt Mary should play a part. I wrote back suggesting a plan: Rather than publish one massive article, we would first propose the new species in a *descriptive* paper, co-authored with Mary and Yves Coppens, and save the *interpretive* discussion— the presentation of our new family tree—for a separate publication authored only by Tim and myself. This would save Mary from being associated with any implication that *Australopithecus* was ancestral to *Homo.*

Mary was scheduled soon for a lecture tour in the States, and late February she stopped in at Berkeley to meet with Tim.

"You know, I don't like it," she said after they'd finished with the small talk.

"What don't you like?"

"That term, *Australopithecus.* I hate the word."

"Why do you hate it?" Tim asked.

"I don't know. I just hate it."

"I don't like it much either, Mary, but we haven't got any choice," Tim said. Then he went over again all the reasons for eliminating *Homo* and every other possible alternative. Finally he convinced her that there was no other way to go. She agreed to join us as co-author of the descriptive paper—so long as it made no mention of *Australopithecus*'s being ancestral to *Homo.* Tim and I finished writing the paper in the late spring, sent drafts off to Mary, and submitted it to *Kirtlandia,* the journal of the Cleveland Museum. We also took the precaution of sending a draft to Ernst Mayr at Harvard University, a doyen of evolutionary biology whose vast knowledge equips him to serve as a final arbiter on the naming of species. Mayr wrote back and approved the logic behind our name.

So encouraged, we wrote up the interpretive paper in May and submitted it to *Science*. Both of us knew that we had just completed what might be the greatest contribution we would ever make to our field—and one that put us on a collision course with some of the oldest, most powerfully defended ideas of human evolution. Naturally we were apprehensive, but we felt prepared to meet any criticism that could be leveled against us. In late May I left for Stockholm. I had been invited to present the Hadar fossils at a Nobel Symposium: a perfect opportunity to announce the new species and present our phylogeny to the scientific community. I had not anticipated that the occasion would also mark the end of my friendship with Mary Leakey, and the beginning of a ceaseless rivalry with her son Richard.

Both were in the audience that afternoon. I gave my lecture as planned, unfolding our reasoning step by step. It was necessary, of course, to talk about the Laetoli fossils at some length, since they played an important role in our hypothesis. I made sure that I gave Mary Leakey full credit for her discovery of those specimens and the development of the Laetoli hominid site—which by this time had also yielded up those ancient footprints. I was unaware, however, that as I talked Mary was growing red with anger. She had planned to discuss the Laetoli material herself immediately afterward and was furious that I had appropriated *her* fossils. She claimed later that she had never been informed that the L.H.-4 mandible had been designated the *afarensis* type specimen, had never consented to be a part of the naming of the species, and indeed had never even believed that there was only one species represented among the specimens from Hadar and Laetoli.

I was completely unprepared for her reaction. Mary had been sent a draft of the *Kirtlandia* paper and had never given Tim or me any indication that she had changed her mind about being a co-author. She later held that she had never given us permission to use her name in the first place, and we were simply exploiting her reputation to bolster interest in our own theory. Richard was angry too. He had been instrumental in organizing the symposium, and he believed it was an inappropriate setting for the naming of a new species. He too accused us of exploiting the aura of the Nobel name to heighten attention to *afarensis*.

I have answered these accusations many times over the last ten years, and I needn't go into them here in detail. Richard's objections are silly; the Nobel Symposium, entitled "Current Argument on Early Man," was as appropriate a forum as any to name a new "early man." As for my discussing Mary's fossils: To cite unpublished fossils is indeed a serious breach of scientific etiquette. The Laetoli fossils, however, *had* been fully published and described two years before, by Tim. As a result, they belonged in the public domain, and I was as free as anyone else to refer to them in a talk. What really irked Mary, I think, was my citing the Laetoli specimens to support a view of human evolution that Mary did not share—first, that man was descended from an australopithecine, and second, that humanity was not nearly so old as the Leakey tradition maintained. The split-publication scheme that Tim and I had developed with her consent was intended to keep her dissociated from those ideas. Apparently it wasn't enough.

To add another twist, Tim was due to spend the field season that summer with Mary at Laetoli.

"She was running an anti-Johanson campaign in camp that summer," Tim told me afterward. "She kept asking me, 'How can you associate with *that man?*' I told her that if she felt so strongly about it, she ought to get her name off the *Kirtlandia* article before it was published."

Mary sent a telegram to that effect to my office in Cleveland. Though the journal issue had already been printed, we were able to halt shipment and reprint the title page of our article without Mary's name on it. A few months later, the interpretive paper presenting the Johanson-White phylogeny appeared as a cover article in *Science. Australopithecus afarensis* was out in the world for all to behold. A front-page story quickly followed in *The New York Times.* Suddenly I found myself swamped by requests for interviews and television appearances. It was an exhilarating time. But amid all the hoopla I remained acutely aware that in Mary Leakey, the birth of *afarensis* had cost me a treasured and respected friend. I worried too about how long my cordial relationship with Richard could last.

On the rim of the great Ngorongoro Crater there is a wildlife game lodge with a magnificent view of the crater floor two thousand feet below. The Olduvai camp was only an hour's drive down the other side of the extinct volcano, but we decided to stop at the lodge for a quick cup of tea before heading out on the last leg of the journey. The lodge possessed a refrigerator—the nearest place to the dig

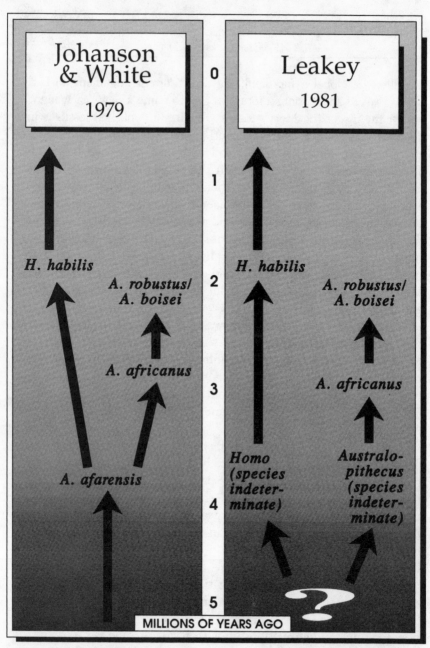

The human family tree proposed by Johanson and White in 1979, compared with another interpretation given by Richard Leakey in 1981. Johanson and White believed A. afarensis was the ancestor of all later hominids, including Homo. Leakey contended that they mistakenly yoked two separate species under the name afarensis, and that the true ancestor of man had yet to be found. Compare these trees with those on page 132. DESIGN BY VAN HOWELL AND DOUGLAS BECKNER, ILLUSTRATION BY DOUGLAS BECKNER where we could keep fresh the snake antivenin we'd brought along. There was little threat of poisonous snakes at Olduvai, but Laetoli was full of puff adders hidden in the grass. The fangs of these thick-bodied snakes deliver a highly toxic venom rendered all the more pernicious by the speed by which it takes effect. Untreated, a bitten arm or leg can turn black and swell up to twice its normal size within minutes; in a few hours internal bleeding sets in, and there is little left to be done to save the victim. I started calculating how long it would take us to rush a bitten team member back up to the lodge from Laetoli on the other side of the Gorge. Then I decided there were some calculations better left unfinished.

From the lodge the road hugged the rim of the crater for another few miles before beginning its descent to the Serengeti Plain. The prevalent mist on Ngorongoro keeps the mountain capped in green, and on either side of the narrow road patches of cultivated crops were wedged in gullies and ravines. Children waved and shouted to us. An occasional Maasai warrior, face and hair coated heavily in ocher, stared impassively at the black and beige van as we passed. Soon the road dropped down onto the shoulder of Lemagrut—another of the extinct volcanoes whose ancient eruptions laid down some of Olduvai's famous beds. All trace of green disappeared. As we settled over a ridge the Gorge appeared teasingly in the distance, a slight, darkened fold pressed into the edge of the dust-dry plain. We'd been chattering through most of the trip, but now all four of us were silent. Now so close to the place that personified the Leakey spirit, I could not help but feel nostalgic for the times when I came this way to visit Mary for a few days of restful conversation, or spent afternoons sailing in the Indian Ocean in Richard's boat. How odd, I thought, that now I was welcome at Olduvai only because Mary was gone, taking her furniture with her.

In spite of the personal irritation that the naming of *afarensis* had caused them, Tim and I had hoped that the Leakeys and their colleagues would oblige our theory with some professional response—perhaps a counterthesis that we could bounce ideas off, even integrate into a more refined synthesis. Our new phylogeny, like all family trees, was not some rigid truth, but rather an interpretive tool—a hypothetical structure meant to help organize thinking. A theory like that only gathers strength as it is tested and retested by competing ideas. I was particularly anxious to hear what Richard would have to say. A couple of weeks after our announcement in

January 1979, he arrived in the United States for a lecture tour. I met him at a symposium in Pittsburgh.

"I think Don was right about the Hadar fossils the first time," Richard said at the symposium, a reference to my 1976 paper with Taieb. He believed that there were at least two species at Hadar, one of them "some kind of primitive *Homo*." His arguments, though, were exactly the ones I had used initially against Tim, so I was prepared to counter them. I even offered to review the fossils with him, point by point. Richard declined.

Finally, a year later, both Mary and Richard responded to *afarensis* in print. Tim and I were amazed: Once again, we had hoped for something substantial we could sink our teeth into. Instead, Mary Leakey and two colleagues attacked us in *Science* only on formal, nomenclatural grounds, offering a thin handful of objections to our choice of name, type specimen, and so forth. Many of their objections centered around the fact that a reporter for a British popular magazine had attended the Nobel Symposium and filed a story on *afarensis* before the name was formally announced in a professional journal. Technically, the magazine story was thus the formal announcement of the species, and since the reporter had ignored various rules of nomenclature, the species name was suspect! Richard Leakey's accompanying response, co-authored with Alan Walker, was almost as meager, challenging the validity of *afarensis* on the basis of a confusing weave of phylogenetic arguments that failed to address the morphology of the specimens at all.

For three years, that was all we heard from the Leakeys. In his public talks, Richard would give only a sprinkling of statements about *afarensis*, always unsupported, implying that Tim and I were mistaken, and that more fossils were needed before anything could be further clarified. I felt I was fencing with a phantom.

"I'm so sick of hearing about the need for new fossils," Tim said to me once in the summer of 1981, soon after I'd moved to Berkeley to establish the Institute for Human Origins. By this time he was a professor at Cal. "If new fossils prove us wrong, *fine*. I hope Richard finds them. But for once, lets see him put his cards on the table."

Tim and I were sitting in a café just across from the campus. *Lucy*, my book written with Maitland Edey, had recently been published, and I had been invited to appear on Walter Cronkite's *Universe* television series. The producers told me that Richard had also agreed to be on the show, and asked if I had any objections. Far from objecting, I was delighted. Richard had been claiming that the "rivalry" between us was a myth, largely the invention of the press. I thought that was misleading, and I welcomed the opportunity to meet with Richard on the record.

"This could be your only chance," Tim was saying. "You've got to press the point that there are major differences in the way we draw the family tree."

The broadcast was scheduled to be taped at the American Museum of Natural History in New York. The producers had asked me to bring along some props, so I carried with me a gorilla skull and a cast of an *afarensis* skull that had been carefully reconstructed by Tim and Bill Kimbel from pieces of several individuals. I had also put together a chart: On one side was the Johanson-White family tree. I'd left the other side blank.

I got to the museum with about half an hour to spare. Richard arrived about fifteen minutes later and greeted me in a friendly fashion. He told me that he too was about to publish a new book, the companion volume to the television series *The Making of Mankind*. He had with him some foundation people, his publisher, and his literary agent. Several paleontologists from the museum were also gathered around. Richard guided me behind a partition.

"Don, I hope this doesn't turn into a debate," he confided. "Our differences are really of a minor nature, and it would just confuse the public if we started going on about jaws. There's a terrible threat of creationism in this country, and we should show a united front."

"I don't agree that our disagreements are minor, but I don't know what's going to happen." I said. "I suppose it's up to Cronkite."

A few minutes later Cronkite appeared and we introduced ourselves. He was something of a childhood hero for me, and I was thrilled to meet him. Cronkite explained how the interview would unfold—first a question to me, then one to Richard, and so forth. Richard told him the same thing he'd said to me—that he didn't want the program to turn into a debate.

"I'm not Dan Rather and this isn't *60 Minutes*," said Cronkite.

The three of us sat down in a makeshift set constructed in the paleoanthropology section of the museum. In the background was a display of skulls. I put my family tree chart beside my chair, and the *afarensis* skull on the table in front of me. As soon as the cameras started to roll, it became apparent that a debate was just what Cronkite was looking for.

"We brought Donald Johanson and Richard Leakey together in the American Museum of Natural History to discuss their different ideas of man's ancestry," Cronkite said. He gave some background information on 1470, Lucy, and the Johanson-White hypothesis. Then it was my turn to speak. I laid out the situation as clearly as I could.

"There has been a controversy that has been going on now for nearly three years between Richard and myself, and it specifically focuses on the family tree," I said. I explained that we had presented our phylogeny in January 1979, but that others, specifically Richard, believed that it did not fit the evidence. Leakey's turn.

"I've heard it all before," he said. "I think it is marvelous. I just don't agree . . . but I'm not willing to discuss specifics. . . . [I'd heard that before too, I thought.] I'm not going to say whether you are right or wrong. But I think you're wrong." Then he gave a little laugh, as if the whole thing was in good fun and we should now move on to other questions. But I wasn't going to let him off so easily. My turn.

"I've brought along a sort of a portrayal of how I look at the family tree," I said. And with that I reached back and took out my chart. "And I've left a spot for you to draw your rendition."

"No, I don't think we can do this," Richard said obviously flustered. "I haven't got crayons, I haven't got cutouts, I'm not an artist . . ."

"I thought of that," I said, and I took a felt-tipped marker from my pocket and put it on the table in front of him. Richard left it lying there and said nothing. But as I started to explain the crux of our differences, he suddenly picked up the marker and asked me to hold one edge of the chart.

"I think in probability I would do *that*," he said, scrawling an angry "X" over my family tree. Now it was my turn to be taken aback. Meanwhile Cronkite was practically squirming with delight.

"And what would you draw in its place?" I said.

"A question mark!" Richard replied, and he drew one in the empty space. Then he sat back in his seat and laughed.

My turn once more. I explained how Richard's family had always believed that man's roots went back millions and millions of years, and that *Australopithecus* had nothing to do with our ancestry. Then I elaborated a bit on finding Lucy, and how we believed her to have everything to do with our origins. Richard had more chances to respond, but each time he dodged. Instead, he talked about how much he'd like to see new fossils discovered.

"I would love to prove him right," he said, "but I might just prove him wrong." One more little laugh, and the debate was over.

As soon as the taping was finished Richard got up and hurriedly left the set. I was told afterward by one of the producers that he refused to sign a release on his way out, declaring that he would not allow the show to be broadcast. Leakey's lawyers called and threatened to sue if the tape went on the air. According to the producer, Cronkite himself had to intervene, apologizing for any misunderstanding but making it clear that the broadcast was news and did not require any release. The show was broadcast as planned. Later, Richard claimed that he did not know about the shoot until the very day of the taping, and that Cronkite and I had planned the whole thing together. Neither statement is correct.

When I next saw Richard, he looked right past me. That was four years ago. We haven't spoken since. In public, he has continued to insist that our "rivalry" is largely the media's creation, and that beneath the hype there lie nothing more than minor professional disagreements. I wish it were that painless.

Through the 1980s, Richard expanded his search for ancient Man to the other side of Lake Turkana from Koobi Fora. The West Turkana region has yielded a lode of new finds—most recently the surprising "Black Skull." Richard should be commended for his part in that discovery. But neither the Black Skull nor any other fossil found in the last ten years lends an ounce more support to his belief in the antiquity of the human line. Richard has stuck to the family tradition nonetheless, believing that further exploration will eventually prove his father right.

It's his privilege, of course, to believe anything he wants, and someday he may well find the proof he seeks. For my part, I am quite happy not having a legacy to uphold. My own father—a barber by profession—died when I was two; I scarcely even remember him. I'm sure I bring prejudices of my own to the worktable when I examine a fossil, but I'd like to think that my belief in a more recent birth to humanity has arisen from the nature of the evidence that we have in hand. Nothing—not even the loss of friendships once held dear—can weaken that conviction. Nothing, that is, except for new evidence. And I will search for it whenever and wherever I am given the chance.

Not all of the critics of *afarensis* turned out to be as evasive as Richard Leakey. Though the 1980s, the legitimacy of the new taxon, and our conviction that there was only one species represented at

Hadar and Laetoli, was challenged over and over again, by seasoned investigators whose own views were threatened by it, and by young Ph.D.s cutting their teeth on a vulnerable target. Phillip Tobias, who had assumed Raymond Dart's chair at the University of Witwatersrand, was one of the first to respond. If fossil species can be "insulted," it was Dart's *africanus* who had suffered the worst affront in our reorganization of the human line: In effect, we had booted it out of its seminal role as the common ancestor of all known hominids, and shunted it onto the robust australopithecine line headed toward extinction. Tobias picked away at our published descriptions, trying to show that *afarensis* was in fact no more than an East African variant of *africanus.* In 1983, we responded with a detailed review of the facial, dental, and skull traits that distinguished *afarensis* as a separate, more primitive species. Tobias was eventually convinced enough to include the species in his own phylogenetic reconstructions.

Most of the other critics of *afarensis* bridled at the notion of one speicies yoking all the Hadar and Laetoli specimens. In each case, the scientist would focus in on a collection of anatomical details and point out how very different one group of Hadar fossils looked from another—at least in the specifics of anatomy that scientist had chosen to focus upon. Yves Coppens, who had joined Tim and me in the original announcement of *afarensis,* changed his mind and declared that he believed there were two species at Hadar after all, citing some differences in the cusps of premolars. His students Christine Tardieu and Brigitte Senut homed in on some differences in the shape of the femurs and upper arm bones of the large and small Hadar specimens. Adrienne Zihlman of the University of California at Santa Cruz declared that the difference in size among the arm and leg bones was alone too much to bear grouping into one species. Meanwhile, Dean Falk of Purdue University scrutinized the Hadar skull fragments and announced that the patterns of blood-drainage channels, faintly perceptible on the inside of the fragments, fell neatly into two groups—one looking like *Homo,* the other resembling those of the robust australopithecines.

Our most vociferous detractor was Todd Olson, a young anatomist at the City University of New York. Olson built his case substantially on a difference he perceived among the Hadar skulls in a region called the mastoid—the hump of bone that you can feel projecting just behind your ear. According to Olson, *some* of the Hadar

mastoids were puffed out—like those of the robust australopithecines—while others resembled the flatter condition of *africanus* and
Homo. Based on his interpretation of the mastoids and a selection of
other features, Olson was convinced that Lucy and some similarly
gracile fossils from Hadar represented the first members of the human
line, a species he called *Homo aethiopicus*. The other Hadar hominids
belonged on the robust lineage.

Tim, Bill, and I responded to each of these critics in turn, even
when we felt that their objections were trivial or had been addressed
before. The bottom line of our counterargument was the same one
we would draw for anyone discriminating species differences on the
basis of a few carefully chosen traits: No two animals have the exact
same anatomy, even if they are members of the same population, let
alone the same species. Meanwhile, through all the salvos launched
against *afarensis* in scientific meetings and journal pages, no one had
ever aimed a shot at the whole corpus of facial, dental, and jaw
characteristics that had brought home to us the clarifying unity of
the Hadar and Laetoli fossils in the first place. If people ignore the
evidence you marshal to support an argument, and instead strain to
find *other* evidence proving you wrong, then you start to think you've
made a pretty good case.

Collectively, the anti-*afarensis* attack was further weakened by
a lack of coherence: Olson and the others all were shouting "two
species at Hadar!," but they did not agree on which fossils belonged
in which of the two groups.

Nevertheless, by that summer of 1986 the mere fact that *afarensis* had drawn such persistent attack seemed to keep the skeptics
going on sheer inertia. Or perhaps something more powerful than
inertia was fueling all the quibbling over femur sizes and blood-drainage channels. Perhaps it was the old hope for the antiquity of *Homo*,
threatened when Tim and I drew the point of divergence between
the two branches of the hominid family tree *after* Lucy's time. If we
were wrong and there really *were* two species at Hadar in the late
Pliocene, then their lineages could again be extended back in time
before three million years, to meet at some distant point in a still-
to-be discovered common ancestor. The unconscious unspoken subtext
of that hope is a belief in the venerable uniqueness of the human
line, distinct from the rest of creation, even as it fades from sight
into the unwitnessed past. Such a powerful idea is not going to die
just because a couple of scientists read some bones and come up with

a different story. After all, it is what humanity has believed about itself for centuries.

The year before, Richard Leakey's team at West Turkana had come up with a new fossil that could be construed to keep that hope alive. "The Black Skull," as it came to be called, was found by Richard's long-time colleague Alan Walker. Alan had brought a cast of the skull with him to a scientific meeting just a few months before we had left for Olduvai Gorge. I had not been able to attend the meeting, but I asked a colleague about it later.

"Walker was the happiest man in town," my colleague told me. "He was carrying that skull around in a blue plastic bag, which he would open up for anyone who wanted a peek. That bag drew people like candy draws kids."

Alan Walker had every right to be proud of his find. For years paleoanthropologists, myself included, had been lamenting the lack of fossil evidence for human evolution from the critical time period two to three million years ago, between the known presence of *Australopithecus afarensis* and the appearance of all later hominids, including *Homo*. Alan's discovery was securely dated smack dab in the middle of that chronological "black hole." It was a beautiful specimen, with much of the braincase and face intact. Only one complete tooth remained; it had fallen out of the upper jaw. The biggest surprise about the Black Skull, or KNM-WT 17000 as it is formally named, was its baffling mixture of very primitive and very advanced traits.

In taxonomy, the word "advanced" does not mean "better," and it certainly does not mean "more human." Advanced traits are simply those that are more specialized—evolved away from a primitive, generalized condition. A less misleading synonym is "derived." Even as Walker was gathering the pieces of the Black Skull off the ground, he could tell that this new specimen was derived in the direction of the robust australopithecines like Zinj, especially in the sheer massiveness of its face and jaws. The one preserved tooth, a premolar, was also enormous, similar to Zinj's own.

But in some other respects—especially in its hind portions—the skull seemed remarkably primitive, bearing the strongest similarities to *A. afarensis*, the most *unspecialized* hominid known. The base of the cranium, for instance, was flat rather than flexed, a primitive condition related to the apelike forward jut of the fossil's face. The size of the braincase indicated a minuscule brain capacity—only 410 cc, smaller than any adult hominid known save one partial specimen from Hadar. To accompany its teeny brain, the skull sported a bony ridge running down the back.

Clearly, this fossil was no ancient *Homo,* and on its own could add nothing to the debate over the number of species at Hadar. But many of the scientists who scorned *afarensis* nevertheless greeted the Black Skull as if it was some samurai warrior come to do battle for their cause. They argued that if the new cranium looked like a derived robust species in the face, but a primitive *afarensis* in the back, maybe that was because *afarensis* was merely a chimera.

At issue was the legitimacy of the *afarensis* skull reconstructed by Tim and Bill—the same one that I had brought to the taping of the Cronkite show several years before. We had never found an intact skull of a single adult at Hadar. To fill that important gap, Tim and Bill had painstakingly pieced together some face and cranial fragments from several Hadar individuals of approximately the same size. No one questioned that the reconstruction had been masterfully handled, but the fact that it was an acknowledged composite left it vulnerable to attack from the two-species adherents, including Richard Leakey. True to form, Richard did not offer his views in print. But in public lectures given soon after the announcement of the Black Skull in 1986, he insinuated that the reconstructed skull was nothing more than a hodgepodge conglomeration of two species.

"I know that Don would not like to agree with my interpretation," he told one audience at Cal Tech, "but science is not the business of agreeing or not agreeing."

Alan Walker's wife, Pat Shipman, also a paleoanthropologist, made the case explicit in the pages of *Discover* magazine. She proposed that Tim and Bill might have force-fit the braincase of an early robust australopithecine on to the faces of more gracile forms. This mistake would explain why the robustlike Black Skull matched up with *afarensis* only in the back, not in the front. Presumably, if an expedition was allowed back into Ethiopia and was lucky enough to find a bunch of new skulls, some of them would look robust both back *and* front, while others would be gracile all around. Two species, not one. Out of the ashes of *afarensis,* the hope for ancient *Homo* would emerge once again.

"Here we go again," I said to Tim when he showed me the *Discover* article. "Tell me, what sort of strange geological circumstances do you think would have destroyed only the faces of the

Bill Kimbel studies the skull of afarensis *he reconstructed with Tim White. No complete crania or skulls were found at Hadar, but Kimbel and White's composite, based on fragments from twelve male individuals, gave researchers a tool for better understanding the anatomy of* afarensis. DAVID BRILL

alleged robust species, and only the braincases of the gracile one?"

There were other problems with Shipman's argument. She claimed that there was no specimen in the Hadar collection of skull fragments in which continuous bone connected the face to the braincase—a bit of evidence that would help determine the accuracy of our reconstructed composite skull. She was simply mistaken on that point. One Hadar specimen, A.L. 58-22, is indeed comprised of both facial and cranial pieces. There is nothing about that specimen that shows it is derived in the direction of the robust australopithecines; on the contrary, it is a perfect example of the primitive, generalized morphology that led us in the first place to believe that *afarensis* was the ancestor to all later hominids. Most important, among the hundreds of fossils in the Hadar collection, we had never located a single anatomical trait that could unequivocably place a specimen on the robust australopithecine lineage.

The Black Skull notwithstanding, today almost every one of our critics has come around to accepting *afarensis*. There is no question, however, that Alan Walker's extraordinary find demands a redrawing of most versions of the family tree—including the one Tim and I had

The enigmatic Black Skull (KNM-WT 17000), found in Kenya by Alan Walker in 1985.

proposed back in 1979. In our original accounting of the known hominids, we had seen the very specialized, robust characteristics of East African *boisei* and South African *robustus* as the end products of a trend in australopithecine evolution. This trend toward massive back teeth and big jaw muscle attachments could be seen faintly in the primitive *afarensis*, became progressively amplified in *africanus*, and reached its fullest expression in *robustus* and especially the "hyper-robust" *boisei*.

In our analysis, we had placed *boisei* in the same species as *robustus*, although evidence was mounting even then for keeping them separate. Yoel Rak, a paleoanthropologist at Tel Aviv University, made a particularly strong case for a species-level distinction for *boisei* in 1983, based on a detailed analysis of australopithecine faces. The Black Skull further strengthened this distinction, defining a separated evolutionary history for *boisei* in East Africa. Indeed, in their analysis Walker and Leakey asserted that the 2.5 million-year-old specimen could be assigned to the species A. *boisei*.

We didn't think things were quite that simple. In the basement lab of the Institute of Human Origins, there is a blackboard set along the length of one wall. Before leaving for Olduvai, Bill Kimbel and I had started sneaking down to that blackboard whenever we could find a spare moment. Sometimes Tim would take a break from his duties at the university and wander over. Anybody looking down on us through the sidewalk-level window would have seen the same scenario repeated again and again: a man stepping up to the blackboard, scribbling something, and stepping back, staring glumly at the result. Then he or another man would step up and erase it, scribbling something else in its place.

On the left side of our blackboard, Bill had chalked in the three most popular pre–Black Skull versions of the hominid family tree. All were essentially two-pronged family trees, differing chiefly in the placement of *Australopithecus africanus*. In the one Tim and I had put forth in 1979, *afarensis* was depicted as the last common ancestor of all subsequent hominids. One branch of our tree led directly to *Homo*, while the other led from *africanus* to the "robusts," *robustus* and *boisei*. A second version had *africanus* shunted over to the *Homo* line instead. A third phylogeny placed *africanus below* the branching of the forks of the tree, so that it and not *afarensis* was the last common ancestor. Bill had sketched these three trees in very small, and indeed their value had shrunk considerably since Alan Walker's discovery had burst upon the scene.

Next, we made a list of the various distinguishing traits of the Black Skull. The rest of the blackboard was reserved for experimenting, trying to squeeze some sense out of the baffling problems the new fossil presented. At this time we were also beginning to formulate ideas for a paper we were to present at a symposium on the evolutionary history of robust australopithecines, organized by Fred Grine at the State University of New York at Stony Brook. We decided to take the opportunity to see just where the Black Skull might fit in the scheme of things.

Like all taxonomists attempting to establish the relationships between extinct species, we were forced to work around a critical "as if": the assumption that a morphological similarity between any two fossils implies an evolutionary relationship. At the same time, we knew that such similarities can often be deceiving. To take just one obvious example, sharks and porpoises both have fins, torpedo-shaped bodies, and numerous other adaptations for swimming, but no one would suggest they are closely related. Porpoises are mammals, of course. The fact that they share some very specific adaptations with sharks is an example of *evolutionary convergence*—two unrelated species converging on similar solutions to an environmental problem.

The very different evolutionary histories of sharks and porpoises are easy to see when you look at them as whole organisms, with many complexes of traits that have little to do with each other. But what if you only had two fossilized dorsal fins to go by, from animals

Paleoanthropologists Alan Walker, Yoel Rak, and Bill Kimbel compare a cast of the Black Skull, left, with that of another robust australopithecine. DONALD JOHANSON

long extinct? It might not be so easy to tell whether or not they represent related species or not. The same goes for extinct hominids. And convergence is not the only pitfall waiting to confound the taxonomist. Sometimes, the same traits can evolve independently from the same starting point—what we call *parallelism.* Old World and New World monkeys, for example, look and behave in surprisingly similar ways. But their evolutionary histories have been kept separated by an ocean for at least forty million years; the traits they share have evolved "in parallel." Another curve ball that evolution can throw is called *reversal.* In this case, a trait that has been lost reappears later on in the same lineage. Perhaps a long-tailed monkey species evolved into a short-tailed one, only to sport a long tail again when new selective pressures demanded it thousands of years later.

The taxonomic monkey wrenches of convergence, parallelism, and reversal have traditionally been treated by paleoanthropologists with a kind of half-embarrassed sleight of hand: We trot them out when we need something to explain an anomaly in an otherwise neat and tidy hypothesis, but otherwise we would rather pretend they don't exist. In a sense, we have to proceed as if they do not exist, though we know that of course they do. This deliberate self-deception is excused by the scientific principle of parsimony: When considering competing solutions to a problem, the one closes to the truth will probably be the simplest. The "best" version of human phylogeny would thus be the one with the shortest list of special pleadings needed to account for the known evidence.

More than anything else that the Black Skull told us, it brought home the realization that there are *no* parsimonious versions of human phylogeny. We began our evaluation of the new specimen by comparing some thirty-two anatomical traits found in the Black Skull and other species of *Australopithecus*. Immediately, we could see that there were problems with calling the skull *boisei*, as Walker and Leakey were maintaining. Twelve of the traits seen in the Black Skull were shared with both *robustus* and *boisei*, establishing the "robust" nature of the skull, but failing to define an exclusive affinity with either one. Indeed, out of the thirty-two traits, only *two* were exclusively shared between the Black Skull and *boisei*.

At the same time, twelve of the remaining traits were primitive ones tying the Black Skull to *afarensis*. So, with its large teeth, sagittal crest, and other "robust" characters, the Black Skull was evolving in the direction of *boisei*—but it still possessed far too many primitive features typical of *afarensis* to be assigned to *boisei*. Indeed, it looked like a good candidate for an evolutionary intermediate—a "missing link," if you will—between *afarensis* and the robusts. Its 2.5-million-year-old date also placed it at the chronological midpoint between them, at 3.0 and 2.0 respectively.

The next consideration was what to call the Black Skull. One possibility was *afarensis*, but in spite of the many resemblances, assigning the new speciment to *afarensis* would obscure its evolutionary meaning. For a name, we turned to a nearly forgotten mandible from the Omo, found in 1967, which had been interpreted by Camille Arambourg and Yves Coppens as being more primitive than A. *boisei*. They called it *aethiopicus*. Like the Black Skull, the Omo mandible was dated to about 2.5 million years. We believed that the Black Skull belonged to the same species, and thus should be called *Australopithecus aethiopicus*.

Now came the fun part—redrawing the family tree. First of all, we realized that *aethiopicus* could qualify as an ancestor either to *robustus*, to *boisei*, or to both. Second, while we had previously believed *africanus* to be the last common ancestor to the robusts, it was obvious in light of the Black Skull that this was no longer a viable arrangement. The Black Skull shared too many primitive traits with *afarensis* to *africanus* to *aethiopicus* would impose too heavy a load of evolutionary reversals—the loss of a host of primitive traits in *africanus* that would make a perplexing reappearance in *aethiopicus*. The Black Skull *had* to be placed between *afarensis* and the robusts—

which unfortunately left *africanus* floating in limbo.

After lots of head scratching and chalk dust, we came up with four alternative family trees, illustrated on page 132, which we presented at the Stony Brook meeting. Not to go into excruciating detail, but all of these phylogenies imply the evolution of certain traits in parallel. Of the four phylogenies, I favor the first. In this version, the old two-pronged Johanson–White tree has sprouted a third branch directly from its fork. *Afarensis* is still the common ancestor of all other hominids, but its descendants evolve in three directions: one toward *Homo*; one through *aethiopicus* to *boisei*; and one through *africanus* to *robustus*. Tim prefers this phylogeny as well. Bill, on the other hand, likes the second tree better, with *africanus* the direct ancestor of *Homo* and *aethiopicus* the common ancestor of both *robustus* and *boisei*. The other two trees are probably less likely candidates, especially the one where *africanus* leaves no descendants.

At the time I am writing this, however, nobody really places a great deal of faith in *any* human family tree. In that sense, it may seem that the Black Skull has led us from clarity into confusion, from conviction into doubt. Such thinking is profoundly misleading. The Black Skull does what the best kind of evidence is supposed to do: It gives unambiguous proof or refutation to existing theories, and in so doing takes us one step closer to the absolute truth. To me, the realization that the truth is more complicated than we thought only makes the search for it more thrilling. Before the Black Skull, it was easier to believe that the ancestral human line was somehow distinct in its humanness, treading an inevitable and inviolate route through time unlike the paths followed by even our closest relatives. That is no longer the case. The very traits that we have assumed to be uniquely human may in fact have evolved in quite separate lineages, giving rise to ancient cousins much more like our own ancestors than we have always believed.

Some of my colleagues—notably Richard Leakey and Alan Walker—contend that until more fossils are found, we should not be wasting our time proposing family trees in the first place. I do not agree. As scientists, our first responsibility is to squeeze the last drop of information out of every bit of evidence we have in hand. But we must also be willing to take the next step, and build from that information theories that will be ready when the next discovery comes along to test their strength. That's what doing science means. Frustrating as it is, the distantly tantalizing truths about our origins will

With its curious combination of primitive and derived traits, the Black Skull forced a rethinking of all proposed human phylogenies. Four possible family trees are compared here. Version B above is probably the most popular, but most scientists agree that the evidence now available does not clearly support any one phylogeny over the others.

probably not be revealed before we ourselves are buried under the earth. But that will not stop me from testing and retesting new hypotheses, exploring further possibilities. The point is not to be right. The point is to make progress. And you cannot make progress if you are afraid to be wrong.

In the summer of 1986, my immediate concern was to find more fossils. We arrived at the Olduvai camp close to 4:00 P.M., the A&K combi surprising a trio of giraffes from a stand of acacia just outside the gate. They floated away with the heart-stopping grace giraffes alone possess, and we drove on through. Some of the camp staff were out in the yard unpacking cooking equipment. There was smoke coming from the cook's shed, and at least one of the two windmills was spinning steadily in the breeze above the Gorge. Gerry Eck came out to welcome us with relatively good news—though Mary had taken the iron stove, Stanley, the cook, had rigged up a serviceable wood-burning stove from a metal drum. Meanwhile Gerry had tended to the one working windmill and had it producing a modest current. He told us that the rest of the expedition members were out surveying in the main Gorge near FLK. Gen and Berhane are by temperament a lot less excitable than I am, but now they were fidgeting like two kids who'd just been dropped in the middle of Disneyland. I knew Tim was exhausted from jet lag, but he agreed anyway to take them down to meet up with the others.

I didn't want to go with them right away. After dropping my bag in what had been Mary Leakey's hut, I walked out across the yard, hopped over the fence, and kept walking in the direction the giraffes had floated, out toward the dusty level plain that stretched beyond to Seronera. Now that we'd finally reached camp, a feeling of uneasiness had taken possession again. What were we really doing here? What could we hope to accomplish in six short weeks? For whatever reason, there were people who I knew would be more than happy if we accomplished nothing at all. Maybe they were right. Maybe Olduvai was a poor proposition, and it should simply be shut down and declared a Tanzanian national monument, as Mary herself supposedly believed. On what presumption did I think the Gorge still held any promise?

Maybe the giraffes had the answers. A hundred yards off to my left I could see them browsing above the thorn trees—"long-stemmed, speckled gigantic flowers," Isak Dinesen called them—their tapered necks kneading the air as they floated tree to tree. They seemed so completely remote from the very notion of worry that I suddenly felt a pang of envy, as if it were somehow a better fate to face the lions of the Serengeti than to struggle along in the anxious environments we create with our own predacious ambitions. I turned around and looked back at the camp buildings, surrounded all around by a fence heaped with thorn branches to keep out lions and other intruders. Olduvai Gorge was my workplace now, though not under circumstances I could have foreseen. We would have to wait and see where that would take us.

PART III:

Hominid
Who?

CHAPTER FIVE:

Hominid Fever

But who knows the fate of his bones, or how often he is to be buried?
—Sir Thomas Browne

A THORN TREE STANDS IN front of the central building of the Olduvai camp, its umbrellalike canopy nearly touching the ground. Years ago Mary Leakey had a stone birdbath built beneath the tree. In the middle of the afternoon of July 21, I was sitting at the table in the open-air common room, watching a flock of weaver birds take turns at the bath. The acacia seemed ripe with chattering, bright yellow fruit. Every few moments a bird would slip off its perch and join the crowd already splashing around in the bath below, squeezing another bird back up into the tree. The weavers were all that moved in my range of sight; everything else was wrapped in the hazy stillness of midday. By the camp road—two parallel tracks of matted grass—a trio of goats dozed in the shade of a smaller acacia. The road passed through the camp gate, buried itself in a thicket of whispering thorn, and descended unseen into the Gorge. On the far side, the Serengeti swelled up toward the ancient eroded slopes of the volcano Lema-grut. It was the season when the local Maasai herdsmen burn the grasslands to encourage new growth, and a tulle of suspended smoke and dust veiled the volcano's summit.

We had been in the Gorge now for three days—time spent fam-iliarizing ourselves with the site, with the work that had to be done,

Members of the 1986 Olduvai Research Expedition. Top: Paul Manega, Bob Walter. Middle: Tim White, Donald Johanson, Prosper Ndessokia. Bottom: Berhane Asfaw, Gen Suwa DONALD JOHANSON

and with each other. There were fourteen of us in camp, including six scientists (two accompanied by their wives), four graduate students, and a couple of visitors. Field expeditions make for strange bedfellows; out in the middle of nowhere you throw some people together who may have little in common, and you hope that somehow an amicable society will emerge. It doesn't always work out—especially when the group is top-heavy with veteran scientists with strongly developed opinions and plenty of ego. I was well aware that in his controversial book *Bones: Ancient Men and Modern Myths*, Lew Binford had sunk his teeth into George Frison's influential interpretations of the behavior of early inhabitants of the New World, based on an important site in Wyoming. Now the two senior archeologists were sharing the same shower bag and latrine.

As it turned out, I needn't have worried on that score at all.

"I made some stabs in the wrong direction, and Lew set me straight," Frison told me when we had a chance to talk. "There's no hard feelings. If you can't take some heat, you're in the wrong business."

I wish more people in academic fields took that attitude—but

George Frison is not a typical academic. He spent his early adulthood as a rancher, entering the University of Wyoming as a freshman at the age of thirty-seven. George finished his undergraduate training in two years; three years later the Anthropology Department at the university had granted him a Ph.D. The following year, at the age of forty-three, he had become chairman of the department. He and his wife, June, are straightforward, friendly, salt-of-the-earth types, sparing of words. I liked them immediately.

I liked Lew Binford too, and his wife, Nancy Stone, turned out to be charming. But one could hardly call him sparing of words. A big, silver-bearded, barrel-chested man, Binford is one of those people whose brain always seems to be working at full throttle. Ideas flow out of him in a stream that at times he seems at a loss to control. It's worth taking the plunge and following him along. Lew is the most influential *thinker* in modern archeology—a prolific iconoclast whose insistence on rigorous self-questioning in the interpretation of sites has opened up a whole new approach to understanding the ancient past. In the process, he had probably set some sort of record for "Most Colleagues Offended in a Single Career." (Given time, Tim White may snatch that trophy away from him.)

The three African students in the group had been hand-picked for their talents by governments keen on developing national research prerogatives. Prosper Ndessokia and Paul Manega were being trained at American universities to assume key roles in Tanzania in, respectively, paleontology and geology. Berhane Asfaw was well on his way to his Ph.D. in paleoanthropology at Berkeley, and would be in an excellent position to help coordinate research in Ethiopia when the time came to push farther into the rich deposits of the Afar and Awash regions. Meanwhile Gen Suwa, already an expert on hominid dentition, was also near the end of his graduate work. He would return to Kyoto University in Japan, remaining active in East African sites.

These students were mature, committed professionals. They were not immune, however, to the flush of excitement that comes when you first arrive in the field. Suwa, finally given a taste of fieldwork after six years buried in the lab, was thoroughly infected with the bug, darting around the Olduvai outcrops as if human fossils were calling to him from under every rock. It seemed that whenever Tim and I sat down to relax after a stint of surveying, Gen would appear in his inevitable blue windbreaker, rock hammer in hand, practically panting to go back out and find an australopithecine skull.

"He's got a bad case of hominid fever," Tim laughed. "Let's hope we all catch it." You have to be optimistic in this business—disappointments come much too often.

While in Berkeley, Prosper Ndessokia had befriended a young Californian named Jeremy Paul and had invited him to spend a few days with us at the Olduvai camp. Jeremy was on the first leg of a round-the-world trek with an ambitiously rugged itinerary. He had outfitted himself with an array of state-of-the-art gear, including a super-lightweight water purifier and a Walkman tape player apparently built to withstand a downpour in Rwanda or a fall from a cliff in Nepal. Jeremy was friendly and ready to help around camp with anything that needed doing, but I could tell that his cool California mannerisms grated on some members of the staff. He had saved up the money for his journey by working in his family's hot-tub business in Marin County.

"Johanson takes over Olduvai Gorge, and one of the first experts he brings in is a Jacuzzi salesman," Tim White kidded me one evening. "Just wait until the boys in the Nairobi Museum get hold of that!"

We had assembled a mixed group, and not surprisingly it was taking a little time for everyone to get accustomed to the others. As it turned out, the initial bonds were cemented with peanut butter. We had all the ingredients needed: plenty of peanuts in camp, my blender from Berkeley, and one working windmill to provide electric current. The peanuts, however, first had to be shelled and divested of their skins. This job required a considerable labor force. On the previous afternoon, everyone had pitched into the business of skinning peanuts. After about thirty minutes we had accumulated enough raw material for several blenderfuls of butter, and a less definable amount of mutual goodwill. We revved up the Waring and soon had a pint of lumpy goo. Served on slices of freshly baked bread, it more than rewarded the effort of carting the machine from the other side of the world.

Halfway into a second batch, the blender abruptly and mysteriously stopped. Gerry Eck took it apart and tinkered with it for a while, growing more involved the longer the blender resisted his mechanical talents. When Gerry took a break, Tim slipped in and took his place, with several others kibitzing over his shoulder. Ten minutes later he threw up his hands and walked off to take a shower.

"*I've* got something that will fix it," Jeremy Paul declared, rooting through his backpack. I half expected him to pull out a featherweight voltmeter and a package of dehydrated blender parts. He reemerged instead with a six-inch length of wire, which he used to bypass the on-off switch. But there was still no sound from the blender. Gerry returned and poked at it for a while, then George Frison had a go, but they only succeeded in further degutting the machine.

Now, a day later, my blender lay strewn about the far end of the table like the remains of a lion kill that had been picked clean by scavengers. Every once in a while somebody would return to it with renewed interest, but quickly the will to tinker would fade. We never did get it to work again, nor did we discover why it had so mysteriously died in the first place.

Bob Walter, the expedition geologist, showed no interest in small-appliance mechanics. I knew Bob well from the Hadar times. A dapper fellow with wide innocent eyes and a wry sense of humor, he always comes in for a lot of kidding in camp, though I'm at a loss to explain why. Perhaps it's a quality he has of seeming perpetually clean, inside and out. After a morning of surveying in some sun-baked gully, Bob would return looking eager and perfectly scrubbed, as if the dust that settled on the rest of us was repelled by some special property of his skin.

Not long after dawn on the first morning in camp, Bob had taken the whole group out to look at the geology of the Second Fault—a five-mile ride along the northern rim of the Gorge. The lorry came to an abrupt stop just a few feet from the edge. A stiff wind pushed against our backs as we walked to the precipice. For a few moments we stared out across the emptiness at the bare, muscular horizons on the opposite side, plunging 250 feet down to the Gorge floor. The fault line was clear: a diagonal gouge running bottom left to top right. To the right, west of the fault, the deposits lay fairly undisturbed, but to the east the entire landmass had sunk down, collapsing the strata into the fault line. Looking down the length of the Gorge, I could see where it narrowed before leveling off into the Olbalbal Depression, a shallow drainage basin lying beneath rose-tinted highlands to the east.

Bob found a little promontory where he could stand in front of us and use the Gorge as an illustration of itself.

"You can get a pretty good perspective here on the entire geological sequence in the Gorge," he said. "Do you see that black stuff at the foot of the cliff and down on the floor? That's the basalt that forms the base of the Olduvai beds. If you walked down to the bottom on this side you'd find almost a hundred feet of it exposed in the cliff face. We know from the original potassium-argon dating done here in the later fifties that the basalt is about two million years old. Above the black lava you've got the sequence of ash deposits that we call Bed I. There's close to a hundred feet of it too, here at the Second Fault, representing some three hundred thousand years. Bed I is composed of volcanic tuffs interspersed with clay stone deposits. Some of the tuffs have very distinctive features, which have been a big help in correlating strata horizontally over the length of the Gorge. Take for instance Tuff IB—that's the band of lighter gray just above the base of the cliff on the right."

Bob continued to point out the successive strata visible across the Gorge, almost shouting to make himself heard over the wind. Bed II, he explained, was a series of clay and sandstone tuffs and deposits, about eighty feet thick at the Fault. It represented some 600,000 years of prehistoric time, and like Bed I had proved rich in fossilized bone and artifacts. These included cranial remains of both *Homo habilis* and *Homo erectus*, along with several extremely important archeological sites.

Lying atop Bed II were the crisply defined sedimentary deposits of Bed III: a rich copper color sandwiched between duller buffs and grays. While certainly the most vibrantly colored stratum at Olduvai, Bed III has yielded few fossils. Bed IV, a brownish-gray series of tuffs visible here only on the collapsed, eastern side of the Fault, has proved similarly sparse in preserved remains. Above Bed IV lies a series of younger ash deposits: the Masek and Ndutu beds, named after lakes at the head of the Gorge, and a bed called the Naisiusiu (pronounced "Nay-soo-soo"), which is the Maasai word for the sound of dry grass rustling in the wind. A lot of local names are Maasai in origin, including "Olduvai" itself, a corruption of the Maasai word *Oldupai*, which means "Place of the Wild Sisal." Found all over the Gorge, the formidable-looking sisal plant grows in clusters of thick tapering stalks, sharp as spears.

Earlier in this book I've referred to the Olduvai stratigraphy as a "layer cake," as if each of these beds was neatly stacked on the one below. As Bob Walter would quickly point out, two million years of geologic upheaval and reworking by the elements produce a much more complex concoction than the cake metaphor really implies.

Consider, for instance, the cake "pan" of hard black basalt underlying Bed I, belched out as molten lava from fissures in the earth's crust. When the lava cooled, it formed an undulating, uneven surface, so that the "batter" of hot ash and detritus thrown down by the volcanoes collected unevenly, filling up depressions in the pan, but only thinly coating the higher ridges. As more layers began to collect, the unfinished cake was further disturbed by violent shifts in the earth's crust—the ravaged strata at the Second Fault forever bearing witness to one of them.

After five major faults and innumerable smaller ones, the layers of the cake would no longer match up horizontally. Meanwhile, the surface of the landscape was being continually stirred and confused by the action of streams, wind, and other natural forces. Next, this disheveled dessert was eaten into by erosion—the cutting of the Gorge itself, beginning some half a million years ago. Only after the older deposits were well bitten into was the "icing" of the cake laid down: more windblown volcanic eruptions, forming the Ndutu and Naisiusiu beds. Here at the Second Fault the stratigraphy might look tidily cakelike, but if we were to get back in the lorry and drive to some other overlook, the geological sequence would be more obscure, and certainly different. It is this horizontal variation running across the Gorge's horizons that has really tested the geologists' patience.

Most of that patience—twenty years of it—was supplied by Richard Hay, now at the University of Illinois. A quiet, unflappable geological detective, Hay walked out, picked at, sifted through, and analyzed the composition of rock in dozens of cliff faces and gullies. His work incorporated a wealth of information to help him correlate the various deposits. By the time he was finished, Dick Hay had not only reconstructed the geological history of the place, but had synthesized that data into a remarkably convincing portrait of the changing Olduvai environment.

Hay found that during the deposition of Bed I and the lower part of Bed II (from about 1.9 to 1.6 million years ago), the region had been dominated by a wide, shallow alkaline lake that lay at the foot of volcanic highlands to the east. Numerous freshwater streams and small rivers flowed *into* the lake, but it had no outlet; consequently the water alternately covered and exposed a wide floodplain. Fed by the intermittent inundation of mineral-rich volcanic ash, the highly alkaline lake could support an abundance of microscopic algae, which in turn supported fish and birds, themselves prey to larger creatures like crocodiles. Plant life in the lake margin also lured a wealth of herbivores—ancient elephant and their extinct cousin, *Deinotherium*, as well as wild horse, rhino, hippo, and a plethora of bovids. The irony of this Rousseauesque vision of bio-abundance is that periodically it would all be chased out by a new blanket of the very ash that had sparked such fertility in the first place.

One of the most informative clues to the ancient ecology of Olduvai is the wealth of fauna preserved in its piled layers of time. A little over a million and a half years ago, the "profile" of the typical Olduvai inhabitant changed. Animals that lived exclusively in swampy habitats, such as hippo, abruptly disappeared, to be replaced by a greater frequency of species adapted to the drier conditions of a savannah habitat. This "faunal break," echoed in the kinds of pollen preserved and the record of windblown and water-worked particles forming the deposits, coincided with the beginning of widespread faulting in the region.

Perhaps aided by global changes in climate, the giant shifts in the earth shrank the lake to a third of its size and set in motion a gradual eastward march of its drainage sump, until it reached its present location in the Olbalbal Basin some 400,000 years ago. The changing portrait of water accumulation and drainage was of course of more than academic interest: Almost all animals, hominids included, need sources of fresh water. Locate the prevailing watercourses, and that's where you'll find bones and archeological sites. In his work with Mary Leakey, Dick Hay found that by Bed III and Bed IV times, the traces of prehistoric humanity had spread out and dispersed along stream beds.

Today, Olduvai Gorge cuts a twenty-five-mile-long Y into the Serengeti. Where the narrower southern arm of the Y—the Side Gorge—meets the Main Gorge, there is a broad, flat area called the Junction. Before getting down to work, we decided to take the students and other newcomers to an overlook commanding a view of this prime fossil area. The lorry barreled through the Junction and labored up the slope on the other side. After a few minutes we pulled up beside the little museum and grass-roofed *banda* that the Tanzanian Department of antiquities provides at the overlook. I took my camera and wide-angle lens and walked away from the others, vaguely seeking a well-composed shot. Near my vantage point, a grand, isolated rock prominence called the Castle rose up almost to rim level, red with the iron-rich silt of Bed III, plunging in a skirt of gray rubble toward the Gorge floor.

A

NAIBOR
SOIT
INSELBERG

Bed I
LAKE

Volcanic
Highlands

CIRCA TWO MILLION YEARS AGO

B

[DRAWINGS NOT DONE TO SCALE ~ FEATURES EXAGGERATED]

SCARPS ALONG FAULT LINES

Olbalbal
Depression

STREAM

(FOSSIL BURIED MANY METERS BELOW STREAM)

CIRCA TWO HUNDRED THOUSAND YEARS AGO

C

PRESENT

A. Lava, ash, sedimentary rocks
(Bed I), settle over ancient basement
rock layer. (Lake gradually fills in)

B. Earth movements cause 100+ meter
drop (at east end of present Gorge).
Scarps appear along fault lines.

C. Erosion by water cuts 100-meter
depth along length of Gorge, exposing
Bed I (& ancient fossils) after cutting
through more
recent strata.

What makes Olduvai such a rich fossil site is its unique geological history. Two million
years ago, the wide, shallow alkaline lake at Olduvai drew an abundance of life to its
shores. The bones of many animals, hominids included, were buried by sediments and
volcanic eruptions. Within the last five hundred thousand years, major earth movements created a depression to the east, and the flowing waters of a stream began to cut
through the accumulated deposits. Today the Gorge is one hundred meters deep,
exposing the fossilized bones buried when the lake still dominated the terrain.

Two hundred feet below, the Junction lay like a tableau, every contour of rock or flush of vegetation crisply outlined by the oblique light of the morning. The dry bed of the Olduvai River wormed its way through a broken patchwork of aloe, acacia, and wild sisal. The scene possessed an inanimate beauty, infinitely receding, like a view through the wrong end of a telescope. I put the camera aside and gazed down, almost hypnotized. Off to my left I could hear Lew Binford and Bob Walter discussing some geological points, but their voices too sounded distant, as if I were caught suspended between the present moment and the unreachable timelessness of the Gorge at my feet.

Suddenly two vivid images seemed to merge in my mind and impose themselves on the scene below. The first was the view of Lake Manyara, where we had stopped the day before. Almost two million years ago, the eastern margin of the similar Olduvai lake lay just where I was looking. Now in my mind I could see the ancient water, its shallow, sun-dappled surface choked with reeds. The cliffs on the opposite side of the Gorge disappeared; I was no longer standing high above the lake, but instead on a gentle rise beside it. I imagined it so clearly that I could almost smell its saline pungency, a mix of brine and rot. Hippo and crocodile basked along the banks, and a gaudy ribbon of flamingoes fringed the water's edge.

The second image was more disturbing. It leaped into my conciousness from the dream I had experienced that restless night in Dar es Salaam. There was a lake in that dream too, brightly colored and inviting, but naggingly out of reach. I wanted to immerse myself in its waters, but something kept holding me back. As in the dream, the air now was full of a insistent murmuring. I looked back toward the museum overlook: Tim, Bob, and the others had all disappeared. In their place, a party of Italian tourists had emerged from a trio of safari combis. They were talking all at once and pointing into the Gorge. I glanced down. Tim and Bob were slowly picking their way across the slope toward the Castle. Prosper and Gen followed behind, and I could make out Lew Binford and his wife, Nancy, farther down. Just then Tim looked back in my direction.

"Hey, Johanson!" he shouted. "You come here to find hominids or to take pictures? Get your butt down here!"

I snapped out of my trance. Buckling the camera strap around my waist, I carefully dropped down onto the slope.

*   *   *

We spent the first day surveying around an area just to the east of the Castle called HWK (Henrietta Wilfrida Karongo) a fossil site defined by the slopes of a dry stream bed. It was at HWK the summer before that we had cleared off the five-square-meter patch of slope. When I caught up to Tim he was squatting on the ground next to the patch, with Gen and Berhane standing beside him. The boundaries of our 1985 square were still clear, but they had filled up with a jumble of debris.

"What do you think, Don?" said Tim. I looked down at the square. Even with a quick scan I could see a piece of horse limb, some tortoiseshell, and a couple of fossil teeth, as well as a beautiful pink-quartz chopper and some other stone tools.

"I think Olduvai must be the liveliest dead site in East Africa," I said. "It will take us a half a day just to inventory this stuff."

"Keep in mind that as far as we can see at first glance, none of this material is *in situ,*" Tim said to his students, meaning that the material was lying on the surface instead of eroding directly out of the deposit on which it was found. "It was all carried down by the rain this spring, from God knows where up the slope. If I've got a gripe about Olduvai, that's it—there's just too much *time* piled up in these deposits. If you don't find your fossil *in situ,* it could be two hundred thousand years old, or two million."

"True enough," I said, "but the purpose of this experiment was to demonstrate that erosion constantly exposes new material, not to ascertain where that material comes from. And I think we've made our point."

"Not until we've got this stuff all plotted and catalogued," Tim answered. He turned one of his sly, lopsided grins on his two students. "Either of you guys want to volunteer for that job, while Johanson and I go on ahead? I got a feeling we're going to find Zinj's girlfriend in this damn gully."

Gen and Berhane knew their teacher well enough not to bite on the tease. He wouldn't ask them to spend the first day in Olduvai Gorge counting rocks and anonymous bits of bone.

"Zinj's girlfriend?" said Gen. "HWK is half a million years above the Zinj floor."

"So, maybe she likes older men," Berhane added softly. We all laughed and started down the stream bed, leaving the work on the square for later.

The four of us fanned out across the western slope above the stream bed, which was heavily carved by rain runoff—a good surface to explore for newly exposed material. I found a deep gully and began to work my way up, eyes on the ground. The light was perfect— plenty of midmorning shadow to add definition to the groundscape.

Still, I knew that the chances of finding anything unusual were slim. Discoveries are rarely made the first few days in the field. It takes time to attune your eyes to a radically different scale. In the landscapes of our normal routines, we're used to scanning for big things—our car in the parking lot, or the gas station on the corner where the directions say we should turn left. And the backgrounds we see in our everyday life are usually simple—pavements, carpets, painted walls. Out in the field, you're asking your eyes to scrutinize a clutter of tiny objects of subtle textures and color, all randomly arrayed. HWK is a fairly rich site, and I could easily make out the larger fragments of bone lying here and there. But these big pieces were the ones that had probably been picked up, evaluated, and discarded by a dozen other fossil hunters who had walked this slope before us. Of course I checked each one again, just to be sure. But I was well aware that at the same time my eyes might be blind to smaller, subtler clues—the faintest sheen cast by bone eroding out of a rain-cut hollow, or an unusual pattern of relief in the dust.

A few yards to my right I noticed a hand ax lying on a little ledge. No hand axes have been found *in situ* at HWK, and this one had no doubt slid down the slope from some level up above. It had little value, therefore, as an archeological artifact. I traversed the pebbly lag anyway and picked up the tool. It was a classic example of the type: a symmetrical teardrop of worked quartz about six inches in length, with flakes knocked off on two faces to form an edge. The broad end fit comfortably in my grip. There's a strange urgency in these ancient axes: As soon as you pick one up its balanced heft seems to compel your arm to *do* something with it, if only to rock your elbow and appraise its weight in your palm. The "biface" hand ax typifies a period called the Acheulean, which endures in the archeological record for a stunning length of time. Tools very much like the one I now held had been found in European sites as young as 500,000 years, as well as in Olduvai deposits dated at a million and a half.

Whatever they were used for, clearly the hand axes and other Acheulean tools were doing it efficiently. Compared to the longevity of the hand ax, the invention of the automobile—or for that matter the wheel itself—strikes me as a sort of cultural whimsy, a fleeting bit of gadgetry. Thousands of generations separated me from the individual who had knocked this flake of rock off a boulder and fashioned its shape. But I, a user of garage-door openers, power saws, and electric blenders, could instantly recognize it as a *tool*, potent with human purpose. Gently, idly, I tapped the blunted point against my palm. For a moment a few thousand generations didn't seem like much time at all. I could count them off in less than an hour with gentle taps of the tool in the palm of my hand—parent to child, parent to child. There was something very reassuring, almost liberating about that thought. I smiled to myself and put the hand ax back on the ledge where I had found it.

I've already mentioned the first stone tool recorded from Olduvai—the one Louis Leakey brought back to camp in 1931 to win his bet with Hans Reck. By the time Mary Leakey retired from the field in 1983, the Olduvai horizons had disgorged over 37,000 more tools—certainly the most grandly informative record of early man from any one site on earth. In addition to their sheer quantity, the Olduvai artifacts are of remarkable quality. Most important, the nature of the tools changes through time, bearing testimony to the increasing sophistication of human culture through its first million and a half years.

The earliest stone tools found in Olduvai Bed I sites date from very close to the beginnings of the archeological record. In Mary's evaluation, the "tool kit" used by the hominids in the very oldest sites, such as the Zinj floor at 1.8 million years, consisted of rough choppers, flakes, and similarly unembellished forms, all created by a few strokes of a hammerstone on one side of a rock core. The forms of these "Oldowan" tools became more complex the higher up she looked in the geological strata—rough-faceted polyhedrons, for example, giving way through time to remarkably smooth spheroids. Twenty years earlier, Louis had believed that this gradual trend toward sophistication culminated in the elegant Acheulean tradition. But Mary could see that in fact the hand axes and other Acheulean tools appeared quite abruptly in the middle Bed II, about 1.6 million years ago. For the next million years, the Oldowan and Acheulean industries continued on side by side, all the way into upper Bed IV—*but never occurred at the same site.* This odd duality led Mary and her colleagues to suggest that perhaps the Acheulean tools represented the culture of an entirely different group of hominids, one that had arrived at Olduvai from some other region. That theory was made all the more convincing by the sudden appearance of *Homo erectus* fossils in the Gorge at about the same time.

Over the years, Mary and her colleagues chiseled from the archeological record of the Gorge a carefully worked portrait of early human activity. At its center was the increasing importance of hunting and the role it played in establishing uniquely human patterns of behavior and social organization. The "hunting hypothesis" was no idle theory: It was bolted to a structure of evidence so broad-shouldered and powerful that no one even considered doubting its validity.

No one, that is, until Lewis Binford came along. Binford's shoulders are pretty broad too, and he plays the game of archeology much the way a good defensive end plays football—with quick intelligence and murderous elan. In his *Bones* book, Binford came down hard on the conventional interpretation of the Olduvai archeological record, questioning the very foundations of the hunting hypothesis and upsetting a lot of people in the process. I will save the substance of that debate for later. Let it suffice to say now that I wasn't sure that I agreed with everything Binford said, but I knew his ideas were worth taking very seriously—enough to invite him to Olduvai.

The evening after that first surveying excursion at HWK, he and George Frison were clearly excited.

"We found tons of evidence of hominid behavior out there," Lew told me after dinner had been cleared away. "There were bones showing cut marks and impact fractures all over the place."

Cut marks are the preserved scratchings from hominid tools found on faunal remains; impact fractures are breaks in bones indicating by their pattern that they were made by the crushing blow of a stone implement. Though he had never visited Olduvai before, Binford knew its topography as well as his own backyard in Corrales, New Mexico. Now he sketched a quick map on the back of an envelope lying on the table.

"The way we see it, there are really two places to look for good sites in the Gorge," he said. "We know that the hominids had to rely on water sources like everything else out there. In the dry season, the place to be would have been over here toward the west, at the Ndutu Stream entrance to the lake basin. In the wet season, you've got drainage from those volcanoes to the east into *this* region." He circled on his map an area around the Castle, including

HWK. "If you could excavate sites in both these areas, you might begin to see the difference between dry- and wet-season usage by hominids. Now *that* would be something worth doing."

I listened with interest. Not many people had done comparative studies of seasonal use by early hominids. In different seasons, the hominids' diet would change—and if their food sources varied, so might the kind and pattern of tools and discarded bones they left behind. Millions of years later, the archeological record would be fundamentally different too. This was just the sort of insight I was hoping for. We talked for a while more around the table, then went to bed.

After a late start, the second day in camp was devoted to surveying in a couple of Bed II sites in the Side Gorge. At a place called FC, Tim stopped to give his students an on-location lecture on field practice. I was fifty feet downslope, but his deep, melodious voice carried well.

"Let's pretend this chunk of equid femur is a hominid," Tim said, picking up a fragment of horse leg bone from the surface. "Is it *in situ*? No. Suwa—any matrix on that bone?"

Tim handed the fossil over to Gen, who shook his head and handed it back. "Matrix" refers to any mineral deposits clinging to the bone that might help identify which stratum in the slope it originally came from. If the fossil is not *in situ*, matrix is the only sure way of pinpointing its age.

"Right. The first thing you'd do now is check the thing for fresh breaks. You can see by the sharp edges that this bone has broken up only recently, so more of it might still be around. So the second thing you'd do is get the hell off this slope before you step on anything. You'd want to systematically put some kind of square around this area to confine your search area. Cut that square into smaller segments, then start at the bottom of the slope and work up, picking every bone fragment out of each segment. Only after the surface is completely checked do you think about digging.

"Let's say you've cleaned the slope and still haven't found anything else," Tim continued. "If you decide to dig, you're looking at a couple of weeks of work. Minimum. So you've got to ask yourself— for Christ's sake, is this worth the time? If what you've got in hand is a five-million-year-old hominid femur, you bet it is. But if it's a chunk of *Homo erectus* limb from Bed III, you might say to hell with it. In the field, you're always running against the clock, and those

The stone circle at DK in Olduvai Gorge, thought by Mary Leakey and her associates to represent the remains of an ancient dwelling

decisions have to be made. Every minute you spend digging here is a minute lost somewhere else in your site."

Tim threw the stand-in hominid bone back on the ground. "Now let's take a look over here," he said. "Asfaw—what can you tell me about this tuff?"

The three of them climbed into the next gully over, out of earshot. I continued on up the slope.

With the students in mind as much as the visiting archeologists, we had planned for today an excursion to a famous site called DK out toward the Second Fault. In 1962, Mary and her team had un-covered a remarkable feature on what appeared—judging from the tools and broken faunal bones scattered about—to be a home base of early hominids. While clearing away some blocks of lava, Mary no-ticed that the remaining blocks seemed to form part of a rough circle about thirteen feet in diameter. Some of the stones were even piled up on each other. The pattern prompted Helson Mukuri, a long-time member of the Leakeys' African staff, to point out that he knew of nomadic tribes in parts of Africa who built shelters out of branches and animal sinks piled on stone bases. Could this "stone circle" be the remains of some prehistoric structure? Mary replaced the lava blocks that she had already removed. Inside the circle, the concen-tration of broken faunal bones was much less dense than outside, suggesting that the resident hominids had tossed away the discarded remains of their meals. Most astonishing of all was the age of the site: The lava blocks rested almost directly on the black basalt at the base of Bed I. Meaning that nearly two million years ago, ancestors of man were constructing and living in rudimentary houses.

Not surprisingly, the stone circle at DK lent new support to belief in the chronological depth of humanity. Through the sixties and seventies, as other archeological sites at Olduvai were excavated, the interpretation of the circle became accepted as fact. "DK . . . demonstrates beyond most reasonable doubt," states an archeology textbook published as recently as 1984, "that early men were already building substantial shelters. . . . Its excavation must rank as one of the most important of all Stone Age discoveries."

Perhaps the writer of that text considered Lew Binford an unreasonable doubter. In Lew's opinion, the DK stone circle was a perfect example of an artifact that had much more to do with modern myths than with ancient men. In the *Bones* book he pointed out that in an area of about 250 yards around the site, the excavators had found nearly 4,600 crocodile teeth shed by juveniles. Obviously, the deposit in which the site rested took a considerable period of time to accumulate all those teeth—perhaps thousands of years. Wasn't it jumping to conclusions to call the site a "home base" in the first place, when so much time was represented? The faunal remains around the stone circle, in fact, were just what one would expect to find at any location near a lake margin, where many animals would have lived and died naturally through generations, without their carcasses having been transported and consumed by hominids. Yes, there were tools on the site—but there are tools almost everywhere in that region of the Gorge, and these were not arranged in any meaningful pattern in relation to the stone circle.

Binford conceded that the circle itself was indeed "enigmatic," but *unless one had already concluded that DK was a home base of hominids,* there was no reason to think that it was deliberately constructed. It might just as well be a random association of rocks laid down by some natural agent—for instance, a peculiar current in the flood margins of the lake, or the action of growing tree roots. Having established the notion of a shelter, however, the excavators then turned around and used that interpretation to confirm their belief in the site as a living floor—precisely the observation that had given rise to the shelter idea in the first place. For Lew Binford, at least, there was nothing circular at DK except Mary Leakey's reasoning.

Toward 8:00 A.M., the lorry dropped us off at the rim of the Gorge above DK. For years the site has been protected from the elements by a sturdy, tin-roofed stone building, erected with funds donated by Gordon Hanes of the Hanes clothing company. We climbed down toward the little building a few hundred yards below, poking around in the deposits along the way. We made it to the bottom of the Gorge by ten. It was hot and windless, the rubble all around shimmering in a baked stillness. When we reached DK, Binford edged ambivalently around the flanks of the site before going in, like an enemy pilot come to pay a surreptitious visit to a city that he himself had reduced to ruins.

Inside the stone building the air was much cooler. As many of us as would fit filed into a narrow walkway in the middle of the room. The place had a solemn, cloistered feel to it, like a secluded chapel. A pale light filtered in from above, so colorless and weak that it barely seemed to reach the floor. For a moment we leaned over the wooden railings of the walkway, contemplating the bones and artifacts strewn on either side. The stone circle was on the left. At first glance it looked like little more than a pile of rubble, loosely piled into small heaps along one side.

"So what do you see?" asked Lew after a while.

"I see a pile of rubble piled up into small heaps on one side," I said. "Though if you look at it a little closer, and keep in mind Mary's plan of the stone circle in her book, I can make out a ringlike shape to it."

"That brings up a couple of points," said Lew. "First of all there's Mary's plan. As Tim has pointed out, it just doesn't correspond to what's here. I'm not saying she drew the plan carelessly. But don't forget that she removed a lot of the lava blocks before she realized that they belonged to the alleged circle. Without intending to, her inclination to see a circle could have influenced the way she replaced the blocks."

"What's the other point?" asked Bob Walter.

"Don said it himself—if you take a *closer look* you begin to see a circular shape. But on that closer inspection, your eyes are *looking* for a circle, so naturally they're inclined to see one. The really odd thing about this site is that you can find circles all over the place, if you look for them—there's one to the right over there, and another one just behind it.

"I think I can see them," said Gen Suwa. "But those circles are a lot smaller—only a couple of feet in diameter."

"Exactly," said Lew. "So what do you think they are? Hominid dollhouses?"

We filed back into the bright heat outside and surveyed for a couple of hours in a series of gullies near the site. There were plenty of croc teeth and some root casts—fossilized plant debris—lying around to bear witness to the marshy lake margin that once lay upon the site. But mammal bones were sparse, especially those showing hominid activity. As the sun rose higher it became increasingly hard to make out anything at all in the deposits. We headed back out of the Gorge, and a little while later I could hear the lorry laboring along the rim, to meet us in time to take us back to camp for lunch. The last thirty meters of slope were tough going, and I was pretty well beat by the time I made it to the rim.

Bob Walter was there ahead of me, smiling, dangling his legs over the edge, and looking as fresh as an off-duty lifeguard sitting by a swimming pool. I flopped down beside him. Below, I could see Lew struggling up the slope, burdened by some video equipment strapped over his back. When his head poked over the rim, the blue bandanna he wore as a headband was drenched in sweat. The three of us stared back in silence down the way we had come. At the bottom of the Gorge, the modern stone building covering the DK site was plainly visible, charmingly incongruous against the raw African landscape.

"I don't care what you say, Lew," Bob said, "that sure looks like a house to me."

We were greeted back at camp by a lunch of cabbage soup, followed by bread served with a gelatinous canned meat the color of aging flesh. I can be pretty sure of the menu, because lunch that summer at Olduvai was nearly *always* cabbage soup, bread, and canned meat. We added plenty of Tabasco sauce and washed it all down with pitcherfuls of raspberry Kool-Aid. The morning's surveying had exhausted everyone and there was not a lot of talk around the table. After lunch, most of the crew retired to rest through the hot part of the afternoon. I decided to stay in the open central room and record the events of the last three days in my journal.

It didn't take me long to realize that there weren't many events to record. Apart from introducing the students to the site, what had we accomplished so far? Systematic surveying had yet to begin. Binford was getting a bead on the archeological possibilities, and he and George Frison had made some tantalizing suggestions about how best to proceed. Their ideas were ambitious, involving large-scale excavations of sites over a wide area of ancient landscape. But that sort of work would require huge expenditures. Where would the money come from? What good were ambitious ideas, when we were hanging on in the Gorge by a shoestring as it was, through the good graces of some private donors? I suspected, furthermore, that when Fidel Masao arrived—and it was Masao who was in charge of archeology at the Gorge—he would be inclined toward a more conservative approach. I put the journal aside and stared out at the weaver birds flitting about in the acacia.

I was anxious for Masao's arrival. I hoped he would bring with him the promised permit to work at Laetoli—as well as the means to get there. Olduvai might be a good bet in the long term, but Tim and I both knew that we'd be better off spending what little time we had this summer surveying in the richer, older deposits at Laetoli instead. Without grant support, however, we were relying on vehicles loaned by the Tanzanian Department of Antiquities. The lorry was needed back in Arusha the following day, which would leave us with a single Land-Rover. It would not be safe to take it to Laetoli and leave those behind without transportation. Laetoli was only twenty miles away, but unless we could put our hands on another vehicle, it might as well have been in South America.

Gerry Eck came around the side of the building, startling the flock of weavers out of the tree. A moment later I saw them descend into another acacia down by the camp gate, catching the sun like a handful of glitter tossed into the air. Gerry walked out to the middle of the yard, where a defunct anemometer—a device to measure wind volume—was mounted on a post. Having given up on my blender, Gerry had decided to take on the challenge of bringing the instrument back to life. For some reason his relentless industry irritated me.

"Look's like Eck is keeping himself busy." I hadn't heard Tim come up the path; he was sitting on the low stone wall in front of me.

"Great," I said. "Any day now we'll begin to know again how much wind is blowing out across the Serengeti."

"You sound a little sour."

"Sorry. It's not Gerry, of course. It's just that I'm beginning to wonder how much we can accomplish here in four weeks. And what happens if we don't accomplish anything."

"I can't say those thoughts haven't crossed my mind too," said Tim.

"There's something about this whole thing that doesn't feel right,"

I said. "I shouldn't complain—the climate's good, we've got clean quarters and enough food, and in the morning somebody whisks away my dirty laundry and returns it washed and folded before lunch. But this is supposed to be an *expedition*, for God's sake, not a vacation. In the Afar, we slept in tents, worked in hundred-and-ten-degree heat and kept one eye out all the time for bandits. Here, the most threatening intruders we have to fear are some overenthusiastic tourists poking around the gate."

We stared out a while in silence. Then Berhane and Gen came around from the other side of the building. They had their rock hammers and canteens.

"We're going down to the Junction to survey," Berhane said. They started to walk off toward the gate.

"Hold on a minute," Tim called after them. "I'd better go with you guys and make sure you don't get eaten by a lion or something." I could tell that he didn't want to go. But it was typical of Tim to use every opportunity to teach his students.

"What about you, Don?" he said to me. "You're not going to find any hominids by moping around up here."

"I might as well keep you company," I said. Tim was right. There was no point in brooding.

Gen and Berhane waited while we fetched our equipment, then the four of us trudged down the road toward the Junction. We were heading for a promising area that Tim had noticed the year before, a low plateau of deposits just to the west of the Castle. In jest, we named the place "TWK," short for Tim White Karongo. There was plenty of stuff visible *in situ*, well-preserved bone with a pretty rosy tint to it. As usual Tim kept his students busy, throwing them bone fragments to identify, pointing out tuffs, explaining procedures as we went along. In one crevice we found a bovid mandible eroding out, broken up into fragments held together only by the pressure of the deposit surrounding it.

"This fossil will be lost next year to erosion," Tim explained. "If you wanted to collect it, you could do one of two things. Either take it out in pieces, put them in a bag, label it and take it back to camp. Then see what you can put together later in the lab. The alternative is to bring some Glyptal or other preservative in here now, and let it penetrate that sucker, freeze the whole thing. Let it dry, then dig away a little and pour in some more Glyptal. Then dig some more, and so on. The point is to take it real slow. It would take a day or two to get it out of here in one block. People make the mistake of putting preservative on the thing, then they try to lift it out two hours later. Take the time to do it right."

We surveyed for a couple of hours around TWK and the base of the Castle. By five o'clock the light was beginning to fade, and we started back for camp. The sun was just settling down toward the rim of the Gorge when we reached the place where the road started to climb back up to the rim.

"There's still twenty minutes of light left," said Gen.

"Let's follow the road across the Junction toward FLK, then climb up from there," said Tim.

It was one of those weightless little decisions that only later, in hindsight, explode out of obscurity. We crossed a flat area, walking along parallel to the road, eyes on the ground. Slowly the Junction filled with dusk. On the slope of a low hill I saw Tim bend down to pick up what looked like a limb shaft of some kind. As he bent over, something else caught his eye—a cylinder of dark-brown bone an inch long. He held it up close to his face and squinted through his thick glasses.

"Damn! This is *hominid*," he said, almost in a whisper. I looked over his shoulder. In his hand was the elbow end of a primate ulna, or forearm. It was small enough to be that of a baboon but lacked the strongly projecting flange of bone in back where a baboon's powerful triceps would insert. That could mean only one thing. I reached down and picked up the limb bone that had first drawn Tim's attention.

"This looks like a piece of humerus," I said. It seemed too incredible to believe—pieces of a hominid skeleton, only a few paces from the tourist road to FLK! Carefully, the four of us got down on hands and knees and started searching through the dust.

"Here's a maxilla," Berhane said after a couple of minutes. His tone was so quiet and matter-of-fact that at first I thought he'd simply found some bovid's jaw. But when I looked up at what he held in his hand I felt a surge of joy and relief go through me like a shock. It was a substantial piece of hominid upper jawbone. There were no teeth intact, but some tooth sockets were clearly delineated. We had fallen upon one of the rarest kinds of discoveries: remains of the cranial region of a hominid found along with skeletal parts from below the neck—a far more valuable association than either skull or limb bones alone. Then it struck me: The first piece of Lucy I had found had also been the upper end of an ulna. The coincidence was uncanny. I got back down on my knees and squinted, trying to pick up the outlines of things in the gathering darkness. Just below my left shoe, I picked up a fossil tooth root, the same purplish-brown color of the other hominid pieces. Another half step, and I might have crushed it.

"Hold it," I said. "We've got to leave this till morning. It's getting too dark to see what we're doing."

"Don's right," said Tim. "This baby's been lying out here on the surface for a few decades at least, and it's not going anywhere tonight. We should mark these finds and clear out of here before we bust anything."

We placed piles of stones where we'd found the fossils. Then Berhane, Tim, and I gingerly stepped away. Gen was oblivious, still prowling on his hands and knees, his face tensed with an almost animallike concentration.

"I think Gen's got the worst case of hominid fever I've ever seen," I said.

"Come on, Suwa," Tim laughed. "You can find the skull for us in the morning."

Tim carefully wrapped the bones in his handkerchief and we started back toward camp. As we crested the rim, the last splash of the day's sun greeted us full in the face, a warm, robust light turning the plain to liquid gold. We walked four abreast toward the camp gate. Later, somebody back in camp told me that we looked like four happy warriors coming home from the battle. For dinner that night Gerry put away the Kool-Aid and brought out a case of Tanzanian beer that he'd kept very quiet about. We talked over the bones and made plans for the next day. I turned in early and got out my journal.

"At last, I can sleep easy," I wrote, and sketched out the afternoon's events. After only three days, the old Gorge had returned our faith in its promise. I fell into a dreamless sleep, unaware that our problems were just beginning.

*There's nothing worse than having a skeleton and you don't know what
it is.*

—Tim White

NONE OF US HAD THE patience to wait for dawn the next day to
begin. We rose early and followed our flashlight beams around in the
dark, wrapped in sweaters against the cold. I washed up and joined
the others gathering in the central room. We warmed our hands on
tip cups of *kahawa*—strong Tanzanian coffee tasting a little of chalk
and smoke. Stephan, the cook's assistant, brought out platterfuls of
crimson-skinned bananas and papaya strips, eggs scrambled with tomato and purple onion, and fresh bread baked over last night's coals.
As we ate, the horizon lifted to the east, the vault of the sky above
losing its stars to the infusion of pearly light from the approaching
dawn. Then the sun crested Ngorongoro, flattening and spreading
out like a flow of magma, as if the ancient volcano were reliving its
youthful devastations.

The hominid we had found was still a stranger to us. This was
hardly surprising, considering what little material we had in hand.
But as scientists, or simply as human beings, we felt an overwhelming urge to probe its identity, find a name for it, pin it down.
Leaving aside the unlikely possibility that this hominid would turn
out to be an entirely new species, our choices were limited by what

SHIFTING SANDS

KNAIBOR
BOIT

MAIN GORGE

OLDUVAI GORGE

SERENGETI ROAD

O L BALBAL

N

SIDE GORGE

NGORONGORD CRATER

LEMAGRUT

ETOLI

LANDSAT-5
Thematic Mapper
image of the Olduvai
region in northern
Tanzania: Carbonate-
rich lavas and ashes
from eruption of
Oldoinyo Lengai in
dark blue/purple;
clouds, white; water,
blue.   COURTESY OF
GODDARD SPACE
FLIGHT CENTER, NASA

LAKE EYASIE

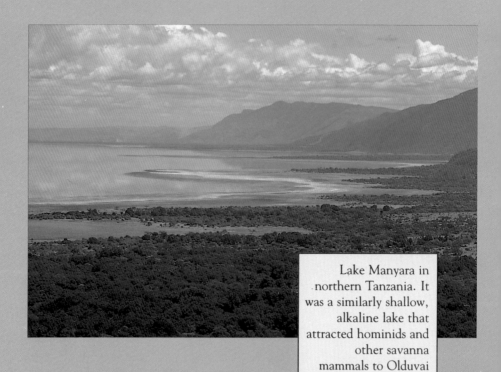

Lake Manyara in northern Tanzania. It was a similarly shallow, alkaline lake that attracted hominids and other savanna mammals to Olduvai in the early Pleistocene, nearly two million years ago.
DONALD JOHANSON

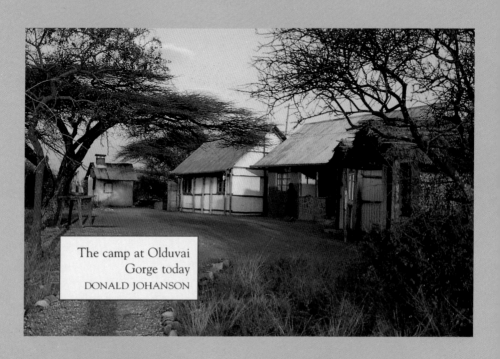

The camp at Olduvai Gorge today
DONALD JOHANSON

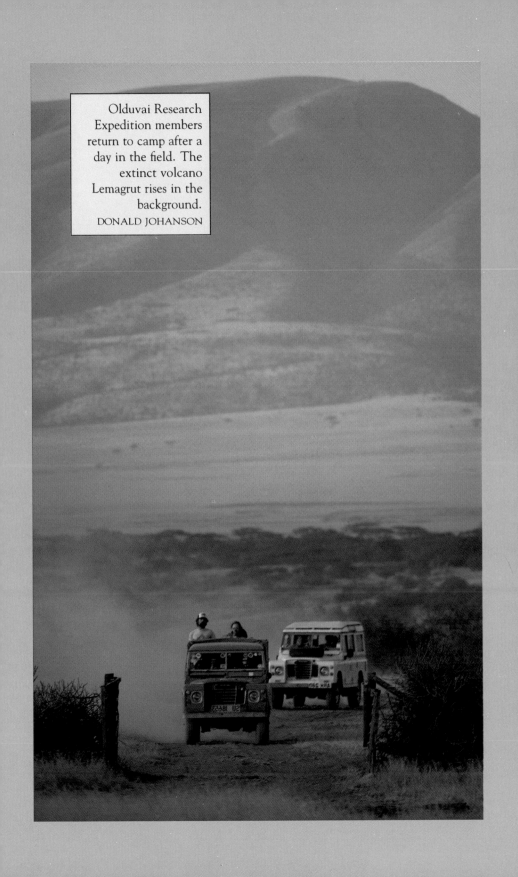

Olduvai Research Expedition members return to camp after a day in the field. The extinct volcano Lemagrut rises in the background.
DONALD JOHANSON

A simple chopper typical of the Olduwan stone-tool industry. *Homo habilis,* believed to be the earliest toolmaking hominid, inhabited the Olduvai region 1.8 million years ago, leaving behind hundreds of artifacts such as this one.
DAVID BRILL

Mary Leakey, with some of the Laetoli hominid fossils arranged in front of her. In addition to her illumination of the archeological record of Olduvai Gorge, Leakey led the expeditions to Laetoli that uncovered these 3.5-million-year-old jaws, and later the fossilized footprint trails proving human ancestors were bipedal by that time.
JOHN READER/SCIENCE PHOTO LIBRARY

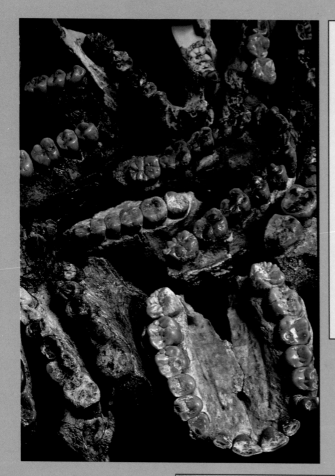

Jawbones and teeth found at Hadar, Ethiopia, in the mid-1970s by Donald Johanson and his colleagues. It was largely on the basis of these 3-million-year-old fossils that Johanson and Tim White named the species *Australopithecus afarensis* and redrew the human family tree, putting them on a collision course with the Leakeys.
JOHN READER/SCIENCE PHOTO LIBRARY

On the left, the Johanson-White phylogeny as proposed in 1979. Johanson brought this chart with him to meet Richard Leakey on Walter Cronkite's *Universe* television series in 1981. On camera, Leakey crossed out the Johanson-White version of the family tree, then scrawled a question mark in its place.
DONALD JOHANSON

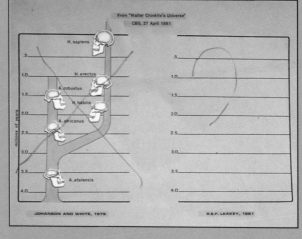

From "Walter Cronkite's Universe"
CBS, 27 April 1981

JOHANSON AND WHITE, 1979

R.E.F. LEAKEY, 1981

*Australopithecus
africanus* (The Taung
child). The original
discovery by Raymond
Dart that ushered in
the modern era of
paleoanthropology
DONALD JOHANSON

*Australopithecus
afarensis.* This
composite cast was
reconstructed by Tim
White and Bill Kimbel
from fragments of
several different
afarensis individuals.
Note the apelike
projecting face and
small braincase.
FRED SCHNEIDERMEYER

*Australopithecus
aethiopicus* (KNM
WT-17000). A cast of
"the Black Skull"
found by Alan Walker
in 1985. Walker and
his colleague Richard
Leakey believe it to
represent an early type
of *A. boisei.*
FRED GRINE

Australopithecus boisei
(OH5, nicknamed
"Zinj"). Found by
Louis and Mary Leakey
in 1959, this specimen
established the
presence of robust
australopithecines in
East Africa.   DAVID
BRILL/NATIONAL
GEOGRAPHIC SOCIETY

Homo habilis (KNM
ER-1470). For a time,
Richard Leakey's
famous find at Koobi
Fora in 1973 was
thought to be "the
oldest man."   DAVID
BRILL/NATIONAL
GEOGRAPHIC SOCIETY

Homo erectus (KNM ER-3733). Found at Koobi Fora in 1975, this specimen pushed the age of the species first known as *Pithecanthropus erectus* back to 1.5 million years.
DAVID BRILL/NATIONAL GEOGRAPHIC SOCIETY

Representative skulls of Neandertal man (left) from La Ferrassie, France, and anatomically modern man (right) from Cro-Magnon, France
JOHN READER/PHOTO SCIENCE LIBRARY

Olduvai Gorge at the
Second Fault, with
Lemagrut behind
DONALD JOHANSON

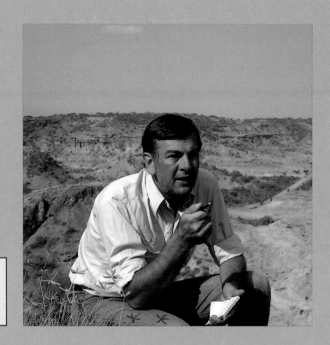

Donald Johanson, with
Olduvai Gorge in the
background

On the day after the discovery of the Dik-dik Hill hominid, Tim White finds another piece of the skeleton.
DONALD JOHANSON

The Dik-dik Hill site from the air. The white dots are markers indicating the places where hominid fragments were found. At top, expedition members dig a trench into the Gorge slope above the site.
DONALD JOHANSON

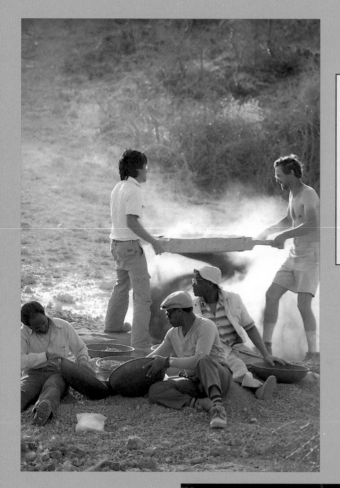

Expedition members and staff at work on the hominid site. Surface debris is first put through a screen to remove dirt, then picked through by hand in the shallow metal bowls called kerais.

DONALD JOHANSON

Don Johanson and paleontologist Gerry Eck work through a day's collection of bone from the site, looking for fragments that might belong to the hominid. In the foreground are already identified bones of the Dik-dik Hill hominid.

TIM D. WHITE

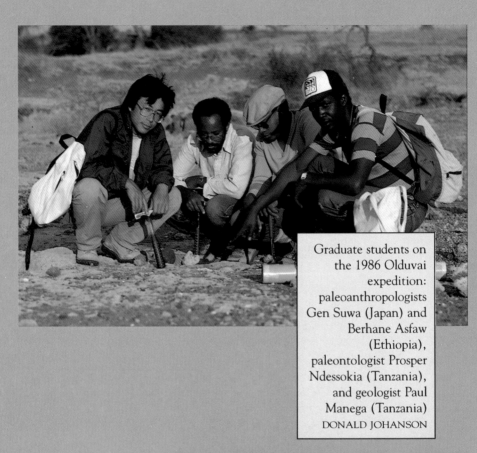

Graduate students on the 1986 Olduvai expedition: paleoanthropologists Gen Suwa (Japan) and Berhane Asfaw (Ethiopia), paleontologist Prosper Ndessokia (Tanzania), and geologist Paul Manega (Tanzania)
DONALD JOHANSON

The dik-dik, a small, pair-bonding antelope native to dry regions of East Africa. It was under a pile of dik-dik droppings that one of the Olduvai expedition members found a hominid canine tooth 1.8 million years old.
DONALD JOHANSON

Lucy's skeleton, as reconstructed in dental plaster by paleoanthropologist Owen Lovejoy and his students at Kent State University. Starting with casts of the original fossils, shown here in dark brown, Lovejoy mirror-imaged the bones and filled in missing parts through inferences drawn from the remains of other *afarensis* individuals. The posture illustrated here shows how interrelated adaptations in Lucy's pelvis, femur, knee, and foot permitted a fully bipedal gait.
DAVID BRILL

Shifting Sands, a moving dune north of Olduvai Gorge. Formed of fine black volcanic ash, the dune has been moving across the Serengeti Plain for the past two thousand years, at a rate of about one and a half inches a day.

DONALD JOHANSON

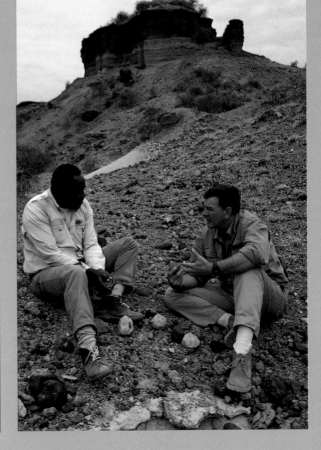

Tanzanian archeologist Fidelis Masao and Donald Johanson discuss the future of Olduvai beneath "the Castle," a prominent geological feature of the Gorge junction.

ALBERTO ANGELA

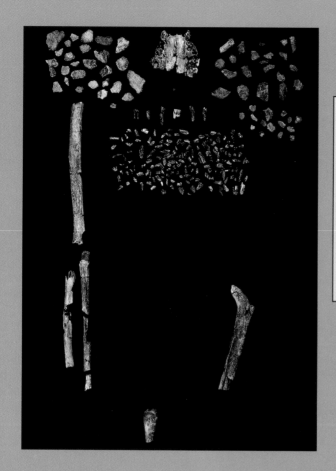

OH62, found by Tim White and colleagues at Olduvai in 1986. The first skeleton of *Homo habilis* with both cranial and postcranial fragments found together, OH62 appears to be the remains of a tiny, long-armed female 1.8 million years old.

Close-up of the OH62 maxilla, or upper jawbone, with heavily worn canine teeth at top, and worn molar teeth indicating her advanced age. It was the anatomy of this jawbone that led the research team to think OH62 was *Homo habilis*.

Four early hominid femurs: *Homo habilis* from Koobi Fora, OH62 (*Homo habilis*) from Olduvai Gorge, and two *afarensis* thighbones from Hadar. Though living much closer in time to the Koobi Fora hominid, OH62's size and body proportions resemble those of Lucy, second from right. Presumably the larger thighbones are male and the smaller ones female, suggesting pronounced sexual dimorphism in both species.
INSTITUTE OF HUMAN ORIGINS

had already been discovered in the lower Olduvai beds. We quickly ruled out *Homo erectus*, best represented at Olduvai by a beautifully preserved skullcap found by Louis Leakey in upper Bed II deposits. The ulna Tim had found was far too small to belong to any *erectus* individual known, even if it *had* washed down from upper Bed II deposits—which, given the flat terrain at the site, was extremely unlikely. A more promising "suspect" was the robust species *Australopithecus boisei*, represented by Zinj himself. A second possibility was *Homo habilis*, the first true species of man.

After dinner the night before, we had cleared away the beer bottles and laid the fossils out on the table. We passed the bones from hand to hand, the light from the one dim bulb overhead barely illuminating the faces all around.

"Look at the size of the root sockets of that premolar," said Berhane Asfaw. I sat down next to Berhane to get a better look. This scrap of jaw held no teeth that could give us an easy estimation of molar size. But the ghosts of some teeth were visible—barely—in the bits of preserved tooth sockets.

"It looks like another premolar root coming in there, and possibly a third one behind," I said. "So you've got a premolar that's three-rooted and real broad. A big Zinj-y kind of cheek tooth."

"Those roots might just be flaring out," said Gen. "The tooth crown might be a lot smaller than we think."

"Maybe. And the jaw itself looks real small. What do you make of it, Tim?"

Tim was across the table, preoccupied with the ulna. He looked up and I handed him the maxilla fragment. For a minute or two he turned the fossil back and forth in his fingers, like somebody playing with a Rubik's Cube.

"If I was desperate," he said, "I'd say this is a female robust australopithecine. But I'm not desperate. Not yet."

After breakfast we loaded the lorry with the equipment we would need to sift through the pebbly epidermis of the area around the find. With the exception of the cameras, the paraphernalia of field paleoanthropology hasn't really changed much since Eugène Dubois was combing the river beds of Java for *Pithecanthropus erectus* a hundred years ago. We brought along rock hammers, whisk brooms, some twopenny nails, a ball of surveyor's twine, and the stack of shallow metal pan called *karai* in Swahili. Though we probably wouldn't need it right away, we also brought along a handmade sieve—a two-foot-square wooden tray with a screen bottom, fitted with handles to allow two people to shake the tray back and forth between them. It was all very primitive stuff, and I suppose I can understand why some laboratory scientists—those who would feel naked without a couple of million dollars' worth of technology purring around them—dismiss field research as some kind of romantic anachronism. But until somebody figures out a better method of looking for needles in haystacks, we'll just make have to make do with our wooden sieves and dented karais.

The lorry dropped us off at the new site and headed back to Arusha; from here on in we would have to make do with a single, elderly Land-Rover. I watched the truck climb the road out of the Gorge. A quarter mile away, the copper-waisted Castle presided majestically over the Junction. Just to its right, the thatch-roofed *banda* of the tourist overlook appeared like a bump on the grassy rim of the Gorge. We couldn't have picked a more public place to find a hominid.

Naturally, all the scientists, students, and guests in camp had come along, and naturally, everybody's urge was to rush in and start looking for bones. But the last thing we needed was fourteen pairs of Vibram soles traipsing about mimicking a passing herd of wildebeest. Tim defined a rough no-man's-land around the spot where Berhane had found the maxilla. Then he asked the students to come up front.

"Ndessokia—what's the first thing you want to do in a surface find like this?" Tim asked.

"Try to get some idea of the provenience of the specimen," Prosper answered calmly. "Place it in the stratigraphy as close as we can."

"Okay. And meanwhile, get the site documented and photographed before we mess it up anymore. Now where are we, geologically?"

We all looked around and took stock of the terrain. We were standing on the north slope of a gentle knoll in what was otherwise a flat wash flanking the road. The knoll was barren of vegetation except for the top, which was capped by a cluster of sisal bushes and other ground growth. Just below the bushes, I noticed a circular patch of leathery brown pellets. Dik-diks—shy, tiny African antelopes—habitually return to defecate in the same place. This was one such dik-dik "latrine." A few yards to the southwest, the Gorge wall rose up about fifty feet in a steep, gully-cut series of deposits. I could trace these horizons on for a hundred yards to the south, while to the north, a finger of low, bush-covered sediments blocked the view toward FLK. From the spot where we'd found the bones, a shallow eroded gully ran roughly eastward for about seventy feet to the road, continuing on the other side into a jumble of black lava outcrops and thicker vegetation bordering the dry Olduvai River bed.

"That's basalt down there across the road," Berhane said, "so here we must be pretty near to the bottom of Bed I."

"Right," said Tim. "And since the fossil wasn't found *in situ*, it could have come from anywhere above. There's no matrix on any of the bones we've found either. All you can do is make probability statements."

"The bones are in pretty good shape, so chances are they haven't traveled very far," Gen offered.

"Good thinking. Also consider how fragile a maxilla is, compared to other cranial parts. If that piece of jaw had rolled a long way to where Berhane found it, there probably wouldn't be that much left of it. So we can hope that it weathered out of the real soft stuff underneath this protective lag."

Tim kicked away some surface detritus, then dug the toe of his boot into the crusty surface to expose the softer sediment underneath.

"Maybe there's more in there, maybe not," he said. "All we know for sure is that last night we found three hominid bone fragments in the dark. And I'll be real surprised if we don't find anything more on the surface today. So Asfaw—where do we start looking?"

Berhane looked around the site before answering.

"I'd start back by the road and work up this eroded gully," he said.

"It looks like everybody was paying attention yesterday," Tim said. "We clear the most disturbed possibilities first, and close in on the area of high bone density—which is right here on the northwest shoulder of this rise. So let's get the area roped off and get to work."

While Tim and Gerry oversaw the preparations for the surface search, Bob Walter took off to explore the surrounding horizons for clues to the geological context. Meanwhile Berhane and I took care of photographing and documenting the locations of the individual finds. In the process I turned up a couple of chips of tooth root—promising material, because it indicated more might be buried just

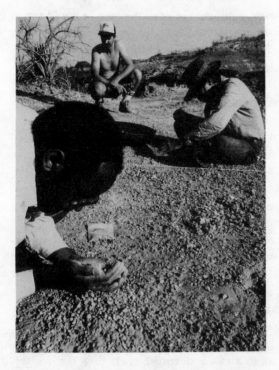

*Berhane Asfaw searches
surface debris at Dik-dik
Hill for signs of the homi-
nid. Behind him are Bob
Walter and Tim White.*
DONALD JOHANSON

below the surface. Scattered around the area I also noticed a number
of crude quartz tools indicative of early Bed I sites—and no hand
axes or other Acheulean artifacts that would have rolled down from
higher levels. Again, this was the merest suggestion—but perhaps
the hominid site was not quite so contaminated by future time as
Tim feared. We'd know a little more after the geologist's report. And
we'd know a hell of a lot more, I thought, after we found a piece of
this hominid *in situ*. I was almost certain that we would—if not today, then tomorrow or the next day.

As if to reward my confidence, Gen Suwa suddenly let out a
shout. He'd made his first find—a brownish-black triangle of hominid cranial bone about an inch square, lying on the surface of the
knoll just a few yards away. It wasn't *in situ,* and it wasn't an australopithecine skull, but it might be a piece of one. Watching his
beaming face, I remembered that just a few days before, we had almost left Gen back in Arusha, cooling his heels until his suitcase
turned up. Instead, he had just recognized what could prove to be
the first clue to a mystery of overwhelming importance. If enough of
the rest of the cranium lay sequestered beneath the surface, we might
be able to piece it together and estimate the brain size of this hom-

inid. *That* would be a discovery worth the sacrifice of a few possessions.

Tim walked over and took a look at the bone.

"Congratulations, Suwa." He smiled. "A couple dozen more of these and we might know what the hell it is we're looking for."

Gerry finished laying out a rectangle of surveyor's twine fastened to nails, framing the gully leading down to the road. This would be our work area. Now he and Tim took another length of string and laid it parallel to the road, about a foot inside the rectangle. The surface search would be done in a line on hands and knees, shoulder to shoulder, one foot at a time, moving the string ahead of us. Tim took a central spot to "quarterback" the search, with the students near him. Gerry, Lew Binford, and I found places on the flanks. Completing the line was Mrisho Ramadhani, a staffer at the National Museum who was being trained for fieldwork. A quiet, bespectacled fellow, Ramadhani was known by the nickname "Mzee," a Swahili term of respect meaning "Old Man." Meanwhile, George Frison, who was troubled by a bad back, would remain upright, surveying around the site.

The procedure for a surface search is simple: We scrutinized the patch of dusty gravel immediately before our eyes, putting anything vaguely bonelike in a marked plastic bag. When every chip of bone and splinter of tooth root had been picked out of the narrow channel between ourselves and the movable string, the two men on the ends of the line would get up and shift the string another foot forward. We then crawled forward ourselves and the process repeated itself. Unambiguously hominid remains were to be bagged separately, their location marked with a flag. Later, the distribution of the bones of the surface could tell us a great deal about where the fossil was eroding out. Meanwhile, any stone tools we found were to be left in discrete piles behind us. If we were persistent, by dusk we might reach the spot where Berhane had found the maxilla—a distance of some seventy-five feet. It was backbreaking, knee-scuffing manual labor, growing harder as the sun climbed in the sky. And we were loving every minute it.

"I'd be climbing over the slopes on either side of you guys, and every once in a while shouts and cheers would carry over to me from the site," Bob Walter told me afterward. "I'd know then that you'd found another piece of the hominid. For once I wanted to be a paleoanthropologist."

The first cheer went up shortly after nine, when Lew Binford, working the southern shoulder of the little gully, turned up a two-inch piece of femur, or thighbone. Limb-bone fragments are especially valuable when they include details of the *ends* of the bones, where they articulate with the neighboring bone to form a joint. Lew's fragment was not one of the articular ends, but it was the next best thing—a two-inch stretch of the femur shaft and neck broken off just where it started to flare toward the proximal end. (In anatomy, *proximal* refers to the part of a limb or other structure nearest to the trunk; the part farthest from the trunk is called *distal*. Think of "distant.") The break on the femoral fragment was fresh enough for us to hope that the telltale end of the bone might be somewhere nearby, perhaps right underneath. But we kept on moving up the gully. An hour later we came across a piece of tibia, or calf bone, the same dark color as the other remains of our hominid stranger—another good reason for high spirits.

The tibia and femur fragments both had another, extremely intriguing feature in common with the arm bones we'd discovered already.

"Don, you know Lucy's skeleton better than you know your own face," said Tim when we broke for lunch. "Now take a look at this thing."

Tim unbagged the piece of tibia and held it up. We were sitting at a worktable in the lab building, an airy stone structure outfitted with floor-to-ceiling shelves crammed full of mammal fossils and boxes of stone tools. In the middle of the room, a fiberglass cast of the Laetoli footprints was propped up on sawhorses.

"It's a little bugger, isn't it," I replied.

"Small as Lucy?"

"Yeah."

"Maybe *smaller?*"

"That doesn't seem possible. A full-grown hominid running around less than three and a half feet tall?"

"Who knows? But it would be nice of Lucy were here to compare it with."

"Kimbel is due here from the Institute in a couple of weeks," Gerry Eck reminded us. He was stooped over a wash pail on a table nearby, scrubbing the dirt off the morning's gleanings from the site. "If we can reach him in time, Bill could bring casts of Lucy's limb bones with him."

Over lunch—potted meat, cabbage soup, and Kool-Aid—we

drafted a telegram to Kimbel, to be sent out with the first vehicle that came through.

HOMINID IN THE BAG, we wrote. BRING LUCY'S RIGHT ULNA, CER-VICAL AND LUMBAR VERTEBRAE, PROXIMAL FEMUR, PROX AND DISTAL TIBIA, PROXIMAL LEFT HUMERUS. Then we detailed some needed supplies that he should bring with him too. Heading the list was TWO POUNDS OF PEANUT BUTTER.

The sun was still high, so there was no point in returning to the site for another hour. Tim gathered his students and we went back to the lab to begin sorting the surface material. He picked up a bag marked "Gully One" and dumped the contents out on the worktable.

"Gerry's washed this stuff, so it's a lot easier to see what we've got," said Tim, picking some pebbles out of the pile and flicking them out the open window. "The next step is to go through each bag piece by piece and isolate anything that has a remote chance of being hominid. If we make a mistake and put a piece of the hominid into the nonhominid pile, we'll never retrieve it—that piece might as well have been washed away to the ocean. Sorting is too critical a process to leave to any one person. Before I relegate anything to the nonhominid pile, I'm going to hand the bone to Johanson. If he has any doubt, then we keep the bone in consideration."

Tim picked out of the bag a concave shard of bone that to an untrained eye might look like a piece of cranial vault.

"I say this one's out," said Tim, handing me the specimen.

"Right. Turtle shell," I said.

"What about all this pale bone?" asked Berhane.

"We can't judge by color yet," said Tim. "Occasionally a fossil has multicolored parts."

One by one we went through the bags brought back from the site. We didn't talk much. We checked the bones for texture and quality of preservation, as well as for hominidlike morphological features. When we came across bones that belonged unquestionably to some other species, we placed them in a separate bag. Information about the fauna commingling with the hominid would help us get a fix on the ecological conditions prevailing at the site. Tim held up each piece to the light of the window, turned it in his fingers, and pronounced his decision: *In . . . Out . . . In . . . Out . . .* In his deep, sepulchral voice it sounded as if he was ruling on the fate of souls. He handed each bone to me, and when there was the slightest shadow of doubt I questioned his verdict. By 2:30 we had gone through most of the bags and had accumulated perhaps a hundred bones that *might* belong to our hominid. These would be part of our raw material when we started trying to put the skeleton together. That would be a far more challenging process—but first we had to retrieve whatever further information the site would yield. With luck, it would overwhelm what we already had in hand.

If the morning's surface search had been promising, the afternoon's was unqualified fulfillment. Shortly after we returned to our positions on the line, Tim plucked a fine piece of palate out of the gravel by his knee. Later, back in the lab, it would fit neatly onto the maxilla found the night before. More finds followed, each one strengthening our hopes. Berhane uncovered the first scrap of lower jaw. It included an eroded remnant of a bump of bone called the mandibular condyle, where the jaw hinges with the skull. Meanwhile fragments of tooth roots seemed to be everywhere. Then Gerry turned up another stretch of limb shaft.

"The rest of the ulna!" Tim exclaimed. "Way to go Eck!"

"We better rewrite that telegram to Kimbel," I said. "Tell him to bring Lucy's whole skeleton."

Berhane's luck continued: Late in the afternoon, he held up what appeared to be the first piece of tooth crown. It wasn't enough to give an indication of the species we were dealing with, but it was a promising way to end the day. We finished the surface search with a little light to spare. As the shadows gathered, we set up for the next day, using twine and nails to divide the entire site into a grid of two-meter squares. Tomorrow we would begin the next step: sweeping the loose lag out of the squares for sifting, one by one.

At five-thirty the Land-Rover arrived from camp. It would require two trips to take us all back, and I volunteered to go in the second load. While I waited, I climbed up the steep slope just to the west and sat down on a comfortable ledge. Looking down at the site, I was suddenly struck by its overwhelming obscurity. Against a background of magnificent cliff faces flushed by the sun lay this stretch of gray nothingness, littered here and there by a spindly wisp of a bush and scarred by the road running along its flank. For decades now, that road had carried tourist combis around the corner to view the plaque erected at FLK, marking the discovery of *Zinjanthropus*. As the combis passed, passengers on the right side would enjoy a view of the cliffs and the river margin below, with its brilliant patches of yellow-green sisal, graceful acacia silhouettes, and stands of aloe vera, their leafy heads perched on rough-barked stalks ten feet tall. Passengers on the left, meanwhile, would have a view of what we were now calling Dik-dik Hill: a brief, apologetic rise in the bare terrain, with a mop of vegetation slapped off center on the summit like a cheap, ill-fitting toupee.

On one side of the combis, in other words, lay Africa, while on the other, the scene resembled a vacant lot. I couldn't help smiling at the irony. The tourists had come to see Africa, of course; but it was the vacant lot that held the treasure—this enigmatic ancestor, all those years lying right out there on the surface. And now we had found it and dressed up the hill with a geometric grid, each square brimming with possibility. Specimens that clearly included both skull and limb bones of either robust australopithecines or *Homo habilis* were not merely rare in the fossil record—they were nonexistent. Thus there was an enormous gap in our understanding of the basic anatomy of these two species, not to mention the problem of some very fuzzy attributions of limb bones and other postcranial parts. Were the isolated femurs found at Koobi Fora really those of *Australopithecus boisei*, or was that just a guess?

And what about *habilis*? OH7, the type specimen, consisted of some skull fragments, part of a mandible, and a handful of hand bones. Were these really part of a single juvenile *habilis*, as the Leakeys believed? What about the foot bones found at the same site: Did they belong to the same individual, or to an adult female? On the Zinj floor itself, the Leakeys had turned up some pieces of tibia and fibula. Did these belong with the other *habilis* postcrania, or were they pieces of Zinj himself, the original *Australopithecus boisei*? Which bones went with which species? It was all too confusing to yield much insight.

If the Dik-dik Hill hominid did no more than help us pin down the identity of such specimens, we'd still be way ahead. But getting the names straight on fossils is always just the beginning, the means to approach deeper questions. Were the robust australopithecines really "robust"? Was *Homo habilis* proportioned like us, as most people thought? Did it walk like *Homo sapiens*? What was the relationship between brain and body size during this critical transitional period in human evolution? Some answers might already be resting on museum shelves in Nairobi, Johannesburg, or Addis Ababa, needing only the right key to unlock their ambiguities. If we could find more of this specimen, it could serve as a sort of Rosetta stone, making sense out of a jumble of uncertainties. Who knows, I thought—maybe Dik-dik Hill would have its own plaque someday.

Back at camp I found Tim and his students at work in the lab, hunched over the fossils like a trio of alchemists about to conjure up the philosopher's stone. They hadn't even bothered to wash up first. Tim looked up and grinned.

"Nothing in the world I'd rather be doing than putting a robust australopithecine skeleton together," he said. "You're just in time to watch these ulna pieces match up."

Tim held one piece of elbow bone in each hand and gently clicked them together. The point of contact was narrow, but there was no doubt about the fit.

"So you're certain it's a robust?"

"These are big teeth, bwana."

"We still can't really be sure of that," Gen interjected.

"Mr. Suwa here has been arguing for *habilis*. He hasn't learned yet that a grad student is supposed to agree with everything his teacher says," Tim said facetiously. "Berhane is a lot smarter. He thinks like me. This hominid's a little robust. Probably female."

I picked up the portion of mandible and ran my finger over the slight, eroded protruberance at the back.

"What about this little condyle?" I said. "It's tough to imagine a great big robust jaw full of megamolars swinging from a joint that size."

"So you think it's *habilis* too?"

"Let's just say I suspend judgment."

"OK, we've got two votes for *boisei*, one vote for *habilis*, and Johanson here is being wishy-washy. What all this tells me is that we need to find a damn premolar crown, bad. Or a molar crown."

"While you're taking orders, how about the missing part of this femur," I said holding the lower limb fragment up to the light. "This break is real fresh."

"We'll get it all. Tomorrow."

We were back on the site early on July 23, eager to begin the sifting operation. I've mentioned before what an advantage it is to have a good, interdisciplinary team in the field. In this expedition the core disciplines—paleoanthropology, paleontology, archeology, and geology—were superbly represented, in some cases by people who

had to be considered among the best in their fields. Our immediate
need, however, was not heavy credentials, but an ability and will-
ingness to haul dirt. Our funding did not provide for paid laborers.
Everyone pitched in with spirit, including camp visitors like Jeremy
Paul and science writer James Shreeve, who was staying with us for
a few weeks. Tim and Gerry worked the brooms, stooping over to
sweep the loose dust and gravel on the hillside into the shallow karais. The rest of us took turns carrying the laden pans to a level area
near the road, to be dumped into the sieve. Two others lifted the
wooden tray and rocked it back and forth to coax the dust through
the screen. If the sievers were lucky, the wind would carry the dust
away, but whenever the wind stopped, the dust puffed up and enclosed them in a blinding cloud.

Once the dust was fully expelled, the sievers dumped the bone,
rock, and other material trapped in the screen into another karai.
The remainder of the team squatted on the ground, tossing the sieved
material one handful at a time into karais, where it could be shaken,
spread out, and scanned through, pebble by pebble. Every splinter of
bone was picked out and put into a wooden box. It was not work
that required a Ph.D.—just a good pair of eyes and a lot of patience.
By lunchtime we had completed three squares and found nothing
that could unequivocally be attributed to the hominid.

The only scientist excused from sifting work was Bob Walter.
The geologist had his own labors to attend to. After spending the
first day getting his bearings in the general framework of the site,
Bob now had the difficult task of determining as closely as possible
where in the Olduvai stratigraphy these hominid bones were emerging from. The gravel forming the surface of Dik-dik Hill was a col-
luvial lag—a term for the accumulation of debris at the bottom of a
slope. This meant that even if we were to find some fossils embedded
in the lag, rather than lying on top, they could still not be considered *in situ,* since the lag itself was not a primary deposit, but
rather a composite formed of material from any number of layers
upslope. With Bob's help, however, we might be able to locate the
primary deposit nearby, where the hominid had originally come from.

The day before, Bob had quickly identified two key marker tuffs
above the site in the surrounding terrain—Tuffs IC and ID. Though
much the same color, the two tuffs could be easily distinguished if
you knew what you were looking for. Tuff ID was characterized by
horizontal layers of pumice chunks, dotting the ash like raisins in a

cake. Tuff IC was finer-grained and showed no such horizontal lay-ering. Toward the end of the day, Bob also got a fix on Tuff IF, a key ash layer that marks the boundary between Bed I and Bed II. Of the three, Tuff IF was the only one that had been dated using the potassium-argon method. The experiments had come up with some rather shaky answers: Tuff IF was anywhere from 1.75 million to 8.5 million years old. Obviously the latter date was incorrect.

"Olduvai is such a classic site that people forget it isn't all that securely dated," Bob reminded me recently. "Most of the Olduvai tuffs aren't very pure—they're contaminated by older rock that prob-ably erupted from volcanoes along with the primary ash. The only firm potassium-argon date is still the 1.8-million-year mark that Garniss Curtis and Jack Evernden got for Tuff IB, in the experiments in the late fifties that broke open the field. Above Tuff IB, you've got a million and a half years of stratigraphy without any firm age control."

Getting some control on the ages of the Olduvai horizons was one of our long-term goals, and I was counting on Bob's expertise. He would have the substantial help of some new radiometric tech-niques being developed by Garniss Curtis and Bob Drake back in the Institute's dating lab. In the meantime, the Olduvai hominids weren't swimming in a completely uncharted ocean of time. Several other dating techniques had been tested over the years at the Gorge and had lent support to some otherwise rickety pottasium-argon dates.

The most informative of these relies on a fascinating property of the earth itself, called paleomagnetism. For reasons no one really knows, the globe acts like a gargantuan magnet. Like other magnets, the globe possesses polarity—it has a negative North Pole and a pos-itive South Pole. To anyone who has watched iron filings arrange themselves under the influence of a bar magnet, it should come as no surprise that as molten volcanic rocks cool, crystals in the rocks also align themselves with the earth's magnetic field. As the rocks solidify, the crystals retain their orientation, like compass needles that have been locked in place. Thus every magnetic mineral in every rock all over the world should point to the North Pole.

In 1906, a French physicist named Bernard Brunhes made the perplexing discovery that *some* volcanic rocks were magnetized in precisely the opposite direction—toward the South Pole. Brunhes concluded that the earth's magnetic field in his study area must have somehow reversed itself. The concept of reversing magnetic fields did not attract much attention until the early 1960s, when three geologists, Alan Cox, Brent Dalrymple, and Richard Doell, became intrigued and began to sample the magnetic polarity of basalt samples from scattered places around the earth. Along with other scientists, they eventually proved that no fewer than nine flip-flops in the earth's field had taken place over the past three and a half million years. And whereas Brunhes had believed that the curious reversals were a local phenomenon, the studies in the sixties showed that the effect was consistent the world over. No matter where the scientists took their samples, the indelible magnetic record of the earth fell neatly into four "polarity epochs," punctuated by much shorter periods of reversed polarity, which they called "events."

The first one of these quick-shot reversals to come to light is called the Olduvai Event, named after a busy little canyon cut on the edge of the Serengeti Plain. Discovered by Hay and Grommé in 1963, the Olduvai Event is a period of normal, northward polarity in an upside-down time called the Matuyama Epoch. Hay and Grommé found that the reversal in polarity lasted through the whole of Bed I times, on up into the lower part of Bed II. There is nothing intrinsically "datable" about a particular paleomagnetic flip-flop: All you know is that it happened before some flips, and after other flops. But since the *order* of events is consistent, if you can pin an absolute age on an event at one location by some other means, then you've got a date for that event that applies the world over. In 1972 geologist Neil Opdyke analyzed the magnetic orientation of some deep-sea cores from the ocean bed at several different locations around the world. He found the Olduvai Event clearly and consistently recorded. By comparing the paleomagnetic data with known rates of sedimentation of the sea bottom, Opdyke figured out that the Olduvai Event lasted from approximately 1.85 to roughly 1.7 million years ago, a period of 150,000 years.

That evidence from paleomagnetism fit very nicely with the potassium-argon date of 1.8 million for Olduvai Tuff IB, which is found near the bottom of the Olduvai Event at the Gorge itself. It also gave some muscle to estimates for the rest of Bed I—including Tuff IF at the top, and IC and ID sandwiched between. According to this technique, at least, all of the tuffs under Bob Walter's scrutiny were at least 1.75 million years old, and no more than 100,000 years older than that.

At the hominid site, Bob Walter's next step would be to try to

MAGNETIC POLARITY   NORMAL   REVERSED

Millions of Years Ago

5   4   3   2   1   0

5.26   3.40   2.47   .73 M.Y.A.

GILBERT   GAUSS   MATUYAMA   BRUNHES

Paleomagnetism is another technique used to provide a chronological framework for ancient deposits. Crystals in cooling molten rock line up with the earth's magnetic field, like compass needles. Over the millennia, the magnetic field of the earth has reversed itself periodically, so that rock crystals point either to the North Pole (normal) or to the South Pole (reversed). The four major polarity chrons—the Gilbert, Gauss, Matuyama, and Brunhes—were punctuated by shorter-term reversals called "events." The Olduvai Event in the Matuyama Chron lasted from 1.85 to 1.7 million years ago.

use these markers to place Dik-dik Hill itself in the larger context of the Olduvai stratigraphy. This would require digging a trench into the steep slope adjacent to the site, exposing the series of deposits that might once have lain over Dik-dik Hill but had subsequently eroded away—leaving behind only the gray shroud of colluvium that we had so suddenly taken an interest in. Bob would then have to dig another trench into Dik-dik Hill itself, hoping to find some correlations there with the deposits exposed by his first excavation.

Most geologists will tell you that digging trenches is not one of the relished delights of the profession. It helps to have some company around—preferably somebody with a strong back. Unfortunately, Bob's student Paul Manega had received notice the day before that he was wanted back in Arusha, and had hitched a ride out of the Gorge with the departing lorry. We could spare no one from the sifting operation, which left Bob to dig alone. He didn't seem to mind at all. Every once in a while through the day I would look up from my karai-ful of pebbles and dirt and I'd see Bob, stripped to his Patagonia khaki shorts and a layer of sunscreen, swinging his pickax into the slope with all the gleeful gusto of one of the Seven Dwarfs. Sometimes I could actually hear him whistling while he worked.

In the afternoon some more hominid tooth-root fragments began to appear in the karais, but not much else that we could definitely put a label on. The day before, the plethora of root fragments had seemed encouraging. Now it was beginning to worry me. One reason that teeth play so large a role in distinguishing between extinct species is their relative abundance in the fossil record. Tooth enamel is harder than bone, and thus is more likely to withstand the pressures of time. But *this* skeleton's dentition had exploded all over the place—which did not augur particularly well for the preservation of softer parts. I'd feel a lot better, I thought to myself, if we could find one intact tooth. Or anything else that would tell us what we were dealing with.

By four o'clock we had swept clean the surface of several more squares on the slope of the hill just below the dik-dik pile. We were dust-caked and bone tired, but had uncovered a curiously meager collection of fossil fragments. Only a dozen or so of the bone chips we'd found were big enough to warrant attention, and of these, none at all belonged unquestionably to the hominid. After yesterday's success, the disappointment was all the sharper for being wholly inexplicable. Tim glared at the cleared square at his feet, looking somber and puzzled, as if he held the ground personally responsible for thwarting his expectations.

"It's late," somebody said. "Let's call it quits."

"There's still light enough for one more square," Tim insisted. "I got a good feeling about the next one up the slope."

He stooped over and began to beat the ground again with his broom. We set to work with the sieve and karais. By the time Bob Walter came by half an hour later and plopped himself down near the pile of dik-dik pellets on the top of the knoll, we were three quarters through. But by then it was clear that this square too was strangely infertile.

"I haven't heard a lot of noise from you guys this afternoon," Bob said, taking a drink from his canteen.

"Whatever the hell this hominid is, it's not being very cooperative," Gerry Eck said.

"Tomorrow we'll finish sweeping the squares down the gully," Tim muttered, still working his broom. "If we get something, I think we should start excavating down in the lag." Then he added, almost to himself, "If nothing turns up tomorrow, I wonder how much time we want to put in here."

If that was a question, nobody bothered answering it. We fin-

ished up the sifting and slowly gathered the equipment together. Bob
Walter sat perched on the knoll, toying with the strap of his canteen
and staring blankly into the dik-dik patch. Even he seemed beat by
the day's efforts. But then I noticed Bob's eyebrows lift up a bit, and
his gaze gather interest and surprise. He leaned down and peered into
the pile of dried-up feces, as if they held some message of deep significance. He bent over and plucked something out of the dik-dik
latrine.

"Holy *shit*," said Bob. In his hand was a hominid canine tooth,
perfectly intact.

Simple gratitude demands that I pay some passing respects at
this point to the dik-dik. These pretty little antelopes are a frequent
sight in the Gorge, and would be even more noticeable if their brown-
and-gray-flecked fur didn't match the stratigraphy so well. If you should
visit the Gorge and catch a glimpse of one scampering up a steep
slope, quickly look for another. Dik-diks mate for life and stick close
by their partners. The females of the species are larger than the males.
Both sexes have big, fleshy noses overhanging their mouths, giving
their faces an expression of perpetual goofiness. (The oversized prob-
iscis acts as a radiator to cool the blood.) Dik-diks live on highly
nutritive but widely scattered foods like buds, fruit, and young green
leaves. Each monogamous pair must therefore reserve for itself a large
and well-defined territory. They remind neighboring dik-diks of their
claim with insistent scent markings. The males are especially well
equipped for the task, their faces adorned by quarter-sized scent glands
just below the eyes, which they use to daub a scenting fluid onto
particular plant stems in the territory. Diligent maintenance of these
territorial signposts envelops the plant stem in a sticky ooze.

Another territorial trick of the dik-dik is the persistent use of
specific defecation spots, anthropomorphically referred to as latrines.
Typically, the female will use the facility first. When she is through
the male will paw and muzzle her leavings before unloading his own.
The ritual, like much of observed dik-dik etiquette, probably reinforces the bond between the pair. Rarely—very rarely—dik-dik feces
will also mark the location of priceless hominid fossils. Whether such
warm attention given to ancient bones represents an integral part of
dik-dik behavior or is merely coincidence is too difficult to ascertain
from the data currently available.

Bob's discovery was enough to send us back to the lab that evening with rejuvenated spirits. But while the tooth Bob had pulled

Bob Walter poses behind the pile of dik-dik droppings from which he pulled a 1.8-million-year-old hominid canine tooth.
DONALD JOHANSON

from the pile was a breakthrough, it was also a source of further frustration. The canine and its root were preserved exactly as they had been when the individual died almost two million years before. Missing from the tooth, however, was what had been lost in life. Almost the whole of the crown had been worn down through years of chewing. Clearly, the hominid had been pretty well along in life when it perished. Judging from the root and what remained of the crown, we could also tell that this canine was surprisingly large. This was an important clue in our search for the hominid's identity. Remember, while robust australopithecines have big molars and small front teeth, in early *Homo* the situation is just the reverse: It tends to have relatively *large* canines and incisors, and relatively small cheek teeth. To make a certain diagnosis, however, it would have helped to know the height and shape of the canine crown. That information was lost forever.

"I'm sorry, Bob, but we're going to have to send you back into the shit to find another tooth," Tim laughed. "Bring me back a big, beautiful back molar. Otherwise I might have to buy the crock that Suwa is dishing out and start believing we're chasing a little *habilis*."

"With a canine root that size its *got* to be *Homo*," Gen said. The three of us were clustered around the bones with only a couple of flashlights illuminating the work. Berhane was feeling ill and had retired early.

"Not necessarily," Tim said. "Look at the bicanine distance. It's really reduced."

The day before we had put together enough of the upper jaw to be able to estimate the distance between the two canines by the position of their root sockets. In this specimen, there wasn't much space between the canines to fit in the large incisor teeth characteristic of *Homo*. It was just another hunch, of course, but the small bicanine distance would lend support to the notion that our hominid was a robust autralopithecine after all.

"Yeah, but look at the back edge of that incisor socket," Gen countered. Having spent much of the last six years becoming intimate with the arcanities of hominid teeth, he wasn't about to relinquish the high ground. "That's bigger than any I've seen on a robust max."

"OK, Suwa, forget the teeth for a minute and check out the guttering of this nasal margin," Tim challenged him, tracing with a finger the contour of what little remained of the side of the nasal opening. "Wouldn't you say it flows smoothly into the nasal cavity?"

A smooth, rounded edge on the nasal margin was another distinct characteristic of a robust. Gen took the bone and studied it from different angles. He wasn't as familiar with nasal morphology as he was with teeth, and I could see that the question bothered him. He pushed his lips forward in a pout of concentration, struggling to get a fix on the anatomy. I noticed that Tim was looking at Gen too, studying his face. Suddenly I realized that Tim was baiting his student, pushing on Gen's memory and conviction to see how well he could defend his position.

"You can't really say that," Gen finally announced. "It could be that the margin's simply eroded. We'll have to find more bone before we can make a judgment."

"Spoken like a born paleoanthropologist!" Tim laughed and slapped his hand on the table, relieving the tension. "When in doubt, shake your head and call for more fossils. OK, we'll say it's *habilis* tonight. But tomorrow I'm gonna find a molar crown under that dik-dik pile big enough to land a helicopter on. Now let's get some rest."

In our map of the site, the two-meter area where the canine had been found was labeled Square 8. The next day we resisted the temptation to dive right into it, and instead spent the morning processing the remaining loose lag. Berhane, stricken by some sort of stomach flu, was on his back in his hut, and without him the work went that much more slowly. Five hours of sifting produced one mottled ridge of palate bone and little else. In the afternoon we cleared away the dik-dik pellets and the other surface detritus from the magical eighth square. Gingerly at first, Tim began to poke into the compacted lag with his rock hammer, trying not to damage any fossils that might be lying beneath. The colluvium proved thicker than we had thought, which meant more dirt for the karais. Nothing was turning up. By three o'clock it was clear that the square was not so chock full of fossils as we'd hoped. Tim muttered and swore and picked up his pace. An hour later we had to concede the truth: The square was barren. The dik-dik had let us down.

That evening in the lab we discovered that the piece of palate we'd found in the morning fit neatly on to the back of the maxilla. It was a small, sustaining consolation to the afternoon's disappointment. And that was to be the pattern over the next several days— we'd bring hopes to the field every morning, and gradually they would dissipate and blow away like dust from the sieve. Then, just when we began to think that it would be prudent to cut our losses and abandon the site, a teaser would turn up in somebody's karai: a bit of cranial vault, a good root fragment, another little stretch of limb shaft. Nothing that would reveal the identity of the hominid, but enough to give us legitimate hope that the next day would yield up that elusive diagnostic piece.

In the lab one day I found Tim staring at the hominid's humerus. A beautiful inch-long chunk of shaft had turned up in somebody's karai that morning, and Tim had glued it neatly in place.

"That's a nice join," I said. Tim didn't look up. He just stared at the bone. For a moment I thought he might be onto something. But he just sighed and leaned back in his chair. Suwa came in and starting poking through the morning's yield of fragments. He handed Tim a thick splinter of limb bone.

"What do you think?" said Gen. "Maybe tibia?"

Tim glanced at the fossil and dismissed it with an impatient wave of his hand. Then he leaned forward again and practically glowered at the humerus. I'd seen Tim in these dark moods before, and knew better than to intrude. But Gen's natural enthusiasm wouldn't allow such circumspection. He wanted more feedback.

"I'm not saying this bone is a hominid tibia," he said. "Just that it might be."

Tim grabbed the fossil from him and pointed to a groove running along its length.

"What do you call this?" he said. "Ever seen a hominid with a groove like that?"

"I admit it's a little weird."

"Weird is right. You've got hominid blindness."

"I didn't say it *was* hominid . . ." Gen insisted.

"And I'm not saying it isn't," Tim snapped. "Just that it's a real low probability. So save it for later." Then, perhaps sensing Gen's pained surprise, he softened his tone.

"Forget that piece of junk, Gen," he said. "Go out and find the proximal end of this humerus. Maybe that'll help us understand the *length* of this damn bone. Because from what I can see now, it isn't making any sense."

Over the next couple of days we expanded the quadrangle of squares at the site and began to dig on the other side of the shallow gully. When that proved fruitless, we excavated on the north flank of Dik-dik Hill farther down toward the road. Those squares were a little richer, confirming our belief that the hominid's bones were eroding out of the hill itself, rather than tumbling down from the steep Gorge slope overlooking the site. Meanwhile Bob Walter had dug a trench into the barren south flank of the hill. He found that the rock fragments in the fossil-fertile lag layer were identical to those found in Tuff ID and below. The absence of any material in the lag originating from higher levels supported the belief that the hominid bones too were no younger than Tuff ID itself. In the absence of an *in situ* find, it was again only an inference. But it was a strong one.

Bob and Paul Manega had done about as much as they could for the time being. They returned to general geological surveying on foot in the eastern part of the Gorge, keeping sharp eyes out all the time for a small pride of lions that they had run into earlier near the Second Fault. Any lion who had stayed in the Gorge over the dry season, instead of following the migrating herds of wildebeest across the Serengeti, was bound to be hungry and unpredictable.

For those of use working Dik-dik Hill, the worst threat was the numbing tedium. After a week, the work had fallen into a rhythmic redundancy—spill your handful of pebbles into the karai, shake it, scan it, spill it out, grab another handful. Other than our own conversation, the only distraction was the occasional tourist combi rolling by on its way to FLK. Every once in a while, the overlook at the museum half a mile away would fill up with bright colors—the T-shirts of the tourists stopping for the view—and we would hear their excited voices filtering across the Junction. Twenty minutes later their vehicle would come rattling down into the Gorge, suddenly appearing around the bend and heading right toward us. The combis slowed down as they passed, then disappeared in the fog of gray dust kicked up by their wheels. I had given instructions to Peter, the guide at the museum, to keep the public away from the work area. That was simply good practice. But now I found myself secretly hoping that the combis would stop to allow their passengers a chance to ask us some questions. Or I could ask them some. Anything to relieve the boredom.

Tim's mood was changing too. His initial sense of triumph at finding the first fragments so quickly ("The Leakeys took thirty years to find a hominid at Olduvai Gorge," he told a visitor. "We got one in three days") had been replaced by a clenching determination to dig as much information as possible out of the ground before the field season was over. Hour after hour he stooped over, legs spread apart, shirt drenched with sweat, scratching at the earth with his rock hammer, then shoveling the loosened dirt into a karai. If the hominid's identify would not spring forth voluntarily, then Tim seemed ready to squeeze it out of the ground by force, one fragment at a time. He worked with such intensity that sometimes even six or seven people sifting through the material were not enough to keep up with him, and the panfuls of unprocessed material would stack up by the sieve. Rather than use the opportunity to take a break, Tim would drop his hammer and squat down to help us, casting handfuls of dirt into a karai and scanning through them with a silent, machinelike precision, then dumping the meaningless rubble out in disgust.

One afternoon the screen in the sieve developed a hole—small to begin with, but threatening to rip wider and bring the whole operation to a halt. If any fragment of the hominid passed through, it would be lost forever in the pile of dirt growing below the sieve.

"Have we got any backups?" I asked Gerry. We were standing around the broken sieve, looking as hopeless as a bunch of stock traders whose computer has just gone down.

"Hell, no," said Gerry. "Somehow I didn't foresee the possibility that we'd be sifting through a few tons of gravel this soon. I'll try to improvise a patch. Otherwise we'll have to go all the way back to Arusha for new screen."

To wait for screen from Arusha would mean the loss of at least two days of work—probably more, given the shaky condition of our solitary Land-Rover. Tim turned around and strode back over to the square under excavation.

"Damn hominid broke our only screen," he swore. "Let's get him!"

Tim spread his feet apart again and set to work, putting behind each controlled swing of his hammer a riveting concentration, as if strength of will alone would ferret out the hominid and banish all disappointment forever. I knew that Tim's frustration was not really directed at the fossil, nor at the delay threatened by the broken sieve, nor even at the shortsightedness of granting agencies that had left us out here without adequate equipment. The object of his anger was stronger, darker, and maddeningly elusive—and approachable only through such bald physical intensity. Watching him probe into the earth with his fingernails, it struck me that at this moment Tim's enemy was manifest in the ground itself. This stretch of ancient earth had entered into a pact with us, and was now betraying that pledge. Several days before, in near darkness, Tim's acumen had recognized a little plug of bone for what it was, triggering the metamorphosis of this anonymous, shit-topped knoll into a hominid site of enormous potential. In return, the perfectionist in him demanded of the earth that it yield under his direction and deliver up its promised revelations.

Instead, Dik-dik Hill—Olduvai ground, don't forget, the Leakeys' "backyard"—had chosen not to reveal but to jealously obscure and obstruct. In so doing, it had allied itself with ignorance. For myself, ignorance defines an absence, a lack of understanding. I'm sure the same is true for Tim's other colleagues—even for Lew Binford, for whom the word carries very special connotations. But watching Tim scrape and swear and drip sweat into the dust under his hammer, I realized that for him ignorance was an active antagonist, never absent for very long. It could take shape as intractable earth, or it might peek out from between some grant-review sheets full of damningly faint praise, or it might put on a suit and tie and lecture to the world on the antiquity of man, all the time restricting access to knowledge that might prove otherwise. In any of its guises, ignorance was the enemy, and if you did not fight it, you were part of its strength.

We worked till the shadows dispersed, tilting the sieve away from the hole and rocking it more gently than usual. The day's efforts yielded two small fragments of tooth crown. That evening Gerry patched the screen, and the next morning we found another molar fragment and some bits of palate. The day after, it was a shard of femur shaft, a chip of cranium. The days of hauling and sifting rub-

Tim White at Olduvai Gorge JAMES SHREEVE

ble turned to weeks. Still there was no breakthrough, but slowly, very slowly, the hominid was coming up for us. I must admit that sometimes, while I pushed the pebbles through my karai or relieved Tim on the hammer, I thought wistfully about the expeditions in Ethiopia, where Lucy's bones and the other *afarensis* specimens had lain out on the slopes for us, to be picked up heavy and whole, like ripe fruit.

Excavating this fossil was more like digging seeds out of winter earth. If skillfully handled, the nameless fragments accumulating in the lab might eventually sprout meaning and matter. At this point, it seemed just as likely that their significance would remain forever unexpressed. Every day Tim and I talked about closing down the site and moving to Laetoli, just as soon as we had a vehicle. We both knew, however, that we weren't going to make it to Laetoli, not this summer, not while there was still hope that this creature who so long ago had died on that spot by the Olduvai lake could tell us something new about the way it had lived. We were seduced by the fossil, and would stay at the site for as long as it took. Too many questions were left to be answered.

CHAPTER SEVEN:

The Primitive Wonder

False facts are highly injurious to the progress of science, for they often endure long; but false views, if supported by some evidence, do little harm, for everyone takes a salutory pleasure in proving their falseness; and when this is done, one path towards error is closed and the road to truth is often at the same time opened.
—Charles Darwin, *The Descent of Man*

BY THE END OF JULY, Dik-dik Hill had lost all of its charm. After the initial excitement, Lew Binford and George Frison had returned to doing what they came for—scouting the long-term archeological possibilities around the Gorge. Eck and Ndessokia were itching to get back to paleontological surveying, and with the returns diminishing at the hominid site, we had no choice but to let them go. The excavation crew was reduced to Tim and his two students, along with Mzee, our lone African staffer, and myself.

I could no longer imagine commemorative plaques being erected on the spot, except to pay tribute to the torments of boredom. My whole past and future seemed reduced to squatting in the dust, picking dark flecks out of an ever-replenishing mound of dirt. I began to take an interest in matters of profound inconsequence—the breadth of silence between each note of a bird's call, the pattern of sweat on somebody's shirt. I grew intimate with each of my co-workers' style of sorting through their portions of sieved detritus. Mzee Mrisho, for instance, sat with his legs spread, hour after hour, his karai cushioned between his thighs. He rooted through the contents of his pan with a forefinger, touching the pebbles one by one. When he came across a piece of bone he picked it out and placed it in the wooden box with an air of proud solemnity, as if he had were returning a stolen gem to its rightful owner.

Gen Suwa's approach was equally formal and precise. He put two handfuls of gravel into his karai, and patted them down with his palms into a neat layer one pebble thick lining the sides of the bowl. Then he raised the whole karai up to his face, studying the dust-covered particles as if each were a character in some ancient text. Berhane had developed a more whimsical technique. He held a handful of gravel up high and let the pebbles trickle out in a stream through his fingers, ringing the karai like a wind chime. When he found a chip of bone, he tossed it into the wooden box with a elegant flick of his wrist. He never missed.

In the mornings, we could usually look forward to a couple of tourist combis rolling by on their way to FLK. By this point even Tim looked forward to the distraction, especially if the tourists took a genuine interest in what we were up to. Unfortunately, many of them seemed reluctant to acknowledge our greetings, much less engage in conversation. I finally figured out that their diffidence rose from our being *outside the vehicle,* which from their perspective defined us as a kind of wildlife—suspiciously communicative, but wild nevertheless. To be fair, the dust blowing out from the sieve had painted us the same dull gray as the ground itself, so perhaps we did not appear quite fully human. But it was a strange feeling, to be so thoroughly objectified. As a combi slowed to a stop, three or four heads wearing safari hats would pop out of the open sunroof, cameras clicking away madly, just as if they had encountered a pride of lions lolling beside the road. Bob Walter suggested we put up a sign: DO NOT FEED THE ANTHROPOLOGISTS.

At the end of one hot, bone-poor afternoon I was standing next to Berhane beside a half-excavated square. Tim had taken a rare break with his hammer, and for a few minutes we had no dirt to sift through. Something in the square caught Berhane's eye. He bent down and picked out an inch-long chunk of limb bone—no doubt a bovid's, judging from the thickness of the bone cortex. This was not a fossil of much importance, but certainly worth collecting. Instead of putting it into the box along with the other fragments from that square, however, Berhane kneeled down and tucked it back into the loosened earth at his feet. He looked up and saw that I was watching him.

"For sieving excitement," he explained with a wry grin.

I couldn't fault him. There was no harm, really, in finding the same bone twice.

A few minutes later we heard the sound of vehicles approaching around the bend. It was unusual for tourists to be in the Gorge this late in the afternoon. The two brand-new A&K Land-Rovers barreling down on us were not behaving like standard safari vehicles either. With horns blaring, they lurched back and forth, then skidded to a full stop right in front of us. Out of the lead vehicle stepped David Koch, one of the board members of the Institute of Human Origins who had helped bring us to Olduvai. He had told me that he was planning a safari to Africa that summer and would stop at the Gorge.

David was dressed in natty khakis and was obviously enjoying himself. The other doors opened and the members of Koch's private safari tumbled out, stretching their limbs after the long ride from Manyara. David introduced his party, which included some close friends and their companions from New York City, as well as a pair of newlyweds from Los Angeles. They all looked fresh, buoyant, and untroubled, like children on a field trip.

Then I introduced my colleagues—glum, unwashed, and staring at the visitors as if they'd arrived from some other planet. Berhane's jeans were sagging down and he had his sweater tied around his head like a fat, artless turban; Tim was glowering, out of habit, from under the rattlesnake band of his battered felt hat; and Gen, bare-chested and scatter-haired, looked like some sort of wild primitive we'd brought in from the bush for physical labor. Only Mzee looked vaguely civilized.

"So what are you guys doing hanging out here by the road?" David asked when I'd finished making the introductions.

"Nothing much," I said. "Just digging up a hominid skeleton."

That broke the ice. Tim put on a grin and started showing people around the site, Gen donned his blue windbreaker, and pretty soon everybody was talking cheerfully and looking like they at least all belonged to the same species. Unknown to us, the support lorry for the Koch safari had arrived earlier, and by the time we got back to camp the front yard was graced with a luxurious little community of tents, shower stalls, and dining furniture. David and his friends were eager to see the hominid, so we went straight to the lab and laid the bones out on the table. Naturally he was ecstatic that his support for the expedition had so quickly borne fruit, and I confess it was a wonderful feeling to have the specimen in hand and a chance to talk about it with new faces, interested people. For the first time since the early excitement at the site, it struck me how *much* we had found, rather than how little, and what a rare stroke of fortune it was that had led us to that fossil. We celebrated with cocktails around a roaring bonfire.

David's visit provided a happy excuse to take a break from digging. With the temporary surplus of vehicles, we decided to drive down to Laetoli. Though we still had no permit to work there, we could at least check on the condition of the footprint site and give the safari a little tour.

When the Leakeys first visited Laetoli half a century ago, the journey from Olduvai took three days. Today the trip takes an hour and a half, even less if you are not too concerned about the longevity of your vehicle. We thumped along, following the Side Gorge as it curved south, steadily climbing up the plateau separating the drainage basins of Olduvai and Lake Eyasi to the south. I sat crammed in the rear of one Land-Rover with Paul Manega and Bob Walter, the view out my window dominated by Lemagrut, flanked on both sides by the great Ngorongoro caldera. These volcanoes are now in their dotage, but in the late Pliocene they were mere molten urgings somewhere deep beneath the earth's crust. The region then was as flat as the Serengeti itself, and with a climate much the same—hot and dry. The only active volcano in the area was Sadiman, now no more than a gentle swelling in the plain, hidden from sight behind Lemagrut. Beginning some four million years ago, Sadiman puffed out a succession of new savanna surfaces, some as fine as filo dough. It was in these famous "Laetoli Beds" that Mary Leakey's team had found the hominid jaws and teeth in the early 1970s. A few years later, they had made an even more sensational discovery: the footprint trails of hominids and other mammals preserved in the hardened ash.

As we bounced along, Tim and I told our visitors about the discovery of the Laetoli footprints and the incredible good fortune that brought them into being. At the end of a dry season some three and a half million years ago, the volcano Sadiman puffed out a series of ash falls over a period of a few days. After a rainfall, these soft surfaces were walked, hopped, and slithered through by all the animals that lived in the area, from elephants to millipedes. Mixed into the fine sandy material that Sadiman was belching over the plain was a very rare ash called carbonatite. When it meets with water, carbonatite goes into solution, and when the water evaporates, a mineral crystal called trona is left behind, which hardens like concrete. The rain that fell was just enough to dampen the ash, so that the footprints were preserved. Then Sadiman erupted again, laying down a protective layer of new ash. The whole process was repeated several times before the deluge of the rainy season began in earnest.

Three and a half million more years of deposits, faulting, and erosion, and the prints were back out in the open, vulnerable once again. Fortunately, they were discovered before they could be destroyed by erosion. Tim was intimately involved in their excavation. It's a touchy subject for him, to say the least.

"The Laetoli footprints are probably the most precious discovery that has ever been made in this science, or ever will be made," he told our visitors. "It took the most unlikely set of circumstances to produce them. We arrived in a tiny opening of time to find them before they were destroyed forever. You can't imagine what luck that was. You can't imagine what a responsibility rested in their preservation. The restoration of the Sistine Chapel—damn it, the *painting* of the Sistine Chapel—was nothing compared to this. And guess what. Mary blew the job."

Tim had joined Mary's team at Laetoli in the summer of 1978, soon after we had completed our analysis of the Hadar and Laetoli hominids and agreed to name *afarensis*. The original discovery of animal tracks had been made two years before, but it was not until 1978 that a verifiably hominid print was found. One day Paul Abell, a geochemist at the site, came across a broken impression that he thought might be such a print. Tim concurred, but anthropologist Louise Robbins, whom Mary had invited to Laetoli specifically to work on the prints, was certain that the impression was actually two antelope tracks superimposed. She convinced Mary that excavating further under the tuff to look for more prints was not worth the effort. After some vehement argument, Tim and some others in camp prevailed upon Mary to at least send Ndibo, one of the African workers, out alone to the site. Ndibo dug for a while and uncovered two beautiful prints. Unmistakably hominid.

At that point Tim took over the excavation. The footprints were extremely fragile, and to uncover them unharmed he had to develop a new technique.

"The footprints had been made in one layer of ash," he explained, as our Land-Rover headed over to the spot where this had all taken place. "But they had made a dent in the thin ash layers underlying them too. The farther down you went from the actual print, however, the more deformed the impression would be. So we first had to be absolutely sure that we did not puncture through that primary surface—or else we'd end up with only a distorted image. Luckily, there was a thin skin of calcium carbonate lying right over the footprint layer, just a little harder than the light gray ash that fell later and filled in the depressions. I poured paint thinner onto the print, and while the gray infilling soaked it up and darkened, the calcium carbonate skin didn't. In that way I was able to discriminate by color between the two ash layers, and carefully remove the infilling without working down into the print itself."

Using this slow, exceedingly painstaking process, by the end of the summer Tim and the other excavators had uncovered a trail of what proved to be the tracks of at least two hominids, and possibly three. Two parallel tracks, labeled G-1 and G-2/3, ran some thirty feet before they were interrupted by a fault line. A small trial trench dug beyond the interruption revealed that the trails continued on the other side, awaiting further excavation the following summer. But Tim would not be in charge any longer.

"Between the 1978 and 1979 field seasons Don and I announced *afarensis*." Tim grinned. "I was finished at Laetoli as long as Mary Leakey was the boss."

With Tim gone, the responsibility for excavating the much-better-preserved footprints in the southern part of the trail was shared by Mary and Ron Clarke, an experienced British paleontologist. Tim had shared with Ron the paint-thinner technique the summer before. Ron continued in the same manner, etching out the impressions with a fine dental probe, working with his eyes practically inside the prints. Meanwhile, Mary chose to use a mallet and a chisellike probe to remove the hardened ash that had filled up the prints. By the end of the season, they had expanded the excavation to include more than seventy recognizable footprints. The length of the trails covered almost eighty feet. Ron made a mold and brought it back to Olduvai for casting.

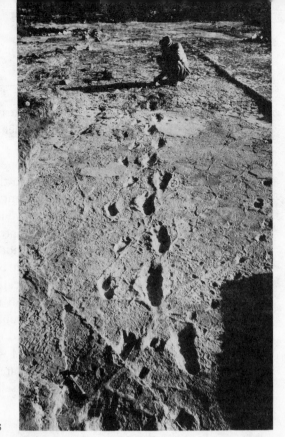

The hominid footprint trail at Laetoli. Discovered in 1978, the footprints proved conclusively that early hominids had walked upright three and a half million years ago.
Copyright © by PETER JONES

Mary still had to face the peculiar dilemma of how to preserve the fragile evidence that her team had exposed. She considered erecting an open-air museum on the site, but unless it could be permanently staffed, a building would serve only to attract the attention of animals and vandals. Mary's only other choice was to rebury the whole trail again, covering it over with layers of sand, plastic sheeting, and lava boulders to protect it from damage from plant roots. And so this remarkable relic of the past was brought to light, witnessed, and returned once again to the earth.

On a brief trip to Laetoli in 1985, we had discovered that Mary's efforts to protect the prints from root damage appeared to have backfired. The footprint site was actually more overgrown than the surrounding terrain. There were even a number of acacia trees growing right over the buried prints. Apparently the microhabitat of the disturbed soil had been improved, rather than hindered, by the human alterations. Of course, we could not tell if any damage was actually occurring to the footprints beneath, but it seemed at the very least a risk.

As we approached the site now, I was shocked to see how much the trees had grown in just a year. Some were almost eight feet tall.

"Welcome to Laetoli National Forest," Tim said grimly, as we got out of the vehicle. Our visitors took a few pictures, then explored around a little, keeping clear of the bushier areas where puff adders might be hiding. After a few minutes George Bunn, a friend of Koch's, walked up to where Tim and I were standing and asked a question that was probably on everybody's mind.

"Is this, well, all there is?"

"Amazing, isn't it?" Tim replied. "People have written reams about this site and what it says about early hominid locomotion— their stride lengths and gait values, toe impressions, weight transfer, mean velocity, on and on. If you believe what some people say, from what you see around you we can tell when the Laetoli hominids curled their toes, exactly how their walk differed from ours, and which of them was blind, pregnant, homicidal, or all of the above."

"But there isn't anything here to see," George said.

The sharp lines of Tim's face opened up into a wide grin.

"Bull's-eye. For all that's been written about these prints, only a tiny handful of experts actually had a chance to see them before they were shoveled over. I was one. Ron Clarke was another. Most everybody else who talks about their meanings and implications is talking from casts, not originals. And that's a real shame. A cast can't tell you anything about texture, about color, about the fine details of the original. It doesn't tell you the difference between the actual footprint and the distorted image below it. It doesn't tell you whether some swelling in the print is part of the morphology of an ancient foot, or just a bit of unexcavated infilling."

Tim paused. His grin turned hard, almost menacing.

"But you know what the casts do tell you?" he said. "They tell you where somebody has cut through them with a chisel. Those marks don't come off. They're part of the record now too."

In my science, discovery is always an act of destruction. Whenever we remove a bone from the earth or dig into and around a collection of ancient artifacts, we contaminate, however slightly, the very truth about the past that we seek to apprehend. Nobody, not even Mary Leakey herself, would argue that the mallet-and-chisel method she used to excavate the footprint trail in 1979 was as precise as the technique Tim had devised the year before and passed on to Ron Clarke. The question is how much it *mattered*. If Mary's technique could recover the prints in the same condition as Tim's could, then perhaps he was being overmeticulous. If, on the other hand, damage done to the prints during excavation was influencing the way people were interpreting their meaning, then clearly the record needed to be set straight.

One of the outstanding issues concerned the number of individuals who were represented in the two trails. The G-1 trail had clearly been made by a single, relatively small hominid walking along on two legs. The G-2/3 trail was more ambiguous; most researchers, Mary included, believed that it represented the tracks of two more individuals, the second walking so as to leave prints partially overlapping those of the first. But some workers, including Ron Clarke, believed that only one individual had made the G-2/3 trail. If the prints seemed disproportionately large, it was because the hominid's feet had slid a little in the rain-slick ash with each step it took.

A strong argument Mary and others cited against this interpretation was the presence of what appeared to be a heel mark in one of the G-2/3 prints a few millimeters inside the rim of another heel mark. Ron insisted that this feature should not be given undue weight, without explaining why. Not surprisingly, his protestations were largely ignored. Finally, at a conference held in 1985 in South Africa to honor Raymond Dart, Ron felt he had to reveal the truth: Among other damage done to the trail, Mary Leakey had inadvertently carved the heel mark into the print with her chisel.

"Although I saw she had dug through the calcareous lining of the print and advised her to stop," Ron told the assembly, "she did not heed my advice."

The audience was stunned. Before the session could be adjourned, Michael Day, a longtime colleague of the Leakeys and one of the few scientists who had actually seen the original prints, demanded to be recognized.

"I cannot let this session pass without responding to the outrageous suggestion made by Dr. Clarke," Professor Day angrily declared. "The suggestion that Mary Leakey was incompetent and damaged those footprints, while she is not here to defend herself, is one of the most outrageous things I've heard in a scientific meeting in many years." His censuring of Clarke's remarks was greeted with applause.

"Ron was in a bind," I explained to David and his friends. "He's by nature a mild-mannered guy with a deep respect for Mary's contributions. But he believed that there were really only two sets of prints on that site at Laetoli. To make his case, Ron had to say things about Mary's chiseling technique that weren't going to make him very popular."

"Most of us disagree with him about the number of hominids who walked here," Tim added. "But today, everyone knows that Ron Clarke was right about that artificial heel. And he deserves respect for having the courage to risk his own reputation and say something about it."

If Tim White bristles when he talks about the Laetoli excavation, it is only because he values the footprints themselves so highly. As evidence, they bear upon one of the most critical questions in the study of human evolution: why our earliest progenitors stood up and started walking on two legs. Between the discovery of Neandertal Man in 1856 and A. *afarensis* in the early 1970s, numerous fossil bones had paid testimony to our ancestors' ability to walk upright. But here at Laetoli, startlingly unforeseen, was even more direct testimony to the function that triggered the human career—the mark of heel and toe, muscle and skin, pushing down upon the ground.

No one questions anymore whether hominids before *Homo sapiens* walked erect. Until recently, however, most scientists were reluctant to believe that Neandertal Man, *Homo erectus,* and the rest really walked *like us*. Their style of locomotion has been variously described as "unique and distinctive," "not fully human," "inefficient," "waddling," and a "shambling half-run." At the heart of this reasoning is the seemingly obvious truism that before our forebears learned how to walk, they had to learn how to walk badly. In the opinion of some other anatomists, however, the people who talked about semihuman styles of bipedalism in the past had fallen into the old anthropocentric trap—the tendency to regard human evolution as a series of inevitable refinements, each of our ancestors becoming a little more refined, a little more like us than the one that had come before.

In the early 1970s, Owen Lovejoy of Kent State in Ohio set out to study the biomechanical properties of *Australopithecus* postcrania from South Africa to see how these early ancestors locomoted. Previously, the anatomy of these pelvic and limb bones had been used as evidence to show that *Australopithecus* was a rather clumsy walker. Working closely with orthopedic specialists, Owen demonstrated that in fact these ancient hominids were *better* walkers than we are today, owing largely to the subsequent compromises that *Homo* had to make in pelvic structure so that human females could accommodate the birth of large-brained young.

Owen went on to take charge of the postcrania that we were pulling out of Hadar—a mammoth responsibility. He subjected the bones to X rays and CT scans, and carefully weighed every anatomical nuance. Nothing that he saw in that wealth of bones shook his conviction: The earliest known hominids were fully committed to a bipedal, terrestrial life-style. Granted, the postcranial bones exhibited some "primitive" aspects. But one would expect that, since *afarensis* was the most ancient hominid. The arms appeared long, especially relative to the short lower limbs. The finger and toe bones were more curved than ours. But the "total morphological pattern"—the important suite of features associated with locomotion in the hip, knee, ankle, and foot—sang out strongly in favor of bipedalism.

For a while it seemed that Lovejoy had had the final word on the subject. But in 1983, two investigators at the State University of New York at Stony Brook announced that *their* study of the Hadar and Laetoli material convinced them that Lucy and her kin had in fact spent a significant amount of their time not walking on the ground but climbing in the trees. Granting that in most respects *afarensis* was bipedal, Randy Susman and Jack Stern detailed more than two dozen separate anatomical traits suggesting that the species was nevertheless a less efficient biped than modern humans. In their opinion, *afarensis* was no less than a "locomotor missing link." They even suggested that the females of the species were better adapted to climbing in trees than their male counterparts. The specter of a shambling, bent-kneed quasi-human was out of the closet again, this time backed by a great deal more evidence than had ever been available before.

Stern and Susman were not the only ones denying *afarensis* a two-legged locomotive perfection. The year before, their Stony Brook colleague Bill Jungers had argued that Lucy's legs were too short, in relation to her arms, for her species to have achieved a fully modern adaptation to bipedalism. At the same time, Russell Tuttle of the University of Chicago was pointing to the fact that the Hadar specimens possessed curved fingers and toes, possibly an apelike adaptation for grasping tree branches. Meanwhile Brigitte Senut and Christine Tardieu in Paris were arguing, on very thin evidence, that the Hadar knee and elbow joints also indicated a much more arboreal animal than Lovejoy's bipedal ideal.

Owen Lovejoy was not at all dismayed that Lucy's status as a full-blown biped was being attacked on several fronts.

"The first rule of anthropology," he told me, "is that when everybody believes what you've said, you've probably got it wrong."

Owen's imperturbability notwithstanding, I felt that what was needed was a forum bringing together all the people whose work was converging on the critical question of Lucy's locomotion. In the spring of 1983 the fledgling Institute of Human Origins sponsored its first scientific conference, "The Evolution of Human Locomotion." Tim and I got together and prepared a list of invitees. Everyone responded enthusiastically, except for the French investigators, who chose not to come. Tim himself agreed to talk about the Laetoli footprints. I would moderate the proceedings and try to make sure things did not get out of hand.

That's not always an easy assignment with Tim White around. When he took the podium early in the conference, Tim immediately challenged a specimen found by Noel Boaz, a scientist who was in the audience. In 1979, Boaz had found what he believed to be a hominid collarbone at a site called Sahabi in the Libyan desert. The deposits where the bone had been discovered had once been covered by a salty sea, and they could be dated by the presence of certain marine-plankton fossils to about five million years. That date could not be more significant: It made Boaz's fossilized clavicle the oldest known hominid in the world.

"The bone has a backward-S curve that is characteristic of hominids," Boaz had reported earlier, "implying that the creature may have been bipedal." If that was true, then hominids were walking erect fully two million years before Lucy.

Before the conference, Tim and his students had done a little study of Boaz's fossil, and now he dropped a bomb. Far from representing a hominid or any other primate, Tim told the audience, the specimen was the fossilized rib of a dolphin. The S-shaped curvature of the bone that Boaz had built his case around was simply not evident in the specimen. Boaz rose from his seat and angrily defended his position, ticking off a number of anatomical points that gave the bone "about a 70 or 80 percent chance" of being a hominid. But Tim was not there to play probability games.

"For those of you who question whether the specimen Dr. Boaz found in Libya is a dolphin or a hominid," he said from the stage, "we invite you to take a look at a dolphin rib and a cast of the Sahabi fossil up here after the talk. I don't think there is a single

The Sahabi fossil (center), found by Noel Boaz and believed by him to be the clavicle of a five-million-year-old hominid. Boaz claimed that the fossil possessed an S-shaped curvature, like that of a chimp clavicle (left). Tim White disputed the claim, declaring that the specimen was the fossilized rib of a dolphin, like the one shown at right. TIM D. WHITE

person in this room—perhaps not even yourself, Noel—who will walk out still thinking that this bone is anything except a fossil dolphin." Later, Tim took to calling the fossil "Flipperpithecus boazi."

"Unseemly behavior," Boaz told a reporter. "It's just his style, so what can I say?" He later claimed that in making his point, Tim had engaged in *ad hominem* sophistry.

"In fact I argued with *ad delphinem* actually," Tim retorted. A picture of the Sahabi specimen is above, flanked by a chimp clavicle on the left and a modern dolphin rib on the right. I'll let the reader decide how much of an S-shaped curve the fossil shows.

The conference then dove into the meat of the dispute over bipedalism in *afarensis*. Russ Tuttle discussed what he saw as an unresolvable discrepancy between the Laetoli footprints and the foot of *afarensis* that supposedly made them. From his analysis of the footprint casts, Russ concluded they had been left by a creature walking more or less like a human. But the foot skeleton we had found in the Hadar had long, curved toes and other features that in his view would have left a different sort of print in the ash. The implication was that an altogether different hominid species—the ancient true *Homo*—had existed at Laetoli and left its tracks behind. If that was correct, then it followed that, in our phylogeny, Tim and I had crammed more than one species under the name *afarensis*.

"You saw Tim White fracture Mr. Boaz's collarbone," Russ joked with the audience, "and I guess he's ready to stomp on my feet."

Tim did have his say later on. Tuttle had based his analysis on the best preserved of the Hadar feet—a large, nearly complete foot skeleton from the First Family site. Tim acknowledged that with its long, curved toes, this foot would not come close to fitting into the prints at Laetoli. But when Tim and Gen Suwa had scaled the anatomy of the specimen down to a Lucy-like size, the *afarensis* slid into the Laetoli prints with a Cinderella-like fit.

Randy Susman, bearded and intense, made the case at the conference for Lucy's climbing abilities. Susman was careful to stress that no single feature endowed *afarensis* with such ease in the trees, but rather a functional complex of traits working together. Chief among these in the upper body were strong, curved, apelike finger bones, and Lucy's long arms relative to her legs—another primitive trait that would facilitate movement among the branches. Below the waist, Susman pointed to what he and his colleagues believed were greater ranges of motion in Lucy's hip, knee, and ankle joints. Lucy also possessed those curved toes, and according to Susman, the anatomy of the base of her foot and her calf bone indicated that powerful muscles once stretched between them. Both of these traits would have given her a grasping prehensility in her feet that would make life a lot easier aloft. In sum, the creature conjured up by Susman's arguments would have been a fairly respectable arborealist, scampering along branch tops, swinging between limbs, and shinnying up trunks with an agility that would put our own attempts to shame.

Jack Stern then took the podium to present the evidence for a less-than-human mode of bipedalism in *afarensis*. He cited Bill Jungers's work on Lucy's short femur, and discussed some fine points of hip, knee, and ankle anatomy. But he leaned most heavily on what the Stony Brook team saw as a peculiarly primitive orientation in Lucy's pelvis. In apes the large flaring bones of the pelvis, called the iliac blades, are tall, narrow, and rather flat back to front. Human pelves are shorter and broader in the beam, and the iliac blades twist around to the side. Everyone agreed that Lucy's pelvis was short and broad. But according to Stern, it still lacked that crucially human twist to the side. This difference has everything to do with locomotion. Without that feature, Lucy could have kept her balance only if she walked with her hip joint flexed, like a chimp.

When it came to the Laetoli footprints, Jack agreed with Tim that *afarensis* was the species that had left them behind. But from the Stony Brook perspective, those Laetoli hominids were walking like missing links. When chimpanzees walk bipedally, they transfer their weight in each step along the outside of the foot. Humans carry their weight from the outside to the inside, so that the last, powerful push-off phase of a stride is supported by the big toe. The ball of the foot should therefore leave a deep impression, especially in the soft surface. But in many of the Laetoli prints, Stern and Susman could find no such deep impression. In one print they actually saw a swelling where there should have been an indentation. They concluded that at push-off, the Laetoli hominids at least sometimes kept their weight on the outside of the foot. Earlier, Stern and Susman had pointed out too that in at least one of the prints, the big toe appeared to be splayed out to the side instead of lined up with the other toes, as in the human condition. Perhaps, they argued, the Laetoli hominids were capable of abducting their big toes outward, almost like chimps.

The Stony Brook arguments about the Laetoli prints made a big impression on some people at the conference. But like almost everyone else, Randy and Jack had been basing their conclusions on studies of casts. Tim knew the originals in detail, and he made it abundantly clear how misleading casts can be. The print that Stern and Susman had pointed to as most obviously lacking an indentation turned out to be one of those excavated by Mary Leakey's chisel probe. Most of the fine detail was obscured. Tim also pointed out that when humans walk on soft surfaces, their tracks do not always show a well-defined imprint of the ball of the foot either. As for the splayed-out big toe, Tim showed that in the ash surrounding that print there were tracks of a Pliocene hare. As the hare hopped through the ash, it left one footstep overlapping the hominid print, creating the false impression of a big toe. This detail could be plainly seen only on the original footprint.

Stern and Susman later admitted that after the revelation that some of the footprints had been improperly excavated, they had "much reduced faith" in their conclusions about them. Instead, they threw their weight all the more behind their arguments from the bones from Hadar. But Owen Lovejoy was quietly waiting in the wings, and now it was his turn. He believed the Stony Brook team had missed seeing the forest while looking for Lucy in the trees. It wasn't enough to simply collect a few simian resemblances and declare a locomotor missing link.

"Bipedality demands a fundamental reorganization of the lower limb," Owen declared at the beginning of his talk. "The animal *has* to give up one form of adaptation for another. There is no such thing as an anatomical free lunch."

A case in point is the human pelvis. The only way to design an animal that can balance the weight of its spinal column in a vertical position is to give it a rounded bowl of a pelvis. But if that remodeling were to be effected on the narrow, keellike pelvis of an ape, the animal would have to sacrifice some 30 percent of its leaping ability—hardly what you would expect in a creature locomoting limb to limb. Stern and Susman had maintained that Lucy's pelvis lacked the human twist to the side, but again they had been deceived by casts. Lovejoy had spent long hours with the original, badly fragmented fossil, carefully restoring it to what he thought was close to its form in life.

Owen's restoration did not reveal a pelvis exactly like that of a modern human, but it did show a much more human like twist to the side in the iliac blades than Stern and Susman had contended. The crucial question was, Did Lucy's hip joint work like ours, or like that of an ape? Owen demonstrated convincingly that the abductors—the hip muscles—employed in stabilizing the hip in bipeds operated in Lucy just as they did in modern humans. He also showed that Lucy's abductors assisted in eliminating potentially dangerous stress upon her *femoral neck*—the thin bridge of bone connecting the shaft of the thighbone to the balllike femoral head, which fits into the hip socket.

A closer look at this vulnerable stretch of bone revealed a telling difference between bipedal humans and quadruapedal apes. An arboreal ape subjects its femoral neck to extreme bending stresses when it leaps and climbs, resulting in a thickening of the bone at the top and the bottom. In a human femur, the femoral neck is adapted only to stresses imposed by walking and running—resulting in a thickening of bone just along the bottom, with only a thin layer of bone at the top. Lucy's femoral neck is identical to that of a modern human, and would fracture if subjected to high stress during climbing.

"Lucy was not just capable of walking upright," Owen later wrote. "*It had become her only choice.*" Point by point, Owen and his student Bruce Latimer showed how, below the waist, Lucy was factory-built for full bipedality. One of the most important bits of evidence that Stern and Susman were using was those curved *afarensis* toes. But as Latimer made clear, in the perspective of the whole functional anatomy of the foot, the toe issue withered in importance. He pointed

Owen Lovejoy's reconstruction of Lucy's pelvis (upper left) compared to those of a human (lower left) and a chimpanzee (right). Lovejoy maintains that Lucy's human-like pelvis is one important indication that her species was fully adapted to bipedal locomotion. C. OWEN LOVEJOY

out that the foot is the most distinctly human part of our anatomy: We have lost the opposable big toe, the prehensile grasping action of ape feet, and gained instead the springlike arch and rigidity of the forefoot needed for bipedal walking. And contrary to the Stony Brook line of reasoning, the *afarensis* ankle, knee, and hip joints were unquestionably human in all but the most trivial respects.

Whichever side one took in this debate, the formal presentations, technically complex but passionately argued, had brought the issue to a fever pitch. On the morning of the second day we brought everyone back together for a closed-door session in the presence of the evidence alone. With no set agenda and no press allowed, the disputants were free to let loose without fear of public scrutiny or the temptation for public grandstanding. Quickly small groups coalesced in pockets around the room. When I looked up an hour later, Tim White, Gen Suwa, and Russ Tuttle were burrowed in one corner, fitting and refitting casts of toe bones into the Laetoli prints. Bill Jungers was running from table to table, measuring bone lengths and ratios. Owen Lovejoy and Jack Stern were pointing finger fossils at each other. Bruce Latimer was explaining ankle esoterics, and Randy Susman had bared one foot, the better to demonstrate toe curling. There were raised voices and arms being thrown up in exasperation, but there was also a lot of listening going on. I smiled to myself. This is why I had put the Institute together. All the work had paid off.

By the end of the conference, I was convinced that Lovejoy and

Co. had made a convincing case, at least with respect to anatomy below the waist. When it came to upper-body adaptations, I was not quite so sure. What bothered me were Lucy's long arms and strong, curved fingers. Both would be a big advantage in moving about in the trees, regardless of whatever commitments a species had made toward bipedality from the waist down. On the other hand, Lucy's long arms and curved fingers might be examples of what Lovejoy calls "evolutionary baggage"—traits left over from a more distant ancestor, not yet lost but no longer needed. I, for one, cannot imagine long arms somehow being a *disadvantage* to a fully bipedal hominid.

Stern and Susman notwithstanding, it seemed to me that Lucy's lineage had already crossed the line over to bipedalism, never to return. I put the question in the back of mind and went on to other things. On that expedition to Olduvai, five years later, it would all come back again.

David Koch had arranged for a chartered plane to fly in from Manyara, pick up his safari, and take it over the Kenyan border to the game-rich plains of Masai Mara. But the soft sand of the makeshift Olduvai landing strip was too perilous for the little Cessna that flew in the next day. After nearly crashing on landing, the pilot refused to burden his take off with passengers. The safari would have to "rough it" back to Manyara by Land-Rover. The decision was unpopular, but it proved wise. Carrying only the pilot, the Cessna barely cleared the runway on takeoff, practically scratching its belly on the thorn fence surrounding the camp.

The near-miss put an end to any grumbling about the bumpy ride back to Manyara. David and his friends crammed into the Land-Rovers and headed out of the Gorge. An hour later another A&K vehicle churned up the road into camp, bringing supplies. The Binfords and the Frisons had been waiting for an opportunity to move on too. While the A&K driver paced impatiently, bags were hastily packed and thrown into the rear. The party was over. It was time to get back to work.

On Dik-dik Hill it was the old story. The hominid hinted at its identity, promised meaning, but refused to deliver. We scalped the top off the hill, hoping that the little knoll might have held on to some bits of the skeleton even as the greater part of it eroded out and washed away. We were rewarded with a single molar crown fragment, not enough to tell whether the hominid was *Australopithecus boisei* or *Homo habilis*. The most likely areas now exhausted, we started in on the longer shots, opening up a new line of squares farther down toward the road. For our efforts we gained a few more tooth roots, a splinter of crown, a handful of brown-black enigmas. By this time the mound of backfill had grown so large we could rest up against it while we worked the karais. There was still much to be done, and in each fresh square there was still the hope of the big find we had imagined from the beginning. But the chances of that happening were tapering away by the hour. Each of us knew, alone, that the best of it was over.

Gradually, imperceptibly, the locus of our expectations shifted toward the lab. On a table by a well-shaded window, we laid out the labeled plastic bags stuffed with bone, dark splinters of possibility. The sheer anonymity of those bones was daunting—thousands of them, of which perhaps one in a hundred really belonged to the hominid, and only one in a hundred of those could ever be recognized for what it was. Yet somehow they all had to be sorted, tested, and worried into order.

The familiar comparison between doing a jigsaw puzzle and re-constructing a fragmented fossil is accurate only up to a point. Yes, the process is much the same—pick up a piece, scan the possible points of connection, test edge against edge until finally something fits. But keep in mind: The vast majority of the pieces in a "fossil puzzle" have been lost. Among those that remain, many have lost their defining edges. In the pile of fragments confronting you, most belong to an an unknown number of *other,* largely irrelevant puzzles. At most, you'll succeed in re-creating only a tiny fraction of the picture you want to see. But if you mess up, a priceless opportunity is gone, forever.

In spite of such difficulties, or perhaps because of them, that table by the window in the cool stone building became an irresistible lure. July turned to August and Dik-dik Hill became a sort of dis-tracting obligation, a chore that took us away from the *real* work. As soon as there was light to see by in the morning, somebody would be over in the lab, pinching a couple of fragments together, rolling them around between thumb and forefinger, searching for joins. The chances of success with each attempt were grotesquely remote, but that seemed only to sharpen the compulsion. After breakfast we'd pack up to go down to the Hill, but if somebody was late getting ready or had to run back to their hut to fetch a canteen, somebody else would slip unobtrusively back into the lab and work the bones for a minute or two. It was the same during the afternoon break, or in the hour before dinner—steal away to the lab and try some joins. In the evening we got out the flashlights and worked until our eyes lost their focus.

Once, in the middle of the night, I got up to relieve myself outside my hut. The lab building was a dense black absence, its shape defined against a horizon built of starlight. A thin halogen glow leaked from the lab window. Somebody was at the worktable, bothering the fossil under the beam of a Mini-Mag flashlight.

People love to hear about breakthroughs, about sudden transformations in understanding that turn ignorance to knowledge, base metal into gold. Science is rarely so dramatic. Before that expedition, however, I would have said that the process of discovery always leaves behind recognizable landmarks, points along the way where outstanding questions were answered, doubts satisfied. Now I'm not so sure. I can easily reconstruct the trail of clues that the hominid left for us, and when we came to solve them. It is all duly recorded in my journal. But what the journal lacks is the one entry you would most expect to find: "Eureka! Today we solved the identity of the hominid!" That entry isn't there because it did not happen that way. There was no eureka. There was no grand turning point. The evidence kept dribbling in, and through hard labor and some dogged thinking we *did* solve the puzzle, not through revelation but through a sort of absorption, just below the level of explicit conciousness. It was as if the truth had slowly seeped in through our pores, until we had come to know it without knowing that we did. So when the final, indisputable confirmation came, we hardly noticed the event. What had once been a mystery had become—in hindsight, mind you—obvious from the start.

Our hope for pinning down the taxon of the hominid had come to rest mostly on Gen Suwa's shoulders. Mary Leakey had taken with her the lab's collection of casts that would have helped in making comparisons, but Gen—deep into his dissertation on hominid dentition—carried a lot of what we needed inside his head. Whenever there was enough light and a little time, Gen could be found squinting over the collection of tooth fragments, bringing his memory to bear on some groove barely evident in a chip of crown, imagining its extension and searching for that image in some other piece.

Once again, the nature of the fossil thwarted progress. The Dik-dik Hill hominid was old when it died. ("A real Mzee," said Tim.) Most of the surface features of the tooth-crown fragments had been worn away. Our best chance of discriminating between *boisei* and *habilis* lay in finding an intact third molar. Like a human wisdom tooth, a third molar would have erupted late in life, and consequently in death might still retain enough of its surface topography to make a positive ID. But just knowing the size and dimensions of the tooth alone might be enough to tip the taxonomic balance. I'll say it again: Robust autralopithecine cheek teeth are huge, relative to the size of their canines and incisors. *Homo* cheek teeth are proportionately small. To make the discrimination, you need one front tooth from your fossil, and one cheek tooth. We already had that canine from the dik-dik pile.

Meanwhile, the fossil's postcranial skeleton was slowly taking on shape. Shortly after Koch's departure we unearthed another inch or so of humeral shaft. When Gerry Eck and I came into the lab one afternoon Tim had just succeeded in grafting the piece on to the existing length of bone. The effect was chilling. We now had virtually the entire humerus save for the articular ends. A peculiarity of the bone, merely hinted at before, was now baldly obvious, laid out on a strip of cotton with the transparency of fact.

"Step right up, folks, and take a peek at the ape lady," Tim said, pushing his chair back from the table.

"Jesus. That is one *long* mother," Gerry said.

"I'll bet you that bone's even longer than Lucy's humerus," I said.

"But what we've got of the femur looks so damn small," said Gerry.

"Right." Tim reached over and picked up the chunk of calf bone we'd found the first day at the site. "But I can't make out this tibia. I just don't see how a tibia that size goes on to that little femur."

"Are you saying it might not be hominid?"

"I'm saying it might not be the *same* hominid. That's been my fear all along. That we might be digging around and suddenly come up with two teeth—a *habilis* incisor, and a great big *boisei* molar."

"Now look who's worrying too much," I said. "Every scrap of tooth crown we've found is worn down to the same degree. And we've got no duplication of any one piece of anatomy. That's enough for me to believe there's only one hominid out there."

"Okay, I'll buy that," Tim replied.

"So we've got a creature smaller than Lucy, but with longer arms in relation to its legs. Just as apelike, but a million years more recent in time!"

"Maybe."

"But that would put hominids in the trees long after . . ."

"Not necessarily. Let other people jump to whatever conclusions they want to. All I'm saying at this point is that this *might* be a very short hominid with unusually long arms. We're going to have to find more of the femur first to nail it down."

I didn't answer. Along with an intact third molar, the rest of that femur, especially the distal end, would be the most exciting thing Tim could turn up with his rock hammer. We had every right to hope for it. The articular end of a femur is just about the hardest piece of bone in a skeleton; you could drive a truck over one without doing much damage. But this fossil had denied our expectations. Since the very first day of surface excavation, there had been no more trace of the femur.

Then, on the first Saturday in August, a possible piece of limb shaft appeared in somebody's karai. When we returned for lunch I dropped my things and went over to the lab. Tim was there, intense as usual. Gen was immersed in the tooth roots. I picked up the morning's find and the portion of femoral shaft we had already glued together. They were the same color and texture. I turned the new bone around and clicked it down on the bottom of the shaft.

"Son of a bitch," I said.

"Let me see that." Tim reached out to grab the bone.

"Wait a minute!" I said, pulling away. I wasn't sure yet of the fit. Sometimes the match between two bones can look good on the outside, especially if you really *want* it to, but when you look inside, the interior edges don't come together. I turned the bones around. They lined up perfectly inside. The new piece added an inch to the length of the shaft: a critical inch more toward the distal end.

"The best part of this sucker is the break on the far end," Tim said when he finally got his hands on it. "Look how fresh that break is. The distal end has *got* to be out there."

Now the fossil was beginning to look like a skeleton, especially in the arms. We had most of the humerus. We had almost all of the radius too, and a solid stretch of ulna. If we *could* find the distal femur, we would be able to accurately estimate the hominid's body size. We could also calculate the length of the humerus relative to the femur. That would be a crucial statistic. In modern *Homo sapiens*, the humerus is approximately 75 percent as long as the femur. Apes have arms longer than their legs, so their "humeral-femoral index" is over 100 percent. We knew that Lucy's was in between, about 85 percent. Where along that spectrum did the new hominid lie? It was commonly assumed that when a younger hominid fossil like this one was discovered, it would have a humeral-femoral index closer to our own. But maybe that assumption was about to go by the board.

Bill Kimbel was due to arrive a couple of days later, and if he had received our telegram he would have Lucy's casts in his duffel bag. On the morning of August 5 we heard a Land-Rover whining in low gear down the far side of the Gorge. It was a Department of Antiquities vehicle, with Pelaji Kyauka, the young director of the Arusha Museum, at the wheel. On board were Fidel Masao and Alberto Angela, an Italian graduate student representing the Ligabue Research and Study Center, who would be helping us with the dig. Masao had with him the permit to survey at Laetoli. They told us that Kimbel and Paul Manega were following in another vehicle, having stopped at Ngorongoro for supplies. An hour later the second Land-Rover pulled into camp. We rushed out to greet it. Bill had received the telegram. He had the casts. He also had the two pounds of peanut butter.

"Things are brewing, Bill," I said as we hurried over to the lab. We crowded around the worktable and Kimbel laid out Lucy's limbs. Then we set each of the new hominid's bones up against the corresponding cast of the famous *afarensis* skeleton.

"Look at that. Holy shit."

"The femur's *smaller*. Smaller than Lucy."

"We thought so. But we couldn't convince ourselves. But check out the humerus. It's *bigger* than Lucy's!"

At that point, we couldn't tell the exact dimensions, the precise proportions. That would require more study back home, and with luck, more bone from the site. But we knew the gist of the story the moment Kimbel laid down those casts. The little hominid was almost certainly female—if it were male, then the females of the species would have been only two feet tall or so, which seemed impossible. More important, the skeleton showed the body proportions of a very primitive australopithecine. Yet it had lived in a time much closer to ourselves, a time when tools were already being used and discarded on the ground, a time when a being with brains and culture enough to be called *Homo* lived at Olduvai Gorge.

And we knew something else. Forgotten in the obsession about finding the rest of the femur was Gen Suwa, patiently fingering his tooth fragments, searching for the fits. Just before Bill's arrival he had succeeded in piecing together much of a third molar. The tooth was big, but not *that* big. It was the confirmation we had sought, and no longer needed. Bill, an expert on hominid-skull architecture, could read the same message in the fossil's face. This little creature, fully mature but standing somewhere around three feet three in its bare bipedal feet, was the same species as other fossils from Olduvai like George Twiggy and Johnny's Child, and most likely the same species as the famous big-brained 1470 from Koobi Fora. The same species that Louis Leakey had found, named, and argued for through the 1960s. This hominid, with a body like Lucy but presumably a brain empowered far beyond her reach, was *Homo habilis*.

Lucy's child. *Homo.* One of us.

That evening Gerry Eck reached into his secret larder and pulled out another few bottles of Tanzanian beer, dark and perfumy. We had cause to celebrate. Good friends, old and new, had arrived in camp. They had brought along an assortment of culinary riches to soothe our goat-numbed palates. Chickens. Fresh eggs and cheese. Peanut butter. M&M's. There was new hope for Laetoli, if we could convince Kyauka to stay on and lend his vehicle to the cause. With the fresh muscle power provided by Bill and Alberto, there was even some hope that the next day Dik-dik Hill might yield more than its meager daily ration of bone chips. Even if it didn't, we had already proved the enduring fertility of the Olduvai beds. We had found the first skeleton known of the earliest species of *Homo*. I was well aware, of course, what such superlatives meant for the future of the Olduvai research project, and the Institute of Human Origins as a whole. Understanding the complexities of paleoanthropology can be taxing to potential supporters, people who have important other concerns and little time to spare. Words like "first" and "earliest" cut to the quick.

But what struck me most of all about the skeleton was its perplexing primitiveness. Most experts on hominid body size would have predicted that a skeleton of *Homo habilis*, when found, would prove to have a stature and body proportions somewhere between those of its *afarensis* ancestor and its descendent *Homo erectus*. Luckily, we had skeletons of both those species to refer to. Lucy, a female *afarensis*, stood about three and a half feet tall. In 1984, Kamoya Kimeu had made a sensational discovery at West Turkana; a nearly complete skeleton of a twelve-year-old *erectus* boy. The skeleton, found in deposits dated at 1.6-million-years old, stood about five feet four inches tall. If one assumes human rates of growth, the boy would have reached six feet in height as an adult—as tall as a modern American male.

If body height in the human line did indeed increase gradually from *afarensis* to *erectus*, then by rights *Homo habilis* should have averaged somewhere between four and a half and five feet tall. Instead, we had found a *habilis* skeleton that appeared to have stood no taller in life than Lucy herself. Judging from the fragments we had of the Dik-dik Hill hominid, from the neck down, she was practically Lucy's twin.

"What an odd luck of the draw," I said to Tim as I turned into my sleeping bag that night, "a diminutive specimen for *Homo habilis*, and a relative giant for *Homo erectus*, only two hundred thousand years later."

Neither we nor anyone else could tell, of course, how representative the new skeleton was of *habilis* female generally, or indeed whether the Turkana boy was typical of *erectus* males. But from the admittedly scant information we now had in hand, and making the fair assumption that *Homo* was no more sexually dimorphic than *afarensis*, then in a span of not more than two hundred thousand years, our ancestors had made a surprising leap in body size. Even more intriguing was the abrupt change in body proportions. The Dik-dik Hill hominid had long arms like Lucy, but *Homo erectus* had upper and lower limbs proportioned more like our own.

A whole stew of ideas was simmering in my mind that night. We already knew that *Homo erectus* brains were significantly bigger than those of *habilis*—and now it seemed evident that their bodies were qualitatively different too. Something extraordinary was happening during those few hundred thousand years of evolution, some shift in behavior that would quite suddenly transform a *Homo* with a comparatively small brain in a primitive body into one with a big brain and a modern body. That *Homo erectus* put that larger brain to good use is evident throughout the archeological record. Its material symbol is the beautiful, biface Acheulean hand ax, an enormous technical advance over the rough cobbles associated with *Homo habilis*. The discoveries of *Homo erectus* fossils all over the Old World testify to the species's ability to solve the complexities of living in colder climates—arid steppes, temperate woodlands, high-altitude plateaus. According to some investigators, the species knew the use of fire, perhaps even language. Indisputably, it was the first hominid species to venture out of Africa—not just to dip a toe into neighboring regions of Europe and the Middle East, but to fling its presence northward and eastward into modern Hungary, Germany, and the far northwestern regions of China. The significance of this vast radiation cannot be underestimated. If *habilis* was a local success, *Homo erectus* was an international phenom.

That's what really thrilled me about the Dik-dik Hill hominid. We now knew that a very primitive creature—from the neck down, little more than a walking ape—was practically rubbing shoulders in the early Pleistocene with a much more modern-looking descendant. Such a profound evolutionary acceleration does not occur without reason. Whatever the cause, an unprecedented evolutionary event had taken place, one that would hold ultimate consequence for the entire subsequent history of the planet. That night again I could not sleep, but it was not for anxiety. I was rethinking the old insights into that mystery, and the new possibilities.

A reconstruction of the Dik-dik Hill hominid is compared to a modern human female. The skeleton found at Olduvai Gorge in 1986 would have stood less than three and a half feet tall. Her long arms and small stature suggest that the earliest human species was much more primitive in body size and proportions than thought.

PART IV:

Becoming
Human

*All the facts gleaned from the [Olduvai] deposits interpreted as living
sites have served as the basis for making up "just-so stories" about our
hominid past.*

—Lewis Binford,
Bones: Ancient Men and Modern Myths

*Because of a variety of weaknesses in Binford's analysis, it is doubtful
that his results on Olduvai are a useful contribution to scientific archeology.*

—Henry Bunn, in a review of *Bones*

This whole book review is an ad hominem *argument effected through
innuendo and self-serving misrepresentation.*

—Lewis Binford, "A Reply to Bunn"

Hamana nale kui,
nale kui.

*Here we go round,
go round.*
—A Hadza dance

IF YOU WERE TO ASK a dozen paleoanthropologists at random to name
the three most important letters of the alphabet, eleven of them
would probably answer "FLK." The *Zinjanthropus* skull was found at

Frida Leakey Karongo, of course, and for that alone the site deserves the concrete plinth that stands there today. A year later the Leakeys turned up those first traces of *Homo habilis* nearby, and soon after the two leg bones practically right under Zinj's nose. But FLK yielded still more: a litter of mammal bones and stone tools so evocatively dense as to all but overshadow the hominid fossils themselves. If there is any one place on earth to ask the Big Questions—How did we begin? What were we doing two million years ago that made us human?—FLK is the spot.

Sometimes after a day on Dik-dik Hill I chose to forgo the Land-Rover and walk back to camp, a route that happened to take me right by the famous site. I remember passing once an hour before sunset. I was alone, and as I turned to face FLK, a robust, coppery light struck the back wall of the old excavation, flooding the intervening space. Mary Leakey's insistence on neat angles in excavations had produced walls so smooth and straight they looked as if they'd been cut into the hillside by a giant cake knife. The floor too was worn smooth. Of course, the thousands of ancient bones and tools that once graced it had long since been swept off to the Kenya National Museums in Nairobi. The only bones there now were the bleached remains of a wildebeest killed by predators only a few weeks before. Lit up by that sudden infusion of sunlight, and with the surrounding slopes and gullies already dimming in shadow, FLK seemed to me like a stage set for some minimalist drama: bare, austere, its props pared down to ephemeral meanings. At stage center rested the monument to Zinj, the marble plaque cracked, the concrete base weathered smooth. As a fixture on the set it would outlast the poor wildebeest, but not by much.

In a sense, I thought, FLK *has* functioned as a sort of theater. I sat down on a mound of compacted backfill opposite the site—a good seat in the house. There was no sound but the faint rustling of lizards and insects in the gravel around me, and the whisper of the breeze threading through the sisal on the hill above. Something occurred on this spot almost two million years ago, some events of no particular importance at the time, except that they involved creatures who would later become *us*. Even so, the events would have lived anonymously in the past forever, had they not left behind an indelible trace of themselves, and had not Louis and Mary Leakey rediscovered that record thirty years ago. Ever since then, what happened at FLK has inspired a series of scenarios attempting to replay those moments in the early Pleistocene, and in so doing explain our beginnings to ourselves. There are other archeological sites, of course, that have given substance to our interpretations of the past—many right here in the Gorge. But for a scenario to have credibility at all, it has to play at FLK.

First a prologue, produced by an old familiar. Before the Leakeys struck it rich in Olduvai Gorge, the prevailing view of our ancestors' habits was an extraordinary vision being put forth by Raymond Dart. In the years surrounding World War II, Dart had returned to the anthropological fieldwork he had abandoned following his disappointing journey to England to show off his Taung child. Instead of looking for hominid fossils, however, he was now searching for signs of hominid *behavior*—evidence of tools, the use of fire, or any peculiar pattern in the concentrations of mammal bones in the South African caves that suggested they had not come there through natural means.

Dart found his evidence in a lime quarry in the Makapan Valley in the Transvaal. There he and his students found several specimens of *Australopithecus africanus*. But more intriguing than the hominids themselves were some dark stains in the deposits, which Dart took to be the traces of ancient hearths. There was also a curious anomaly in the collection of seven thousand mammal bones also recovered from the site. When he tallied up the numbers of anatomical parts in the collection, Dart found that he had many more skulls, mandibles, and lower legs than could be accounted for by the number of ribs, vertebrae, and pelves also present.

Very curious. When an animal dies, all the parts of its skeleton will of course be present just as they were in life—so many ribs, limbs, and so forth. If you find a collection of animal fossils where there are more of *some* body parts represented than you would expect to find judging by the number of other body parts counted, then you have to assume that something has tampered with the animal's bones after it died. There are all kinds of forces that can influence the fate of a bone after death—scavengers can carry off parts of a carcass and leave others behind, for instance, or gnaw them to splinters, or water action over time can wash some smaller bones away from their original location, leaving larger ones behind. There is even a name for the subdiscipline of paleontology that deals with the forces acting upon bones after death—we call it taphonomy.

Dart reasoned that the force responsible for the balanced number of anatomical parts at Makapansgat was the hand of our ancestors. The most dramatic evidence for hominid involvement was a collection of forty-two crushed baboon skulls, fully two thirds of which had been smashed in on the left side. Dart believed that the baboons had all been slaughtered by right-handed australopithecine hunters wielding lethal clubs.

These weapons were manufactured of bone and other hard body parts—which explained the plethora of some kinds of bones at the site. He called the culture that produced them the *osteodontokeratic*, meaning "bone-tooth-horn," and painted a vivid portrait of its members:

"Man's predecessors," he wrote in 1957, "seized living quarries by violence, battered them to death, tore apart their broken bodies, dismembered them limb from limb, slaking their ravenous thirst with the hot blood of victims and greedily devouring livid writhing flesh."

With Dart serving up such high-protein prose all by himself, his "killer ape" hypothesis, as it came to be called, hardly needed a professional writer to escort it out of the scientific literature and into the public domain. As it happened, an American journalist and playwright named Robert Ardrey met Dart on a tour of Africa around this time, became enamored with the professor's osteodontokeratic bad guys, and wrote a best seller about them called *African Genesis*. Ardrey's writings, translated into many languages, spread Dart's word around the world. Possessed with a deeply cynical mind himself, Ardrey used Dart's grim vision of man's beginnings as a key to understanding—or even excusing—mankind's persistent tendency toward violence:

"Man is a predator whose natural instinct is to kill with a weapon," Ardrey wrote. "The sudden addition of the enlarged brain to the equipment of an armed already-successful predatory animal created . . . the human being."

Compared to that brute ancestor, the version of humanity that Louis Leakey was simultaneously re-creating here by the Olduvai lake seems positively dainty. Spurred on by the discovery of Zinj, Louis and Mary had spent the rest of the 1959 season digging further into FLK. On the same layer of silty green clay where Zinj had rested, they soon uncovered an interesting assortment of crude tools, and a litter of bones as well—bird's eggs, little birds, tortoises, and small, immature mammals. The complexion of this "faunal assemblage" fit neatly with Leakey's belief that the earliest toolmaking ancestor of Olduvai Gorge was essentially a vegetarian who ate meat only when he happened upon it. Certainly nothing about Zinj himself, with his big millstone teeth, contradicted this portrait of his life-style.

With the aid of the National Geographic Society, the Leakeys expanded the excavation the following year on a scale they could only have dreamed of before, exposing over three thousand square feet in their effort to find more of Zinj. The rest of him never turned up, but in the process, the faunal remains uncovered on the same level took on a compelling new character. Along with the scraps of tortoise, catfish, and lizards, the Leakeys found the bones of more impressive prey densely intermingled with stone tools: Pleistocene pig, horse, antelope, and giraffe. Suddenly Dart's killer ape did not look so out of place in East Africa, especially with the larger-brained *Homo habilis* specimens turning up to steal the lead role from *Australopithecus.* One of the *habilis* juvenile skull bones that had turned up nearby showed a curious fracture pattern. Leakey himself suggested—though he later regretted it—that the fracture might have been caused by "a blow from a blunt instrument." Other researchers speculated that "true *Homo*" might also have killed and eaten Zinj too.

Now, with the shadows gathering in the gullies around me, I imagined a band of Dart's deadly apes running amok on my FLK stage, like demons in a Bosch landscape. This image of man continued to enjoy immense popularity through the 1960s, reaching Hollywood stardom in Stanley Kubrick's film *2001: A Space Odyssey.* But at the same time, scientists were beginning to ask some pertinent questions. Could these small early hominids really perform such prodigious feats of carnage as Dart had detailed? Couldn't some other agents be responsible for the smashed skulls and peculiar patterns of bones found at Makapansgat?

In the mid 1960s, a young geologist named Bob Brain decided to look a bit closer at *all* the taphonomic forces that could have influenced the accumulation of bones-not only at Makapansgat but at the key South African sites of Sterkfontein, Swartkrans, and Kroomdrai as well. Brain's work was a masterpiece of prehistorical detective work. He noticed, for instance, that the trees on the savanna landscape in South Africa did not grow stunted and scattered as one might expect in such a rain-parched habitat, but instead grew in clumps, with many of the trees surprisingly large. Brain found that their roots had tapped into isolated reservoirs of ground-water formed in natural fissures had developed beneath the trees, exposing the subterranean caverns to the open air. All sorts of debris from the surface could fall into these fissures—including bones, especially if carcasses were being eaten in the trees above.

Brain knew that the leopard is the only living predator that regularly eats its prey in trees.

He analyzed the makeup of the bones accumulating beneath trees attractive to leopards, and discovered that the number of anatomical parts included far more lower limb bones and skulls than ribs and vertebrae. This was much the same pattern that Dart had found in the supposed leftover meals of his killer apes. The skulls of the leopards' victims too were often smashed in, the same as the Makapansgat baboons. In *African Genesis*, Robert Ardrey had also cited as evidence of a case of "intentional armed assault" a juvenile australopithecine skull bearing two curious puncture wounds. In the course of his study Brain took a pair of calipers and measured the distance between the two puncture wounds on that skull. The gap matched the space between a leopard's lower canines. Far from being the chief consumer on the ancient South African savanna, *Australopithecus* appeared to be merely one of the consumed.

Brain's work did not end with leopards. He studied other animals who might have contributed to the contents of a cave over its life history. To better understand how scavengers might affect the pattern of bones in ancient sites, he undertook a study of the Khoisan pastoralists in Namibia—or rather, a study of their garbage. Khoisan raise goats, which they regularly butcher and eat in their villages. They also keep dogs, who are naturally accustomed to chewing up, carting around and otherwise leaving their imprint on the remains of their masters' goat meals. Brain found that after the dogs had finished their scavenging, the litter of goat bones left behind also resembled what Dart had found at Makapansgat. Apparently, scavengers had contributed their part to the complexion of the cave deposits. Thus the lives and deaths of leopards, owls, porcupines, hyenas, and yes, hominids too—the imprint of the whole ecosystem through thousands of years—was written in the record of bones in a limestone cave, as long as it remained open to the surface. Eventually the opening would collapse under its own weight or fill up with new deposits, sealing the record until a lime quarryman's dynamite brought it all back to light.

*   *   *

C. K. Brain's studies of South African cave sites helped put to rest the theory of "the killer ape." The accumulations of mammal bones—including hominids—were more likely the remains of prey devoured by leopards in trees above natural sinkholes. Puncture wounds in the skull of one juvenile australopithecine, once thought to be evidence of murder among ancient ancestors, proved to match the spacing between a leopard's lower canine teeth. ILLUSTRATION BY DOUGLAS BECKNER

Bob Brains's work confirmed something about the killer ape that others were beginning to suspect: The hypothesis may have had as much to do with recent events in the quarryman's world as with human behavior in the early Pleistocene. Dart's view of our beginnings was heavily colored by post war gloom. In the 1950s, the self-image of our society was aching from the revelations of its darkest potentials, and just coming to terms with a new, nuclear *Homo*. In a sense, the killing instinct—"this common bloodlust differentiator, this predaceous habit, this mark of Cain"—that Dart planted in our origins made it all make sense: No one was at fault, except humanity itself.

Certainly the Pleisto-drama that replaced Dart's scenario had a sunnier plot, as well as more tangible evidence to lend it credibility. Right here on the Zinj floor, the concentration of stone tools that the Leakeys found was far more solid testimony to the activities of early hominids than Dart's imagined bone weapons. There was also a telling pattern in the way the stones and bones were distributed across the site. Small flake tools and thoroughly smashed-up bones dominated a central area of about four hundred square feet. A semicircle of barren ground bordered this concentration on its eastern edge. Beyond the barren patch, the debris thickened again, but was characterized here by more complete bones, and larger tools. Desmond Clark visited the site and made the inspired suggestion that the quarter-moon of cleared ground might represent the former location of a windbreak—perhaps some sort of thorn fence—protecting the central living area of the tool-using hominids of FLK. Beyond the windbreak lay the debris chucked over the fence by the hominid occupants.

That the Zinj level at FLK represented an ancient "living floor," to use Mary Leakey's term, seemed self-evident; the only questions was what the residents were doing for a living. The many large animals represented on the site had all but convinced most scientists, including Louis Leakey, that the earliest Olduvai toolmaker was doing more to procure meat than just aimlessly stumble around tripping over lizards and baby gazelles. More evidence was soon unearthed: a disarticulated elephant skeleton found in upper Bed I deposits at the nearby site FLK N, and a skeleton of a massive *Deinotherium*, the elephant's shovel-tusked relative, found near the bottom of Bed II on the same site. Both were surrounded by stone tools. Whether these behemoths had been hunted down or scavenged, there seemed little reason to doubt that the hominids of Olduvai Gorge were getting their hands on large quantities of meat. Apparently, *Homo habilis* had already embarked on a hunting way of life, almost two million years ago. Just a little farther up in the Olduvai stratigraphy came evidence of even bolder ancestors: a skullcap of *Homo erectus*, and the fine Acheulean tools associated with an increasing frequency of larger mammal remains.

Louis Leakey drifted away from work in Olduvai during the 1960s, leaving Mary and a steady stream of visiting archeologists to elaborate Olduvai's crucial contributions to the "hunting hypothesis." At the same time, Clark Howell was busy excavating two sites in Spain that would provide abundant evidence that man had become a confirmed hunter some 400,000 years ago. At a place called Torralba,

Howell discovered the remains of almost thirty elephants, along with various skeletons of rhinos, red deer, horses, and wild oxen. Nearly eight hundred Acheulean tools punctuated the debris—and even some weapons made of wood. No hominids were found, but based on the time period and the form of the tools, it was safe to assume that the inhabitant of the site was *Homo erectus.* The archeologists also discovered bits of charcoal suggesting the use of fire, and a strange logic to the placement of some of the bones. Almost the complete left side of one elephant skeleton was found arranged as if for display, each bone turned over and replaced in the position it would have held in life. At the nearby site of Ambrona, Howell found several elephant leg bones lying end to end in two perpendicular lines.

Along with Leslie Freeman, Howell pieced together a scenario that neatly accounted for the complexion of the sites. Apparently, bands of hominid hunters had deliberately set fires to the grassland, driving a migrating herd of elephants into a bog. Mired and weakened in the swamp, the elephants were pelted with rocks from above, then finished off with spears. The hunters closed in to carve up the carcasses with stone tools. The perpendicular lines of leg bones found at Ambrona may have been a walking bridge of elephant limbs, set up to haul the bonanza of flesh out of the muddy swamp. The oddly symmetrical half-carcass was harder to explain—perhaps it was the remnant of some ritual, though no other signs that *Homo erectus* indulged in ceremony had ever been found.

Vividly illustrated by painter Stanley Meltszof in Time-Life books on early man, the Torralba-Ambrona massacres epitomized the "Mighty Hunter" vision of our ancestors rapidly gaining strength in the late 1960s. But the hunting hypothesis was much more than a supposition that humans had been hunting for a very long time. It was a unifying theory arguing that hunting was what made us human in the first place.

"Human hunting is made possible by tools, but it is far more than a technique or even a variety of techniques," wrote Sherwood Washburn and C. S. Lancaster in *Man the Hunter*, in 1968. "It is a way of life, and the success of this adaptation . . . has dominated the course of human evolution for hundreds of thousands of years. In a very real sense our intellect, interests, emotions and basic social life—all are evolutionary products of the success of the hunting adaptation."

Adding force to this view were new studies of contemporary hunter-gatherer societies, principally the !Kung San and G/wi people of the Kalahari Desert, the Hadza of Tanzania, and the aborigines of the Australian outback. Unlike earlier observers of these "primitives," anthropologists like Richard Lee and Irven DeVore did not hold these societies to be quaintly preserved remnants of Stone Age Man. They believed, quite rightly, that the hunter-gatherers alive today had developed patterns of existence unique to *Homo sapiens* and, incidentally, just as viable for their purposes as those of other modern men. They reasoned that since the hunter-gatherers did not practice agriculture, however, their habits—especially as they pertained to procuring food—might reveal something about the principles governing the lives of ancient hunters as well.

One principle that seemed to be universal among hunter-gatherers was a distinct division of labor between the sexes. The males did most of the hunting, while the females took care of the bulk of the gathering. This division of labor, completely unknown among the other primates, formed the central post of the hunting hypothesis. A whole constellation of uniquely human behaviors spun out from it. Hunting and butchering the dangerous game found at Olduvai and Torralba would require efficient cooperation among males—something rarely found in nonhuman primates. Unlike their ape relatives, human hunters also had to maintain large territories, which would put a premium on learning and on a rising capacity to store knowledge of the environment. Increasing brain growth, more sophisticated weapon making and communication skills, the sharing of food, the origin of monagamous pair bonding and the nuclear family—everything essentially human could be traced back to hunting. Warfare too, of course—the killer ape lived on underneath it all. Washburn and Lancaster also proposed that in the symmetry of the Acheulean hand ax lay the beginnings of aesthetics—an appreciation of an object as beautiful beyond its function.

"For those who would understand the origin and nature of human behavior," they concluded, "there is no choice but to try to understand 'Man the Hunter.' "

No choice? I thought about that for a minute, as I listened to the silence gathering around me in the Junction and watched my empty stage. I had no trouble conjuring up some ancient hunters who would fill the space and fit the scenario: a band of near-men armed with hand axes and spears, huddling in a circle to plan their strategy, while a dimwitted *Deinotherium* grazed nearby, oblivious to its impending doom. The scene was easy to imagine, of course, because I had seen it illustrated in textbooks and popular magazines so many times that it had established a kind of verisimilitude simply through repetition. I had to admit too that the hunting hypothesis had potent "explanatory power"—a phrase used to describe a theory that ties together a lot of loose ends. Many anthropologists today still believe in its essentials. But *no choice?* I shivered at that. If the last twenty years of discovery have taught us anything, it is not to trust *anything* so faithfully.

In fact, there were plenty of other choices waiting in the wings— and critics gathering in the audience. One aspect of the hypothesis that drew a lot of fire in the early 1970s was the emphasis it blithely conferred on hunting. Female brains are of course as large as male brains: Why assume that human cerebral capacity was spurred on by an essentially male activity? Richard Lee's own studies among the !Kung had also shown that hunting accounts for only some 30 percent of that group's diet—the rest is supplied by the nuts, tubers, and other plant material gathered primarily by females. The same seemed to be true among other modern hunter-gatherers. If hunting was apparently a secondary activity, why grant it such overwhelming significance? In sum, how could any theory explain the evolution of a species when it ignored the contributions of 50 percent of the population?

Feminist anthropologists, notably Nancy Tanner and Adrienne Zihlman, sized up these shortcomings of Man the Hunter and offered in his place a version of our beginnings launched by Woman the Gatherer. They contended that the prime mover for the split from the apes was indeed the development of tools—not weapons for hunting, however, but digging sticks, hammerstones, and various containers, all used to gather plants, eggs, honey, termites, and perhaps an occasional burrowing rodent. In this hypothesis the fundamental social unit was that of mother and child, with the female sharing the fruits of her foraging with her long-dependent offspring. Through generations, this economic alliance between mother and child might expand to include sharing between the gathering female and other kin, and eventually a more generalized sharing with adults outside the kin group, including males. Since the most important food sources were gathered, however, it would have been females, not males, who were in charge of the technical innovations that nurtured the growth of intelligence and set *Homo* apart from the other primates. Hunting played at most a peripheral role: that of a hit-or-miss, inefficient activity that males could afford to pursue because they could count on the women back at the living site to provide the steady source of food.

There is no doubt, in my mind at least, that the gathering hypothesis helped to correct a view of human origins that was woefully out of balance. (Mentally, I shooed my band of hunters offstage. To take their place I ushered in a clutch of resourceful she-hominids. Their young ones watched, engrossed, as they coaxed tubers out of the Olduvai earth.) But there were problems with this theory too, not the least of which was the replacement of one sex bias for another. Why should a female activity be any more exclusively responsible for the development of human intelligence than a male one? Certainly plant foraging played an extremely important part in early hominid evolution—but it doesn't necessarily follow that we have to shrink the role of the Mighty Hunter to that of an Idle Sportsman. It is simply a fact that in all present-day hunter-gatherer societies the males in the social group *do* hunt, while the females by and large do not. If hunting served no purpose, it is very difficult to see how it would have survived so long in evolution, let alone how it might have developed in the first place. The hunters would have long since disappeared, outcompeted by the industrious males who spent their time in more profitable pursuits—like foraging along with the females.

Another shortcoming in the gathering hypothesis is the lamentable lack of evidence either to support or refute it. Meals of meat and marrow leave bones behind; tubers and termites leave nothing. Likewise, a stone tool is forever a stone tool, while a digging stick is very soon a pile of dust. Until we can find some way of more accurately quantifying the amounts of meat and plant matter consumed in the past—and some interesting progress is being made in that direction—the hard archeological evidence of bones and stones will carry more weight than the most elegant speculation.

Which brings us back to the real stuff of FLK. In the late 1970s, the litter on the Zinj floor, along with what had been discovered at some sites at Koobi Fora, provided the props for another version of humankind's beginnings—balanced, persuasive, and enormously appealing. The designer of the new hypothesis was Glynn Isaac, the tireless and influential co-director of Richard Leakey's expeditions for many years. Isaac began by asking the same question that set off these reflections: What was it that our ancestors were doing differently from other primates that led them to become human? He reasoned that "using tools" was not an answer, since it begged the question

The excavation at FLK today. At center is the marble plaque marking the spot where Zinjanthropus was found in 1959. DONALD JOHANSON

of what the tools were being used *for*. "Hunting," however mightily, was not a satisfactory answer either. For one thing, new field research on chimpanzees and savanna baboons was revealing that among primates, humans were not so unique after all in their taste for flesh. Modern hunter-gathers clearly hunted more systematically than non-human primates, and with larger animals for prey, so hunting might be part of an answer. But for Isaac, the hunting hypothesis put the emphasis in the wrong place.

In an outcrop about fifteen miles east of Lake Turkana, Isaac and his co-workers had uncovered the remains of a hippopotamus that had died in a delta channel some 1.6 million years ago. Among the hippo's bones were over a hundred stone tools, mostly small flakes. Several cores were found, along with a battered river pebble that evidently had been used to knock the flakes off the cores. Whether the hominids had killed the hippo themselves or merely come across its dead carcass was not really important. (Given the primitive forms of the tools, Isaac suspected scavenging.) What mattered was that no other stones in the sediment were larger than a pea, so it was certain that the raw material for the tools had been *carried* from somewhere else, then fashioned into usable implements on the spot. At another site nearby, Isaac's team found more stone tools, together with a scattering of mammal bones—hippo, giraffe, pig, porcupine, and various bovids. Unless one presumed that the toolmaking hominids had simply happened upon a menagerie of dead or dying animals, then this site had to represent a living floor—or "home base," as Isaac put it—and so did the Zinj level at FLK. The bones had been *transported* here, presumably when they still had meat on them.

For Isaac, that was the crucial issue. In all known human societies, "bringing home the bacon" (not to mention the vegetables) is an utterly commonplace activity. Isaac concluded that the most reasonable explanation for transporting food away from its original location *is to share it with somebody else.* Like the proponents of the hunting hypothesis, he believed that a division of labor was the critical human innovation. But the methods of obtaining food—hunting, scavenging, gathering, whatever—were not as significant as the act of sharing itself. At its most fundamental level, a subsistence strategy based on food sharing would provide the economic advantage of expanding the resources available to all members of a group. This economic security would be especially important to a species whose females were kept closer to the home base by young who stayed dependent for a long time.

The beauty of Isaac's theory was that it did not account just for the home bases evident at FLK and the Koobi Fora sites—it made human evolution impossible without them. In time, the economic advantage of sharing food would give way to an array of uniquely human social behaviors. For instance, hominid groups who could share not only food but *information* on the location of resources would be favored by natural selection over those who could not—leading to the development of language. Food sharing might also play an intrinsic part in the development of a sense of reciprocal obligation, giving way to the extremely complex social and economic alliances found in human societies. Finally, the food-sharing hypothesis could also help explain human marriage patterns, as an outgrowth of the division of labor that allowed males and females more efficiently to exploit the available resources in their environment.

We're ready now for another change of set on my ancient proscenium. I did not have to use my imagination to bring a food-sharing scenario into being; Isaac wrote one himself in 1976. He meant it to describe life at Koobi Fora in the early Pleistocene, but it will play just as well on the FLK stage. The scene is the swampy shores of a lake, full of hippos, crocodiles, and birds. Beyond stretch some open floodplains:

Far across the plains, a group of four or five men approach ". . . striding along, fully upright, and in their hands they carry staves. . . . As the men approach the observer becomes aware of other primates below him. A group of creatures have been reclining on the sand in the shade of

*a tree while some youngsters play around them. . . . They seem to be
female, and they whoop excitedly as some of the young run out to meet
the arriving party . . . the object being carried is the carcass of an impala
and the group congregates around this in high excitement; there is some
pushing and shoving and flashes of temper and threat. Then one of the
largest males takes two objects from a heap at the foot of the tree. There
are sharp clacking sounds as he squats and bangs these together repeatedly.
. . . When there is a small scatter of flakes on the ground at his feet, the
stone worker drops the two chunks, sorts through the fragments and selects
two or three pieces. Turning back to the carcass the leading male starts to
make incisions . . . each adult male finishes up with a segment of the
carcass, and withdraws to a corner of the clearing, with one or two females
and juveniles congregating around him. They sit chewing and cutting the
meat with morsels changing hands at intervals. Two adolescent males sit
at the periphery with a part of the intestines. They squeeze out the dung
and chew at the entrails. One of the males gets up, stretches his arms,
scratches under his armpits and then sits down. He leans against the tree,
gives a loud belch and pats his belly.*

For all their bad manners, Isaac's hominids were more generous
and humane than the mighty hunters who had preceded them on
stage and infinitely more appealing as ancestors than Dart's demon
apes. The food-sharing hypothesis, embraced by Isaac's friend and
colleague Richard Leakey in a series of popular books, enjoyed tremendous acceptance in the late 1970s, and still does in some places.
Is it just a coincidence that the late 1970s was a time when modern
males too were beginning to embrace a more sensitive, caring self-
image? I don't think so. Nevertheless, no one before Isaac had so
neatly accounted for the hard evidence of bones and stones.

Though perhaps not neatly enough. Sitting on that mound of
excavated earth by FLK, I decided to add a little coda to Isaac's
published scenario. I pictured again those hominids hunched over
their shared meat and entrails. Unbeknownst to them, another figure
was approaching across the floodplain, also walking upright, with just
a hint of a swagger in its gait. As the figure came closer, I could see
that it was wearing baggy workman's trousers and a lightweight sweater.
A dirty blue bandanna was tied around its forehead. The figure stopped
in front of me and leveled a cold stare at the happy hominid group.
Then it turned to face me, shaking its head.

"You can believe this poppycock, if it makes you feel all warm
and gooey," said the figure. "But if you want to explain human evolution, you got to *go for it.*"

Lewis R. Binford had arrived at FLK, and the stage would never be the same again.

Throughout his career, Lew Binford has never once been praised for his humility. As a grad student at the University of Michigan, his contempt for current fashions in archeology so alienated his thesis adviser that the man declared Binford would receive his Ph.D. "over my dead body." Binford got the degree. From Michigan he took a teaching position at the University of Chicago. His first lecture there nearly caused a riot; he was not allowed to finish. Later, he team-taught a course with the eminent Robert Braidwood, a doyen of Middle Eastern archeology and a powerful force in his department. The forty-three students in the course were given the choice of writing papers for Braidwood or Binford. Forty-one chose Binford.

Lew describes himself in those early years as "intolerably arrogant." But sometimes arrogance is just what is needed most to shake up a science. His generation of archeologists had inherited a very idealistic approach to understanding the past. Their more traditional predecessors had long held to a view that placed enormous value on the role *culture* plays in determining the material record from the past. The artifacts that archeologists deal with—stone tools, potsherds, broken bones, and the like—were looked on as cultural texts, left behind by primitive people almost in the same way that later individuals left behind documents, diaries, and other accounts that form the historical record. But whereas historical texts could be read and interpreted, the leavings of prehistoric people were essentially mute because there was no way of ever knowing how the minds that produced ancient cultures were working in the first place. The best that could be done was to examine the *forms* of tools and other artifacts and organize them into categories that would in essence reveal the cultural progress of the human species through time—leading (naturally) to the pinnacle achieved by modern Western civilization.

Early on, Binford decided he was not about to spend his career poring over the forms of artifacts and assigning dates to collections. He and some other young investigators suspected that some new approaches to site interpretation could squeeze more meaning out of the stones and potsherds than their mentors realized. They began to look for new ways to see, searching for patterns in the distribution of artifacts on a site, for instance, or analyzing stone tools for clues to their manufacturing techniques and original function. But what was needed was more than a few new tricks in a researcher's bag of techniques: Archeology required a complete new set of rules and a rejuvenated sense of itself as a science.

One of the notions dispelled by Binford's "New Archeology" was the false assumption that the job of archeologists was to "dig up the past." If you think about it, no shovel, pickax or bulldozer is capable of digging up the past, unless the implement has a time-machine attachment. Archeological sites exist *in the present;* they are as much a part of the contemporary world as the rocks, trees, houses, and billboards that also occupy a given landscape. Furthermore, an archeological site is static and lifeless. On its own, it cannot say anything meaningful about the living processes that brought it into being. In Binford's view, archeologists had been consistently confusing the past and the present when they came to the task of interpreting a site—a messy situation made all the messier because they failed to realize that the observations they were making were *also* part of the contemporary world.

Let me give you an example of where this might lead. In their summation of the hunting hypothesis, Sherwood Washburn and C. S. Lancaster had speculated that the beautiful symmetry in Acheulean stone tools may have developed because symmetrical projectiles when attached to a shaft, travel more accurately through the air than lopsided ones. Likewise, a hand ax fixed on the end of some kind of handle is easier to balance when it is equally weighted on both sides, so symmetry has a functional advantage there too. This observation is undoubtedly true and makes exquisite good sense. But it is nonetheless an observation made in a *contemporary* landscape, one that, to put it crudely, includes not only an ancient hand ax site, but a modern hardware store too, where a selection of good-quality ax handles can be found in aisle three. Considered on its own, there is nothing about the symmetry of an ancient hand ax that suggests a handle was once attached to it, or that the implement was used to clobber antelopes, skin elephants, or mash potatoes. Come to think of it, there is nothing about the symmetry of a hand ax that says anything at all, beyond the obvious statement that its maker was capable of fashioning a symmetrical tool.

In Binford's world, what you know about such things is much less important than what you don't know. Put another way, the first, crucial task of any scientist is to deliberately and unsparingly take stock of his own ignorance—because only when he knows the level of his ignorance can he begin to carve away at it, leaving the truth behind like a sculpture brought forth from raw stone. Instead of wasting time building theories on what we have already assumed to be true, we should instead cast a critical eye on those assumptions and see if they hold up to the facts.

Binford accused his peers of making one common assumption in particular: that everything found associated with human artifacts is by definition a product of human activity. Remember that pile of dik-dik feces back at the new hominid site? Let's say that a similar pile became fossilized a couple of million years ago. (Fossilized feces are called "coprolites," and they are by no means rare.) Now let's say that in the process of excavating a living floor at Olduvai Gorge, an archeologist uncovered that long-buried pile. He finds it surrounded on all sides with stone tools and flakes, and nearby is a scattering of broken bones. If he knows anything about dik-dik behavior, he will quickly recognize that the concentration of feces was a defecation spot for an ancient pair of dik-diks. *But if he is ignorant of the natural process that forms such piles,* he might well assume that the hominids who once lived on the site had collected the pellets, one by one. Based on that commonsense inference, the archeologist might then begin to build a plausible argument that Man in the early Pleistocene had already developed the slingshot, and had tapped into a naturally available supply of ammo.

Nobody would be that silly, of course. But as Binford pointed out, plenty of people were assuming that the existence of a bunch of broken bones together with a bunch of stone tools at such sites as FLK meant that hominids had used the tools to break up the bones. In fact, any number of natural, nonhuman forces might account for bone concentrations. Perhaps they were carried there by the waters of a stream. Perhaps, like the bones of Makapansgat, they had been accumulated over time by carnivores. Before they were buried, the bones could have been broken up by passing herds of animals, or they might have been crushed after burial by geological forces. Perhaps hominids were responsible for *some* of the broken-up bones, but not all. How could an archeologist discriminate which ones? How could he accurately reconstruct the *dynamic* processes of the past, based on the lamentably *static* record that survives in the present?

Binford's answer to that question is called "middle-range research," a term he invented to embrace any kind of investigation needed to justify whether an assumption about the past is true or false. Most middle-range research involves looking at the *present*. If this seems like an odd way for archeologists to be spending their time, keep in mind that living human beings and animals, like their counterparts in the past, leave behind an archeological record too— but their "static" litter can be traced back to real, observable, dynamic behaviors. Once something quantifiable is known about the relationship of modern processes to the litter they leave behind, then you can feel more secure about reconstructing ancient processes from the remnants they left behind too. Take for instance Bob Brain's research on the bone accumulations in the South African caves—a classic example of middle range research. Instead of assuming that the bones had been accumulated by ancient hominids, Brain looked to the modern world for living processes which would create similar bone concentrations. In that case, it turned out to be leopards feeding in trees.

While Brain was digging into the mystery of the South African caves, Binford was applying middle-range research to another enigma, trying to make sense of the puzzling variations in the stone tool kits of Neandertal Man in Europe. He studied the bone rubbish of Navaho Indians and the debris left behind by stone knappers in Australia. His quest sent him to the Arctic, where he spent years with Nunamuit hunters, examining the cut marks, patterns of bone fractures, and the distribution of bones left behind when they butchered a kill. At the same time, he began to accumulate data on wolf kills, hyena dens—any activity, human or otherwise, that might influence the complexion of litter on a modern landscape. Somewhere along the way, Binford came to realize that the huge amounts of modern-day data he was accumulating might have some bearing on FLK and the other early Pleistocene sites. It was hardly what the specialists wanted to hear.

"Let's face it, you guys were getting away with murder," Binford told me once before he left the Gorge. We were sitting around the camp table in the dark, smoking some small cigars I'd brought along. "Mary Leakey, Glynn Isaac—the whole African group didn't even know they had a problem. They'd just go out and have a good time, and when they'd find something, they'd call a press conference and open up the champagne."

Binford's first target was an archeological site in Kenya called Olorgasailie. Glynn Isaac had found seemingly solid proof there of large-scale hunting by *Homo erectus* some 400,000 to 700,000 years ago. His most dramatic evidence was an area less than fifty feet in diameter, where the shattered remains of ninety giant baboons lay together, along with a large number of hand axes. Isaac's interpretation: The baboons—an extinct species the size of female gorillas—had been slaughtered and butchered en masse by a band of hominids.

"I jumped all over Glynn for that," Binford said. "There was no evidence at all that those baboons had been killed all at once, or even that they'd been hunted by hominids at all." He showed that the pattern of bones could have been influenced as much by running water as by hominid hunters. Other smashed-up bones Isaac had cited as evidence of hominid predation might just as well have been broken up by trampling hooves or other nonhuman forces.

Having drawn blood at Olorgasailie, Binford charged headlong into battle against Man the Mighty Hunter. The oldest *indisputable* evidence for systematic hunting by hominids was Clark Howell's famous elephant massacre site at Torralba; Binford disputed it. He agreed that there was a pronounced concentration of large animal remains on the site, especially elephants. But even Howell admitted that the deposits in which they were found could have accumulated over a great length of time. Since the area was a swamp, and elephants are known to migrate to marshy areas to die, why rule out the possibility that these animals might have died natural, insignificant deaths over the centuries, unembellished by human intervention?

"Clark had observed that these elephant remains were found along with lots of Acheulean stone tools," Lew told me, helping himself to another cigar. "So he and Les Freeman developed that dandy four-color picture of mighty hunters butchering herds of elephants. Les even calculated the amount of meat on that many elephants and estimated that it would have taken fifty men six trips apiece to cart the meat out. So now you've got *Homo erectus* organized into cooperative labor groups, half a million years ago! Well, I showed that the tools they found at the site weren't really associated with the elephant bones. In fact, there's an inverse correlation—where you find the elephants, you don't find the tools. The artifacts were actually correlated with the lower limbs and mandibles of red deer, bovids, and horses—what you'd expect to find if the hominids were scavenging, not hunting. So much for the classic mighty hunter site."

Armed with his heavy core of data—honed to a fine cutting edge by sophisticated statistical techniques—Binford hacked away at the evidence for hunting at sites covering four continents and extending from the early Pleistocene all the way to the upper Paleolithic, only some 30,000 years ago. All over the world, he believed archeologists had grossly overestimated the sophistication of the ancient people they were seeking to understand.

But he saved his most pointed attack for Olduvai Gorge—which brings us back to our FLK theater. You'll remember we had Glynn Isaac's hominid family up onstage, with Lew Binford standing to one side, giving them the cold eye. Under his skeptical gaze I saw the apparitions quiver and disappear, leaving Lew alone, hands stuffed in his pockets, probably puffing on one of my cigars. I didn't have any trouble imagining this, because Lew and I had visited FLK together a day or two before the discovery at Dik-dik Hill put an end to such sightseeing. He had his own Pleisto-drama ready to replace Isaac's, executed with the sweeping bravado of a Broadway veteran come to show the yokels how to act.

"Okay, Don, we're positioned now on the Zinj occupation site, alias Mary's living floor, alias Glynn's home base," he said, as if he were briefing me on an impending military encounter. "How do we know it's a home base? Because it's got lots of tools and broken bones, right next to where a lake used to be. But think about it, Don—why would these hominids want to establish their camp next to a lake?"

"There's bound to be a lot of other life around," I answered, "and obviously a water source . . ."

"That makes sense for Boy Scouts in Yosemite Park, but if you're some three-foot diurnal biped out on the Pleistocene savanna, it'd be the worst place to be. The lakeshore is where the lions and other predators will be hanging out, waiting to eat you. Even today, hunter-gatherers in remote regions, with fire and bows and arrows and other sophisticated weaponry, almost never camp by a water source."

"Maybe they were sleeping somewhere else," I countered. "They could still be bringing food back to a central place to eat."

"Sure they could. And if you just want to feel all warm and cozy, you could even imagine them sharing the food around in the social group. The alternative is to try to justify those inferences. Get your hands dirty in some real science."

I'd read Lew's book, so I knew what he was getting at. If we take as the inference to be tested the existence of a home base where hominids were transporting meat to be eaten, then that dynamic process should have left some very specific trace of itself in the static archeological record. For instance, among the debris on the site there should be more meat-bearing bones, like the upper limbs of bovids, than the total number of other kinds of bones can account for. Before you can make that judgment, however, you first have to factor out all the *other* dynamic processes that added their traces before the site was buried. Hyenas may have carried some bones away, or brought others in, or gnawed the ends off still others. Perhaps some carnivore made its den here once. And there's always stream action to consider. Once you've subtracted the contributions of all the nonhominid agents from the Zinj-floor bone pattern, the bias in the representation of one kind of bone over another can be attributed to the actions of hominids with some real confidence. It's not just an assumption anymore.

"I went to work on Mary's data, and sure enough, there was a surplus of some anatomical parts among the bones on the Zinj floor," Lew said. "But the surplus wasn't in the meaty upper limbs predicted by the home-base model. Quite the opposite. There were significantly more *lower* limb bones, as well as skulls and mandibles, than could be accounted for. The hominids were transporting carcass parts, all right. Only they were carrying around the pieces of a skeleton that would yield the least amount of meat!"

Standing on the spot where it had all happened two million years ago, Lew then offered his own version of the FLK play.

"In my opinion these guys were continuously feeding, moving through the landscape like a damn troop of baboons. Tubers, grubs, seeds, whatever. So let's say one of them looks up and sees some vultures circling. With a few whacks on a core he makes one of these choppers, then off he goes. He gets to the kill site, but by this time there's been lots of scavengers and there isn't much left of the prey. All that's left of any value is the little bit of marrow in some lower-limb bones, but to get at it he has to soak the limb in water to soften the skin. So he carries the thing over to the lake shore. Then he smashes up the bone, gets what he wants, and leaves tools, bones, and everything else behind. That's the stuff we find at FLK. There's nothing suggesting a living floor, a home base, a thorn windbreak, a social system based on sharing, or anything other than a place where some tool-using creatures broke open some already defleshed bones to dig out the morsel of marrow inside."

Naturally, Binford's trashing of the conventional wisdom was not based on his interpretation of the Zinj level alone. He also de-

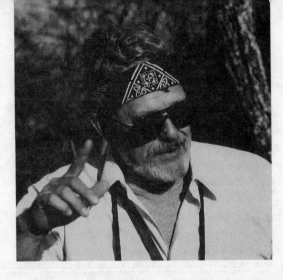

*Lewis Binford holds forth
at Olduvai Gorge.*
DONALD JOHANSON

bunked Mary Leakey's elephant and *Deinotherium* sites nearby, the famous DK stone dwelling, Isaac's hippo site near Lake Turkana, and anything else recovered from *Homo habilis*'s time on earth that vaguely suggested large-scale meat-eating. In Binford's view, there was indeed a battle for meat going on here in the early Pleistocene—but the combatants were well-established, specialized predators like lions, saber-toothed cats, and hyenas, not hominids. After all the other meat-eaters had had their fill of a carcass, the hominids scuttled in last and made off with what little scraps of marrow remained.

"It's clear from the bone distributions and the way the limbs had been busted up," Lew told me on the site. "The Olduvai toolmaker was no mighty hunter of beasts. He was the most marginal of scavengers."

So much for romance.

Lew Binford is endowed with infectious conviction. By the time we walked away from FLK that afternoon, I had become a believer: *Homo habilis* was an unspecialized opportunist whose tool-assisted scrounging of pre-ravaged carcasses had little to do with "becoming human." But now Lew was gone, and except for an crowned plover darting in and out among the gullies, the old excavation was empty. The scene was set for the final act of the drama. Before it was over, my FLK stage would start to look more like a boxing ring.

While Binford was preparing his full-scale assault on Olduvai Gorge, Glynn Isaac was hardly waiting around for the ax to fall and crush his food-sharing tableau. He had a knot of talented students working full tilt, principally at a new site near Koobi Fora. Called FxJj50—or Site 50 for short—the new excavation had yielded more than fifteen hundred pieces of worked stone and two thousand fossilized bone fragments strewn about a river bank 1.5 million years old. What was intriguing about the site were the indications that it had been occupied by hominids for only a very short time, then quickly and gently buried. In this regard, it provided an even better "snapshot" of ancestral life than the jumbled and overabundant record at FLK.

Working Site 50 with Isaac was a young man named Nick Toth, who later joined us at the Institute and is now on the faculty at Indiana University. Toth's target of research was the collection of stone artifacts, in particular, the patterns of fracture evident on their surfaces. To make sense of their meaning, Nick taught himself to make stone tools and used the results of his handiwork to butcher animal carcasses. This sort of modern-day modeling of hominid tool use was nothing new in itself. (Louis Leakey, for one, was wowing Olduvai visitors with his stone-age butchering techniques before Nick Toth was born.) But the conclusions were radical.

Most archeologists had been focusing on the various forms of the worked tools—the discoids, end choppers, side choppers, and so on laid forth in Mary Leakey's descriptions of the Oldowan artifacts. What Toth found was that these forms were simply the result of knocking small, sharp flakes off a core. The little flakes themselves, which previous investigators had been interpreting as the waste by-product of tool manufacture, were in fact fairly handy implements for cutting up a carcass. It Toth was right, *Homo habilis* would not have needed a great deal of stone-knapping expertise to gain access to the meat beneath an animal hide.

Just because the flakes *could* cut meat did not mean, of course, that they were being used for that purpose. While Nick was busy at Site 50, Larry Keeley from the University of Illinois at Chicago Circle was examining under a microscope some flint tools from upper Paleolithic sites in Europe. Keeley had found traces of "micropolish" on the cutting edges of the tools, indicating that some had been used to cut meat, while others had been variously applied to bone, hide, wood, or some softer plant material. Toth wondered whether the same kind of discriminations could be found on the much older Koobi Fora tools. The two archeologists decided to collaborate.

Unfortunately, most of the Koobi Fora tools had been made of rough lava, a stone too coarse and too sensitive to weathering to show signs of micropolish. But Toth was able to find fifty-nine finer-grained tools in the collection, mostly flakes of chert. Keeley's microscope revealed micro–wear polish on nine of them—four with polishing marks indicating animal butchering, three characteristic of woodworking, and two others showing the sort of polish produced by contact with soft vegetation.

Out of the hundreds of thousands of stone artifacts from the early Pleistocene, the testimony of one technique focused on nine little flakes was hardly enough to inspire a chorus of "eureka,"even among the food-sharing faithful. Nevertheless, it provided a tiny morsel of evidence for meat processing, much more useful in its way than the beautifully reasoned "Just So" stories abhorred by Binford. Meanwhile, another Isaac protégé, Henry Bunn, now at the University of Wisconsin, was squinting over the bones collected from the site, looking for the telltale cut marks and fracture patterns that the hominids' tools would have left behind. His research eventually led him to the FLK bones in the Kenya National Museum in Nairobi—and smack into the path of Binford's *hominid* scavenger hypothesis.

Unless a bone is very quickly buried, it will bear on its surface the markings of its fate after death. The scars on a fossil bone fall into three general categories: cut marks and fractures left by hominids wielding stone tools; gnaw marks and tooth punctures recording the munchings of carnivores; and the pits, cracks, and scratches produced by natural forces such as weathering and abrasion. People had been interpreting these surface hieroglyphics in paleo-Indian remains for years, but until Bunn and others came along a decade ago, nobody had paid much attention to them in older collections.

Bunn had little trouble distinguishing the cut marks on the East African bones from the gnaw marks that were also present. Bob Brain's work in South Africa had shown that a stone tool leaves a distinct V-shaped groove in the bone, while a carnivore's tooth leaves a broader, U-shaped impression. Not surprisingly, Bunn found plenty of both kinds of damage. What was interesting was the *location* of the tool-inflicted cut marks. In many instances the cut marks were clustered around the articular ends of upper-limb bones—precisely where a hominid with a tool would scrape against the bone when attempting to detach meaty limbs from a carcass. Some of the upper limbs were also severely bashed up, enough to convince Bunn that the bashers were almost certainly hominids wielding hammerstones, going after the big bones' rich trove of marrow. If the hominids were butchering substantial amounts of meat at particular places on the landscape, then whether or not the meat had been hunted or scavenged, Isaac's food-sharing hypothesis looked pretty good after all. So much for marginal scavengers. In his report in *Nature*, Bunn was icily exact about the implications of his work for Binford's theory:

"This direct evidence of early hominid diet," he wrote, "allows us to dismiss models of human evolution which do not incorporate meat-eating as a significant component of early hominid behavior."

Henry Bunn was not the only young investigator burning the midnight oil in the museum in Nairobi. At the same time, Rick Potts of Harvard University and Pat Shipman of Johns Hopkins were also taking a closer look at the cut marks on the Olduvai bones. Using a scanning electron microscope, Potts and Shipman discovered that different kinds of tool use were distinguishable by microscopic features of the mark left behind. Tools used for slicing, for instance, left fine, parallel grooves within the V-shaped cut mark. Like Bunn, Potts and Shipman believed their evidence proved that the hominid tools and the faunal bones at sites like FLK weren't there together by accident. But they disagreed with Bunn on some key observations. Whereas Bunn had looked at the thirty-five hundred FLK bones and found cut marks on more than three hundred of them, Potts and Shipman could identify only a few dozen.

Most important, they also disagreed on the critical issue of where those cut marks were located on the bones. Bunn said most were on the articular ends of meaty limb bones, but Potts and Shipman found a greater number on the bone shafts—an odd place to be slicing away with a tool if your aim is to detach flesh from a carcass. Furthermore, Potts and Shipman could find no indication that the hominids had given any more attention to meaty bones than they had to the meat-poor lower limbs. They concluded, contrary to Bunn, that there was no evidence at all that hominids at Olduvai and Koobi Fora had been systematically butchering meals of meat. Bunn countered that they had simply been counting the wrong things. Trained as paleontologists, Potts and Shipman had included in their study only bones whose taxon could be identified. Bunn himself, on the other hand, was using every scrap of bone on the site in his calculations, nameable or not.

When it came time to expand upon the meaning of FLK and the other Olduvai sites, not only did Potts and Shipman disagree with Bunn—they disagreed with each other as well. In his Ph.D. thesis Potts analyzed the whole complexion of Bed I archeological sites and came up with a novel alternative to the traditional home-base model. Using a sophisticated computer modeling program, Potts showed that foraging hominids would have saved energy by "caching" stone tools at specific locations throughout their territory.

Whatever food they found could be carried to these caches to be processed. Rather than representing the remains of a home base, the Zinj floor was perhaps the vestiges of just such a stone cache, frequented over and over again through a period of several years.

Pat Shipman's view swung even further away from the popular wisdom. Since her analysis had shown that the cut marks on the Olduvai bones were not where they *should* be if the hominids were stripping meat, then either the hominids were very stupid or they were after something else on the bones besides the meat. Shipman searched through the literature on modern hunter-gatherers and discovered that cut marks encircling lower limb bones are commonly left behind when a carcass is skinned. There were no encircling marks on the ends of the fossilized lower limbs, but there were plenty of cut marks there nevertheless. Shipman concluded that the hominids were scavenging carcasses and removing *tendons*, perhaps to use as thongs in the making of primitive carrying devices. They were probably eating what little meat was left on the bones as well, and perhaps using the skins too to make "sack-like carrying containers."

Shipman had also noticed that among the Olduvai bones were a few with hominid cut marks laid directly *over* the toothmarks of carnivores—direct evidence that these little ancestors were scavenging the kills made by others. Gradually a more elaborate portrait of "Man the Scavenger" began to emerge in her mind: Unlike hunters, scavengers need a very efficient means of locomotion over long distances, so they can search for carcasses. Walking upright would provide just such an energetically efficient means of getting about, though it is a pitifully poor adaptation for the short bursts of speed needed in hunting. Bipedalism would also leave the hands free to carry the tools needed to exploit whatever carcasses one might find. Finally, a confirmed scavenger would need to have some other source of food to fall back on in those trying times when carcasses were hard to come by. Pat Shipman's husband, Alan Walker, had already done electron microscopic studies of fossil hominid teeth, which he believed suggested they ate a diet composed primarily of fruit.

Nowhere in Shipman's view is there room for a home base, food sharing or large-scale butchering of carcasses. You might think that Lew Binford, who had been stressing scavenging for years, might be pleased to have found an ally. Think again.

"Shipman's hypothesis is shot through with unjustified inferences and a complete disregard for logic," Lew told me when we were at Olduvai. "She tells us that early hominids were scavengers, but what are they scavenging? Tendons! She argues for a whole shift in a way of life based on extracting tendons to make tote bags. It's nonsense."

"Well, what about Potts's stone cache theory?" I asked.

"Calling it a theory is kind," Lew answered. "What Potts did was invent a computer model that predicted that it would have been more efficient for hominids to cache stone tools around the landscape. And since the computer said it was efficient, it followed that the hominids were actually *doing* it. But there's no evidence at all! It's just a computer's idea of how to live in the Pleistocene."

Binford believes these investigators, like their forerunners, make the mistake of beginning by endowing early hominids with considerable humanity, instead of framing arguments that will help us find out how human our ancestors really were. Stockpiling stone tools for the future and using tendons to make carrying baskets are activities that imply more foresight—or what Binford calls "planning depth"—than we have any reason to believe *Homo habilis* possessed. The same goes for *habilis*'s descendants; wherever Binford casts his eye on the archeological record—at *Homo erectus* sites in Spain and China, or the leavings of premodern *Homo sapiens* in South Africa—he sees a much less capable, less human ancestor at work than we have been led to believe. In Binford's final analysis, the adaptation to hunting, far from forging humanity for millions of years, did not play a significant part in our evolution until a mere seventy thousand years ago, when fully modern humans began to cope with the harsh conditions of Europe by systematically hunting large game.

And what about Henry Bunn, the Isaac student who had "dismissed" his model of human evolution? Initially, Binford had regarded Bunn's critique much the way a six-hundred-pound saber-toothed cat might look upon a three-foot *Homo* juvenile brandishing a pebble. But Bunn was not going to be easily intimidated. Chosen to review the *Bones* book for *Science*—apparently at the suggestion of Glynn Isaac—Bunn praised the book's opening sections on methodology, but pummeled Binford's view on FLK.

Chief among the weaknesses he perceived was Binford's reliance on Mary Leakey's data to draw conclusions about which kinds of limb bones were more highly represented at key sites like the Zinj floor—the meaty upper limbs, or the nonmeaty lower limbs. Bunn pointed out that Leakey herself had stressed that her tabulations should be looked on as preliminary. Binford had disregarded her caution, and by applying "numerical acrobatics" to the incomplete data, had

The late Glynn Isaac at Koobi Fora.
DONALD JOHANSON

come up with a completely unwarranted conclusion—that Isaac's food-sharing hypothesis was dead. In contrast, Bunn himself had gotten *his* Olduvai data straight from the equid's mouth, so to speak, lying on the shelves of the Kenya National Museum. And *he* believed that food sharing was very much alive.

His usual combativeness exacerbated by the perceived insult that a graduate student had been deputized to review his book, Binford fired off a response to Bunn. In the meantime, Isaac himself had begun to back off from the more romantic assumptions of his hypothesis. Most important, whether hominids were hunting, scavenging, or both, Isaac now acknowledged that there was no evidence that they were sharing the proceeds among themselves. If they weren't sharing food, then the concept of a home base was meaningless, and the whole pattern of human social organization he had outlined came tumbling down. He still firmly believed, on the other hand, that FLK and Site 50 proved that hominids were transporting bones and butchering them for meat—on that crucial point Binford was "very probably wrong." Isaac concluded that much more research was needed before we would really know what had happened at FLK.

Tragically, Glynn Isaac did not live to continue that research. In 1985 he died suddenly at the age of forty-seven. With Isaac gone, the mantle of battling Binford fell upon his former students—and in particular Henry Bunn. Together with his wife, Ellen Kroll—another former Isaac protégée—Bunn went back to the bones, employing exactly the sort of middle-range research methods Binford had marshaled to attack the food-sharing hypothesis in the first place. Bunn and Kroll's results, detailing their view of what happened at FLK, would be published in *Current Anthropology* soon after I returned from Africa.

Judging from the proportion of stone flakes that had been retouched, the great number and location of cut marks, and especially the preponderance of meaty limbs on the site, hominid life 1.8 million years ago clearly included the transport, systematic butchery, and sharing of meat. Whether the meat was hunted or scavenged from fierce predators was not really the issue: Both involved "coordinated group activity" and "repeated participation in dangerous subsistence pursuits." Brave *Homo* was back, this time armed with some hard data. Binford's claim that the Zinj site was dominated by meat-poor bones such as lower limbs "should be regarded as a myth that is flatly contradicted by the archeological facts." Binford quickly responded.

"This study has no intellectual anchor beyond an imagined picture of early hominid life," he wrote, later referring to Bunn's evidence as "wishbones."

Nevertheless, he could no longer regard Bunn's studies as a grad student's rearguard attempt to blow life into a dying theory—especially since he sensed that other people were beginning to take them quite seriously. In his reply in *Current Anthropology*, Binford attacked Bunn and Kroll's cut mark evidence, leaning heavily on Pat Shipman's observations that the meaty limb bones at FLK were in fact more often inflicted with the gnawing marks of carnivores than with cuts from hominid tools. He called Bunn and Kroll's conclusions about hominid access to meat-rich limbs "nonsense," unless they could explain how the bones got to the site in the first place. In order to do that, they would have to account for these hundreds of gnaw marks on the FLK bones—an issue that Bunn and Kroll did not address. Previously, Bunn had declared that the simplest explanation for the gnaw marks was that scavenging carnivores had come upon the bones *after* the hominids were through with them.

"That may be the simplest assumption," Binford had countered, "but it's also the assumption that saves the consensus view of the past." Now he pointed out that carnivores rarely gnaw bones where they find them. Instead, they take them off to some protected spot, where they can eat undisturbed. If hyenas were scavenging *after* the hominids were finished with the bones at FLK, then you wouldn't expect to find many gnaw marks, since any bone juicy enough to attract a hyena would have been carried away.

"Hyena behavior is not such a simple thing, and Binford knows that," Bunn says in response. "He is only using the gnaw mark argument to distract attention from the real issue, which is the overrepresentation of meat-bearing upper limbs on those ancient sites.

Binford is just plain wrong. He just won't admit it. But that's nothing new for him."

Bunn has a right to his confidence in how many upper limbs he sees among the FLK bones—after all, he counted them. Or at least he counted all the bone splinters and used them to determine a reliable estimate of how many whole bones had originally been on the site. It probably won't surprise you that Lew Binford doesn't buy Bunn's method of counting bones. He believes that Bunn, ignorant of the number of splinters formed when a bone is smashed up, has given too much weight to each splinter, and thus overinflated his estimates. Binford has his own way of determining the number of each anatomical part that is represented at a site—a complex analysis taking as its starting point the number of articular ends of bones left on the site, rather than the number of bone splinters. It won't surprise you either that after his analysis is completed and his disc drive has cooled down, his figures wind up supporting the "marginal scavenger" hypothesis.

Binford's densely detailed reply to Bunn and Kroll, published in *Current Anthropology* in 1988, was followed by a longer counter reply from Bunn and Kroll, which was followed in turn by a short note from the editor declaring an "end of the Binford/Bunn-Kroll exchange in these pages." Which is the equivalent of the referee in a fight suddenly throwing up his *own* hands and crying, *"No más!"* And there it stands.

I began this little drama by asking big questions. What made us human? What was going on two million years ago that changed us, rendered us unutterably and forever different from the other animals? We have never suffered from a shortage of answers. Killer ape, mighty hunter, family man—and now, perhaps, lowly scavenger. In a span of three decades, the image of our original selves reflected in the archeological record has shown all the permanence of a view through a kaleidoscope. The hard data of bone and stone have not changed, but like the colored glass shards, they shift and tumble into new mosaics of meaning, borrowing their order from the stress and bias in the theories that guide our sight.

In retrospect, there's no question that the political and social times we have lived through have distorted our view of the ancient past—the harsh realizations of the human capacity for evil that produced the killer ape in the fifties, the imperial, space-exploring *machismo* of the sixties' mighty hunter, so quickly superseded by a vignette of human beginnings as soft around the edges as a John Denver lyric. Does that mean that prehistorians are concerned more with illusion than truth? Is paleoanthropology really just a sort of high theater? I don't think so. The real progress—the chipping away at our ignorance—goes on strangely independent of the theory making, though it seems to depend on the theory makers to bring it into being. Today everybody knows that Raymond Dart's visions of bone-wielding australopithecine cannibals was farfetched; but it was Dart who first had the insight to look for traces of human behavior in a collection of mammal bones. Sherwood Washburn, Irven DeVore, and other promoters of the hunting hypothesis overplayed the role of hunting as the prime mover of humanization, but in so doing, they taught everyone else how to synthesize the evidence from the archeological record, nonhuman primate studies, and research on modern hunter-gatherers.

What Lew Binford has taught us is to beware of our tendency to invest every chipped stone or pile of bone with a human dimension, a human depth. Personally, I think that his marginal-scavenger theory is also extreme. I believe that the Olduvai archeology really *does* tell us something about bone transport and butchering going on at specific hominid activity places. I'm not ready to take it the next step and buy in to a food-sharing scenario—but *something* was going on in the diet of *Homo habilis* that would soon explode into truly human behavior patterns. That explosion—and what our new Olduvai hominid can tell us about it—is what the next chapter is all about. My point now is that whether Binford is right or wrong, we can only progress further toward the truth by following the difficult path laid down by his methods. We can no longer be satisfied with answers that are merely "satisfying."

"The question 'Is this true?' doesn't lead anywhere," Lew told me once. "The question to ask is 'Does this open up new learning opportunities?' "

One certain truth about FLK is that it is not a healthy place to be alone after dark. As I'd been sitting there, the dusk had moved in and swallowed my stage, pulling a cold wind behind it that bit through my light cotton shirt. In twenty minutes it would be pitch dark. The camp staff had lately reported seeing a small pride of lions in the Junction at night—perhaps the same pride that Bob Walter had run across down by the second Fault. I did not intend to wait around to make a positive ID. Besides, it was dinnertime back at the camp, and I was getting hungry.

CHAPTER NINE:

Lucy's Children

Nothing of him that doth fade
But doth suffer a sea-change
Into something rich and strange
        —The Tempest, I ii

"EAT PLENTY OF BREAKFAST," TIM said. "You'll need the strength. We're going to dig a trench."

We were sitting around the table just after dawn on the last working day of the season. Most of us were only half awake, but for some reason Tim was all fired up, acting like we'd just arrived in the field.

Bob Walter looked up from his coffee.

"A geological trench? I've already dug two trenches."

"And lovely trenches they are. Mary Leakey herself could not have made straighter walls. Only both of them came out sterile. No bone at all. That's been bugging me ever since. You'd think that there would have been a stratum somewhere above the site that held some bone. It's a long shot, but if we were to dig a third trench directly upslope from Dik-dik Hill, maybe we could pinpoint the stratum where this hominid is coming from."

I glanced at my colleagues around the table. Most of them would have looked about as eager if Tim had asked them to spend the last day in camp spooning out the latrine. Frankly, I wasn't too keen on digging a hole into the side of the Gorge myself. There was already too much to do—specimens to be sorted and packed, paperwork that I'd been putting off for days. I was also hoping that we might still have a shot at getting some aerial photographs of the hominid site. The day before, I had received word that a bush pilot named Hans Schneider was to fly in from Arusha and help us out with his two-seat Cessna C150, a plane light enough to land and take off from Olduvai without any trouble.

But Tim is hard to dissuade once he's got an idea in mind. We threw some pickaxes into the back of the Land-Rover and headed down to the site. If the bush pilot made it in, I thought to myself, I would have no choice but to abandon trench digging to the others—with deep regret, of course. I could then spend the rest of the day flying over the Gorge in the Cessna, occupied with the heavy labor of snapping my camera shutter and changing rolls of film.

You may recall that when Bob Walter had dug his original trenches—the first, big one a dozen yards south of the find, the second directly into the sterile southern side of Dik-dik Hill—he'd been trying to get his bearings on where the site fit into the overall geology of the Gorge. It would have been a tremendous bonus if he had found some more of the hominid *in situ* in a deposit above the site, but that hadn't happened. Tim was pinning his hopes on running into some *in situ* hominid bone with his new trench, which would tell us exactly where—and when, geologically speaking—the hominid was coming from.

I'd like to say we took a few swings with the pickaxes and uncovered that distal femur we'd been looking for. But we weren't quite *that* lucky. At the price of a lot of sweat, the new trench revealed very much the same stratigraphic pattern of tuffs that Bob's first trench had shown—with one important addition. Just beneath the coarse-grained ashfall known as Tuff IC, Bob's ax exposed a small, isolated patch of dark sand. This "sand lens" did not extend even as far as the two sides of the trench, so it was no wonder the first excavation had missed it entirely.

Tim knocked some of the sand into a karai with his hammer, poked at it with his finger, and pulled out a fossil. It wasn't hominid, but it was stained the exact brownish-black color as the bones of our hominid, and its condition was similar too. Further digging revealed more of the same—no hominid bone, but fossils in the same state of preservation, all *in situ*. We could not be absolutely sure, but it was a pretty good bet: On the last day of our stay, we'd located the original resting place of our little *Homo* of Dik-dik Hill.

With that last-minute discovery, we could now understand in much better detail what had happened to that little hominid from the time of her death almost two million years ago to the moment Tim spied her broken elbow bone lying on the surface in the fading afternoon sunlight.

"This sand lens was probably deposited by a little rivulet draining into the Olduvai lake through the margin area," Tim told his students when we stopped for a midmorning break. "Judging by the assortment of anatomical parts we found so close together, I'd say the hominid died pretty close by, leaving her bones in one of these sand distributaries."

"From the weathering on the bones," I said, "they probably sat around on the surface for a year or two, maybe as much as five."

"Why aren't there any carnivore marks on the surfaces?" asked Berhane Asfaw.

"Who knows?" I said. "Maybe they missed it. Maybe there was better stuff around to eat than a scrawny three-foot hominid."

"Or maybe they took away the bones that they wanted," Tim suggested, "like that damn distal femur. There's plenty of grease for a hungry hyena inside a big articular joint like that."

"What if it *isn't* gone?" Gen Suwa offered. "We could dig deeper, follow the sand lens farther into the Gorge wall . . ."

"Sure, if we had another couple of summers and twenty guys to help us move dirt." Tim frowned. "If we'd turned up some of the hominid today, I'd say go for it. But the farther you move from the original find, the less likely your chances of finding anything.

"There's one thing I still don't understand," Gen Suwa said. "If it happened the way you've reconstructed it, why were the bones broken up so much?"

"To answer that you've got to look at what happened to the fossil after it was buried," said Bob Walter. "There are a lot of clays in this soil, which expand and contract, putting stress on the bones they surround. Calcite crystals and other minerals also grow in the cracks of the bone, wedging them apart. Meanwhile, you've got deposits piling up above. So while the fossilized bones might be shattered, the pieces are held tightly together by their surrounding matrix. A long time later, along comes some big erosional event, cutting down against the grain of all those layers. Later still the Olbalbal Basin sinks lower, cutting the Gorge deeper. Pieces of the Gorge wall

The possible fate of the Dik-dik Hill hominid after death. Top, left to right: The corpse of a mature Homo habilis *female dies near the Olduvai lake margin, vulnerable to scavengers. Over time, lake deposits and volcanic eruptions bury the skeleton deep under the surface. Natural underground forces shatter the bones, but the surrounding deposits hold them together. Bottom, left to right: Major erosional events cut down across the grain of the accumulated deposits. As the Gorge deepens, pieces of the wall break away. Centuries of wind and rain remove soft material unprotected by hard volcanic tufts, slowly bringing fossils and other denser materials to the surface again. Once exposed, the skeleton falls apart. Before all of it is washed away, the fossil-hunting team discovers the remaining bones on "Dik-dik Hill."* ILLUSTRATION BY DOUGLAS BECKNER

break away, like icebergs calving off a glacier. That's what Dik-dik Hill is, or was, before most of it eroded away.

"Where the wall is still intact," Bob continued, pointing up the slope, "hard caps like Tuff IC and ID protect the light material like the sand lens we found this morning. But where it is exposed, sand and other loose stuff washes out in the rains, or just blows away. The surface erosion slowly brings up the fossils and other hard stuff buried underneath. More of it rolls downslope. Which creates this hard 'desert pavement' you've been digging through all summer."

"Don't forget that the fossils are already shattered while still underground," said Tim. "So as soon as they hit the surface, they fall apart."

"So what you end up with is a couple of hundred tooth fragments, and only one complete tooth," said Gen, completing the answer to his own question. Tim grinned.

"Right. And when we get back to Berkeley, think of the fun you can have trying to put some more pieces back together."

Hans Schneider, the bush pilot, flew in just as we were finishing up lunch—too late to save me from trench duty, but still a welcome sight. Gerry and I got into the Land-Rover and drove out to the strip to meet the pilot. We found him tinkering with the engine, a rugged-looking man with smiling blue eyes and a disarmingly gentle manner. He was up to his elbows in grease, with Schubert's Unfinished Symphony booming from a tape deck in the cockpit. We introduced ourselves and told him what we were hoping to accomplish.

"You will not get good pictures now," he said. "The smoke from the grass fires on the plain is too heavy."

Hans would have to stay overnight. We all agreed that he and I would try to document the site on the way out the next morning, with a detour down to Laetoli before heading to Arusha. Tim, Bob, and most of the others would finish up work on the trench and then head to Arusha by Land-Rover bringing the hominid with them. Bill Kimbel and Alberto Angela would stay on at the Gorge and work Dik-dik Hill for a few more days.

We took off shortly after dawn, the nose of the plane pointed straight into the sun rising over Ngorongoro. It was a gorgeous morning, the air clear and cool. Hans motioned to me to put on the headphones. He slipped a cassette into his tape player, and the sunny opening theme of the Beethoven Pastoral Symphony tripped into my ears. Below me the Gorge looked like an emerald necklace thrown down on the spreading gold of the Serengeti, the light catching on the sisal spears lining the heights, carving shadows into the deep ravines. We banked over the Olbalbal Basin, dipped down into the main Gorge and breezed up its length, under the bronze cliffs of the Second Fault, past the stone hut sheltering the DK site, straight toward the Junction. In my ears the music swelled with optimism, the whole orchestra embracing that sunny theme in a bear hug, basses humming, flutes trilling, and for a moment it felt as if the airplane and the music were one, and I was being held aloft by the sheer, resolute joy of that melody.

As soon as we rounded the red-earth shoulder of the Castle I could see the Land-Rover parked beside the hominid site. The crew was already at work, puffs of dust rising from the sieve between Bill and Prosper. I took a couple of shots as we flew past. We were continuing up the belly of the Main Gorge when Hans abruptly pulled the plane up and banked to the north. He tapped me on the shoulder and pointed down. Ahead of us a small family of elephants was feeding below Granite Falls, a series of black cliffs near the western margin of the Gorge.

"The noise scares elephants," he said. "They panic, wasting energy that they badly need this time of year." He pointed down again, and I saw a pair of giraffes gliding across the plain toward the Gorge. "Them, they don't mind the plane," Hans explained.

We had seen plenty of giraffes around camp that summer, but the sight of the elephants surprised me. All summer long, preoccupied with the bones of the dead, we had been sharing the Gorge with these enormously obvious beings, without giving their existence a thought. How much other life breathed down there in the dry ravines? How many dik-dik pairs were domesticating the karongos with their scents and feces, how many lions and hyenas fed on the Olduvai night? As we banked for another run through the Junction, I saw a dozen oryx striding across the plain below Naibor Soit—graceful, big-bodied antelope with horns straight and long as lances. When the rains came they would be joined by a flood of other hoofed mammals washing in from the north—zebra, wildebeest, gazelle of all kinds, and the predators on their traces.

Two million years ago, when the Olduvai lake shone like a great silver coin in the middle of the plain, the mammal abundance would have been richer still. Below me I would see giant baboons, saber-toothed cats, pigs the size of buffalo, giant antlered giraffes, pachyderms like *Deinotherium* sharing the landscape with the animals still living there today. And amid all that heavy undulating mass of life there would be our little *Homo*, a naked two-legged thing with long arms and a body no bigger than a modern human child. How strange, I thought, that this little creature, this insignificance underfoot, had presaged an animal to come who would invent airplanes, write symphonies, and soar higher than a hawk above the ravines, a creature who would have the phenomenal presumption to wonder how he got so high in the first place.

For twenty years I had been trying to figure out how that transformation might have begun, but at that moment the mystery had me more baffled and enthralled than ever. Hans steered the plane back toward the Junction. Below, the excavations at FLK and FLKNN stood out like dead flesh, scars dug into the landscape by hungry, acquisitive hands. Around the bend, Dik-dik Hill bore a fresher wound. Tim was bent over an excavated square, worrying the earth with the pick end of his hammer. I kept my camera shutter clicking as we flew by. I thought about the effort we had expended there and the prize we had won for it: some three hundred chips of bone, which put together added up to one more morsel of information to feed this insatiable urge to know.

We took a few more runs over the site, and then followed the Side Gorge southwest toward Laetoli. My work at Olduvai was over for the year. Hans slipped another tape into the player, and Bruch's Violin Concerto sang through the headphones. Below me now lay the brush scrub of Laetoli. I shot my last two rolls of film and told Hans I was ready to head east toward Arusha. Instead he continued south along the Garusi river, flying only a few dozen yards above the dry riverbed.

"There is something I want to show you," he explained with a sly smile, and as he spoke the earth fell away beneath us. We had reached the Eyasi Escarpment, a sheer drop of three thousand feet. Far below, the parched bed of the salt lake shone with a pale brilliance, as if the crust of the earth as far as I could see was made of mother-of-pearl.

"Now we have a view, eh?" said Hans.

"Beautiful," I said.

Hans banked steeply and headed back to the east, skirting the south flank of Lemagrut, it shoulders pockmarked with grass fires. As we came into the lee of the volcano, a sudden downdraft hit the little plane with an audible thump. My head banged up against the ceiling and we began losing altitude. The sensation was less like falling than like being forcibly pushed down by an oppressive weight. Hans tried to pull the nose up but the plane kept falling, the engine screaming in protest and a half-charred ravine coming closer into focus. He gripped tight on the controls and gradually urged the plane sideways, away from the volcano. We had about five hundred feet to spare when the downdraft released us.

"That was not a scheduled part of the tour," Hans said when it was over. He was more upset than his words implied. We both had known people who had been caught in downdrafts like this one, and had not been so lucky.

As we rounded Lemagrut I looked back once more at the Gorge, now a mottled blemish on the edge of a plain stretching endlessly west. Through the years Olduvai had been such a fertile place for fossil hunters that sometimes it seems that early human evolution was an event staged at Olduvai Gorge. That is illusion, of course. Olduvai is a gift, a glorious accident of geology that punched a hole in the fabric of time and spilled a little of its contents. The same might be said of Koobi Fora, the Omo, the Hadar, the cave deposits of the Transvaal—all holes in the fabric. But time, and evolution, were happening everywhere.

The fossil we had found had revealed to us that the earliest humans were much smaller, much more primitive than we had imagined. But it could not reveal how such an animal managed to survive in the competitive world of the savanna. It could not explain why this diminutive ancestor had so suddenly become something far more human, in the transition to *Homo erectus*. It could not tell us what had become of its close cousins, the robust australopithecines. And it could not answer the question that I believed lay at the heart of the mystery: To what end had *Homo* evolved its appallingly oversized brain?

So where is one to look for answers? The best reply is "In better questions."

"The first step toward understanding is to stop assuming that humans win out in evolution *because they are human*," says Robert Foley, a young paleoanthropologist at Cambridge University in England. An archeologist and ecologist by training, Foley believes that far too much homage has been paid to the uniqueness of humankind, at the expense of understanding our genesis as a product of evolutionary forces shaping a whole community of other organisms at the same time. Our self-fascination has led us time and again into the same tautological trap: We look for some trace of uniquely human behavior in the ancient record, and once it is found, we point to it proudly and declare that we now understand the origins of humanity. If you define man as "the technological animal," for example, then of course you have only to find the first evidence of tools, and *presto,* you have discovered the beginning of man.

As Lew Binford would say, that is *post hoc* thinking, studying the past with one eye in the mirror. Toolmaking. Bipedalism. Brain growth. Hunting. Food sharing. All of these things *did* develop at some time in the human career, but we'll never comprehend how or why or what for unless we stop thinking backward from the *result.* Only when we strip early humans of their future can we begin to understand the secrets of our past.

I want to talk about hominids. But I first have to review a few points about *species,* whether they be hominids, hippos, or hibiscus plants. Point number one is easy: All species are adapted to the habitats they live in. You cannot ask a hippo to rise from her watery niche and populate the grassland, any more than you can expect a desert flower to thrive, transplanted into the jungle. Some species may be specialized to live in *one* kind of habitat (marsh lilies, penguins), while others are adapted to a range of habitats (cockroaches, us). But you still won't find any species dwelling for long where it is not physically or behaviorally adapted to make a living. It needn't be perfectly in tune with the environment; it need only be adapted *enough* to reproduce another viable generation of hominids, hippos, or hibiscus.

The second point follows from the first: Species tend to be very *conservative*. In most circumstances they do not show much change generation after generation, and for good reason. So long as their habitat remains fairly stable, those members of the species who are best fitted to the prevailing conditions will be those most likely to survive and reproduce, passing on the same old conservative traits that allowed them to succeed. If and when new species arise in stable habitats, the change is likely to be so subtle, so gradually paced, that the dividing line between the ancestor and the descendant is quite impossible to detect. Some theorists, including many who subscribe to the well-known "punctuated equilibrium" model of evolution, believe that new species cannot originate *unless* there is a substantial change in the environment first. I do not think this has to be true— but I do agree that it is in times of environmental instability that evolution really begins to heat up.

Point number three: While the environment outside provides the impetus for change in a species, the response that the species makes will be constrained from within. The biology of every toad, daffodil, and tsetse fly is a legacy of its evolutionary history. That heritage is inescapable; whatever anatomical or behavioral innovations are offered by the next generation of toads, they will always be Variations on the Theme of Toad. For this reason alone, you cannot focus a narrow beam on the earliest *Homo* and understand what it was doing to become "human," unless you consider too its australopithecine and primate pasts.

My fourth and last point: The creation of a new species requires that a population of its ancestors be blocked from reproducing with others outside the population. Usually this reproductive isolation comes about geographically, resulting in what is called allopatric speciation. Allopatric means "in another place." Brought to prominence by the Harvard evolutionist Ernst Mayr, the allopatric theory holds that new species usually originate in small populations isolated on the periphery of the species's ancestral range. Closer to the center of the range, the large, stable populations enjoy a sort of built-in genetic inertia; the conservative traits of the many tend to obliterate the evolutionary innovations offered each generation by the few. In the small, peripheral populations, on the other hand, random genetic variations are more likely to catch hold and express themselves in the next generation. Natural selection works with a sharper edge in these marginal habitats, since they offer unfamiliar environmental challenges.

Now let's work our way back to hominids. As Hans Schneider and I flew east over Ngorongoro, I peered down through the mist and could just make out the lush greenery covering the volcano's slopes. Ngorongoro is an island of forest in the surrounding plain. During the early Miocene, some sixteen to twenty million years ago, this kind of forest would have stretched uninterrupted across the Serengeti and all the way to the west coast of Africa, and northward across the Sahara Desert, blanketing virtually all of Africa and much of Europe and Asia as well. Living under that endless canopy were dozens of species of hominoids, among them the ancestor to all existing apes. The environment was stable, and for an arboreal, fruit-eating ape, making a living was relatively easy.

But nothing is stable forever, least of all the planet itself. Unbeknownst to the apes, the continents were sliding around under their feet. Long before the Miocene, Africa, India, South America, Australia, and Antarctica had all been part of one megacontinent that scientists call Gondwanaland. Over hundreds of millions of years the movement of the tectonic plates making up the earth's outer shell had been pulling the gigantic landmass apart. By sixty million years ago, only Australia and Antarctica were still connected, and Antarctica enjoyed a relatively temperate climate. But when the two other continents broke free and drifted north, an ocean current developed around Antarctica that effectively blocked warmer water from reaching its latitudes. (Today this circum-Antarctic current is the strongest on earth, transporting some twenty million cubic meters of jater per *second.*) The isolation of Antarctica led to massive buildup of the continent's polar caps, causing a significant drop in the level of the world's oceans.

Until just a few years ago, it was thought that the buildup of ice at the earth's poles led to increased rainfall and vegetation in the tropics. We now know that exactly the reverse is true: Global cooling leads to more arid conditions around the equator. And so, gradually, the Miocene rain forest began to break up. From the nature of pollen preserved in soil, and from the kinds of animals we find inhabiting the regions, we know that open woodlands and even some grassy expanses were gaining territory at the expense of tropicalforest.

Then came a deeper catastrophe. With the help of some local tectonic movements, the drop in sea level began to squeeze shut the narrow channel between the Mediterranean Sea and the Atlantic Ocean. As the bottleneck between the two seas grew shallower, enormous quantities of salt began to accumulate in the Mediterranean. Between six and a half and five million years ago, the Mediterranean trapped in its shrinking volume as much as 6 percent of the world oceans' salt.

The "Mediterranean salinity crisis," this quirky aberration in the simple chemistry of the ocean, may have been a kind of climatic trigger to the human career. Fresh water freezes at a higher temperature than salt water, and a world ocean 6 percent fresher than normal is no exception. The result was a sudden, accelerated buildup of sea ice around Antarctica, further lowering the sea level to the point where the Mediterranean basin was left high, dry, and a mile deep in salt. The earth's temperature took an abrupt plunge, a much steeper drop than the gradual cooling trend that had prevailed for millions of years.

Think back to the theory of allopatric speciation—new species erupting on the periphery of their ancestral habitat. Now think about a forest breaking apart, becoming not one far-flung mass but a scatter of smaller patches, ever more scattered, ever smaller. In some areas, the forest might be reduced to the greenery clinging to the mountains. Ngorongoro beneath us. Mount Meru north of Arusha. Kilimanjaro. Mount Kenya. And as the forest goes, so go the species who depend upon it. Instead of one large ancestral range bordered by peripheral areas, the hominoid apes, along with everybody else, ended up in many "islands" of the old preferred habitat, *each* isolated, *each* surrounded by the kind of iffy, marginal zone where rapid evolution is likely to occur.

Elisabeth Vrba, a South African paleontologist now at Yale University, has an elegant way of describing the choices * facing a

---

* Biologists use words like "choice," "strategy," and "solution" to describe the responses of species to their environments. But species, including our own, do not make conscious decisions about the course of their evolution. The language of consciousness is used merely as an analogy for the way natural selection and adaptation work.

species whose habitat is breaking apart under its feet. Elisabeth says the species can take any one of the three paths offered by the "Hindu Triad" of gods. It can follow the way of Vishnu the preserver and migrate to a new area, where the old environmental conditions still prevail. With this option the species need not give rise to new forms, nor even undergo much change within itself. The second choice is to stay put geographically, and be led by Brahma the creator, bringing forth new species better fit to the conditions that have taken over the home region. The third choice is to fall into the waiting arms of Siva the destroyer, and become extinct.

From what we can see in the fossil record, by six million years ago most of the dozens of hominoid species which once inhabited the rain forest had followed Siva the destroyer out of existence. Of those few that remained, most followed Vishnu to the patches of forest resembling the original habitat. In the late Miocene, coinciding with the Mediterranean salinity crisis, one ape took the path of Brahma, and a species it spawned walked there on two legs. It became adapted to more open habitats, where a bipedal primate could forage with success at least equal to that of a quadrupedal one. Not everyone thinks that the first hominid developed bipedalism *because* it was a more efficient way of coping with open landscapes. Owen Lovejoy, for example, is convinced that Lucy's ancestor was bipedal while still adapted to the Miocene forests. But whatever the prime motivation for bipedalism, the fragmentation of the forest gave this novel trait room to establish itself: an evolutionary innovation of a small group of prehominids, tucked away out of reach of their four-legged ancestral stock.

There is no fossil I would rather find than one plucked from that population of transitional bipeds. But the chances of that wish coming true are vanishingly remote. The transition probably would have taken place too fast and in too restricted an area to be viewed from one of the geological "windows" represented by the fossil sites of Africa. My guess is that the end result of that innovation was *afarensis*—or something very close to it. The oldest signs of *afarensis* in the fossil record are the fragments of frontal bone and femur that Tim and Desmond Clark found on the expedition to the Middle Awash in Ethiopia in 1981. These have been dated to be roughly 4 million years old. Meanwhile the *youngest afarensis* from Hadar carries a date of approximately 2.9 million years. That means that the species survived at least a million years, perhaps far longer. By any-

SAVANNA AND WOODLAND

RAINFOREST

LATE MIOCENE THROUGH TO PLIOCENE

MONTANE FORESTS

EARLY HOMINID SITES

1 - ETHIOPIA
2 - LAKE TURKANA
3 - LAKE BARINGO
4 - OLDUVAI REGION
5 - TRANSVAAL, S. AFRICA

SAVANNA AND WOODLAND

RAINFOREST REFUGIA

DESERT

GLACIAL

SAVANNA

DESERT

SAVANNA

SAVANNA

INTER-GLACIAL

LAKE MEGACHAD

RAINFOREST

SAVANNA

BASED ON BONNEFILLE 1984 AND ROBERTS 1984

DESERT

PRESENT

SAVANNA, WOODLAND, SHRUB

RAINFOREST

SAVANNA, WOODLAND, SHRUB

DESERT

African HABITATS

The pattern of change in the environments of Africa helped to shape the evolution of the hominid lineage. In the late Miocene, the tropical rain forest that once dominated the continent began to give way to savanna and open woodlands. Over the next 10 million years, polar glaciers exerted a profound effect. Cooler temperatures and lower rainfall during glacial periods shrunk the forest into scattered patches, isolating the species within them. The rain forest expanded again in the warmer, wetter periods between glacial advances, bringing together species that evolved in isolation.

one's standards that is a stable, successful evolutionary experiment.

What is surprising is that the Pliocene environment of East Africa was anything but stable. From what we can tell from fossilized pollen samples and from the record of the animal inhabitants, the mosaic of forests, open woodlands, and savanna flickered through time, regions first wooded, then open, then forested once again. At the same time, volcanoes, lava flows, and earthquakes were constantly reworking the landscape, altering the course of rivers, raising sheer fault scarps out of level plain. Hardly what I would call a stable environment.

How could *afarensis* endure such commotion and remain unchanged for a million years? For a clue, look to the species's heritage. The ancestor of *afarensis* was an dietary generalist, an omnivorous primate, like its own ancestors. But it took the generalists' strategy one critical step further, broadening its menu and extending its reach beyond the forest. The low-cusped, thick-enameled molars of *afarensis* reveal an animal accustomed to a diet that regularly included hard items like nuts and seeds, as well as softer fruits. Under an electron microscope, the patterns of wear on its teeth are those of an eclectic feeder, their surfaces scratched, pitted, and flaked by a greater variety of foods than seem to be consumed by living apes. We know, moreover, that *afarensis* frequented the dry environment of Laetoli, as well as the open canopy forest of Hadar. It may have sometimes foraged in the trees, but at the same time the terrestrial mobility granted by bipedalism probably stretched its range beyond that of the other apes. As a result it was able to exploit the resources of a number of different habitats.

If you think the old way, backward from ourselves, you might say that once a uniquely human trait like bipedalism was established, the rest of the package—big brains, tool use, food sharing and so forth—would inevitably follow. *Nothing is inevitable in evolution.* I see no reason why Lucy's descendants could not have persisted just as they were for another million years or more, well-endowed generalists in a fairly rich habitat, apes with brains hardly bigger than other apes, walking on two legs because it suited their *present* circumstances, not because it augured some glorious future. But *afarensis* did change. Between three and two million years ago, East Africa became an even harder place to make an easy living, perhaps quite suddenly. And *afarensis*, like its own ancestor, was forced to choose between the paths of Vishnu, Siva, or Brahma.

I've talked about the changes wrought upon Africa by the global temperature plunge in the late Miocene. Recently, Elisabeth Vrba drew my attention to a rash of new evidence pointing toward another climatic catastrophe later on. Deep-sea sediment cores record a surge in polar ice between 2.5 and 2.4 million years, perhaps marking the first glacial advance in the Northern Hemisphere. Pollen studies on land deposits tell the same story: In Holland, palm forests give way to open steppes; in Colombia mountain forests wither into plain. Pollen samples from the Omo in Ethiopia show an abrupt shift from woody plants to grasses and low shrubs. The Omo's record of microfauna—rodents and the like—neatly parallels the vegetative switch, with forest-living forms giving way to arid-adapted types between 2.5 and 2.4 million years ago. Most recently, deep-sea cores from the ocean off West Africa are coming up full of dust at the same point in time. From modern studies, we know that dust settles in the ocean where there is desert on the adjacent land.

Elisabeth's own work on African bovids comes up with the same conclusion, and in spades. Bovids are especially good indicators of evolutionary change in Africa simply because there are so many of them. Two and a half million years ago, the bovid family underwent an explosion of new species well adapted to savanna conditions: the hartebeest and wildebeest, the gazelles, impala, springbok, and similar forms.

"All the continents are saying the same thing," Elisabeth told me, with obvious delight. "The climate is changing in some places, with dramatic force. The cause of the change is not clear—perhaps tectonic movements closed the Isthmus of Panama, reshuffling the circulation of currents in the Pacific and Atlantic oceans, which in turn affected temperature and precipitation patterns. But that it *did* happen is almost beyond doubt."

According to her "turnover-pulse" theory, this sudden shift in the global climate might have sent a surge of extinction and speciation through the food chain. The pulse would hit the early hominids too, possibly triggering the appearance of *Homo*. We do not have any direct evidence for *Homo* that early in the fossil record—not yet—but we do have the next best thing. The discovery of those very primitive stone tools near Hadar matches the date exactly. Equally important is the *absence* of tools any earlier. Stone tools are not time-fragile like fossils. If we look for them, and we can't find them, then they probably weren't there to begin with. If Elisabeth Vrba is right, and I think she is, the *Homo* emerged in East Africa some 2.5 million years ago, one among many species struggling to adapt to radically altered conditions.

"What is true on a personal level is true for evolution too," she says. "You are not going to change much if you sit around doing the same old thing in the same familiar habitat. But when you are thrown into situations of stress, of unfamiliar risk, you are pushed to change. We are the product of catastrophe."

We have to look a little more closely now at this new world facing "Lucy's children"—the descendants of *afarensis*. So far, I have been talking about habitats in rather two-dimensional terms, sliding in words like "forest," "woodland," and "savanna" as if they were painted backdrops to the real action taking place stage front. That is convenient shorthand, but it reinforces the notion that human evolution was somehow special and distinct. Humans did not evolve *in* habitats; they were *of* them, like other animals, the way that molecules in an electrical wire are part of the energy running through. An animal's habitat is the temperature of the air next to its skin, the rainfall dampening the dust beneath its feet and its cycle through the seasons, the height of the mountains and depth of the winters, the salt in the earth and the oxygen in the air. By day a habitat sucks up energy from the sun, by night it gets hungry and eats its own tail. A habitat is *alive*. It moves. It runs away from you or snaps at your hooves. It gets to the food before you do, or it paces nearby while you eat. It may steal your meal, your portion of the energy, from under your nose, or it waits in your gut and steals it later. A habitat is dynamic. It is more than the physical environment and the sum of the organisms that live and die in its boundaries; it is the conflicts and interdependencies that bind them together. A habitat doesn't stand still while you evolve to master it. It evolves too.

"Savanna" is a broad term embracing everything from gallery forests lining rivers and lake margins to semi-deserts with scarcely a tree in sight. In between are moist woodlands, drier woodlands, bush country like Laetoli, and vast grasslands punctuated by the occasional solitary acacia. In spite of this diversity, there are conditions that all these habitats share in common. Savannas do not support much "primary production"—the foundation of plant material that carries the hierarchy of animal life in the food chain above. In spite of the apparent barrenness of the bottom line, however, savannas often show a great abundance of animal life. Anyone who has had the good fortune to witness the annual, horizon-spanning migration of wildebeest in the Serengeti Plain knows what the word "abundance" can mean in this context. The key to this mammalian munificence is *grass*. Grass is low-quality food; it does not hold much protein, and what is there is locked up in tough cell walls. But on the plus side, grass regrows quickly, so supplies are constantly renewed. Hoofed ungulates like the wildebeest, zebra, and gazelle "solve" the problems posed by grass feeding through behavioral routes (eating all the time) and anatomical ones (specialized digestive equipment capable of breaking down the cellulose in grass). These prey species naturally attract predators. Savannas are also home to a few primates and pigs that feed on high-quality, scarcer plant foods.

Our ancestors did not enter the plains like Oklahoma land-rushers racing to stake a claim in virgin territory; they were thrown into an environment already populated with highly successful savanna veterans. Like any species trying to carve a niche for itself in a new habitat, the hominids would have to sniff around the edges of the energy system, looking for food resources left unexploited by more established species. I doubt very much that *Homo* joined the ranks of the carnivores and took to hunting. Tools or no tools, how is a fruit 'n' nuts kind of generalist supposed to muscle a niche for itself between a five-hundred-pound lion and a pack of sly hyenas? The first hominids on the savanna did not have to compete with carnivores—they had only to stay out of their reach. Their real competitors would be other high-quality plant-food eaters, like the baboons, monkeys, and pigs. Like these other species, the hominids would have to come to terms with a fundamental fact of savanna habitat: Premium resources are rare and scattered. To keep alive, you will have to forage farther, with greater reward attending whatever extra effort you put in.

But that's only half the problem. The savanna confounds the search for food in the dimension of *time* as well as space. People tend to think of savannas as dry, which is only partially true. Some savannas receive as much as 100 inches of rain a year. What matters, however, is the *timing* of this rainfall. The most distinguishing characteristic of the savanna environment is seasonality. The rain comes in bursts. The periods in between—the dry seasons—may last anywhere from two and a half to ten months. The dry-season savanna is not just a thirsty version of the wet-season savanna. It is a different place altogether. In the dry season the grass shrivels to a useless brown mat. Where there was food, there is dust. In low elevations the heat is intense, and even on the relatively cool plateaus like the Serengeti, there is little shade to escape to from the sun. The herbivores, dispersed during the wet season, either migrate away or flock to permanent sources of water. There many die of starvation, or fall victim to the predators who await their coming. Animals adapted to higher-quality plant foods suffer just as much. They stand in double jeopardy: As each parcel of their range grows increasingly impoverished, the drying up of water holes keeps them bound to a smaller and smaller foraging area.

To every animal on the savanna, the dry season represents a chasm of lean times that has to bridged year after year. The first thing an animal does when faced with a lapse in resources is cut down on activity to save energy. Not many mammals have evolved the radical extreme of hibernation, but most show a falling off of play, socializing, and reproducing during the hard months. But rarely is energy saving alone enough to allow survival until the rains return. Each animal has to make a crucial decision: either to start eating lower-quality foods like mature leaves, seeds, and stems that are still abundant in the dry season, or to find ways to win access to higher-quality foods previously out of reach.

I think it was this dry-season "decision" that really forced the branching in the hominid line. In response to the seasonal stress, some populations of *afarensis* developed the customized chewing equipment—those massive jaws and heliport molars—that would enable the robust australopithecines to cope with the tough, low-quality vegetation available in the dry season. But another population took a second route. Building on their phylogenetic history as resourceful, omnivorous primates, the ancestors of *Homo* began to poke around in the dry season looking for new opportunities to get at out-of-reach foods with high payoffs. They did not use specialized jaws and teeth to get at these prized goods. They used their heads.

Brains are wonderful things. Speaking from the admittedly biased point of view of a large-brained primate, I would say there is no better solution to one's environment—no claw so sharp, no wing so light that it can begin to bestow the same adaptive benefits as a heavy ball of gray matter. What a big brain gives you is *flexibility*. With a brain you are no longer a creature dependent on the moment, doomed to programmed responses that may or may not be equal to the task posed by the new challenges you face. With a brain you can learn from past situations, foresee the advantages of two different courses of action, and calculate the best alternative. Big, powerful, calculating brains are so useful that at first glance you might wonder why so few species have developed them—the primates, some cetaceans, to some extent elephants, a few carnivores.

The answer is that their cost is prohibitive. Modern humans spend about 20 percent of their metabolic energy keeping their brains running, as opposed to about 10 to 13 percent in a relatively cerebral nonhuman like a monkey. In human infants and children under four, the brain devours closer to 50 *percent* of total body metabolism. Half the blood supply pumping for one organ. The brain's demands are relentless. They go on even when you sleep, even when you watch reruns of television shows you thought insipid the first time around. Brains are also freeloaders. They hold no energetic reserves themselves. If the supply of oxygen and glucose is cut off, the brain quickly collapses into stupor, with vast and irreversible damage to its tissues within minutes. When you add up all its costs, a brain makes evolutionary sense only if you really need what it provides.

What early *Homo*'s brain provided was *access*, the means to break through the inhibiting protections around food pockets and scoop out their rich, sequestered rewards. Leaning on sheer versatility, they eked out a living where none was there to be found, borrowing a little from the fringes of one species's niche, taking the crumbs that fell from the mouth of another. Some of these rich nutritional sources would be virtually invisible. The African savanna is full of "drought-evading" plants that keep a large part of their energy reserves stored underground. In the dry season, when edible vegetation aboveground grows scarce, the tubers, roots, bulbs, and other nodulous larders of the drought evaders make up a huge proportion of the total plant biomass—all of it available to rooting pigs or clawing bears, or to a primate clever enough to conceive the idea of a digging stick. Other dry-season energy sources are highly visible, but more difficult to catch.

"One of the best solutions to getting through hard times is to eat somebody else who has already taken the trouble to come up with a different solution," says Lew Binford.

When Lew told me that, he was referring to the hunting behavior of Ice Age humans a mere forty thousand years ago. As you know from the last chapter, he scoffs at the notion of *habilis* as a hunter, and by and large I have to agree with him. But to rule out that early *Homo* was eating *any* live prey is too extreme. I find it hard to believe that a large-brained, undoubtedly social animal like *habilis* would eschew a rich food source that some modern nonhuman primates regularly exploit. When Jane Goodall first observed chimpanzees hunting twenty years ago, it was assumed to be a rare, isolated phenomenon. Through her subsequent studies and those of others, we now know that the hunting of other animals, often planned, deliberate, and highly cooperative, is characteristic of many chimpanzee communities, though some do it more than others.

And chimps are not the only primate killers. Humans aside, the most predacious primates known are the members of the "Pumphouse Gang," the group of olive baboons in Kenya that have been under the scrutiny of Shirley Strum of the University of California at San Diego for over fifteen years. Strum's baboons have developed sophisticated strategies like relay chases and long-distance pursuits to capture young Thompson's gazelles and other small ungulates. In one year they averaged one kill *every twelve hours*—hardly what you would call gentle herbivores. Granted, the Pumphouse Gang might be an unusual extreme. But they stand at one end of a very suggestive trend: In both chimps and baboons, the groups that inhabit savanna environments include a much greater percentage of meat in their diets than do their forest-dwelling counterparts, and they hunt most during the dry season.

Oddly, today few chimps or baboons appear to avail themselves of that other method of obtaining meat—scavenging. Early *Homo* was not so choosy, and according to Rob Blumenschine, now at Rutgers University and a member of the Institute's research team in Tanzania, the opportunities were there to be exploited. In 1983, Rob conducted a study of what happens to a carcass after death on the savanna—how much the killer eats, what kinds of scavengers come to sup upon the carcass later, and what they leave behind for others—to see if there would have been anything left on a regular basis for a hypothetical early hominid to exploit.

After several rather messy seasons of fieldwork, often up to his elbows in half-eaten wildebeest carcasses, he concluded that a "scavenging niche" might indeed have been vacant in the Plio-Pleistocene, ready for hominid occupancy—but only in certain habitats. Among all the carnivores on the savanna, only the hyena eats all of a carcass, leaving nothing of worth behind for subsequent scavengers. Rob reasoned that the places where hominids might have profited from the kills of predators would be where hyenas weren't around to consume everything first. Hyenas prefer open plains or lightly wooded habitats. In the infrequent times when Rob encountered them in more densely wooded areas, such as the forest fringes of lakes and rivers, they seemed "skittish," apparently wary of lions. In these areas the marrow and head contents of a lion's kill often sat untouched until they finally began to rot. Rob's study did not prove that hominids were scavenging—only that the opportunity may have existed. From sites like Olduvai Gorge and East Turkana, however, we know that the lake and river margins seemed to be a preferred habitat of *habilis,* and that they appeared to be using stone tools to break open bones.

The lasting testimony of *Homo*'s heightened foraging access is the ancient tool, used to coax tubers out of the dead ground, deflesh carcasses, and hammer marrow out of barren bone. But because an activity requiring intelligence just *happens* to have archeological permanence does not mean that toolmaking is the sine qua non of the human mind. The ecological opportunity I see opening to *Homo* extends far beyond what we see expressed in a chopper or flake. *Knowledge,* not its manifestation in stone, is what pried out the hidden scraps of energy dotting the ancient landscape. The first humans survived the dry season by knowing their habitat in intimate detail. They were opportunists armed with information, and probably relied a great deal on each other to communicate knowledge of food patches separated by long distances. They knew from the shape of a dessicated stalk what pithy tumescence lay in the ground beneath. They knew the promise implicit in the circling of a vulture, a monkey's scream, the urgent trilling of a honey guide bird as it led them to a bee's nest. They knew that adult antelopes, while impossible to catch, sometimes "park" their young in grass and go off to browse. Though invisible to the motion-sensitive eyes of a carnivore, a generalist with a primate's color vision could pluck the infant like ready fruit—if he knew where to look.

Obviously, the big-brain flexibility evolved to cope with dry-season stress would be available in the wet season too. The early humans understood that the pattern of food on the landscape shifts in complex but predictable patterns: that fig tees in the gallery forest ripen at specific times, that toxic berries can be separated from the edible ones that mimic them by shape of leaf or feel of bark, that the termite's nuptial flight attends the first drops of rain and for a few days fills the air with food. Bird's eggs are rich morsels too *if* you can get access to them, perhaps by knocking down a nest with a well-aimed stone, or remembering what kind of cover a nesting pair used in earlier years. Later on in the wet season, when the fledgings take their first independent flights, there may be some who fail the test, their panicked thrashings revealing that they are ready to be fished out of the avian gene pool. What set *Homo habilis* apart and defined the human niche was not hunting, not scavenging, not digging sticks or any tool per se, but the apprehension of possibility in an unpromising landscape. An animal on the make.

On the flight east from Olduvai I looked down upon the Kainam Plateau, wearing its pallid late-summer complexion. We soon reached the escarpment above Lake Manyara, and then, abruptly, Manyara itself, a dark ribbon of forest threaded between the lake and the highlands to the west. The fringes of the lake were dappled with bird flocks and slow mammalian motions; I could see elephants browsing in fever trees near the shore, and in the shallows, an archipelago of wallowing hippos. Nearby a herd of zebra bulged around a stream. I could not see the lions sleeping in the trees, the warthogs quick-stepping in the thickets with their purposeful gait, or the other small creatures picking out a living in the sunlight or curled in their burrows, waiting for dark. But they were there too, and if you took away the hotel perched on the escarpment, the cultivated fields, the shadow of the plane and other signs of later men, it wasn't so hard to imagine *habilis* in this world after all. There would be no stone dwellings by the lake, no little families waiting in the vestibule for Daddy Homo to sharpen his chopper and carve a thick steak off his latest kill. But there would be small, brown figures darting among the shadows of the umbrella thorns, drawn to the lakeside because that was where the energy resides—in the trees, in the ground, in places where no one else thinks to look. They could scrounge out a living that way, if they relied on each other and assiduously avoided known dangers. Early *Homo* survived, barely, without a sheen of special destiny protecting its progress toward dominion. Personally, I find that more impressive than any of the old myths.

And what of the hominid siblings, the robust australopithecines? They would be down there too, of course. Because the path they took led eventually to extinction, the robusts are often thought of as innately inferior to *Homo* from start to finish. Nonsense. Judging from the sheer number of fossils we have found, *A. robustus* and

A. *boisei* were very successful species in the early Pleistocene, often outnumbering their *Homo* counterparts by two to one. By definition, the adaptive strategies of the two lineages would have overlapped in the beginning, including the ability to access food resources through ingenuity. Chimpanzees use tools effectively, and it is almost inconceivable that the australopithecines would not have done so too. From a level at Swartkrans associated with *robustus*, Bob Brain has recently unearthed long-bone splinters that appear to be polished and may have been used as digging sticks. *Homo* is represented by only a few fossils at Swartkraus. Is it possible that *robustus* was using the digging sticks? Perhaps, but we cannot be certain.

Another prevalent myth has it that the robusts were driven to extinction by competition from their smarter *Homo* relatives. That idea is unlikely, at best. The robust and *Homo* lineages would have competed for resources intensely near their point of divergence, when their ecological niches butted up against each other. But as time progressed, their differing strategies for coping with seasonal stress would have taken them ecologically farther apart. The robusts did not disappear until just after one million years ago, long after *Homo habilis* had evolved into *Homo erectus*. Robert Foley speculates that if the robusts *were* squeezed out of existence by foraging competitors, the pressure would have come not from *Homo erectus* but from the bovids and other herbivores who could better exploit the low-quality plant foods to which the robusts had become adapted. Alan Walker sees a different role for *Homo* in the extinction of the robusts: as a member of an efficient new guild of predators. Meanwhile, Elisabeth Vrba points to the possibility of another episode of global cooling near nine hundred thousand years ago. She suggests that the demise of the robusts might be understood in the context of another massive wave of mammalian extinctions and speciations. The truth is we do not really know why the robusts faded from existence. But all species do, eventually.

There are still a great many questions to be answered about Lucy's other child as well—the *Homo* lineage. For starters, the controversy surrounding *habilis* remains unresolved. *Homo habilis* was an ill-defined taxon when Leakey, Tobias, and Napier named it back in 1964, and none of the dozen or so fossils found since—not even the famous 1470 skull from Koobi Fora—have made things any clearer. Some anthropologists, such as Chris Stringer at the British Museum and Bernard Wood of the University of Liverpool, have recently ar-

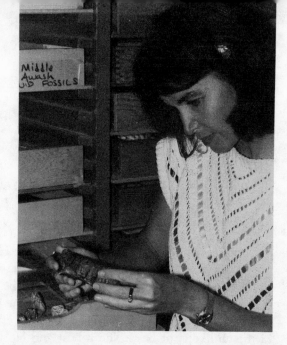

Elisabeth Vrba examining afarensis *fossil vertebrae.*
DONALD JOHANSON

gued that there is too much variation among the accumulated *habilis* specimens to fit comfortably into a single species, and that there may in fact be two species represented in the fossil sample. The diversity they point to is most evident in cranial capacity, which ranges from just over 500 cc to about 750 cc—too great a reach, perhaps, to be spanned by the single name *habilis.*

Stringer's and Wood's interpretations imply more than just a little taxonomic housecleaning. If there *were* two species of *Homo* living contemporaneously in East Africa, then probably only one of them could be an ancestor to *Homo sapiens.* Taking that thought one step further, you end up with a sort of shadow human lineage, evincing many of the characteristics we thought to be ours alone, then disappearing from the fossil record. It is a fascinating possibility, and unlike the arguments for two species roped under the name *afarensis,* deserves to be considered very seriously.

At this time, however, I do not think we have sufficient evidence to justify splitting the *Homo habilis* sample in two and naming a new *Homo* taxon. J. Miller of the University of Southern California recently showed, for instance, that large samplings of gorillas, orangutans, chimps, and humans show a range in cranial capacity equal to or greater than that of *Homo habilis*—and nobody doubts that these are single species. My working hypothesis is that the variations found among the *habilis* specimens have a great deal to do with sex, geography, and time. The big individuals are probably males, the smaller ones mostly females. The sites where the specimens have been found are as far apart as five hundred miles and may cover as much as three or four hundred thousand years.

Which brings us back to the mystery so potently underscored by the Dik-dik Hill hominid. If this little skeleton is a typical *habilis* female, then the transition to *Homo erectus* in that critical time-slice between 1.8 and 1.6 million years ago was sudden and dramatic. We do not know why that transformation occurred, but we do have a few leads. So far there is no indication of another global climatic trigger at that time, but Richard Hay's geological work tells us that the local Olduvai habitat, at least, dried out about 1.7 million years ago. The lake shores shrank in. The fauna switched from species comfortable in moist conditions to those adapted to open grassland. The same change can be read farther north in the Omo's Shungura Formation, and perhaps in South African cave deposits too. A big-bodied creature like *erectus* could exploit the larger home range necessary under such conditions, and would be in a better position to face predators in the open. A big body would also be needed to metabolically support a bigger brain, since neural activity consumes considerable energy. Certainly a lineage already committed to intelligence as a foraging strategy would use that flexibility as it continued to adapt to new habitats farther down the evolutionary road.

That swollen cerebrum would bring with it some inflated costs. In addition to its even greater need for water, the absolute energy requirements of a big *erectus* individual, like the five-and-a-half-foot skeleton of an adolescent that Kamoya Kineu found in 1984, would have been much greater than those of the tiny Dik-dik Hill hominid. Alan Walker believes that beginning with *erectus*, our ancestors became much more dependent on live prey, so much so that the species might be described as "a stalking species of hunter, as men are today." The hindsight perspective implied in that statement bothers me, but I suspect that *erectus* *was* relying on more meat, especially in the dry season. I do not see how a dietary generalist with that kind of body bulk could have survived without leaning more heavily on animal protein than its compactly proportioned predecessor.

And of course the Acheulean tools appear in the archeological record along with *erectus*. The temptation remains to put man and tool together, and see the advance of technology as the driving force in the evolution of *erectus*. But be careful—we might start reading the text backward from the conclusion again.

"I'm sick and tired of hearing people say that '*erectus* equals

Acheulean', as if there was a gene at position twenty-two on the fifteenth chromosome programming that particular hominid to start making hand axes," says Tim White. There is no reason to assume, in other words, that the biological transition to *erectus* was somehow *dependent* on an advance in technology.

"Tools were adjuncts, not the means of adaptation like they are today," adds Lew Binford.

To my mind, it was probably the pressure of an increasingly impoverished habitat working upon the hominid heritage that brought forth big *erectus*, much as it had earlier initiated our divergence from the robust australopithecines. But that cannot be the whole story, not by a long shot. Environmental stress may have provided the "kick," but other influences were in play as well, amplifying the direction, quickening the pace, reinforcing each other. It makes no more sense to look upon *Homo* as purely an ecological entity than it does to consider the invention of stone tools in isolation, or to attribute our evolution to some one, uniquely human behavior. Simple answers might be satisfying, but they will not lead to the truth.

Before descending from this flight over the landscape of our beginnings, I have to bear witness to one evolutionary "amplifier" in particular—the role that hominid society itself must have played in shaping our intellects. Generally speaking, paleoanthropologists today tend to shy away from speculations on early human social behavior. We relish hard evidence, and start to squirm in its absence. (Not once during a field expedition have I glanced down to see a fossilized social interaction lying at my feet.) But to ignore the pressure of society upon our ancestors just because it leaves no permanent record would be ridiculously shortsighted. While my colleagues and I have been busy scanning the ground for physical testimony to the human past, primatologists and animal psychologists have been looking for other clues in the social lives of our closest living relatives. What they have been finding there most recently bears directly on the origins of our intelligence, and is too disturbing to be ignored.

As Hans Schneider brought the Cessna around to land on the Manyara strip, I looked west one more time toward Olduvai. Beyond the Serengeti, over the horizon and across Lake Victoria lay the Virunga mountains, where Dian Fossey had so long studied and lived with the mountain gorillas. In the early 1970s, a young British psychologist named Nicholas Humphrey spent some time working in the

Virungas with Fossey. Like other researchers before him, Humphrey was struck by the apparent ease of gorilla life: They had no natural predators other than man, and to eat, they had only to reach out and grab a handful of leaves. Humphrey knew that gorillas, like other apes, show amazing intelligence when put to the test in laboratory experiments. Therein lay a powerful paradox, for if intelligence evolved in response to environmental pressure, why was so unchallenged an animal so manifestly smart?

In an essay called *The Social Function of Intellect,* Humphrey answered that society itself was the driving force behind primate intelligence, and even more so the spur to the astonishing intelligence of man. Society acts as a sort of double-edged knife to shape the intelligent being. On one side, a social group provides the context for learning about the nature of the habitat that every young animal will need for its future survival. Chimpanzees, for instance, do not come into the world knowing how to fashion a twig into a probe that can be used to fish termites from their nest; nor are they likely to discover the trick on their own. They learn to fish by watching older, more experienced members of their group.

In Humphrey's view, this "collegiate community" would become increasingly complex and cooperative as new environmental pressures added to the usefulness of intelligence. But this complexity brings the other side of the double-edged knife to bear upon human intelligence, and it cuts just as deep. Though the members of a social group behave cooperatively, especially toward close kin, the bottom line is that every individual is out to ensure the survival of his or her own genes. Each will be competing *within* the group for a piece of the resource pie—and that includes chances to mate, as well as opportunities to feed. Humphrey's collegiate community thus harbors the seeds of considerable political strife. As much as each individual relies on intelligence to confront the environment, his real intellectual enemies become the other members of his group. It is one thing to try to "outwit" a fig hanging just out of reach, or to fool an infant gazelle whose flight is governed by unthinking fear. But it requires a different sort of mind altogether to outwit an intelligent adversary who is simultaneously trying to outwit *you.*

Humphrey likened this intellectual challenge to the game of croquet Alice plays with the Queen of Hearts in Wonderland. Alice's mallet is a flamingo, the balls are hedgehogs, and the hoops are card men who can jump out of the way:

"You've no idea how confusing it is, all the things being alive," says poor Alice.

Without really meaning to, Nicholas Humphrey provided with his essay the harbinger of what has recently taken on the dimensions of a new paradigm for understanding the origins of our intellect, even the nature of what we call the human psyche. Some of its advocates—mostly primatologists and psychologists—call this social function of mind "Machiavellian intelligence," which should give you an idea of how much emphasis they place on the frankly political advantages of being smart. Cunning and calculation are not the only tools in the inventory of Machiavelli's model Prince, not do they exhaust the repertoire of the socially intelligent ape. Nevertheless, according to the new way of thinking, what matters is not so much *what* you know, but *whom*—and how effective you can be at keeping critical knowledge out of the hands of those who might oppose you.

Thirty years ago, when Irven DeVore, Sherwood Washburn, and others were coming back from the field with the first good data on the social behavior of baboons and other primates, the interactions between any two individuals were seen in terms of their place in a dominance hierarchy. The outcome of encounters between two individuals was fairly easy to predict: The bigger, nastier animal almost always prevailed. DeVore and Washburn's observations were not wrong, but they now seem misleadingly incomplete. Primatologists watching baboon, monkey, and chimp interactions in the wild today believe that one-on-one encounters, far from being the essence of social structure in primates, may be relatively unimportant. Rather than be doomed to submission, a physically weak member of a group might recruit stronger allies who can be depended upon to come to its aid when needed. Most often, these alliances are formed between kin.

What the primatologists are seeing in the field is basic playground politics: If somebody is bullying you, go tell your big brother so he will come stand behind you. Chances are good that the bully will gain sudden new respect for you—unless, of course, he fetches *his* brother, who happens to outrank yours in the group, further complicating the social equation. Among the primates, mothers more commonly serve as recruited allies than older siblings, but the analogy holds true. A young rhesus macaque, for instance, quickly discovers that she can intimidate members of the group far larger than herself because her high-ranking mother will always back her up in any conflict. Eventually the daughter will come to occupy a place in the female hierarchy just below her mother.

Thus the most basic kind of social intelligence is the ability to understand and remember the web of kin relationships that form the heart of a social group. What intrigues me more, however, are the political alliances that primatologists are discovering among *unrelated* individuals in a primate group, who have no shared genetic inheritance that might otherwise explain their favored treatment of each other. Primatologist Meredith Small of Cornell University recently reported the case of Becky, a low-ranking Barbary macaque in a captive community in southern France. Over a period of months, Becky managed to defy the normally rigid female hierarchy in macaques, and advanced several rungs on the social ladder by judiciously grooming and caring for the infants of females well above her in rank. To do so, Becky had to know who was powerful enough to merit the time spent currying their favor, and more importantly, she had to have some conception of a "payoff" weeks, even months down the road. Becky was one smart macaque.

In a longer-term study, Barbara Smuts of the University of Michigan found that among the fifty-odd adults in her study group in Kenya's Amboseli National Park, tight "friendships" often formed between members of opposite sexes, some lasting as long as six years. A female had one or two "special males" who tended to stay close to her even when the female was not in a mating period. When the female was attacked, her male friends rushed to her support. If the female gave birth, the male friends were often equally solicitous to her infant. In return, the special males could better count on the female's support in conflicts with strange males, and were probably favored when the time came to mate. Shirley Strum's observations of the Pumphouse Gang baboons bore this out. Generally speaking, the baboon male who mates in not the most aggressive newcomer, as Devore and Washburn believed, but the one who knows that success comes from cultivating social relationships and understanding the patterns of alliance in the group.

If the behavior of these baboons were unique, or if Becky the macaque were the only ambitious monkey forming alliances with unrelated big shots, the idea of a social origin for intelligence would not be gaining the momentum it now enjoys. But these examples just scratch the surface. All over the primate world, the reports from field biologists are giving shape and substance to Nicholas Humphrey's germ of an idea. Forming alliances is only the beginning. If it takes smarts for a baboon or monkey to keep track of all the *facts* in his social relationships, imagine how much intelligence is required when he and his companions begin to lie.

Take Paul, for instance, a young juvenile chacma baboon observed in Ethiopia by Richard Byrne and Andrew Whiten of the University of St. Andrews in Scotland. One day they noticed Paul watching an adult female named Mel dig in the ground for a large grass root. He looked around. There were no other baboons nearby, though the troop was well within earshot. Suddenly, and with no visible provocation, Paul let out a yell. In an instant his mother appeared, and in a flurry chased the astonished Mel out of sight. Meanwhile, Paul walked over and ate the grass root she left behind.

Deception is a natural art. You find it everywhere in nature: insects mimicking the appearance of plant stems or leaves, harmless snakes that look like deadly poisonous ones, fish who puff themselves up when threatened, cats who arch their backs and bristle their hair to seem bigger than they really are. On a very general level, all of these animals can be said to practice deception because they fool other animals—usually members of other species—into thinking they are something which they patently are not. Even so, it would be incorrect (not to mention odd) to accuse a stickbug or a blowfish of being a lying scoundrel. Their biology leaves them no choice but to dissemble, and so their behavior is in fact perfectly honest.

Tactical deception, to use the term coined by Byrne and Whiten, is another matter entirely. In tactical deceptions, somebody does something that fools somebody else into believing that a normal, honest state of affairs is under way, when in fact something quite different is happening. The intention to deceive is quite deliberate, and the misinterpretation is designed to play into the hands of the deceiver. Byrne and Whiten also happen to be the scientists responsible for the provocative term "Machiavellian intelligence."

"It is good to appear clement, trustworthy, humane, religious, and honest, and also to be so," Machiavelli himself advised his aspiring Prince, "but always with the mind so disposed that, when the occasion arises not to be so, you can become the opposite."

In Paul's case, the occasion that arose was his own hunger. He misled his mother into believing that he was being attacked—the "honest" reason for his scream—when in fact nothing of the kind was taking place. Again, this was not some isolated case. Paul pulled the same trick several times on other unsuspecting adults. Byrne and Whiten recently sent out a questionnaire to their primatologist colleagues, asking for similar examples of deception among primates. The responses flooded back—dozens of anecdotes telling of one chimp, baboon, or monkey duping another, or concealing some piece of information vital to his own advantage.

Sometimes it was simply a matter of one animal hiding a choice bit of food from the awareness of those in the group who were strong enough to take it away. In one case, a subordinate chimpanzee, aroused by the presence of an estrus female, covered his erect penis with his hand when a dominant male approached, and thus avoided a likely attack. Another chimp, locked in a struggle for power, hid his "fear grin" by tugging at his lips, literally wiping from his face the smile that would have betrayed his anxiety to his rival. One researcher reported watching a female hamadryas baboon slowly shuffle over toward a large rock, pretending to forage, all the time keeping an eye on the harem male in the group. After twenty minutes she ended up with her head and shoulders visible to the big male, but her hands happily engaged in the illicit activity of grooming a favorite subordinate male, who was hidden from view behind the rock.

In all of these cases, the deceivers executed a prodigious mental leap. They set upon a course of action based not only on what they *knew* of the social milieu—who is strong, who is weak, who is most likely to help—but also on what they *imagined* to be going on inside another animal's head. The female hamadryas baboon knew, for instance, that she risked attack from the harem male if she were caught grooming her favorite "other male." But she also understood that she could get away with it so long as from harem male's viewpoint, no grooming was actually taking place. By placing herself within his mental space, she had become what Nicholas Humphrey calls a "natural psychologist." This is a talent—or more properly, an adaptation—that our own species has evolved to perfection.

"The pervasiveness of deception in our everyday lives," says Richard Alexander, an evolutionary biologist at the University of Michigan, "can be glimpsed by anyone willing to reflect on how often he or she bathes, shaves, puts on deodorant, makeup, or artificial eyelashes, chooses clothes with concealing and flattering effects such as shoulder pads, dons shoes with elevated heels, pops a mint into the mouth, or enters the workplace wearing a polite smile."

More than anyone, Richard Alexander has picked up on the

On the right, "Becky," a socially intelligent Barbary Macaque, ingratiates herself with the higher-ranking female on the left by tending her infant son. MEREDITH SMALL

ideas of Nicholas Humphrey and applied them directly to a scenario of our origins. Out of all the species on earth, we are the only one that has achieved what Alexander calls "ecological dominance." We can and do live practically everywhere, under almost any ecological condition, simply by eliminating whatever threat the environment might pose to our survival. The elemental forces of natural selection—pestilence, predators, parasites, drought, climate, or what Charles Darwin called "The Hostile Forces of Nature"—no longer act upon us as they do upon other animals, and have not done so for some time. Human beings deal with predators, for example, by attacking them back—and as Alexander points out, we have done so with such thorough success in the past that we must now strive to preserve their remnants. But in the process of freeing themselves from the normal, external pressures of natural selection, our ancestors created a new force to drive human evolution forward—especially the evolution of the brain.

"The only plausible way to account for the striking departure of humans from their predecessors," Alexander says, ". . . is to assume that humans uniquely became their own principal hostile forces of nature." For better or worse, mankind invented itself.

The human mind, Alexander maintains, is the product of an evolutionary trajectory—a runaway intellect fueled by "interminable and intense conflicts of interest both within and between groups." However much a group might harbor internal conflict, the social unit whose members cooperated most effectively would have a genetic advantage over neighboring groups who were less adept at getting along for a common purpose. A "balance-of-power race" between groups would thus emerge, each forced to evolve ever finer cooperative skills simply to keep from being outcompeted—not to mention annihilated—by neighbors trapped in the same evolutionary spiral. The cliché of a "vicious cycle" can be taken quite literally here, for the net result would be a species intensely loyal to fellow group members, and viciously hostile to those on the outside. Us and them.

In Alexander's scenario, the runaway human intellect snowballs through prehistory, across the vestibule of recorded time, to eventually take up residence in the complexity of modern society, with vast communities—nation-states—engaged in an ultimate balance-of-power struggle played with nuclear weapons. This grim version of our origins leans heavily upon some recent, rather bloody revelations about the behavior of wild chimpanzees, our closest genetic relatives. After long believing that chimp society was fundamentally peaceful, in the 1970s Jane Goodall discovered to her horror that chimpanzees were capable of remarkably effective aggression against neighboring chimp groups, none the less violent for being carefully planned in advance and cooperatively perpetrated. In the most celebrated case, the males of one powerful community in the Gombe National Park study area systematically hunted down, attacked, and destroyed the males of the community next door. In three years time, the neighboring group had been utterly annihilated, its home range—and many of its females—taken over by the aggressors. Such violence, never before witnessed in the history of mammal research, was not the work of some band of simian sociopaths. In subsequent years, the victorious group was itself threatened and attacked by males from another nearby community. Similar territorial battles have been observed by researchers in other areas too.

If waging war (I see no reason to call it something else) is unique to chimpanzees and humans, then you have to wonder what traits the two species might share that would make it come about. Richard Alexander's answer is *female exogamy*. In chimpanzee society, the females of a community are the ones to leave the communities of their birth when they reach maturity. In almost all other mammal societies, it is the males who emigrate, with the females staying behind to form the social core of the group. The result among the chimps is a social structure centered around related males—all of them fathers, sons, brothers, half brothers, or close cousins.

You might expect such a tightly knit genetic fraternity to behave cooperatively, and they do. Chimps tend to forage alone or in small groups, but when one locates a tree heavily loaded with ripe fruit, he will often give forth excited pant-hoots and even drum with his palms on the resonant trunk of the tree—a din that quickly brings others to the food source. I have already mentioned their ability to hunt cooperatively. Chimpanzee males even show remarkable, if hardly perfect, mutuality when it comes to sex, sometimes lining up to copulate in succession with a single estrus female. Now we know they will also cooperate to kill their own kind when it suits their territorial interests.

"No wonder [chimpanzees] are territorial," explains field biologist Michael Ghiglieri, who has studied the chimpanzees of the Kibale Forest in Uganda. "If they were pacifists, or even individualists, their more coordinated neighbors would carve their territory into parcels and annex them. Thus armies are introduced into the natural arms race. Once this happens, solidarity between a community's males becomes essential."

Sound familiar? It should come as no great surprise that most human societies are also based on female exogamy, the males retained in the natal group to form potently cooperative, territorial units. Most modern hunter-gatherer groups also share the chimpanzee's "fusion-fission" pattern of social organization—small, impermanent groups in a community constantly separating and coming together again as resources allow. Among both chimps and humans, these reunions are often accompanied by noisy and elaborate displays of greeting, reaffirming the political unity of individuals who in fact are rarely all assembled in one place at one time.

Alexander's theory places a high premium on the social skills of manipulation and deceit. (Indeed, he believes it quite impossible that a thinking organ as powerful as the human mind would have evolved in a universe where everyone told the truth—there would simply be no need for it.) The best deceivers would be those skilled in *self*-deception, for no ruse is so successful as the one where even the deceiver is unaware of his own ulterior motives, and thus avoids the risk of betraying them. Self-deception would carry a powerful advantage in intergroup conflicts, especially as groups became increasingly larger. The members of small social units would be predisposed to cooperative behavior simply because they are closely related to each other. But as group size grew, the *us* in "us and them"—one's clansmen, countrymen, whatever—would no longer be close kin, and might in fact be total strangers. Any self-deception that would promote unity under such circumstances, such as a binding belief in tribal ritual and myth, organized religion, patriotism or ideology, would give the group a selective advantage in its conflicts with other groups. Even the human enjoyment of group-against-group forms of play—including modern sports—can be seen as a kind of no-risk practice for serious and deadly conflict.

Throughout this chapter I have warned against the dangers of drawing conclusions about human origins by thinking backward from modern humans. It would be easy to dismiss this harshly expedient view of the evolution of humanity as just another narrative told with its conclusion already in mind—Raymond Dart's killer ape again, warmed up with some sociobiological motivation and granted a scheming mind to go with his bone bludgeon. Richard Alexander admits that there is no unequivocal evidence in the fossil record revealing that our intellects rose on a tide of violence, manipulation, and deceit. But he quickly adds that there is no evidence to the contrary either. He can cite the mass of material documenting the ubiquity of warfare and aggression since the beginning of recorded history. In the modern world he can turn for support to the savage lives of the Yanomamö of the Amazon, where a quarter of all males die in warfare, or to the Hewa of New Guinea, where the murder rate is reported to be eight people per thousand per year, or for that matter to Auschwitz, Nigeria, or Cambodia. He can then point to the newly discovered belligerence of chimpanzees, and declare that the burden of proof lies with those who insist that long ago when the curtain was drawn, Lucy's Children matured under a halo of altruism and mutual trust.

At the very least, Alexander's theory, and the recent emphasis on social intelligence in general, suggest some exciting new questions for research. Did the origins of the "Machiavellian" mind have anything to do with the sudden emergence of *Homo erectus*, or were humans in the early Pleistocene still struggling more with the environment than with each other? When did our ancestors achieve "ecological dominance"? What about brain size—did it grow gradually through human evolution, or did it accelerate through time? If humans and chimpanzees exclusively share the social conditions for an intellect-enhancing balance-of-power race between groups, then what accounts for the cleverness of the other great apes—or for that matter, the keen intelligence of dolphins?

Before we can answer these questions, we need to know more

about the environments that our ancestors lived in. We need more knowledge on the intelligence of living primates, and how it is shaped by social conditions. We need to better understand the structures of the human mind, the roots of consciousness, the origins and evolution of language. We must have more information about human group sizes and population densities on the ancient landscapes. We have to comprehend more about the genetics of behavior, and the way evolution proceeds in a species struggling free of the mechanisms of natural selection that bind all others to their habitats. Above everything else, as a prerequisite to progress, we need more fossils—fossils that can tell us more about what our ancestors really looked like and how they might have behaved. Every specimen we have in hand is like a brushstroke on a canvas that has been bleached out, pulled to pieces, and scattered by the wind. We need to find more of the canvas and re-create its original colors. We need to know more. We need to know.

Epilogue

Of all the wonders, none is more wonderful than man,
Who has learned the art of speech, of wind-swift thought,
And of living in neighborliness.
                                        —Sophocles, *Antigone*

THIS STORY BEGAN IN A hotel room in Dar es Salaam. Scarcely a month later I was back in Dar again, staring out a window of the Embassy Hotel. The city moved through its day with the same, familiar rhythms of amiable confusion and ragged purpose. On the crowded sidewalks, street vendors displayed frankly utilitarian objects on wobbly card tables: pads of colored paper, sewing needles, thermos liners, secondhand rubber stamps. In the streets, the overstuffed buses lay in traffic jams like beached whales, waiting for a light to change and carry them away on the flow.

All was as it had been, except for one tiny addition. Ten blocks away, a handful of blackened bone rested in a locked safe at the National Museum. I was waiting for a VW minibus to take me to the airport, with a stop at the museum to pick up the fossil. The day before, the Department of Antiquities had agreed to loan the skeleton to the Institute of Human Origins to complete research on the specimen, publish an analysis, make casts, and give American scientists a chance to examine the original. The Dik-dik Hill hominid would then return to a permanent home in the museum in Dar. The Tanzanians were delighted by the summer's success. The discovery confirmed their hope that Olduvai Gorge would have a future as well as a past, a future growing under the management of Tanzanian scientists with their own national interests at heart.

The discovery of the new hominid would mean a great deal to the future of the Institute too, in winning support for subsequent expeditions to Olduvai and beyond. But as I sat in that hotel lobby in Dar, I was thinking more about what it meant to me personally. Field paleoanthropologists are often called "fossil hunters," as if our discoveries were trophies to be brought back and held up as testimony to our prowess. If I felt any satisfaction, it was not the hubris of the hunter, but the quieter pride of someone who had participated in a successful rescue mission. We had snatched those bones from the nameless obscurity that awaited them, and given their long-vanished owner a new, empirical identity. Two millions years after her death, this little female's remains had taken on a meaning incalculable to those of her time. We had given her a part in the organized wonder we call science.

But pride was the least of my emotions. I knew that a more important rescue mission had taken place, one in which the roles were reversed. In a real sense, *I* was the one imperiled a few weeks before, and it was the Dik-dik Hill hominid who had done the rescuing. With the fossil in hand, what I felt most was *gratitude*, understandably to Tim and to the others who had worked so hard to bring it to light, but in an oddly personal way to the hominid itself, who had shown the consideration to turn up just in time to save me from my own devils. For years I had been pinning my career on a return to Ethiopia, the locus of my early success. Over time that success had become a kind of curse, as if my future were in hock to my past, with "another Lucy" the only hope of redemption. This hominid was not Lucy. She was a fascinating new piece of the human puzzle, but one that would generate as many bewildered looks as cries of "Eureka." Precisely for that reason, she was much more typical of the way this science proceeds toward its goal: each new discovery a tiny prism to catch the light from what we know and split it apart into new patterns of possibility, sharper questions, more certain uncertainties. Thanks to the Dik-dik Hill hominid, I was part of that process again. To have organized the expedition that found the skeleton, to have experienced the exuberance and the disappointments in the field, made me feel like a scientist again, not a "spokesperson." I did not need another Lucy anymore. I just needed a chance to work.

A day later, I was flying across the Atlantic, sipping a glass of wine and listening to *Tosca* over the earphones, the hominid in an orange North Face bag beneath my seat. When I got back to Berkeley, one of my first acts was to write Mary Leakey to let her know about the discovery. Late in September I received a brief note of congratulations from her.

"The last hominid allocated by me was OH61," she wrote. "Your skeleton thus becomes OH62."

So now the specimen had an official name. What it lacked in romance it more than made up for in economy: "The Dik-dik Hill hominid" was too long a label for so tiny a creature.

Through the fall Gen Suwa worked on piecing together the tooth fragments, trying to complete as much of the puzzle as was humanly possible. His efforts helped us correct a few mistakes we had made in the field when we had been joining fragments without the advantage of casts of other hominids to refer to. But nothing Gen discovered overturned our initial characterization of the fossil as a female *Homo habilis*. In May we announced the find in *Nature*. There, and in the press reports that followed, we told it the way we saw it: To judge from this specimen, in body size and build the first human species was a lot more primitive than had been thought.

We were curious about how our colleagues would receive the new addition to the hominid family. One of the first to pay it a visit was Henry McHenry, a paleoanthropologist at the University of California, Davis. As it happened, Henry had just completed an extensive study estimating the body sizes of early hominid species, including *habilis*. When I laid the bones of OH62 out on a table for him, Henry laughed.

"Such a tiny body!" he said. "It looks like I've got some more work to do." Fortunately, there was enough time before it was published for Henry to revise his study to include mention of OH62.

Meanwhile, the skeleton's long arms did not go unnoticed by the combatants in the debate over how much time our ancestors were spending in the trees. Randy Susman and Jack Stern had earlier analyzed the original *habilis* foot and hand bones from Olduvai, and had concluded that the first *Homo*, like earlier hominid species, was still committed to a partially arboreal life-style. Needless to say, they were delighted by our discovery.

"People said we were crazy," said Randy in an interview with *Science* magazine. "But now look at OH62. It's wonderful. The very long arms go perfectly with what we've said about the hands."

"*I've* looked at OH62, and I *still* think they're crazy," said Owen Lovejoy when he read that article. Owen had first seen the skeleton a few weeks after we'd returned from the field. Nothing about it made him an ounce more charitable than before to the Stony Brook team.

"They've got it ass-backwards again," he said. "Sure, OH62's arms are long relative to modern humans, just like Lucy's. But what matters is that they are *shorter* than the arms of their ape ancestors. If a species is still climbing in the trees, but it has sacrificed to bipedality all the advantages of a lower limb adapted for climbing, then why on earth would it further hobble itself by reducing the length of its arms?"

Clearly, it will take more than one new fossil to settle this dispute. Perhaps Bernard Wood's evaluation of OH62 comes closest to the truth:

"The new find rudely exposes how little we know about the early evolution of *Homo*," he wrote in *Nature*.

Since the summer of 1986 I have led two more expeditions to Olduvai. Meanwhile Prosper Ndessokia began to direct his own field team at Laetoli. One of our long-standing goals was to train local scholars to conduct their own research projects, and it was very gratifying to visit Prosper's excavations and see the A. *afarensis* fossils his team was finding. In 1988, Prosper also found a hominid lower molar near the type site of *H. habilis* in the Gorge. The same summer, high up in Olduvai Bed III deposits near the Castle, we discovered the fossil skull of a giant baboon that had been washed out by the spring rains. I had surveyed the area the year before, and I would almost swear that the baboon skull was not visible then. Soon the rains will come again to Olduvai. I wonder what treasures they will wash out next.

During those expeditions I would often pass by Dik-dik Hill. The edges of our excavation were already eroding, and the mound of backfill we had accumulated was compacted by the weather, rapidly becoming just another feature in the landscape. I could not go near the place without feeling an itch, a tickling absence. After two years, I still had an urge to find that missing distal femur of OH62. We had already announced the find and speculated about its weirdly ape-like build. But without the rest of that thighbone, we were resting on hunches—educated hunches, but hunches just the same. How nice it would be, I thought, if I could sit down here on a lump of basalt, reach down, and pull that distal femur out from under a sisal bush. But OH62 had already obliged us as much as she was ever going to.

Without the rest of the bone, there was still a way we could firm up our estimate of the femur's length, which by extension would tell us how long the hominid's arms had been in proportion to her legs. The shaft of thighbone we had in hand revealed many important anatomical landmarks—holes where blood vessels passed through, for instance, and grooves, crests, and ridges where muscles had once attached. We would easily measure the distances between these various landmarks. And we could do the same on whole femurs, whose overall lengths were known. By plotting some ratios, we could work backward and predict the length of OH62's femur based on the distances between key anatomical landmarks on the bone. In essence, we could "find" that missing distal femur statistically. We would need to conduct the same kind of analysis on the humerus too. Though its shaft was intact, we lacked the articular ends.

To do the job right, we had to allow for the natural variation in bone proportions that exist within any sampling. We would have to take measurements on scores of femurs—modern humans, and chimps too—and calculate a range, which could then be applied to OH62. The best place I knew for that sort of work is the Hamann-Todd Anatomical Collection—racks upon racks of catalogued bones, housed in the basement of the Cleveland Natural History Museum, where I had started my career twenty years before. Cleveland held another lure. Owen Lovejoy could come up from Kent State and lend his considerable intellect to the analysis. Bruce Latimer, Owen's former student and curator of the Hamann-Todd Collection, could contribute his expertise as well.

In October of 1988, Tim White, Bill Kimbel, and I, accompanied by Israeli anthropologist Yoel Rak, flew out to Cleveland with the OH62 bones. Owen and Bruce met us in the museum lab.

"How do you know that all these bones belong to the same creature?" Owen challenged, even before we'd had a chance to say hello. He had hinted at this possibility before—that what we were calling OH62 was really a mix from more than one skeleton. Wasn't the radius too big for the ulna? The tibia too large to match the rest? Of course, if we really had found the remains of more than individual, then all our speculations about limb proportions were so much wind.

"Come on, Owen," I said. "What are the chances that there would be two hominids lying out there so close together? We've got no duplication of parts. The same color, the same degree of wear—it all adds up to one hominid."

"Prove it to me."

We attacked that problem first, taking measurements on dozens of chimp and human skeletons randomly selected from the collection. If the dimensions of OH62's bones, matched up against each other, fell out of the range of variation in our random sample, then we had a real problem. After the better part of two days of work, Owen was convinced.

"Okay, one hominid," he said. "But you still don't know how long the femur is."

"That's what we came here to find out," said Tim.

We got back to work. It did not take long to pin down the length of OH62's humerus to a range of only a few millimeters. The femur was trickier. After a couple of days spent hunched over our calipers, we realized that the fragmentary nature of the bone would never let us accurately reconstruct its exact length. But based on the distances calculated between a number of different anatomical landmarks, we could estimate the femur was slightly longer than Lucy's, somewhere between 300 and 330 millimeters, or roughly a foot long. When we compare the humerus of oH62 to its femur, it proved to be about 85 percent as long, suggesting proportions much like Lucy's.

Before returning to Berkeley, we had the chance to put the fossil through one more series of tests. A former student of Lovejoy's, Jim Ohman, had taken a job at Picker International, Inc., a leading manufacturer of CT scanning machines and other X-ray medical equipment. In Picker's factory just outside of Cleveland, Ohman had a demo of their latest, most powerful machine set up and ready to go. Picker had generously offered to lend us some time on the machine.

We were thrilled. With a CT scan, you can look *through* fossils at their interior structure. You could do the same with a hacksaw, of course—but no one would ever let you near a museum again. CT scans do no damage to the specimens. In the past few years, they have often proved useful in rooting out otherwise unreachable information beneath a fossil's surface. It was only on the basis of a CT scan, for instance, that the four-million year-old femur fragment that Tim had found in 1981 was proved to be that of a bipedal animal—the oldest sure hominid known. The main problem with the technique is its cost—hence our gratitude to Picker for the loan.

On a rainy morning, Bruce Latimer and I drove out to the Picker plant, a huge, hangarlike building filled with a dull hum of activity. Bruce introduced me to Jim Ohman.

"The machine we'll be using is a Picker 1200 Expert, absolutely state-of-the-art," Jim told me. "There is no other machine available with this kind of resolution."

News had gotten out that a two-million-year-old human ancestor was going to be paying a visit, and several engineers were already gathered around the demo machine when we arrived. The scanner was huge, sleek, and black—almost regally high-tech. The centerpiece was a seven-feet-tall doughnut, called the gantry, surrounding a long platform. Housed in the gantry was a laser X-ray emitter and detectors. The whole unit could move up and down the platform, while the laser spun around to project from any angle. Each beam of the X ray through the subject on the platform—in normal circumstances, a patient's head—provided a cross-section of its interior. By compiling the data from a series of these "cuts," a computer attached to the unit could generate a three-dimensional view of interior anatomy.

It was into this futuristic device, designed for medical specialists to reach into the living human brain and pinpoint abnormalities, that we placed our ancient *Homo habilis*. We started with the humerus. Jim devised a cradle to hold the specimen steady under the laser beam, and I carefully set the bone in place. He made a series of adjustments to the controls, and then another engineer turned on the laser. We watched through a protective screen as the thin red beam struck the fossil at one end, moved a millimeter forward and spat out again, proceeding down the whole length of the shaft. The procedure took all of twenty minutes; ten minutes later, we had a clear 3-D image of the fossil dancing on a video screen. By sending directions to the computer, we could turn the image around, magnify it, stand it on end, or peer into its depths at any point we wished. After we'd gleaned what data we could from the humerus, we moved on to the ulna, then to the radius and the rest of the skeleton. The cortex of the arm bones appeared to be amazingly thick—more robust even than that of many chimpanzees. OH62 may have been a little hominid, I thought, but she was far from defenseless.

In the span of a few hours we had completed the electronic metamorphosis of the fossil, her most intimate dimensions securely reiterated onto hard disk. At some point along the way I was struck by the dizzying symmetry of this event: On a gray, wet October morning in Cleveland, a sample of the most sophisticated technology

Donald Johanson prepares the ulna of OH62 for CT-scanning. BRUCE LATIMER

ever devised was whirling around this little fossil, trying to help us fathom what made the first toolmaker tick. I listened in the darkness to the gentle whirs and throbs of the equipment, and to the engineers murmuring to each other in the argot of their calling. Each time Jim Ohman placed a bone in the cradle, I thought back to when we had pulled it out of the Olduvai earth—the quick joy of discovery, and the frustration that followed. I remembered too the first morning of surveying, when I had picked up that quartz hand ax off the slope at HWK, and felt in its heft the urgency of an ancient purpose. If the Dik-dik Hill hominid were not just a collection of bones, I wondered, but instead were lying here whole and alive on the platform, would she be as impressed by *our* tools, and by what we had made of the world?

I found myself thinking about another moment later on in the field season. One afternoon, we had quit work on Dik-dik Hill a little early and decided to take a ride out to a place called Shifting Sands, about five miles west of the Olduvai camp. It had been a particularly frustrating, particularly tedious day on the site—hours spent staring at dust and pebbles, silently picking out bone chips that we knew were meaningless to our purpose. We just wanted to relax and watch the sun set over the Serengeti.

Shifting Sands is a moving mountain—or more properly speaking, an "active dune." It was formed some two thousand years ago out of a shroud of black ash that lay across the plain miles to the east—very fine, windblown volcanic sand that pulled up into a bulky mass and began to march westward before the prevailing wind. As it crawled along (just over one and a half inches a day), the dune left behind two parallel sand ridges that extend from its flanks—sand that has been blown off by crosswinds and trapped in the grass. A person looking down from a plane can trace these ridges back two miles. As the dune moves along, it continues to lose its substance to the wind. Not long ago, Shifting Sands was only one of a number of such dunes dotting the plain in this area. From the air you can see the evidence of little geological tragedies—parallel tracks of sand, tapering to a "V" that marks the spot where the other dunes ended their brief journey and vanished.

We climbed up to the top of the dune and looked to the west. The sun obliged and descended gorgeously, like a thick bronze ball melting into the edge of the earth. But to me, the sun seemed to take with it more than the light. As soon as it slipped over the horizon, I felt a sudden draining of energy, as if the tiredness in my own body were somehow connected to a falling off, a giving up, in the whole visible world around me. While the others in the group slid down the windward side of the dune, I slipped down the front, into the leeward cul-de-sac formed by its flanks. I could hear Tim White and Bob Walter talking on the other side, but the sound of their words had no resonance, no depth.

It was a place that inspired bleak thoughts. I sat there on the ground, my back up against the cold black wall of sand, and I began to wonder why I was doing what I did, what purpose this obsessive search could really serve. You find the funding, you assemble a team, you work through the politics, then you fly across the ocean, and if you're lucky you find a scrap of bone or a tooth. When you get back, you poke and probe it and make as big a deal about it as possible. A question seemed to come from the depths of the dune itself. *Why do it?* I thought about going into some other kind of work, though I could not think what it would be.

Two years later, as I sat there in the Picker International factory watching the luminous, purloined images of OH62 coalesce on a video screen, I thought I could answer the question posed by the dune. The whole human career is the story of a species never relenting in its effort to pull itself free, by the sheer force of intellect, from the natural constraints that bind all other species to their biological fates. In one sense, that is a fantastic triumph—witness the machine before me, that would soon be leaving the factory to begin its real job of saving lives—lives that might have been lost only a few years before. But the cost of this "ecological dominance" has been equally fantastic. In playing out the full extent of our uniquely unaccommodating relationship with the environment, our species has engendered a powerful self-deception: the belief that we were separately created for a special destiny, with all other life on earth subservient to our own needs.

This self-deception must once have carried with it a real evolutionary advantage, helping our species spread over the globe and overcome the challenge of virtually every known habitat. But the rules are changing. In the last few decades, our belief in the earth as *merely* a resource for humanity has led us to waste and destroy whole ecosystems, even poison the biosphere itself. The idea of a special human destiny has never been true—now it is no longer adaptive either. Simply put, we are losing our ecological dominance. The environments we have created are becoming uninhabitable, and we may not be able to control them any longer. The ozone layer above us grows thin and tears, because our life-styles depend upon refrigerators, air-conditioning and Styrofoam cups. The Greenhouse Effect may or may not be a real threat to global agriculture in the next few decades, but either way, we do not appear able to do much about it. The "us and them" balance-of-power race between human groups that Richard Alexander talks about threatens to lose its adaptive value too. No matter whose side you are on, nuclear war will hardly increase your reproductive potential.

Under these circumstances, any effort to get the truth out about who we really are and where we fit into the rhythms of the earth seems to me passionately worthwhile. I would like to think that my vocation, the search for our origins, is a part of that truth-quest. It is not simply the romantic dalliance of a species in love with itself, a species that, having led the rest of creation to the edge of annihilation, has nothing better to do than dawdle in front of a mirror, reimagining its rise to greatness. Our shared curiosity about our beginnings is the emanation of a deeper urge, felt as wonder, to discover the true humanity that lies beneath and beyond the old deceptions, the outmoded beliefs. To my mind, the primitive little human we discovered at Olduvai Gorge underscores how closely and how recently we really are bonded to our primate pasts, and by extension, to the rest of life on the planet. It is not the final word on the subject, because there are no final words. Human origins will always be enigmatic. But if we keep up the search, each new fossil we find will tell us something more. I hope we will listen to what they say.

Bibliography

Of General Interest

Johanson, D. C., and Maitland Edey. *Lucy: The Beginnings of Humankind.* New York: Simon and Schuster, 1981.

Lewin, Roger. *Bones of Contention.* New York: Simon and Schuster, 1987.

Pfeiffer, John. *The Emergence of Humankind,* 4th ed. New York: Harper and Row, 1985.

Reader, John. *Missing Links.* Boston: Little, Brown and Co., 1981.

In addition to the popular works above

Alexander, Richard. "The Evolution of the Human Psyche," in *The Human Revolution,* eds. P. Mellars and C. Stringer. Princeton, N.J.: Princeton University Press, 1989.

Ardrey, Robert. *African Genesis.* New York: Atheneum, 1961.

Binford, Lewis R. *Bones: Ancient Men and Modern Myths.* New York: Academic Press, 1981.

————. *Debating Archeology.* New York: Academic Press, 1989.

————. "Human Ancestors: Changing Views of Their Behavior," *Journal of Anthropological Archeology,* 1985, 4:292–327.

————. *In Pursuit of the Past.* London: Thames and Hudson, 1983.

Blumenschine, Robert J. "Characteristics of an Early Hominid Scavenging Niche," *Current Anthropology,* August–October 1987, 28:383–406.

Bowler, P. J. *Evolution: The History of an Idea.* Berkeley, Calif.: University of California Press, 1984.

Brain, C. K. "The Evolution of Man in Africa: Was It a Consequence of Caiozoic Cooling?" Alexander L. du Toit Memorial Lecture No. 17, Geological Society of South Africa, 1981.

Brown, Frank, John Harris, Richard Leakey, and Alan Walker. "Early *Homo erectus* skeleton from west of Lake Turkana, Kenya," *Nature*, August 29, 1985, 316:788–792.

Bunn, Henry T. "Animal Bones and Archeological Inference" (review of *Bones: Ancient Men and Modern Myths* by Lewis R. Binford), *Science*, January 29, 1982, 215:494–495.

———. "Archaeological Evidence for Meat-Eating by Plio-Pleistocene Hominids from Koobi Fora and Olduvai Gorge," *Nature*, June 18, 1981, 291:574–577.

Bunn, Henry T., and Ellen M. Kroll. "Systematic Butchery by Plio-Pleistocene Hominids at Olduvai Gorge, Tanzania," *Current Anthropology*, December 1986, 27:431–452.

Byrne, Richard, and Andrew Whiten, eds. *Machiavellian Intelligence*. Oxford, England: Oxford University Press, 1988.

———. "The Thinking Primate's Guide to Deception," *New Scientist*, December 3, 1987, 54–57.

Cheney, D., R. Seyfarth, and B. Smuts. "Social Relationships and Social Cognition in Nonhuman Primates," *Science*, December 12, 1986 234:1361–1366.

Coles, Sonia. *Leakey's Luck*. New York: Harcourt Brace Jovanovich, 1975.

Dart, Raymond. *Adventures with the Missing Link*. Philadelphia: The Institutes Press, 1967.

Day, M. H., M. D. Leakey, and T. Olson. "On the Status of *Autralopithecus afarensis*," *Science*, March 1980, 207:1102–1103.

Delson, Eric, ed. *Ancestors: The Hard Evidence*. New York: Alan R. Liss, Inc., 1984.

Foley, Robert. *Another Unique Species*. Essex, England: Longman Press, 1987.

Foley, Robert, ed. *Hominid Evolution and Community Ecology*. London: Academic Press, 1984.

Ghiglieri, Michael. "The Social Ecology of the Chimpanzees," *Scientific American*, 1985, 252:102–113.

———. "Sociobiology of the Great Apes and the Hominid Ancestor," *Human Evolution*, 1987, 16:319–357.

Goodall, Jane. *The Chimpanzees of Gombe*. Cambridge, Mass.: Harvard University Press, 1986.

Harcourt, Alexander. "All's Fair in Play and Politics," *New Scientist*, December 12, 1985.

Harding, R.S.O., and G. Teleki, eds. *Omnivorous Primates*. New York: Columbia University Press, 1981.

Hay, Richard. *Geology of Olduvai Gorge*. Berkeley, Calif.: University of California Press, 1976.

Hay, Richard L., and Mary D. Leakey. "The Fossil Footprints of Laetoli," *Scientific American*, February 1982.

Herbert, Wray. "Lucy's Family Problems," *Science News*, July 2, 1983, 124:8–11.

Howell, F. Clark. *Early Man*, rev. ed. New York: Time-Life Books, 1973.

Isaac, Glynn. "The Food-Sharing Behavior of Protohominids," *Scientific American*, April 1976, 90–108.

Isaac, Glynn, and Elizabeth R. McGown, eds. *Human Origins*. Menlo Park, Calif.: W. A. Benjamin, 1976.

Johanson, D. C., and M. Taieb. "Plio-Pleistocene Hominid Discoveries in Hadar, Ethiopia," *Nature*, March 1976, 260:293–297.

Johanson, Donald C., Fidelis T. Masao, Gerald G. Eck, Tim White, Robert C. Walter, William H. Kimbel, Berhane Asfaw, Paul Manega, Prosper Ndessokia, and Gen Suwa. "New Partial Skeleton of *Homo habilis* from Olduvai Gorge, Tanzania," *Nature*, May 21, 1987, 327:205–209.

Johanson, D. C., and T. D. White. "On the Status of *Australopithecus afarensis*," *Science*, March 1980, 207:1104–1105.

———. "A Systematic Assessment of Early African Hominids," *Science*, January 1979, 203:321–330.

Johanson, Donald C., et al. "Pliocene Hominids Fossils from Hadar, Ethiopia," *American Journal of Physical Anthropology*, April 1982, Vol. 57, No. 4 (complete issue).

Keeley, Lawrence K., and Nicholas Toth. "Microwear Polishes on Early Stone Tools from Koobi Fora, Kenya," *Nature*, October 1981, 293:464–465.

Kimbel, W. H., and T. D. White. "A Reconstruction of the Adult Cranium of *Australopithecus afarensis*," *American Journal of Physical Anthropology*, February 1980, 52:244.

Kimbel, W. H., T. D. White, and D. C. Johanson. "Implications of KNM-WT 17000 for the Evolution of 'Robust' *Australopithecus*," in *The Evolutionary History of the "Robust" Australopithecines*, ed. F. E. Grine, in press.

Kinzey, W., ed. *Primate Models of Hominid Behavior*. New York: Plenum Press, 1985.

Leakey, L.S.B. "Exploring 1,750,000 Years into Man's Past," *National Geographic*, October 1961, 120/4:564–589.

———. "Finding the World's Earliest Man," *National Geographic*, September 1960, 118/3:420–435.

Leakey, L.S.B., P. V. Tobias, and J. R. Napier. "A New Species of the Genus *Homo* from Olduvai Gorge," *Nature*, April 1964, 202:7–9.

Leakey, M. D. *Olduvai Gorge, Volume 3*. Cambridge, England: Cambridge University Press, 1972.

Leakey, M. D., R. L. Hay, G. H. Curtis, R. E. Drake, M. K. Jackes, and

T. D. White. "Fossil Hominids from the Laetoli Beds," *Nature,* August 1976, 262:460–466.

Leakey, Richard E. "Hominids in Africa," *American Scientist,* March–April 1976, 64:174–178.

Leakey, R.E.F., and A. Walker "On the Status of *Australopithecus afarensis,*" *Science,* March 1980, 207:1103.

Lewin, Roger. "The Origin of the Human Mind," *Science,* May 8, 1987, 236:668–669.

Lovejoy, C. Owen. "Evolution of Human Walking," *Scientific American,* November 1988, 118–125.

———. "The Gait of *Australopithecus,*" *American Journal of Physical Anthropology,* 38:757–780.

Olson, T. "Basicranial Morphology of the Extant Hominoids and Pliocene Hominids," in *Aspects of Human Evolution,* ed. C. Stringer. London: Taylor & Francis, 99–128.

Potts, Richard. "Home Bases and Early Hominids," *American Scientist,* 1984, 72:338–347.

Potts, Richard, and Pat Shipman. "Cutmarks Made by Stone Tools on Bones from Olduvai Gorge, Tanzania," *Nature,* June 18, 1981, 291:577–580.

Rak, Yoel. "Australopithecine Taxonomy and Phylogeny in Light of Facial Morphology," *American Journal of Physical Anthropology,* 1985, 66:281–287.

———. "Lucy's Pelvic Anatomy: Its Role in Bipedal Gait," unpublished manuscript.

Shipman, Pat. "The Ancestor That Wasn't," *The Sciences,* March–April 1985, 43–48.

———. "Baffling Limb on the Family Tree," *Discover,* September 1986.

———. "Scavenger Hunt," *Natural History,* April 1984, 20–27.

Shipman, Pat, Wendy Bosler, and Karen Lee Davis. "Butchering of Giant Geladas at an Acheulian Site," *Current Anthropology,* June 1981, 22/3:257–264.

Small, Meredith. "Ms. Monkey," *Natural History,* January 1989.

———. "Social Climber: Independent Rise in Rank by a Female Barbary Macaque," unpublished manuscript.

Stern, Jack T., and Randall L. Susman. "The Locomotor Anatomy of *Australopithecus afarensis,* *American Journal of Physical Anthropology,* 1983, 60:279–317.

Stringer, C. B. "The Credibility of *Homo habilis,*" in *Major Topics in Primate and Human Evolution,* eds. B. Wood, L. Martin, and P. Andrews. Cambridge, England: Cambridge University Press, 1984.

Susman, Randall L., Jack T. Stern, and William L. Jungers. "Arboreality and Bipedality in the Hadar Hominids," *Folia primatologica,* 1984, 43:113–156.

Tattersall, Ian. "Species Recognition in Human Paleontology," *Journal of Human Evolution,* 1986, 15:165–175.

Vrba, Elisabeth. "The Environmental Context of the Evolution of Early Hominids and Their Culture," in press.

———. "Late Pliocene Climatic Events and Hominid Evolution," in *The Evolutionary History of the "Robust" Australopithecines,* ed. F. E. Grine, in press.

Walker, Alan. "Extinction in Hominid Evolution," in *Extinctions,* ed. M. H. Nitecki. Chicago: Chicago University Press, 1984, pp. 119–152.

Walker, A., R. E. Leakey, J. M. Harris, and F. H. Brown. "2.5-Myr *Australopithecus boisei* from west of Lake Turkana, Kenya," *Nature,* Augsut 7, 1986, 322:517–522.

White, T. D., and J. Harris. "Suid Evolution and Correlation of African Hominid Localities," *Science,* 1977, 198:13–21.

White, Tim D., Donald C. Johanson, and Wiliam H. Kimbel. "*Australopithecus africanus:* Its Phyletic Position Reconsidered," *South African Journal of Science,* October 1981, 77:445–470.

White, Tim D., and Gen Suwa. "Hominid Footprints at Laetoli: Facts and Interpretations," *American Journal of Physical Anthropology,* April 1987, 72:485–514.

Index

bones (*continued*)
  fracture patterns on, 150, 216, 217,
    218, 231, 237
  predator marks on, 218, 237, 239,
    242, 247
Bones: Ancient Men and Modern Myths
    (Binford), 138, 150, 153, 213,
    233, 240
Bones of Contention (Lewin), 95n
bony crest, on skull, 67, 68, 125, 130
Boswell, Percy, 62
bovids, 267
  fossil, 144, 225, 232, 259
Brace, Loring, 105, 106
Braidwood, Robert, 228
Brain, Bob, 217–219, 231, 237, 267
brain capacity, 19
  of apes, 54, 268
  of australopithecines, 83, 106
  of *Australopithecus afarensis*, 86, 107,
    108
  of *Australopithecus africanus*, 54
  of *Australopithecus boisei*, 67, 68
  of Black Skull, 124–125
  of chimpanzees, 86, 107, 268
  as criterion of humanness, 49, 50, 70,
    83
  of 1470 skull, 83, 106
  of *Homo erectus*, 50, 208, 269
  of *Homo habilis*, 70, 268–269
  of humans (*Homo sapiens*), 49, 223,
    263
  of Java Man, 50
  in microcephalism, 50
  of Neandertal Man, 49
  range of variation in, 268
brain enlargement, 194, 252, 262–266,
    276, 279
  flexibility conferred by, 262–263, 265–
    266, 269
  food access enhanced by, 263–266,
    267, 269
  knowledge of habitat conferred by, 222.
    265–266
  metabolic energy required by, 263, 269
brain fissures, 54
breccia, 54, 64
British Association, 51
Broom, Robert, 63–64, 65, 66, 67, 98
Brown, Frank, 96
Browne, Sir Thomas, 137
Browning, Robert, 17

brow ridges, 46–47, 48, 54
Brunhes, Bernard, 172–173
buffalo, fossil, 66
Bunn, George, 191
Bunn, Henry, 213, 240–243
  paper by, 237–238
Byrne, Richard, 274–275

C

caches of tools, 238–239, 240
canine teeth, 84, 177–178
carbonatite, 188
carnivores, 230, 234, 237, 239, 247,
    261, 263, 264, 265
  feeding behavior of, 218, 231, 242
  see also predators
Case Western Reserve University, 81
casts, 200, 203, 283
  endocranial, 53–54
  of Laetoli footprints, 189, 191, 196,
    198
  of Lucy, 33, 199, 206
  original fossils vs., 191, 192, 198, 199
caves, limestone, 218, 231, 251, 269
"Celebrity Chef" contest, 41–42
cetaceans, 263
  see also dolphins
cheek teeth, 177, 204
chimpanzees, 46, 56, 79, 80, 84, 86–
    87, 287
  bipedal locomotion by, 197–198
  brain capacity of, 86, 107, 268
  fear grins of, 275
  female exogamy of, 277–278
  hunting by, 225, 264
  male cooperation among, 277–278
  in primate studies, 225, 264, 275, 277–
    278
  territoriality of, 278
  tool use by, 267, 271
  warfare among, 277, 279
China, 57, 58, 67, 240
Cinderella (OH13) specimen (Olduvai
    Gorge site), 70, 76
Claiborne, Craig, 41
Clark, Desmond, 26, 27, 28, 29, 220,
    256
Clarke, Ron, 189, 191, 192–193
Cleveland Museum of Natural History,
    20, 28, 113

hominid behavior (*continued*)
transportation of food in, 225–226, 233–234, 241, 242, 244
violence in, 216, 219, 243–244
see also tools
Hominid Gang, 91, 96
hominids, 19–20, 26, 129
ages of, 111
contiguous cranial and post-cranial remains of, 158, 169
dolphins vs., 195–196
at Hadar site, 19, 21, 82–83, 84–88; *see also Australopithecus afarensis*
hiatus in fossil record of, 124
at Koobi Fora site, 81, 83–84, 89, 92, 96–97, 99
at Laetoli site, 101, 104–105, 106, 114, 187; *see also Australopithecus afarensis*
locomotion styles of, 193
at Olduvai Gorge site, *see* Olduvai Gorge site
at Omo site, 79, 130
teeth and jaws of, 107
at West Turkana site, 121, 124, 208, 269
Homo, 27, 50, 60, 62, 70, 83, 85, 123, 207, 283
australopithecines contemporary with, 88–89, 104–105, 111, 266–267
Australopithecus robustus vs., 266–267
emergence of, 260
in human phylogeny, 109, 111, 123, 128, 131
teeth and jaws of, 86, 177, 178, 204
see also human evolution
Homo aethiopicus, 123
Homo erectus, 96, 111, 208–209, 240, 252, 267
Acheulean tools associated with, 209, 220, 221, 269–270
age of, 208
brain capacity of, 50, 208, 269
diet of, 269
emergence of, 267, 269–270, 279
fire used by, 209
height of, 208
hunting by, 232, 269
Java Man as, 49–51, 58, 60, 161
language and, 209
locomotion style of, 193
at Olduvai Gorge site, 142, 150, 161, 220

Peking Man as, 58, 60, 67
population radiation of, 209
at Torralba site, 221
at West Turkana site, 208, 269
Homo habilis, 69–71, 83–84, 110, 111, 214, 235, 240
age of, 70
brain capacity of, 70, 268–269
diet of, 220, 244
foot structure of, 70
habitation patterns of, 265
hands of, 70
hunting by, 220, 263–264, 266
OH7 as type specimen of, 70, 169, 207
at Olduvai Gorge site, 69–71, 94, 142, 207, 214, 217, 283, 284
range of variation in, 267–269
taxonomy of, 71, 267
teeth and jaws of, 70, 71
tools and, 70–71, 209, 236, 265, 266
unresolved questions about, 267–269
Homo habilis OH62 specimen (Dik-dik Hill site), 201–209, 244, 250, 269, 281–290
age of, 207, 247
analysis of, 161, 166, 170, 177–180, 202–206
announcement of, 283
Australopithecus afarensis compared with, 166–167, 168, 204, 206
bicanine distance in, 177–178
colleagues' reactions to, 283–284
CT scanning of, 286–288, 289
death scenario of, 247
designated by Mary Leakey, 283
gender of, 206, 208, 283
height of, 166, 207–208, 283
Homo erectus compared to, 208–209
humeral-femoral index of, 206
indications of agedness in, 177, 204
missing distal femur of, 205–206, 246, 247, 284–286
morphology of, 178, 204, 206–208, 283
nasal margin of, 178
number of fossils found of, 250
primitive traits in, 207–208, 209, 283
reconstruction of, 170, 177–178, 202–204, 248, 283
taxonomy of, 160–161, 170, 203, 207, 283
teeth and jaws of, 158, 159, 161, 170,

JIM
LEWIS

SISTER

A NOVEL

Graywolf Press, Saint Paul

Copyright © 1993 by Jim Lewis

Publication of this volume is made possible in part by a grant provided by the Minnesota State Arts Board through an appropriation by the Minnesota State Legislature, and by a grant from the National Endowment for the Arts. Additional support has been provided by the Jerome Foundation, the Northwest Area Foundation, the Andrew W. Mellon Foundation, the Lila Wallace-Reader's Digest Fund, and other generous contributions from foundations, corporations, and individuals. Graywolf Press is a member agency of United Arts, Saint Paul. To these organizations and individuals who make our work possible, the publisher offers heartfelt thanks.

Published by *Graywolf Press*,
2402 University Avenue, Suite 203,
Saint Paul, Minnesota 55114.

9 8 6 7 5 4 3 2
First Printing, 1993

Library of Congress Cataloguing-in-Publication Data

Lewis, Jim, 1963–
    Sister : a novel / by Jim Lewis.
        p.   cm.
    ISBN 1-55597-178-4
    I. Title.
PS3562.E94755S4   1993
813'.54—dc20   92-34194

To my father and mother.

For my friends.

Preface

A life of rational planning, a happy life that owes nothing to luck, is necessarily independent of others; so it's a life without love, without deep company. There are careers devoted to indiscernible causes, to mere thinking or interminable prayer. They are not ours. There are hermits who prefer their seaside caves, armies made of forgotten mercenaries, astronomers who see only stars. But for us one motion of individual want sends trembles around a circle of dependents, until the whole helpless ring knocks and shakes like a tray of wine glasses in an unsteady waiter's hands. Any music they might make is random, involuntary and brief: one can't be still unless they all are, and they never are. How unbearable.

It's true I'm a singular creature, a mooncalf, a monster if you will, equally knocked about and knocking. I have been and I've known as much for as long as I can remember, and I remember everything. Still, I don't know why: maybe my mother had a scare while she was carrying me, or some cold spirit or spirochete wended its way into my company during the first days of my term, or some gene jumped from its proper place. Something happened, something moved or went astray and marked me as I lay there bathing blindly. I don't know: I have no myth or miracle to sustain me or help me understand, so I sustain myself with these idle dreams and inventions, and wonder if the weather will end. It hasn't ended yet.

My name is Wilson. Once when I was young I knew a pair of fierce young girls, was taken by one for love and by the other for rage, and we rattled the glasses until they broke. That's my story. I will pursue it now like a boy chasing an errant firefly with open hands on a dark summer lawn.

One Mississippi

1

On my seventeenth birthday I left my home in Lincoln, Nebraska, and went out for a walk into the world. It was a clear day, a Friday late in March. The sky was a deep and noble blue, the sun was invisibly bright, and the air was warming, though the shifting breeze still harbored traces of winter's bitterness. As birds chirruped outside my window I threw some clothes, a toothbrush, and a book into a large duffel bag, and then I closed up my house, locked it carefully, crossed the brown lawn beneath the still-bare trees, and without a last look back started down the muddy road. I was heading south towards the summer and whatever waited for me there; it had been years since I'd been able to tell a day when I wondered about it from a day.

There was a spring in my step as I passed the end of the city, and for a few hours I walked along the shoulder of Highway 80, heading east past the city limits, past the intersection where it met the road north, past the final mile of strip malls, gas stations, motels and convenience stores. Soon there was nothing to watch but the fence posts and farmhouses, so I began to sing a song of my own invention:

Snakes are quick and crows are bold
Rain is wet and snow is cold

Coal is black and gold is gold
I'll be young until I'm old

Over and over again I sang my little verselet, with the mood changing according to the slow entrances of opportuning noise; as I went by a herd of mooing cows it became a chorale, then it rocked with the rattle of chains on a passing truck, and as an airplane passed slowly overhead the drone added a meditative touch. This last tone lingered for a few minutes after the plane had disappeared, leaving me content and happily humming, and when a fat man in a beat-up station wagon took it upon himself to pull his car to the side of the road and ask me if I needed a lift, I thanked him and said No. He tipped his cap back on his forehead and without a word started off again, leaving me to myself.

As I went on my mind wandered, from the home I'd left behind to the world I hoped I would find ahead, and most of the day had disappeared beneath my feet before my thoughts were interrupted: I looked up from the ground as I rounded a long bend and saw a line of trucks parked out in a field by the side of the road, with their cargo spilled out onto the grass: it was a carnival under construction. In the fading light of day the multicolored lights and bright paint seemed like futile stuff, no match for the amber after-noon. A Ferris wheel already rode above the grass, with its dark spokes spinning in place; next to it was a spider-armed contraption holding motionless cars; then a jerry-built street lined with painted booths, and a series of commission carts standing by the side, waiting for night and the folks who would make their way out in the darkness, their pockets filled with jangling coins. As I passed I could hear faint candy-colored music coming from the far end, but I kept walking; I was afraid some barker might spot me slouching across the state and come out to the highway to sign me up.

I wouldn't have stopped, no matter what he offered: I was look-ing for some concoction of pleasure and peace, a bottle full of unstable combinations, sealed like a pharmacist's healing syrup to prevent the fragile base from evaporating. My song went:

What's yours is yours, what's mine is mine
And I don't mind dying—
No, I don't mind.

2

In time the houses thinned out, and as evening began to fall I came upon an abandoned farmhouse. I couldn't tell how long it had been since a farmer had lived there and cared for the place, but it must have been a while: the house had been reduced to tatters by the weather, shutters hung slantwise from the face by single screws, and all that was left of the roof were strips of fading tar paper. On the ground by the side door there was a small pile of bricks that had once been a chimney. In places I caught glimpses of the horizon through missing slats in the walls, as if the house was a half-solved puzzle—Complete the Picture, or Find the Hidden Face—in a Sunday supplement. It seemed an inviting place to spend the night, so I walked up to the front fence and hied myself over it and into the mud in the yard.

I'd just started towards the doorway when—lo!—a group of pigs came trotting around from behind a backyard shed, big, black creatures with plug eyes and brutish snouts. They drove one another back and forth across the ground as they came towards me on their piggy-sharp feet. Ha! I yelled, and they broke into a seesaw gallop and abruptly turned away, kicking up clods of mud as they collided, and giving out with grunts and alarmed squeals. Their voices became dimmer as they disappeared around a corner, and then at last it was quiet again. There was no door to the house at all, and I found more pigs inside, lying lazily in the rooms; one turned her face up to look at me, snuffled loudly, and then dropped her head again and went back to sleep. I could hear the heavy scuffling of hooves on distant floorboards and feel the lingering heat from their hides; I could smell the deep odor of mud, of shit and sweet hay. There was a cast-iron stove lying on its side in the living room, and the door to the kitchen had been pulled off its hinges and propped against a wall. I made my way to the hallway and started upstairs, stepping carefully over the missing boards. On the second floor I found a landing, two or three decrepit rooms, and a second flight of stairs disappearing up into a dark attic, above which, through two separate holes in the roof, I could see the sky, already faded and softened like well-washed cloth. I put my pack down in one corner of the master bedroom and sat beside it with my back propped against a wall.

It was growing dark out: there was a mighty grey on the plains, and the air was suddenly flushed. From the open window I could see clouds gathering in the sky, grey-green with rain and electricity: it was as if my room were the housing inside some giant, archaic experimental apparatus, and I was the quivering element. I lay myself down in a corner, pulled my shoes off, put my pack under my neck with the sharp corner of my book pressed into my shoulder, and listened to the cars passing from time to time on the road outside. Shush . . . the sky thickened, a few fat drops fell at the head of night's advancing column, and then a full parade of rain began, to celebrate my first day of independence.

3

That night I dreamed about a man with arms that were wings. When I saw him his hair was burned and his skin blackened from some punishing fire that escaped his belief, as if he would always wonder what he'd done wrong. I was lying on my back and he came down to me suddenly, wrapped in a cloud of luminous mist amid which sheets of fire snapped in the wind, as if he were a refugee running from some imaginary, superlunar war. I was afraid he was going to speak, afraid of whatever blessing or brief he might bring, but he was empty-handed and silent. He looked at me, pecked once at my hip, and then bent his head down until it rested on his birdlike breast. Then he hid his face under the feathers, not out of shame, but as if to prevent me from recognizing him. I was so transfixed by the sight that I couldn't move; nor did he stir again; and the dream went on in a kind of stasis, as if some mechanism were stuck, until finally it began to fade, the figure slowly dissolving into a smear of grey and black. At the end the light flickered, until at last it was dark. I slept on another hour or two without any companion but the cold.

When I woke up it was morning and the room was bright with sunshine, and smelled of charred hair. There were ashes scattered across the floor; my back was stiff. In the opposite corner my visitor slept, with his arms folded over his chest and his body curled in on itself under a blue army jacket. I lay there, drowsy and half-awake for a few minutes, and watched him as he dreamed, thinking maybe it was me. I had my leg cramped beneath me, and I slowly stretched it out, too tired to rise. He turned over and briefly shook himself. Shuffle, edit. In time he opened his eyes and turned his small head towards me until I could see his face; it was expressionless, sallow and worn, and the flesh of his features hung from its bones so that his thin mouth dangled open. I could hear his short, fast breaths escaping. He was a grotesque, with his tiny, yellow eyes, dull hair, and his body bent and damaged.

As soon as he seemed to be awake enough to hear me I greeted him, but he didn't answer, didn't even nod or shake his head; still, his eyes moved from my face to the corners of the room, and then back again, and he put one small finger up to the side of his beak, bent over, and abruptly blew out the contents on the floor beside his bed. Then he got up and began to dress. I watched him as he hid his long, thin limbs underneath a flannel shirt with a tear in the sleeve and then pulled on a filthy wool overcoat, which he buttoned all the way up with cold, fumbling fingers. He had no hat. I got up and splashed some water on my face from a puddle under a leak in the roof, and then began gathering my things into the bag. By the time I'd finished he was standing shyly in his corner of the room beside a hole in the floorboards, beneath which I could see the fat black hillocks of the pigs as they rooted into the corners of the living room below. I motioned to him and he raised his eyebrows, but he didn't move, so I approached him and reached my hand out slowly. He offered his forearm to me like a blind man, and I felt the fragile bones beneath his clothing as my fingers closed around it; and then in soft slow motion I drew him out of the room and into the hallway, and we made our way to the head of the stairs. Together we paused while I shook the last sleep from my eyes, and then, while he leaned lightly on my arm, I guided him slowly down the steps with me, each one in turn, as if, like a cat caught in a tree, he'd scrambled up and couldn't get to the ground again without my help.

We stood together on the ground before the house, blinking in the clear blue light, with the morning horizon ahead of us and the night horizon behind, while the sky opened mechanically overhead like the slow ocular roof of an observatory. It was too early in the morning for there to be any traffic, so we crossed the yard, climbed carefully over the fence, and began down the road on foot, my paces outmeasuring his by half. After a mile or so had passed I stopped to look back at the house for one last time, perched there on the barren crest of the globe like the poorhouse in a cautionary fable. When I turned back again I found my companion staring at me with black pupils set in a yellowish cast. He quickly averted his eyes when my gaze met his. I'm not one to be looked at, he said.

I'm not either, I replied, and we set off again. As we walked I explained myself. I told him that I was a doctor's son, and that I'd left what home I'd had a year or two after my father died. I told him about my pursuit. I said I was prepared to ride as far south as

Mexico. The country, I said, was open below me like a stadium from the stands.

He nodded each time I paused, but when I told him I'd dreamed about him the night before he immediately stopped, turned to me wide-eyed, and said No! so forcefully that I shut my mouth. We passed a few long minutes in a silence broken only by the cold, quiet grinding of the gravel beneath our feet. A car.

Today is Saturday? he asked.

March twenty-first.

That makes it a fucking month, he said, and kicked a dun-colored stone out onto the blacktop. That seemed to be all he could come up with for the moment, so I waited. A yellow tractor went past, leaving behind parallel chevron-shaped mud tracks on the road, a small plume of black exhaust in the blue air, and a slowly Dopplering rumble in between. I could feel him gathering himself, drawing in the particles of his confidence and molding them into an invisible substance within him, and when the mass was reached he stopped again and cleared his throat with a rattle. Have you got any money? he said while he stared at the rubber marks where a car had skidded off the road. I reached into my pocket for a coin, but I thought better of it when I caught the look on his face, and in-stead I fetched my wallet out of my jacket, plucked out a bill, and turned it over to him. He treated the note as if it might be made of flash paper, holding it between his fingertips and watching it for a moment to see if it would disappear in a burst of pale green, spend-thrift light. When he was satisfied that it was immutable he folded it carefully and tucked it into the breast pocket of his shirt.

He began to walk again, but I stopped him by putting my hand on his chest and I asked him his name. Well . . . he paused and cocked his head. Jones, he said, then he shrugged. All right. Jones, I said. He looked out across the field at the ho-rizon. Are you leaving?

I guess I am, he said, as he reached out and took my hand in his. It was dead cold and dry. Then he leaned forward, tugged my arm until I stood above him and my face passed a shadow over his, reached up on his toes, and kissed my mouth . . . I could feel the sun on my neck and his heart beating against my chest, smell his dirty breath, see his white eyelids lowered an inch from mine. It was a long moment before he released me from his grasp, and when he did he turned and started out into the field by the side of the road. I stood on the shoulder and watched him for a while as he walked out into the long grass, tilting from side to side on his paces, until he dwindled into a dark point and then disappeared. I could taste the salt and smell of his mouth all morning.

4

I walked alone for a few hours, a raggedy man by the side of the road, covered in dust from the rigs that blew past me. By midafternoon I'd come to a small town over the crest of a dry hill. In the general store I bought a sandwich and a bus ticket to Chicago. I was a sightly thing, but the woman behind the counter was passing time with a delivery man, and she would have sold passage to the devil himself without noticing.

I'm going down to Reno in June, said the man, gesturing towards my ticket as she filled it out. She had one of those midwestern faces that looks like it's been drawn on a balloon; the string jerked and she nodded. He leaned over the counter and began to watch what she was doing, as if he was thinking of applying for a job along the same lines and wanted to see what it would take. Get a cheap ticket down and try my luck.

Oh, boy, she said. Just don't sit there and lose everything. My friend Katey . . . She turned the ticket around and slid it across to me, then disappeared behind the refrigerator case. He pulled a pack of cigarettes out of his shirt pocket and lit one, shiffed his breath in through his teeth, and sighed out a small plume of ashen smoke.

Fifteen-fifty, she said to me when she returned. They stood qui-etly while I counted out the money, but neither of them looked at me; they were simply being polite to my parting wages. He scanned the covers of the magazines in the rack beside him, and as I took the bag and started for the door he pointed to a copy of a tabloid and made a comment that I missed, and she laughed so loudly that I looked back, and saw her hand clasped over her mouth to keep her teeth from showing.

As I sat on the curb outside and waited a state trooper's car pulled to the corner and stopped. The signal changed to green, but the car didn't move; the officer had his head tipped up while he watched me through his rearview mirror. I brought out my sand-wich and slowly unwrapped it. The signal was red again. A black-bird on a telephone wire across the way raised his wings and started up into the sky, and I removed a flaccid green spear of pickle from the waxed paper and deposited it back in the bag. When the signal changed the trooper pulled away from the curb, made a U-turn, and disappeared. The bus was the next vehicle to heave up the road.

It was night when I arrived in Chicago, and the city was glitter-ing in the misty sky, hovering like an enormous craft in the hot, tangerine glow of its own illumination. I immediately felt a kind of rapture, and I spent an hour or two just wandering north, duck-ing past the pedestrians on the narrow sidewalks, stopping to stare through a store window. When the lights and the traffic began to thin out, I turned right and strolled over a few blocks, crossing the highway and making my way across a wide strip of grass until I reached the deep edge of the lake. There were orange lights out in the water, the faint sound of wavelets slipping at the shore. As I walked south along the stone wall I came upon a man and a woman, lying out in the darkness. She was long-limbed and red-haired, and she was stretched out on her back with her hands clasped behind her head. He was half-reclined beside her. As I ap-proached I heard him laugh as she said, I hit him with a piece of, like the thing from a bicycle. I must have been eleven. The black lake swelled up to meet the black sky. Slowly he bent over her, big-shouldered and dark. She closed her eyes, smiled slightly, and let him gently kiss her. Then she pushed him away and sat up, looked quickly at me, and pulled her white jacket around her middle. Molly, he said, and started to protest, but she shushed him softly as I passed.

The depot was empty by the time I made my way back. According to the clock over the door it was two in the morning; according to another near the ticket windows it was ten to three. For a few hours I slept on a brown bench in the waiting room, dreaming quick, static dreams interrupted by night's obscure motions around my real body, until they melted together into a single strange document in which the pictures don't illustrate the words. When I woke up the next morning there were people all around, making a traffic island out of my bed. I caught the first bus south.

It was seven hours just to Missouri, and I dozed by the window as the blue fields and small towns passed. For a while we raced a train on a set of tracks beside the highway; we gradually lost. My first seatmate, a silent man with a long, pale face, disappeared somewhere in the lower Illinois plains, leaving behind a Chicago newspaper that car sickness prevented me from reading. My second was a sweaty woman with a fidgety daughter across the aisle, whom she ignored until the shining parabola of the St. Louis arch appeared on the horizon. Is that where Grandma lives? asked the girl. It's not Grandma, it's Julie, her mother snapped. Now hush up.

And I remember Memphis the following day, the bus stop a tin building on the south end of town where we sat for an hour or so. The driver left the engine idling, and it rumbled as if it were restless. Across the road there was a diner, and I stretched my legs and stopped in for some listless breakfast, taking a booth so I could stare out the window. We were at an intersection and it was the middle of a weekday morning; a pickup passed with an old man planted in the driver's seat, staring carefully out through the windshield, his hands gripping the wheel. There were some black children walking in the street, laughing, and a teenaged boy lying back on the hood of his car in the parking lot of the gas station across the street.

South of Memphis the highway rose and sank as it passed through uneven fields. From time to time the bus would pull over to an exit, and we'd take a few minutes to stop at some small town and drop off a passenger. We were headed towards Louisiana when I first saw the Mississippi River in daylight, running wide, great and brown at the edge of the highway, a thick spine, storied home to Br'er Rabbit, and John Henry, and Stagger Lee. We followed by its bank for a few hours, and then the driver turned off to stop in a small city that spread east from the bluffs.

It was the county seat, a few hundred years settled, and there was profit there, collected like silt from the river; I could see it in the big old houses we passed, in the neat shops and flush air of the townspeople as they went about their business. When we pulled into the depot I asked the driver to get my bag from beneath the bus. Your ticket's to Houston, he said as he climbed down from his seat. You sure? I was sure: I had felt a prescient shiver, a bit of un-caused knowledge as I sat, and I believed it was the right place for me to settle.

Diesel smoke hung in the afternoon air, and a few cabdrivers leaned against their cars. One of them answered my first question by pointing across the highway to a motel. I scrambled between the traffic, and within a minute I was in a room with my bags dropped inside the door. After I showered and shaved I turned the television on and began a nap that lasted until I was awakened by the sound of the couple next door arguing. From the window I looked out into the alley and the houses beyond, anonymous buildings with shut windows and broken roofs, left in a pile beneath the darkening sky like playthings on the floor of some busy child's bedroom. With one fingertip I tapped the glass a few times, and then I turned away and went to bed.

5

The city was small enough that I could circle it in a long day's walk; I would leave my room in the morning, stroll from one end of the shopping district to the next, and then hike out for a mile or so to the high school and come back around, past pretty churches and quiet, carefully trimmed lawns, and I was always home before dinner. Each day I made a slightly different course, down shady streets fragrant with magnolias and oaks, across a footbridge that spanned the highway, along a path above the river. Within a week I had the whole town fixed in my mind, and I bought a copy of the local paper.

That first morning I went looking for a place to stay, and by noon I'd taken a room above the garage behind a house on the south side of town. My landlady was an elderly woman who lived alone among the sort of impeccable furnishings that only those one step above ruin bother to maintain; every picture and brass lamp was perfectly placed, the carpets were newly vacuumed, the curtains were drawn just so, as if housekeeping alone would keep the specter of poverty away. I don't usually take in tenants, she had said as she sat me down with a cup of tea at one end of a firm couch and slowly lowered herself onto the other end. I just have to these days—she quickly glanced at the floor—because my paycheck, I work for the local school board, you know, isn't enough, even with my husband's pension. I set the cup of tea down on a coaster and nodded. Anyway, she continued, you seem like a nice young man. She paused for a second as if waiting for me to contradict her, and I suddenly noticed, from the tentative way she reached for the plate of cookies on the table before us, that without the glasses suspended from a string around her neck she was nearly blind. Would you like one? she asked. I said, No, thank you, and she set them down again carefully.

As she walked me up an outside set of stairs to a room above the garage she talked on about the town and its history and what there was for a fellow like me to do there. I don't get out much myself, she said as she fumbled with a rusty key in the rusty lock. They were lines from a country movie that she had memorized years before, and she played the part slightly nervously, as if she were trying to please a director in the shadows over my shoulder. Things were certainly different when my husband was alive. You couldn't keep me in then.

The room was small and the ceiling was low, and as I listened to her I looked around; there was a bed and a desk, and through a half-open door at the top of a few stairs I glimpsed the corner of a small, dark bathroom. She reached up to touch a polished lens, and asked me if everything was to my liking. I said it was and dropped my bag down on the bed, and she resumed her talk.

Age bores some into quietude; others it makes chatter like bone white dice on a hardtop table. She went on for a while ... Somewhere outside a phone began to ring, rang and rang, and stopped. The sun moved a shadow from the window frame across a stain on the floorboards. Thank you, ma'am: long company is a lesson in time's disorder, which every lingering child must learn someday. Well, I won't bore you anymore, she said at last, but if you need anything you just come down and ask me.

9

The next morning I walked into town, bought a paper from a newsstand, and settled down to breakfast in a hotel restaurant. Weather mild, the bond bill failed, a suspicious fire in a riverside warehouse, Congress debates the law of averages. When I reached the help wanted ads I began to circle the paragraphs. At midmorning I called a gardening firm called Turner's from a phone booth on the street; just after lunch I stopped by (berry blue trucks in the parking lot, grass green bench inside) and had a short interview with a distracted manager. Ageless, boyish, mannish, mischievous, I added a full seven years to my age. He never bothered to look up from my application, and I was hired to start as an assistant the next day.

At first it was just work, and no more. With the dispatcher's assignment in hand by ten we used to arrive at a house by mid-morning, park in the driveway, and get straight to it. I was on my knees pulling weeds in the morning, planting bulbs in the after-noon, mowing lawns in the evening. I was left alone most of the time, and before long I'd found a rhythm that helped me pass the days effortlessly. It's true I hadn't settled into a proper life — I had no friends, no pastime — but I didn't worry. On the bus to work one morning I spotted an old Ford in a passing driveway, with a hand-lettered *FOR SALE* sign in the window. I went back for a sec-ond look that evening; it seemed solid enough, so I rang the door-bell and asked after it. The owner was an eccentric, excitable man with a white, waxed mustache who jabbered as he popped the hood and touched each of the engine's parts as if they were talis-mans. As I counted out the money into his open hand he danced from one foot to the other, and as I drove off I saw him in the mir-ror, waving good-bye.

7

Standing on the deck of a standing ship, a sailor looks for coming waves in the subtle swells of the grey-green hori-zon. The dark water rises far in the distance, and he waits for the long causes to build — but it's simply the random motion of the sea; it never approaches; it has no effect. So I stood and watched for my future, looking for a reason in the distance that would pick me up like a wave and bring me up onto the shore. It never came: in-stead, a creeping tide, an undertow, moved me quietly along.

One morning about a month after I'd started work I received a new assignment. Wilson! the dispatcher said sharply, and as I ap-

proached he wiped his hands on his shirt before picking up the yellow slip that lay on the desk in front of him. Scratch. He folded it
carefully in two, flattened the crease with a dirty thumbnail, and
pushed it through the mouse hole in the bottom of his window.
Brand new, he said. Don't fuck it up.

The address was far down a street called Cypress. I remembered it from my first survey of the town; it was on a hill that began
where the playing fields of the public high school ended, and as
our truck rattled through the wide, tidy rambles, with their
wrought-iron lampposts and broad sidewalks, their centuries-old
trees making dappled shadows on the unbroken asphalt, I rolled
down my window and took in the confident scent of lawns and
flowers, and I remember wondering what hidden manufacture
made such perfume possible.

The house itself was hidden behind tall, well-groomed hedges,
marked only by a yellow barn-shaped mailbox with a nameplate
that said THE MILLERS. I stopped, shifted into half gear, lurched,
shifted again, and started to nose the truck into the driveway just
in time to miss colliding with a mouse-grey sedan that was coming
down. The driver, a plump man with a grey beard, braked and
pulled to one side, then waved to us peremptorily as we passed.
The oaks that lined the driveway were hung with Spanish moss,
but the house itself was nowhere to be seen, only knotted branches
with their mannered freight, and between the rough trunks the
edge of an immaculate lawn. A quarter of a mile passed before the
trees parted to reveal a great wooden frame in the shape of an oc-
tagon, with windows on every side, columns before the door, and a
balcony with a white railing on the second floor. I brought the
truck to a stop, quietly, gently, so as not to break the glassy picture into pieces, and my partners and I got down from the cab to
survey the place.

The grounds were cast back behind the house with the ease and
grandeur of a kept woman's blanket thrown lazily over her bed.
Out the kitchen door there was a patio built of flagstones, which
ended in a strip of grass leading to a stone square with a small

fountain in the middle. To one side of the square there was an herb garden, flanked with myrtle trees. To the other there was a hedge-row, and beyond it a long, gentle slope leading down to a few rows of flower beds, azaleas arranged so that paths of turf waded through them, and daffodils, camellias, begonias, and tea roses. On the far side, away from the house, the square ended in a short flight of brick steps, after which there was a wide, rolling field dotted with flowering dogwood, and among the boxwoods at the end there was a small pond stocked with goldfish, with a wrought-iron bench beside it. At the very bottom of the garden, as far away from the house as possible, a large gazebo, long in disrepair, peeked out from behind a large willow tree.

We spent the rest of the day poking around and preparing: the lawn had grown long since the last workers had been by, and the edges of the flower beds were ragged. From time to time I'd see a shade that slipped into the house behind the slamming of a screen door, or the flash of an anonymous midriff exposed as a window was raised, but aside from those glimpses there might have been no one there at all. The grounds were so large that a shout at one end wouldn't be heard at the other, and the house presented such a diffuse facade, as if to scatter attention back into the garden around it, that it seemed more a monument, solid, sufficient, and uninhabited, than a dwelling. But it was the garden, rather than the house in it, that enthralled me. It was as big as a mother's pride, and it was still untested. It begged for me, and I knew right away that it was the medium of my next years: I loved the place, and I vowed that afternoon to do whatever I could to keep it in my purview.

Over the following two weeks I made such a show of my efforts that I managed to have myself assigned there regularly, and soon it was simply understood that the Miller's garden was Wilson's trust, and Wilson's song was:

It's hard to know, it's hard to say
How we ended up this way

But work we must if work we can
Down to the last poor powerless man

In the evening I would return to my room, wash my hands, fix my-self dinner, and sleep.

8

My landlady had a back neighbor, a plump, white-haired old woman who was as deaf as my landlady was blind, though she didn't have the gadget to correct it. One weekend after-noon I'd helped her by moving a compost heap from one side of her tiny, perfect garden to the other, and I'd listened to her sing-song mumbles the whole time without once understanding a full phrase. From that afternoon on I was her second-best friend, and she used to hang her head over the fence behind the garage and watch me with her watery eyes as I walked up the stairs to my apartment. When I was halfway up she would call to me — well, not my name, but some collection of consonants — and I'd turn and watch her gesture as if she were trying to initiate me into some ur-gent, secret, and solitary society. I never knew why she was beck-oning, but I'd come down the stairs again until I was close enough for her to reach through the fence for my shirttail, which she held tightly between her fingers as she turned my ear. She would ask me a question — I knew it was a question only because her wordless voice rose — and then pause for an answer, and I'd nod and smile and finally insist that I had to go. As I walked away I could feel her eyes at my back. Her name was Mrs. Robbins, and I liked her; she struck me as a funny old woman, and I appreciated the comfort-able emptiness of her company.

One midnight when I couldn't sleep I let myself out and went down the stairs to the black ground, then crept to a clearing be-hind the building, between the back wall and the fence that separated it from Mrs. Robbins' house. I would have stared at the sky but the trees overhung the ground and I couldn't see, so I shinnied up the side of the building, passing from window frame to roof beam and then up onto the roof itself, where I could sit on the pitched tiles and watch the night sky. Mrs. Robbins' dog, a huge German shepherd with yellow eyes that were caked with unwashed sleep, came to the fence below, and together we sat there and listened to the breeze through the oaks. There was no moon, so I thought I'd serenade the stars, and this was the song that I sang:

If I don't get to sleep tonight
I'll lie awake instead,
And ask the lonely summer sky
Into my lonely bed

As I repeated the verse and began a chorus I heard the old dog below me: first he whined, then he keened, then he tipped his head back on his throat and began to howl, and together we harmonized, from ground and rooftop. When my throat became so sore that my voice cracked and I couldn't keep the tune, I applauded the animal, got back down again, let myself into my room, and immediately fell asleep.

The work I had was hard, and I slept well most nights, but once a week or so I'd find myself hopelessly awake, and I'd get up from my bed, leave my apartment, and climb the roof. As soon as I had reached the peak I'd look down and find Mrs. Robbins' dog waiting by the fence with his tongue hanging from his slavering mouth, and we would sing. In time our book grew into a makeshift and varied thing. There were songs to woo the sheriff's daughter and bad-luck ballads, gun battles, ghosts, and lovers' leaps. I would beat out the rhythm on the shingles, and get to my feet and bow to the neighborhood when we were done.

One night we drew old Mrs. Robbins out her back door. The

sky was cloudy and the moon was hidden, so I didn't have light enough to see her as she made her way tentatively across her back lawn, and my ears rang from my own voice, so I didn't hear her when she first called out curiously. I'd just paused between verse and chorus when she called again, and I immediately shut my mouth. But I'd forgotten which woman was deaf and which blind: I stood up on the rooftop and made a gesture to shoo the dog away, showing myself in the light of the moon. Her eyes met mine for a moment. – And the dog started barking and then ran at his mistress and began to circle her, howling and showing his teeth. She put her hand to her chest and screamed, stepped backwards quickly, and then planted her feet, threw up her hands, and said – Glory! as I slid down the tiles and hastened down a drainpipe on the far side of the garage. By the time I reached the ground she was scurrying towards her house, and I heard one last, embattled Ooh! as her back door shut behind her.

The following morning was wet; a shower just before dawn had kindly watered the begonias in the backyard and left a small shallow puddle in an ear-shaped indentation in the driveway. I could hear my landlady coming, hear the knock of her shoes on the wood, and then the double rap of her hand on my door. When I opened it I found her standing there, her glasses perched on her nose, two fingers from her right hand gently stroking the frame. Her voice quavered slightly as she spoke, and she was so quiet that I'm still not sure of the story she gave me – her nephew, his bad chest, the damp air, a favor for her sister. Between clauses she glanced up quickly to see my expression, but I could think of none to wear. She was asking me to leave, and rather than let her finish her painful story I held my hand up to interupt her, shrugged, tried to smile, and told her I'd be out in two days.

There was no singing either that night or the night after; it was bed and boredom, and by the time the sun came up on the second morning I'd packed my bag, put it in the trunk, eased the car out of the driveway, and was gone.

9

I had twenty-four dollars in bills and another two in change, and a week and a half to wait before my next payday; so I had no choice. The following morning I drove to work with my suitcase still in the trunk, and for the next few nights I parked my car in a riverside lot behind a highway restaurant about twenty miles out of town and arranged myself as comfortably as I could in the backseat. It was cold outside, and no matter how many layers of clothing I wore I couldn't keep warm enough to sleep well, so I lay awake for hours and watched the dark trees through the windshield, and between them, among them, the lazy river, the brown, loggy river, with its animal coils and heavy flow, and tortured myself with a ditty I learned in nursery school, a rhythm for spelling its name, with its improbable yips and hisses: MIS-SIS-SIPPI. I couldn't shake it; it stuck in my dry mouth like crumbs from a soda cracker even when, at last, I slept.

When morning came I'd wake before my little alarm clock had a chance to sound, peer out the clerestory behind me, taste my salty lips, and brace myself for another day. In the cold tile bathroom of a gas station a mile from Turner's parking lot I'd splash water on my face, and I'd swallow a cup of bitter coffee from a convenience store along the way. Eight hard hours later there was nowhere for me to go but back to the parking lot.

10

I've tried to write these, my confessions, many times, and each time I've stopped no farther than a few impoverished pages in, collected like so many useless pennies in a cup; and here I am, with a full fifty done. Will the book end so soon? Will our strange and powerful child now slink home, his ragged tail between his legs? No. Everything that I have promised will pass, or I am endlessly nothing.

The Mansion on the Hill

1

Oh, it's true I'm a magician. My mother was a witch, a Sycorax of the North Plains. When she left, she left me occult powers: I can conjure action at a distance, I can bring about the past, I can see around corners. I make accidents, and I can take them back. I put the stars in the sky, and I hung the moon among them; and I can move it at my will. I had no home, so I created one out of wishes and purpose.

It was a little past noon on a Thursday. I'd just finished clearing out the area around the Millers' fish pond and I'd stopped to wipe the sweat from my purblind eyes. It had been a long and tiring morning, and I found myself leaning on the handle of my rake, staring across the shimmering lawn at the gazebo at the foot of the garden, suddenly trapped in one of those dreamy moments when one's senses fix on a single spot while one's concentration evaporates into rare, alcoholic fumes. A brilliant red oriole – an omen I will always owe – darted across the scene, and when I blinked and broke my reverie I noticed the structure for the first time.

A few stairs led up to a hardwood floor that was elevated about four feet above the ground. There was a white painted rail around it and a semicircle of benches at its outer edge, with armrests that were worked up into pillars wound with yellow jasper, supporting a steep-sided roof. Behind it the Millers' property ended in a strip of trees, and beyond them there was another road; it had been placed so far from the house that it had no view to speak of. But it was a welcome little thing to me, because as I looked at it the point of its being gradually came into view. It was a forgotten folly, the generous whimsy of some past estate. I couldn't have known what had happened there once upon a time, a first kiss, say, or a late summer dinner, or tears from a runaway child; I couldn't have known how many days had passed since someone had last considered it. But I knew I could live beneath it peacefully, and if I could, I would. Anywhere I hang myself is home.

2

The rest of the day, spent tying saplings to stakes, passed so slowly that at one point early in the afternoon I thought it might have stopped, as if the sun had been rigged to a watch that had wound down. The evening crept along, my untasted dinner was endless, the time afterwards was a desert without dunes. I drove around for a while; I parked by the river, walked up the levee, and watched the dark barges glide by in the night. I counted the shivering pins of light on the far side. Then I got out and went down to the bank, crouched down in the tall grass, and found stones to throw out into the water, listening for the faraway *lunk* as they broke through the surface and sank. The sky was clear, the moon half full. The car steered like dirigible as I made my way back to the house.

There was a loose spot in the rusted fence and I wriggled under it and crawled on my hands and knees through the underbrush, pushing my pack ahead of me until I reached the edge of the grounds. There I paused, waited. . . . In the distance the dark house sat, strangely diminished, a shack under an enormous spiral projection of stars. The grounds were dark with gloom; it hung in patches in the air like morbid bunting. The trees were shivering in the breeze, the breeze smelled like sugar blossoms, and I could hear the high surrounding rasp of cicadas. A single light stared from a first-floor window. I raised a tentative foot and wondered. I could: who is more mooncalf than me?

The ground was spongy under my first step. With my second I trod on my breath and broke it in two; I left one half on the ground behind me and took up the other, and slowly tracked across the strip of lawn that separated me from the structure, with my back bent to make myself small. When I reached the base I tugged at a part of the lower fence until it came away in my hands . . . peered into the dark space . . . did, no, did something behind me move? I dropped down to a crouch and squeezed through the fence posts. The air inside was dank and mossy, and I could feel the crust of dirt beneath my splayed fingers. I pulled myself in, turned, and immediately shut out the pearl grey light and the shadows of the yard by pulling the section back into its exact place.

Inside it was cool, damp, and quiet, and so completely enclosed that I could feel the dark pressing against my fingertips when I put my hands up. I couldn't stand upright, but I could get to my feet, provided I stayed low on my legs, and I could move around freely. For a few minutes I followed the edge of the enclosing wall in a waddle, stopping here and there to feel for the right spot to make my bed, and when I'd settled on the proper place I unpacked my bag of things, stacked my clothes carefully in one corner, and put my book on the ground beside them. Then I lay down on the hard ground with my empty pack beneath my head and waited.

My ears rang from the silence. Ninety-nine, ninety-eight, ninety-seven, ninety-six . . . My eyes stopped searching. Nowhere. A minute went by. A blue black day. A month of Sundays. – And then with a sudden rush the room sprang open into the world, expanding until it became the world, a dark and unbounded globe that marked the limit of my possible life, a universal night in which I might meander, perfectly invisible, an invisible night, an unmoving giant in whose cavernous mouth I was soon asleep.

3

I was very comfortable that first thick night. I slept so soundly that my dream (I was the stage manager for an opera cast with orangutans) took in the ringing of my alarm clock (a warning that it was almost curtain time), and I was late for work. By the time I got to Turner's it was almost noon and the place was almost empty. I wandered down the cool, dark corridor, listening to the rhythm of my own footsteps and thinking of my new home; I was as spellbound and woozy as a lover on the morning after.

I found the dispatcher in the waiting room, frowning over some papers in piles on his desk. When he looked up and saw me standing in front of him he raised his hand and silently waved me away, accidentally knocking over half a cup of cold coffee with his paw. I waited while he bent down awkwardly to retrieve the mug, and when he stood up again he looked at me impatiently. Go on, go on, take the day off, he said. We'll make it up later.

So I went to town, where I mingled with the housewives saying hello to the shopkeepers and the men sunning their skins on the bench before the bank. In the hardware store I bought a little tin camping light and a few wool blankets, and then I stopped at the stationer's for a dozen sheets of black construction paper and a roll of tape. After I dropped the things off in the trunk of my car, I headed to the supermarket for some food and bottles of water. Along the way I counted the elm trees planted in little fence-squares at the edge of the sidewalk and began to write a song out loud, starting and stopping and searching my head for rhymes. As I passed an alleyway I noticed a figure loitering in the shadows of a loading dock – and just as I stepped up on the far curb he called my name – I recognized the voice as one I'd heard before, but I couldn't say where or when. I stopped and turned back.

He stood dead still in the shadow of a supporting post, did Jones; he waited patiently while I made my way down the block to him. As I neared him I noticed that his shoes were scraps and his

clothes were rags, and not even the bright sun shining on the immaculate town could make him more than a wretch. He greeted me
by waving a little and came up with a kind of pleasantly surprised
smile. You found this place? he asked, as if it was a secret town full
of legendary pleasures, an El Dorado of unspoken qualities.

I've been here about a month and a half.

Found work?

Gardening.

You'll like it here, he said. A refrigerator truck turned into the
bottom of the alley and started up towards us, bouncing on the
ruts in the road. It passed noisily, and when it reached the corner
of the main road it stopped at the sign, and then headed off around
the corner. Gardening. Fine, he said when it had disappeared.
Then he patted me on the shoulder, turned, and began down the
street in the direction from which the truck had come. He was
limping slightly, as if his feet hurt, and as I followed him with my
gaze I imagined him having shuffled across cornfields and grasslands, over hillsides and through woods, a mile at a time, tracing a
long, unlikely longitude line that intersected with my own path at
just that spot, fixed, in that town.

4

I spent the rest of the day sitting in the town library,
looking at engravings of gardens, and when it was dark I went
back to the Millers' grounds, let myself in under the gazebo, and
went to work on my shelter. The paper went up to cover the gaps in
the grillwork, and then I lit the lamp. The floor was scattered with
debris, a few pieces of wood that a careless workman had left
there, along with a single empty beer bottle and a sodden yellow
newspaper. A woman's black leather shoe lay unreasonably in one
corner. In no time at all I'd cleared them to one side of the space,
and when I was finished I swept the floor with a piece of card-

board, carefully bagged the trash, and set it inside the door. With my housework done I blew out my lamp and lay down for the second night.

5

The first pair of men who worked the garden with me made an early, dramatic exit, and I never had a chance to get to know them. Even their names are lost to me now, though I still remember a thirtyish man with a fortyish face, and a strange and unconscious habit of asking me to repeat everything I said to him, and then finishing the second sentence for me. One afternoon they had an argument in Turner's parking lot about a ten-dollar loan that one – I don't know which – had made to the other. Words turned to insults, and insults to blows; they were pulled apart by a passerby. Then the debtor went to his car, took a small handgun from the glove compartment, and chased the lender towards the warehouse. Just as the latter reached the front door a bullet caught him in the backside. The sun was just setting in the western sky; at the sound of the shot a bunch of birds in a tree started screaming. The victim crawled inside and lay there moaning. The shooter sat on the curb outside and wept until the police came.

I'd already gone home for the day, but I noticed the bloodstain on the floor the next morning, and the dispatcher called me into his cubicle so that he could relate the story to me in close quarters. Gave him another asshole, he said, his face creased in ugly amusement. When the cops came they just laughed and handcuffed him. They came around here again this morning; turns out he jumped bail in Michigan a few months ago. He rested his hand on my shoulder, raised his furry eyebrows, and guffawed until tears came. Hell. Anyway, he said, giving my forearm a warning squeeze, you're in charge of the Millers'. There are two fellows waiting outside; they'll be working with you now.

The first was a boy about my age whose maker had cemented his bones together with sticky wit, and had given him little more to hang on them. He didn't mind much; he said his name was Spot, and there seemed to be nothing that he minded much, and I who minded everything envied him just a little. The second was an older man, a small fellow called Baker, who was quiet and gruff to the point of sullenness. By noon of that day his face was the color of burning anthracite from a combination of the midmorning heat and the contents of a small, tin flask that he kept in his side pocket, and later that afternoon I found him napping beneath the shade of a tree, his hands folded across his belly, his face, with its half-open mouth and half-knitted brow, made stupid by sleep. I gently woke him and put him to work again, though not without having to ignore his grumbles. Well, I could ignore them: there was so much to do, a patch of ground that needed to be pampered into giving up its colors, a hedge that needed clipping, fat bags of smelly fertilizer to be spread among the roses. The garden as we got it was pretty enough, but it had nothing on my manhood dreams, which climbed like ivy and opened like irises, and if I had to muscle them out of the ground, I would. I thought the three of us were a team, however unlikely – a winning hand, three jacks in hearts, clubs, and spades spread beneath a king and queen who remained face down and of unknown suit, at least until the bet was finally called and the accounting began.

6

Late one breezy Sunday evening I settled onto my mattress to read by the low light of my lamp. I'd spent the after-noon window-shopping in town and had picked up a bag of ripe cherries from a grocer's before I drove back home. As I lay on my back with the book propped on my abdomen I was popping them one by one into my mouth, depositing stem and pit into the palm of my hand and then transferring them to a small pile on the ground beside me. By then I'd come to see the garden as mine – I was its keeper, and it was my front yard – but the book distracted me as well; if I hadn't been so caught up in the familiar pleasures of its pages, and so careful not to mark them with pale pink juice, I might have heard my neighbors coming, but I felt as isolated as a man in his manor, and it wasn't until I heard the muffled sound of a pair of footsteps on the stairs outside that I was drawn from the words to the world. In a hurry I put out the light and sat as quietly as I could.

In time the sound of a girl's voice drifted down through the floorboards, but I couldn't make out the words, only a mash of syllables and squeezed vowels that went on for some time, evenly cadenced and blunt, as if she were reciting a story that she'd practiced for days. In some places she was emphatic, in others amused, in still others resigned, but her voice never rose or fell by as much as a fourth. Eventually she wound down, started up again abruptly, and then stopped. Another voice appeared, again a girl, but softer, more patient, and slightly drawling. . . . The first answered briefly, and with a note of assent. I heard a fit of coughing, which I used as cover to get to my knees. Then there was quiet for a time, the trembling of proximate thoughts, and light footsteps leaving.

I did follow them. I couldn't resist it, though I swear I tried; I sat on my hands, I pressed my ankles together and rocked back and forth, I squeezed my eyes shut until shards of ingrown light impressed themselves on the black of my lids. But as the two girls strolled slowly across the grounds back to the house I found myself slipping from my shelter and following their voices, and while I lost them among the azalea bushes, still I kept on, pulling shadows over me as I moved towards the great house. There were lights on in a first-floor window, and I saw figures darting across the facade of the house and then swiftly disappearing just before the back door banged shut. A few moments later I came onto the cold deck out back, and I got down to my knees and crawled behind a wicker chair to peer through the window into the golden glow of the living room.

There were four. An oldish, portly man with a neat grey beard sat in a deep black leather chair in the center of the room, with a large book open and face down on his lap and an unlit pipe pressed between his lips. His wife, a fine-featured woman with her hair pulled back, sat on a couch that faced him, one arm lying along the back. Beside her sat her eldest daughter, half-reclined on the cushions with her legs drawn up underneath her to make room for her little sister, who sat on the floor before them with her head resting against the seat behind her. The two girls were still flushed from their trip through the garden.

Father was speaking softly – the pipe wiggled in his mouth until he reached up and removed it. I crawled a little closer to the window, hoping I might hear a little talk, but I felt light on my back, and I scurried back into the darkness. By the time I was hidden again he'd finished. He put the pipe back into his mouth, tipped his head back with the satisfied look of a man who's just put out a small, harmless fire, and folded his pink hands across his stomach. His wife reached down and gently stroked little sister's long brown hair, and little sister shifted her luxurious lap on the floor and pursed her lips into a cherry red pout. Her mother gave her a tender glance and murmured a word or two to her. Her father brought his head up again and spoke a sentence out loud; big sister sighed, bent her head back and lowered her eyelids, shook the hair off her forehead, and opened her hands on her lap. She spoke some words of whatever mark to the ceiling; it was the same voice I'd heard from within my cave. Mother arched her eyebrows in lazy surprise, and little sister turned her head, but not far enough to see the other. (Pause.) All resumed their original positions. It was the entire cast, full stage and floodlit. I wasn't bored; I waited there and watched until one by one they shook their evening off and started upstairs to bed, leaving me to myself.

Late that night I lay awake in my hiding place, nursing circus visions, dreams of flight, and terrible, longing cramps. Lights burn bright in Hollywood; in New York couples cut across avenue traffic; children play evening games in Dallas yards. Saturday night beckons like a distant bonfire. Surrender for a moment, will you, to my misery, and sing along to whatever tune you like:

> Who is this who spies my home?
> What worm is it that turns the loam?
> As green a boy as ever was
> Monster is as monster does

7

House warm, proud house, with a chimney on the roof and a Wilson in the yard. By noon the next day they were all gone, and under the guise of detaching a green cellophane garden hose from a spigot by the back door I stole over to the kitchen window, cupped my hands around an invisible pair of binoculars, and pressed my nose against the dark glass to see what I could see. The room inside was ringed with a gleaming white countertop and equipped with a number of mysterious appliances. The ceiling fan spun slowly above a black-lacquered wood table, on which someone had left a still life of a fruit bowl and a half-empty honey jar. A tap on my shoulder made me jerk and spin around: it was Baker, standing behind me with a pair of gardening gloves in his right hand, very carefully not smiling. The thing is out of gas, he said solemnly, and then he stuck the tip of his index finger in his ear and gently waggled it.

Well, go on and get some more, I replied, trying hard to seem annoyed.

I need the keys to the truck, he said, and slowly held out his hand.

I drew them from my pocket and gave them over to him, and he absent concentration on her face, her head tilted slightly to one side as she watched her hands work.

There she is again, yawning, stretching on the back porch one Saturday morning, her shirt raised on the soft, pale isthmus of her stomach as her arms strain behind her head; or coming up the walk from school, her brown eyes half closed against the afternoon sun; or alone in town just before dinnertime, waiting at a traffic light with her bicycle. And there she goes, leaving me hiding, doped.

8

In time I decked out my crawl space with trinkets and toys. I bought a rug and I placed it on the floor, and some pieces of wood made a sort of low table and stool to sit on. Empty crates pilfered from the garbage pile behind Turner's served as a dresser without drawers, and from my occasional trips into town I gradually acquired whatever things accumulate in a house, magazines and a pair of sunglasses, a pillow, pens and pencils, a set of tableware, a second chair for an imaginary houseguest, a wastebasket, and a second lamp – this one battery-powered, because I worried about fires.

It was a warm and wet spring that year, and while I was snug at night, I still had work to do during the day, and it was often interrupted by rain. At the first sign of cloud cover, Spot, Baker, and I would retreat to the eaves of the mansion, where we'd wait and listen to the water drop around us. The dampness would remind me of Olivia, filled as it was with mixed and inviting notes, and I'd smile to myself and count the shivers in my attention. When the rain ended we'd step off the patio and resume our work in the garden, and within a few minutes the sun would begin to show in the sky, less as the familiar liquid yellow pool than as a brightening source in one corner, still occluded by clouds; I would spy the noble frame of my gazebo down the hill and make a note to pick up something or other on my way home from work. A butterfly would flutter by. Then, as the bumblebees began to buzz loudly in the heat, I'd wander the wet acres, while water dripped down the fat, full veins of the green leaves around me; my shoes would soak through, and then the cuffs of my pants, as my garden passed beneath my padding feet.

Baker would glare at me whenever I asked him to take up a shovel again, and then walk as slowly as possible towards the spot I'd pointed out, stopping every few steps to hitch up his pants, or to blow his nose into a rag that he kept in his front pants pocket, or to light one of the cigarettes that, no matter how many times I asked, I couldn't keep him from stamping out in the grass. Spot, on the other hand, just said, Done, boss, lowered his eyes, and smiled to himself – somewhat mysteriously, I thought, as if it was all, ridiculous as it may have seemed, exactly as he had predicted.

When we were finished for the day we'd drop the truck off and check our tools into our lockers, and once, when Spot and I were walking slowly back through the silent parking lot, he invited me to join him for a beer. The sun was low in the sky, and the air was warm and hazy with golden pollen. He stopped for a moment, placed his hands at the base of his back, and stretched his spine. A little pinball maybe, he said. Maybe chase some, you know . . . He laughed shortly, and I watched his Adam's apple travel an inch up his throat and then drop back down again.

What about Baker? I asked.

Hell no, he replied, looking around to make sure we were alone. God. Come on, you have a car, right?

I nodded.

Then let's go.

I wanted to head back home, to take in the last hour of fragrant daylight before the sun went down, but he followed me to my car as if I'd already agreed. As I unlocked the door on the driver's side he rested his arm on the hood, peered through the window at the dark interior, and said, Nice. How much was it? I told him and he shook his head. Got to get one of these, he said.

The car glided to the gate. Where to? he asked.

I don't know, I said. I could feel his eyes on me as I spoke.

There's this bar . . . He pointed left with one long finger.

With Spot providing delayed directions – Left here, back there, he said as we passed a boulevard, and I braked so suddenly that a bottle on the floor of the backseat bounced up against the gearbox and broke – we came to a dark wooden building at the back of a grey gravel parking lot, a mile or two past a decrepit racetrack in the fallow fields north of town. Inside there were a dozen or so tables, extending back into the dim recesses of the room, but only one of them was taken. Three boys and one girl sat there, less another girl who had left a half full glass of beer while she used the pay phone by the bathrooms; I could see her small, dark form against the rear wall, one hand flat against the top of the coin box while she held the receiver to her ear with the other.

I had never been in a barroom before, and I was still standing in the doorway, staring at the rows of dusty pharmacy glass behind the counter and thinking how similar it all was to the bars in books and movies – though I hadn't expected the sour smell of stale beer – when Spot took a stool and motioned me to the one beside him. The bartender brought us two dark brown bottles and then turned back to watch a basketball game on the television above the old refrigerator at the far end. You're not from around here, Spot said speculatively. Nope, you're from another land, far, far away – another world, where, um, trees grow upside down, and, and women give birth to ponies.

I laughed. Nebraska, I said.

Of course. One of these days . . . He shook his head and raised his bottle to his lips.

What?

What?

One of these days what?

He looked back over his shoulder to the table by the telephone.

He scratched the side of his soft nose. See this? he said, flattening the point above his nostrils against his face. No bone. No bone at all, boss. I got it broke so many times they just took it out. Anyway ...Look at that, and he nodded his head towards the table. Should have stayed in school, don't you think?

The girl on the phone had finished talking and was making her way back to the table, her eyes mnemonically glancing down and to one side while she bit contemplatively at one corner of her lower lip. In her dark clothes, and with her hair arranged so that the parted side was tucked behind one ear while the other half fell over her eyes, it took me a moment to recognize her. It was the gesture she made as she took her seat that tipped me off, the way she opened her hands, palms up, as if she expected her friends to hand her answers. I've got to go, she said resignedly. My mom wants me home for dinner. She stood up again, jammed her hand into the pocket of her jeans, and came up with a few bills, which she dropped like trash in the middle of the table. Close. Where is her sister? Somewhere.

No bone at all, Spot said again, looking carefully at Marian as she pulled on a grey sweatshirt, several sizes too big, with the word Trinity written in purple across the chest. A girl sitting with her back to me said something that made her laugh and nod her head as she lingered over leaving. Finally she raised her hand in an absent good-bye and started for the door. Nope. I turned back and watched the girl through the mirror behind the bar. She paused in the doorway so that her eyes could adjust from the cool shadows of the bar to the glare outside, and then with a sun-wet shiver she disappeared through the door like a swimmer into a clear summer sea. Spot turned back to me and drummed briefly on the bartop with his fingers, a tattoo that gradually faded. He turned his bottle around in his hands and then peeled off a corner of the label. At length he said, I guess I'd better go too, boss. He lapsed into a parody of his own open accent: I'm plumb tuckered out. Besides, my mom wants me home so she can remind me that I'm . . . a disgrace.

I'm buying, he said, and put a five-dollar bill on the bar. You're driving.

On the way to his house he asked me to stop for a moment at a convenience store. I watched through the window as he pointed to a rack behind the cashier's back, but I didn't see what he'd bought until we were back on the road. Look at this, he said, and pulled a magazine out of a brown paper sack. A police car passed. I glanced down just as he flipped it open to a picture of a young woman on all fours on a bed, naked but for her crimson high-heeled shoes, a pair of thigh-high crimson stockings, and a string of pearls that hung down to the bedcovers. She was kneeling away from the camera's eye, with her head turned up so that her bleached blond curls fell down her shoulder blades. Her back was arched, and her legs were parted to reveal the damp, dark, en-folded cleft where they met, and with the long fingers of one hand she was gently gripping herself. Her skin had an unnatural tex-ture, and I noticed that her toes were slightly spread, as if the film had caught her just as her efforts were being wrung out to the last, eccentric border of her body. It made me think of a butter truck overturned on a highway, but Spot was gazing at it as I turned my eyes back to the road, and for the rest of the ride he flipped through the pages, pausing now and again to compliment an image that he admired.

9

Within a few weeks the blossoms began to bud, and by the middle of May the grounds were composed of pages of open-ing leaves, operatic folios and quartos. Wine ran through the earthly spine, and honey dripped from the fat stamens of the plants. As the air warmed, scents appeared like notes on a staff, monster clef, in the key of me.

That land was my first medium, and as I practiced it I grew more adept at judging myself; I saw its resistance and my own response, measured my powers and met my personality. In making my gift I made myself, in colors more vivid than I brought to the piece. I soon became so absorbed in the green work of gardening that I would sneak from under the gazebo after midnight and do a little digging, a little weeding, a little planting; but never mind, I made the landscape open itself up. I don't know where my talents came from, unless it was simply desire, but there they were, and my monsterpiece grew greater with every day that passed. I was a Demiurge, filling the world with the reluctant stuff of creation, the something that I made out of nothing, by casting it away from the dull silence before its existence. Passing the herb garden set my nostrils to quivering, and the hedges were full and deep green; when I walked among them I was embarrassed, the way some women are embarrassed by the lusciousness of their own bodies (Olivia, in a pair of shorts, looking down at her thighs as she sat on the kitchen counter and quickly hopping down again). The water in the pond became sweet and clear, the soil was damp and brown, and every blade trembled in the dolorous sunlight, each one complementing the next, until their individual shades and spears mingled in a humid expanse, a blanket so soft and heavy that it trapped every sound, and apart from the occasional song of birds and the noiseless hum of flourishing, the garden was silent.

These are notes of a long transformation, compressed by necessity: I find it almost impossible to account for the individual days that made it up — not because I've forgotten, but because in retrospect their qualities have been rewritten. They flash by like the jerky cinema stories of a flip book: three characters make their way in from the gutter where the pages are bound, stopping once or twice and bending to make some vague motions on the ground. We don't look at one another. Drops of cartoon sweat appear on Baker's forehead; he abruptly wipes them away with the palm of his hand. An awkwardly flapping bird crosses above us, then a tiny dot appears in one corner, a point that gradually expands, swells, its details becoming clearer: it's a whole planet, with rivers and valleys, and as it grows it overwhelms the scene, filling the sky. Spot disappears under its shadow, and then Baker, leaving me alone to stare up from the garden as a city materializes on its surface, a street in the city, a house, and in the backyard the accelerating image of a girl in jeans and a striped T-shirt, who waves to me from the sky, her ground, as she swoops down on me – and then the last page unexpectedly flaps through my fingers, and the book falls to the floor.

10

One Thursday evening I found the house glowing with soft gold, and through the windows I could see Holiday and Anne bustling about as if on the distant stage set of some amateur parlor drama. Then she crossed to the left and sat down at the kitchen table to write out a long note, and he went up to their bedroom and began to draw clothes out of his closet and dresser. In time she followed him upstairs and disappeared into their bathroom, and he began to pack a large suitcase that lay open on their bed. When he was finished he stood it neatly by the door, then went down to his desk and began to put papers into his briefcase. They were going away.

At first I balked at the thought, since I was afraid that I'd be lonesome with the family gone. But neither of the sisters moved: while their parents packed they sat and watched television, and when the suitcases had been placed by the front door Marian patiently received a final word, kissed her mother good night, and saw them to the car. From some foliage at the side of their property I watched as their ember-red taillights floated down the hill to the street and then disappeared.

The note was a set of instructions, but I never did have a chance to read it. While her sister watched uncomfortably, Marian set fire to it over the stove three minutes after they'd gone – and the two of them jumped identically when it suddenly flared in the pan, leaving a black smudge of soot on the ceiling that no one but me ever noticed. For the rest of the evening they sat in the kitchen, talking over a bottle of their father's red wine, until Olivia grew so tired that she could barely hold herself up, and she went to sleep.

Her sister moved to the couch in the living room, turned out the light, and lay alone with the television, stretched back against the cushions with her eyes lowered, her hand pressed between her closed thighs. The minutes didn't change, but the girl herself gradually became glassy and bare; and her nerves began to fire, tying urgent knots in a long, slow loop. Her hand moved, then she turned slightly and wriggled her hips a bit farther down the cushions. Her mouth opened slightly, and a few seconds later she pressed it tightly shut, as if to block her tongue . . . she was night fishing by lamplight, waiting, intent on a string in dark water, on an invisible jerk below the lapping waves. Her brow furrowed as if she was intensely curious about something, breathing. – Suddenly she winced, shivered once, and then twice more in quick succession, and then again, and then she relaxed back against the pillow and slowly let out her breath.

For a few moments she lay there, relieved, motionless in her daydream, and then she sat up slowly and glanced around the room. It was still there, so she went to the front door and locked it, turned out the lights, and walked swiftly, surely, upstairs to bed.

I was still asleep the next morning when the two sisters left for town, but I was awake by the time they returned, with the back of their mother's car filled with grocery sacks, and I was wide-eyed as I watched what they unpacked: bags of cookies and chips, dips, pretzels, and all kinds of fruit – grapes, apples and oranges, peaches – and two cartons of cigarettes and a bag of stacked plastic cups, and several large containers of juice and coffee-colored soda, and so many bottles of beer and liquor that I was stunned – was that what a parent prevented? – until I realized that they were going to have a party. They'd planned it for the next night, a Saturday.

That evening I lay awake with jitters, my head filled with unruly plans that stood in a ragged line at impatient attention, while I inspected and then dismissed them, one by one; and when they'd fallen away I found only one that remained in place, standing unsteadily under nervous clouds on the parade grounds. It was necessary because it was possible, and possible because it was left. The sheer momentum of the act's modality pricked me to it; I never would have been so brave.

11

The following day brought the first truly hot weather of the year. The dew had dissolved by mid-morning and the air grew heavier as it warmed; by noon it had turned to steam, and as I sat beneath the gazebo, reading the morning paper in a diamond of light that came through a hole in the floorboards above, drops of sweat fell from my forehead and mottled the newsprint, and my shirt became pasted to my back. A local church bell struck twice and then quit, as if it had just managed to compress a pair of brass droplets from the summer sky before retreating back into the darkness of its tower, exhausted. At three in the afternoon two girls with bright yellow hair appeared out of the brilliant sunshine, coming up the drive in a bright yellow car; a little later a boy with a bicycle arrived, propped the thing up against a tree and untucked the ankles of his pants from his socks, and then came through the front door without ringing the bell. In the cool, hazy darkness inside the house I could see Olivia moving about in a polka-dot summer dress, her calves and the plump white flesh of her upper arms exposed. She stopped and touched her bare neck to remind herself of something, and then started again. The plants needed to be watered, and she padded into the kitchen, emerged again a few moments later with a long-nosed green plastic watering can, and started over to a cactus by the back window.

Marian was leaning forward on the couch, with her arms crossed over her crossed legs. She gave a faint, wilted wave as their friends entered stage right and collapsed into chairs, and her friends didn't respond at all. Olivia finished her chore and lowered herself next to her sister with her pretty feet up on the coffee table. I could see black ovals of dirt on her soles. She wriggled her toes and sighed. After half an hour she and one of the girls began to get ready; they unbagged the food and put it out on a table in the living room. Afterwards the five of them sat in the dining room lazily sipping iced tea.

Then Olivia and the bicycle boy disappeared in a car. When they returned a half an hour later they had two or three bags of ice, which they emptied into a tin bucket from the basement, and the bucket, in turn, went into the refrigerator. There was nothing left then but the waiting. For several hours they sat, as their boredom and impatience grew. The television talked on endlessly, applause, laughter. They tapped restlessly on the armrests of the couch, they checked the bathroom one more time . . . And then it was nine. It was ten-thirty before the first guests arrived.

By eleven there were a dozen in the house, and by eleven-thirty two dozen. I went back to the gazebo and changed into the only clean shirt and pants I had. Numb hands, not mine, let me out of my bedroom. The yard was very quiet, and the steps I took were long and bouncy; they settled slowly, like a balloon, while I thought – not thought, exactly, but dazed and dozed, and listened to nothing as I thoughtlessly crossed the shadowy lawn. Then I stole down the side of the house and sidled up the front path to the door, attaching myself to a group of a half dozen other boys, taller than me and older than the sisters. They were completely unimpressed with the preciousness of their position, but more I can't say; not a feature or gesture remains. I remember only that they were laughing easily at something that I, my head filled with damp fog, had missed. When Marian opened the door she greeted each one with a kiss on the cheek while I held back in the shadows and then, just before the door shut, pushed my way in – Oh, sorry, she said, as she tried to shut the door on my shoe. She wouldn't give me a second look or a third word for the rest of the night; she left me standing on the threshold, the living room open before me, while I gazed into the noise and the featureless faces.

12

Was I nervous? I was. Was I afraid I'd be exposed? Of course. Was I monstrously self-conscious? Yes. Did anyone approach me? One did. And who was it?

13

She caught my eye in a mirror that hung above the couch in the living room. I was standing against the far wall, with a small, empty plastic cup in my hands. I was watching their friends; I wanted to box them all together in order to have a little container full of rivals. The glass shone against the wall like a window onto another room, and through the crowd I saw Olivia's profile reflected, one cheek framed with rococo curls of chestnut hair showing as she faced me across the room. She'd changed her clothes, and the soft grey man's shirt she now wore was so large that, untucked, it fell almost to her knees. I watched her watch me for a few moments, watched her glamorous blush in the glass. When I shifted nervously she fixed the angle and frowned, glanced over again, and silently laughed as she realized I was watching her reflection. She turned towards the mirror and I could see her eyes on me, and then she was obscured; the room had become so crowded that it was only through the figures of her friends that I glimpsed her open gaze, once, twice, gone, and a third time again. You're crazy, no way, someone said. It can't be more than about eighty. A boy in a red windbreaker was nodding vigorously at his sandy-haired friend.

She came carelessly towards me, without effort or thought; she didn't look at me again, and I suddenly wasn't sure if she'd seen me at all, or if she had some other reason to move so. She raised her hand briefly to touch a girl's shoulder in greeting as she passed, and smiled distantly. It's a hundred twenty something. This is before he went to Oakland. I swear, I know, I lost a bet on this. I felt slightly sick. The tape player howled with music, over which a man sang in a low, lazy voice: Sometimes I don't thrill you. Sometimes I think I'll kill you. Just don't let me fuck up, will you. 'Cause when I need a friend it's still you. What a mess. The lights were too bright in the room, the music was too loud, and it felt like a cell, a noisy, frantic capsule falling swiftly through time and the quiet darkness outside, turning over and over again. I wondered how the furniture stayed in place, why we weren't tumbling onto one another like dolls in a box. A tall girl with long brown hair turned to the wall, tipped her head back, and swallowed something small, a piece of candy or a pill, or a bug. Sandy-hair was gesturing violently as he shouted at his friend, and still she made her way towards me, raising her eyes to mine as she neared, slowed, and stopped by my side. My features turned to soft clay.

My name's Olivia, she said, and she held out her small hand and smiled as if at some secret joke. I felt the warm pads of her palm touch mine. What's your name? she asked, as if she'd known once and just needed to be reminded. Wilson, I hissed, my tongue a flopping fish in my mouth.

She laughed. What's your first name?

Wilson, I said. I could hear my own voice: it was wrong.

She shook her head as if to clear it, and laughed brightly again; I saw a sweet pink kiss flash past. Well, Wilson Wilson, she said.

I hope you're enjoying yourself. You're not drinking anything; can I get you something to drink? There was a slapback echo on her voice, a ringing around her words that lingered in my ears. Sweeter than wine.

No, thank you.

So, she said abruptly, aiming her eyes at mine for a moment and then turning them away. You know Marian, right? Have we met before?

I don't think so. (I'm a goblin that lives like an ornament in your garden, a garden I made for your family.)

. . . .

I was invited here by a friend, but I don't think he's shown up yet. I said: I'm sorry.

She smiled shyly, hugged herself gently, and twisted a bit on her feet as if she were dancing to some music; she stretched in her skin, she bit her plump ruby underlip. She tucked an errant curl behind her pink ear and I saw the tiny glitter of a diamond-drop resting in her lobe. She moved like a girl on holiday in her own prettiness. Don't be, she said. I'm glad you could come. She glanced up and waved to a boy who'd just come through the door, then looked at me again with her eyes wide. Don't be sorry, I mean. I hope you'll stay.

(I'll stay for months, for years. I have nowhere else to go; this is my green island.) Actually, I think I'm leaving now, I said.

No, stay. Do you know why a whale is like a picket fence? Let me go get you something to drink. She became mock stern and waggled a finger at me. Don't you move, I want to talk to you.

All right, I said. She turned away and headed towards the kitchen, and when she was out of sight I pushed my way through the room and let myself out the back door, and as the funhouse echoes faded behind me I slipped quietly away, a shadow on the back patio, a scape, a goat in the garden, a poltergeist with a knocking heart sprawled on a thin mattress under the gazebo.

14

Congratulations, climbing vine; and to you, black beetle, on the opening of your pale, iridescent wings; and to you, Wilson, on having made such a fine occasion, a celebration: little sister, with her affections, her liquid moods and long lashes, her cinema faces, had finally risen in my mind like a full moon above the Atlantic:

> What did you learn this palace spring?
> When you are queen I will be king.

15

Two days later Anne and Holiday returned from their trip to a spotless house (less one crystal drinking glass, now slivers and shards in an outdoor garbage can), a pair of daughters with no particular news to tell, and a boy still hiding in their backyard.

I know my desire for Olivia's company will seem like a terrible decision to some. The chorus is already restless, gossiping, worrying, predicting a bad moon, terrors, a broken tower. Good players, we'll let it pass. Olivia knows, I know, that as much as I chose I was chosen. I admit it was bad, but not because she or I was bad: it's just bad to be. Anyway, this is not a case of beauty consorting with beastliness; for if I'm not handsome, neither am I entirely impossible to look at, and as a child I received my share of favors. I have an afternoon preserved in my memory like a chip of ruby glass in a box, when a youngish widow visiting my father's office touched my cheek as she was leaving, then brushed my hair back and left a quick kiss of lipstick wax on my lips, and an invisible cloud of perfume about my head. My father saw, and when she'd gone, with an icy flash of her jewels and a bright smile that lingered in the waiting room for a few moments after the door closed behind her, he took me into his examination room, sat me in his chair, and paced the floor in silence while my reddened ears rang with what was left of her laughter. Finally he stopped, turned to me, and said, Be curteous, and remember what you are. I do remember, and the woman's compliment means nothing to me now — it makes up for nothing.

16

Where were you then?

Hiding.

Hiding?

I was in the garden, you know. I was afraid.

Oh, no. You didn't have to be. Come here, put your head here.

There wasn't much else I could do. I didn't have anything to give you, so I don't know.

(Smiles.) You're so serious sometimes. You, mmm, I love this, the way your hair, goes . . .

Suppose I'd just come to the door one day and asked for you.

Asked who?

Whoever answered. If it was you, just asked to see you.

I'd have been flattered. And then what?

I don't know. How does this go? A movie, or, what do I say?

A walk.

A walk?

A gentleman comes calling, if a gentleman comes he asks a lady out for a stroll, if the weather's nice.

If it isn't?

Then he comes back.

17

The next Monday was a school holiday. Holiday went off to work that morning, leaving room in the driveway for our now clutch-sick, lurching green truck, but both Marian and Olivia were in and out all day. I was trimming a hedge in the back of the house when I heard their mother's car start, and then late in the morning the sound of the two of them calling to each other came across the great lawn, but I was careful to keep hidden. I made myself invisible: it's one of the things I can do.

That afternoon barefoot Olivia emerged on the back porch, wearing blue jeans and a loose white T-shirt and carrying a pitcher of iced tea that her mother had made for us. From the fish pond I saw her wave once, her arm tracing a wide, awkward arc over her head, and I turned my face away and sent Spot up to thank her. A minute later I glanced up to see him stop on the flag-stones, smile, and start towards her, and I watched with agonized frustration as he spoke to her, one hip slightly bent as he rested easily on his feet. For a moment I saw my dreams drive up to the edge of a cliff, but she politely answered whatever comment he'd made and then turned back into the house. I only went for my own cool and bitter glass, with its sun yellow slice of sour lemon and its shiny cubes knocking together like my knees, when I was sure she was inside the house. No luck? I said to Spot as he passed me on his way back into the humid garden. No nothing, he said, without looking up. I couldn't help but laugh with relief, an outburst of chattering and indiscreet glee that rankled him. Fuck you, too, he said, and left me there with a cold face.

18

A drop of water hangs from a wrought-iron rail, qui-vers and glitters with captured light, a shining globule trembling with the tension of its own tiny gravity. Beside it another drop appears, and then a third, this one excruciatingly bright from the newly emergent sun. The first drop hangs, falls in a vanishing quicksilver streak, and another one replaces it.

A brief gust of wind rustles the trees, and a moment later they shake loose a sudden, late epilogue of secondary rain, a sort of softer playlet about the downpour that's just ended, and Holiday, who has come out onto the back porch, and whom I've been watching from the rose garden, a pair of pruning shears frozen half-open in my hand, feels a hundred unexpected drops striking his shoulders, lowers his head, and hurries back into the house.

19

According to the notes that I have kept in the soft sentences of my undying memory, the next morning was clear and dry. When I awoke, stuck my head out of the back of my gazebo and peered blinkingly up at the sky, I found that someone had painted a cloud in one corner, but it had disappeared by the time I arrived at work, and the day promised to be perfect. I took my place on the end of the bench and waited, but an hour passed and the dispatcher forgot to call my name: Baker and Spot were sent to the house, my house, with another man I'd never seen before, a fat, bejowled beast with tiny eyes. His name, I learned when I overheard Baker introducing him to Spot, was Willie. When everyone was gone, the dispatcher called me over and told me that I was wanted in the office. There the manager sat, behind a long table covered with slips and papers. Without asking me to sit, without meeting my eyes, he began to speak.

Gardening is a cooperative thing, he said. Everyone's personality has to be, what's the word? . . . everyone has to get along for everything to work, so the client will be satisfied. We provide a service; that's what we're paid for. You've been a promising worker, he said, and you're a bright boy. We were happy with your work, and we thought you'd do well around here (with the unhappy tense my smile slipped to the floor). But Mr. Miller came down here yesterday and complained for an hour. So we sent a supervisor out this morning, and he came back with . . . well Jesus, it's a fucking jungle over there, it's a wilderness, it's—are you doing any work at all? I started with astonishment and opened my mouth, but he looked up for the first time from the stack of invoices on his table, and with a wave of his hand he silenced me. There was a pair of oversized red plastic dice on his desk, and he picked them up and began idly trying to match the dots. So it's been decided that you aren't working out. He set the dice back down again: boxcars. He was sorry. He thought for a moment and his face changed, as if he had been struck with a sudden sincerity. You are a strange one, he said, as if I wasn't there at all. Strange.

I paused to allow my blood to settle, and when the roiling in my ears had faded I got up from my seat, smiled to show my teeth, turned abruptly, and walked out the door. I could find other work; but the garden was mine and always would be.

20

It was particularly warm that night, and because it had rained in the evening the grass was wet and the smell of undergrowth drifted through the meshwork of my walls. As it grew dark I rose from my bed, opened my door, and peered out at the garden. That afternoon we'd mown the back lawn, and the air was thick with the sweet smell of cut and rotting grass. It was a cloudless night, and the stars circled above me in dizzying whirls, spotted bands of white in the darkness. In the time it takes to tune a guitar I had my clothes off and had begun a kind of unemployment dance. I trailed my hand along a row of buds; I scratched my bare back against the rough trunk of a tree; I somersaulted down a small slope; I wriggled my toes in the dirt of a flower bed; from the herb garden I picked sprigs of mint, crushed the leaves between my fingers, and rubbed my flesh until it stung with the sweet oils. I picked berries from the bushes, popped them into my mouth, and spit their skins onto the ground. I tore up a handful of grass, revelling in the ripping sound it made and scattering the blades onto the crown of my head until they mixed with my hair and fell onto my face. Am I alone? I asked myself. Yes, I am. The whole house is sleeping, the whole world is sleeping, and I'm all alone again. But I am the Genius of the Place.

I loped over to the fish pond with a weed stalk between my teeth and found my own familiar reflection in the black glass. Wilson, Wilson, he called you a strange one, I said. I reached into the water to stir it until my features distorted and dissolved, and then I jumped through the ripples with a giant splash. Ooze sucked at my toes when I touched bottom; weeds wrapped round my feet when I launched myself over to the other side. When I got out, dripping wet and shivering in the starlight, I shook myself like a soaked dog and turned towards my home. It was going to rain.

I could see a yellow flickering in the darkness; it lay like a slick of phosphorescent fluid on the ripples in the black water, and when I looked behind me I found tiny licks of light on the far windows of the house. With dark clouds in chase I hurried across the bottom of the grounds in a crouch, pulling branches over me as I stopped behind trees, pressed my cheek against the bark, and looked around. What's that smell, what fine burning grain in the air? Hot smoke: I was almost at the light before I realized it was a fire at the foot of my gazebo. I could see the door to my crawl space propped up against the bottom of the structure; there was a man outlined against it, an adipose figure who stood tossing dark objects into a small crowd of flurrying flames. As I watched he paused and looked around him, and I saw his face clearly, with its expression of permanent contempt. Behind him I could make out the dark outline of my chair, the slats on its back bowing like ribs behind translucent leaves of fire. Next to go were my clothes, and then a box that had contained an envelope with a month's worth of savings in it, now money gone to smoke. Then he bent down and took hold of my rug by one corner, and with a motion like a bull-fighter turning a satin cape he raised it up and brought it to settle over the flames. A plume of black smoke and orange sparks flew into the air, and for a second I thought he might have smothered the flames; but then the edges of the cloth began to flicker, the flickering widened towards the middle, and the whole thing went up like some giant, light-giving flower, the brightest bloom in the garden, with petals of fire that mocked me with the work of my undoing.

I stopped myself from crying out by biting my lip until the skin split and my mouth filled with the thick taste of my own blood. Holiday paused, puffed on his pipe, watched the fire. After a moment he crouched down in the darkness, and when he rose again he was holding my book; and as the fire with its brass band cadence suddenly grew again he balanced its weight in his hand, bent his head until his glasses caught the firelight, and flipped the pages . . . paused at a plate, frowned, and then casually tossed it into the flames.

The old man stood there until the fire was finished, kicking at the ashes to be sure there weren't any embers left, and then he glanced once around the garden and started back for the house. As soon as he passed me I started running towards the gazebo in hopes of saving something, but it was too late: I could see as soon as I arrived that while the fire had died, my last poor things were ashes, mixed with the charred and blackened logs that he'd used as fuel.

As I hid and crouched that endless night, covered with a crust of dirt and salt, I thought about the meanness of my weather. All I'd wanted was to make nature in peace, I said to myself. No, I don't know how the world was made, and what's more, I don't know why. I don't know why I was made it in it, and made to make it back: I could hazard fifty guesses, and get fifty cuffs for my troubles, fifty insults, and five hundred lies. Holiday stood for Holiday, and stood behind every one.

If he'd taken my job from me, but left me my shelter, I would have been content. If he'd evicted me from my shelter, but left me my things, I would have been content. Even if he'd set my things on fire, but left me to work freely in the garden, I would have been content. But he left me nothing, and at last my fury descended upon me in a flock of winged w's, like birds before their sharp beaks nip into flesh: if it was a war he wanted, well, I would wage my own, and begin it by singing.

Some say men were given tongues to praise whatever heaven they admire, but I have mine to curse my enemies, and lungs to blow the insults on them. I howled until I was hoarse. This was my song:

> What is a man? What does he know?
> He's a coward, a bully, vulgar, low
> A fool with a vain and tempted eye
> Fickle clouds in a summer sky
> Greedy, sullen, pompous, mean
> Feeble, dull, a mere machine.
>
> And what, instead, can we say of me?
> What purpose do I fail to see?
> I'm proud and gentle, brave and just,
> So full of desire that I'm going to bust,
> Dispensing my uncommon joy.
> Light a candle for the boy.

What employment could I desire, now, beyond the pursuit of my future?

Stranger in the House

1

Self-portraiture is a kind of folly, like trying to grasp the fingers of your right hand in the same fist. The sky on which we write our constellations is not a mirror, since once hung the stars shine by their own fire, and while the course we plot assumes that they're fixed we'd never know if they wandered. It's true nonetheless: I was born over my senses, and I was a very difficult birth. I struggled with all of my tiny might. We all know that there's no comfort or calm equal to the dark solitude before birthdays, but that wasn't why I was reluctant to be born: I didn't want to be at all, and I fought for hours, for days, to keep away from the world. Having been born, and now having lived, I sometimes think it would have been best if I'd used the moment of my first gasp to go right out again, but I was instantly impressed by the smart light of the delivery room, the shining metal tables and floors, the beeping of the instruments, and I reached my pink hand out towards the masked features of some doctor or nurse, and couldn't turn back.

I can see my father standing in the hospital hallway waiting for the news: I was the news. I can imagine him watching impassively as the nurse brought my soft, swaddled self up to the glass so he could get a look at me. Sir, a boy. He was a strict and quiet man, my father, a man with an incalculable and unexpectedly clear soul, which was absorbed by his work like well water in a dry flower bed. That day fulfilled one of those ironies of generation, of being born and begetting, that warp stories into sacredness: my grandfather was both a doctor and a tyrant, a tough and difficult man, so my father was scrupulously principled; he thought of himself as a name under a moral law that he sustained only by correcting himself through the years as a man corrects a dray, using his own doubt as a bridle and his capacity for shame as a bit. I was the third issue, and he would bear it without complaining, as if an otherwise absent providence had determined it. I don't know what grief he might have kept alive over the years, but I'll ask you to believe that his life from then on was an attempt to concentrate, as if to sharpen away the brute moment of my being under the small abrasions of his duties. For a long time he had studied deserving, the way a foot soldier studies war, and he'd taught himself to see everything: he stood in the bright hallway, his thoughts carefully hidden: he simply watched, and slowly nodded.

And there in my imagination is my mother, damp, pale, exhausted, and relieved, lying in a hospital bed with her hair unpinned and cast out on the white pillow. My father is in a chair beside her, waiting anxiously for her first look at the son she delivered. He holds her hand. A knock comes at the door, she turns her head expectantly, the nurse pushes her way into the room with her arms full of clothes, and there I lie, quietly covering my face with my tiny hands.

About a year later my mother died in an accident – I see an airplane landing in a rainstorm, though I don't know why – leaving me with my father. All that remained of her was her signature in the front of the poetry books that were sorted on one shelf in my father's study, an old-fashioned signature made in fading blue ink by practiced penmanship; and there were three photographs in which she appeared – one on my father's desk, the second on the mantle above the fireplace, and the third, which I saw only once, in his wallet. I was unconsciously young when she entered heaven, as my father, in a lapse from his usual plain-speaking, put it, so I have no memories of her at all. I have no suit against her. I don't know what kind of woman she was, and I never asked, since it seemed to be the last thing my father could have answered; I was afraid he'd turn as brittle as old paper, and then dissolve into dust under such a bright light.

2

My parents had moved to Lincoln just before I was born, to a blue frame house on the edge of town. It was huge and hollow inside, with a front hall laid with black and white diamond-shaped tiles that I used to slide over in my stockinged feet until the soles of my socks were grey with dust. Towards the side there was a porch which was seldom used, because it was cold in the winter, and the winters were long. My bedroom was at the start of a long second-floor hallway, and my father's was at the opposite end. He and my mother had bought the place expecting to fill it with children—there was a bedroom for each of four—but his sense of a house died with her, and he simply left the unused rooms empty; there was a single rickety chest of drawers pushed against the wall of one, a rolled-up carpet laid against the baseboard of the next, an unplugged lamp on the floor of the third. Absurd, but I think he was also a little sentimental, so we never did move.

I used the rooms as a diving bell. I wasn't happy, and as a boy I liked to imagine a sea in place of the Great Plains, with a hole in the bottom where I could live, passing midnight days among the translucent ferns, the shells and silt. In school one afternoon they pulled the shades and showed us films from diving ships, dark flickers of what they found near the boiling springs as far below as a man could go: giant white worms, fat mushrooms, flathead fish and eels. They did nothing but swim the currents and feed. I didn't even know how they went about making more of themselves, but I knew I wanted to live with them, because I knew that I belonged to nature, too—and why not? Freaks and sports of all kinds are hers to make and keep, spiny fish, moss and mung on trees, mandibles and hammered features, and choking smoke from fires, and crawling dirt, and brackish water, and me. If my father was bothered he never showed it. We lived together, he and I, in a house that was far too big for us alone, and in which half the rooms had furniture the way months have full moons.

Like him, I can now grant that nature's insults aren't insults; but when I was a child I reckon I made things hard for him. From my bedroom I could imagine him, after one of my wildcat tantrums, returning to his study to sit silently in his chair, his head lowered into thoughts of his gone wife and my improbable unhappiness. I know he found it difficult and bewildering. At the bare blank and diminishing end, now, I'm grateful to him for his generosity. What use can I make of sympathy? My dear father, small-town doctor with a spook for a son, a boy who made fears.

3

Daddy never brought stories of his patients home; their sufferings were secrets, and he took the privilege of his invitation into the systems that sustained them very seriously. But my curiosity about the patterns of disease was insatiable, and like a wind chime it could be set trembling and ringing by the slightest move. I used to watch him carefully while we sat at the dinner table, looking for some sign he might show of the travels of his adversaries; if he sighed softly just as he lay his fork across his plate at the end of his meal, I'd imagine that a patient had worsened during the night before; if he lingered over a forkful of potatoes, I decided that a new possibility had just come to him, and the next day would bring brisk arrangements; if he fixed himself an extra cup of coffee after dessert, I guessed that he was rewarding himself for having effected a cure—unless he added an extra spoonful of sugar to it, in which case I could tell that he was expecting to study late into the night.

When he did have work left ahead of him he used to take the kitchen table to pore over the illustrated journals that arrived regularly in the mail, looking for a new therapeutic treatment, or something to suggest that a diagnosis might have been off. As I passed from the empty living room to the empty dining room I'd see him, his grey head bent over his wonderful research while the illnesses of men and women all around the world formed swirling, page-bound currents of blood and compounds. The magazines he read would be open to their difficult maps, the charts of deep waters and undertows that some anonymous second had prepared and published. He watched them all like some quiet, latter-day Poseidon, with his favorites and battles, redirecting Furies and tides to achieve his ends, the health and completion of the men and women who came to him with their aches, their breathing troubles, their messy cavities and miseries, their numb limbs, their sleepless, bedridden bodies.

I remember leafing through his books from time to time; I used to sneak into his library when I came home from school and choose from the leather-bound medical volumes that lined the shelves. Had I had the proper temperament I might have learned something, but I never thought to wonder how the things they described might have had a place in the causal order. I wasn't born to be a doctor; I'd rather think of the singular, the particular, the actual, than spend time making real sense of the general world of symptoms, or cures. I used to look at the pictures and try to imagine the body that had posed for them, and then recite passages aloud for the rattle of the syllables, without knowing or caring what they meant.

One fine day I came across a pathology textbook, as devoted to viscera as a slaughterhouse. It began with a special inset: on the end paper there was a pair of skeletons, like exotic musical instruments, half violin, half vibraphone – though one, with its deep, curving centerplate, looked as if it would be much richer and more resonant than the other. Over them successive transparencies could be laid, thin plastic sheets on which were printed, first the shaggy skein of nerves, then the fatty organs, then the tubules of blood (red with oxygen, blue as a drowned child), then the fibrous muscles, and then translucent, pale pink skin, until a whole and very patient couple finally appeared, standing like sentinels over the carnival inside. I read through the book with the devotion of an initiate, skipping over the technical terms that seemed to multiply as the pages made their way towards the distorted glimmers and gazes, the pulp and sordid perfume that lead to the blots of flesh from which you and I, in our several ways, began; but I always returned to the frontispiece, and I never tired of assembling that map, with all its clever, interlocking layers.

I wrote stories of my own, in a notebook that still sits in the bedroom desk drawer where I hid it. It was a school composition book, bound fat with a strip of black tape over the spine, and the lines on the pages were wide enough for a child's hand like mine to keep its characters under control. The cover was a painterly abstraction, black ink spotted over a white background until the individual flecks melted together, making a sort of camouflage pattern; in the center a space was cleared for my name and home address, an oasis that I, inclined towards invisibility even then, left uninhabited. Inside I carefully wrote out little tales about a wild, illiterate, and helplessly destructive Wilson; I hid in swamps, in ship's holds, in other people's houses, where I stole daughters and murdered fathers; I ate insects and stray, misfortunate men, and when I was done I belched loudly, bent down, and beat the ground with my fists until the trees shook in Africa.

For every empire, even of a child's limpid imagination, there is an emperor, and I liked to imagine the great day when I was crowned. There would be a hall so huge that I wouldn't be able to see the ceiling. The light would come from rows of flaming, smoking torches that hung on the walls. At one end I would stand, boyish and unembarrassed, raised on a platform and gazing out with a slight smile over an assembled mob of monsters. They'd groan their cheers, they'd stamp their stumps on the ground, they'd shake their staffs in the air, and I would be declared President for Life.

4

Lincoln in those days was a small, quiet city under a huge blue sky. It wore the smell of the fields that surrounded it the way a farmer's wife wears a cotton dress, and like a farmer's wife it was bare-legged underneath. Within a few blocks of the main street the houses fell down to two-story frames as if on their knees before the sublime beauty of the Plains: there was so little substance to the whole, from limit to limit, that if the University and the Capitol hadn't held it down like nails I think it would have become detached from the earth and floated silently up into the sky, leaving me alone at last and unwatched in the dirt below.

Our house was on the south side, and our nearest neighbor was the Widow Foster. She had always been the Widow Foster, and had always lived there, but in all the years we lived next door I never did meet her; I seldom so much as saw her in the open air. Still, on afternoons when I played lordly games in our yard I'd occasionally catch a dark glimpse of a serpentine form behind the windows of the French doors that led to her porch, and I'd seen the shadow of her figure often enough to know that she was a pleasant-looking old woman, with white hair and a white throat and a body as bent as a bicycle after an accident. All services were delivered to her door, and we grew used to the sight of a grocery delivery boy or florist standing at the top of her front stairs, waiting patiently for her to make her way up from the back of the house. Then one day when I was eleven, under the spell of one of my father's funereal afternoons, I first contemplated the mysteries of mortality, using our neighbor as an example. I never even left my room: I just wondered, and the next day a man with a package rang and rang, paused, rang some more, peered through a window, and then came over to our house and spoke to my father for a moment. I was sitting in the kitchen when he came to the phone, and I watched as his index finger drew the dial in a circle. I remember asking myself what law had been suspended to reduce the familiar seven digits, with their inconsistent rhythm (a measure that waltzed, a measure that marched) to a brief and urgent three.

In the Widow's place came a family from Kansas City, a young couple somehow connected to the University. I spied on them from my window as soon as the enormous green and yellow moving truck pulled up to the curb in front of their door. For the rest of the day the movers carried their furniture into the house, while a girl in a grass-stained dress played among their legs, sat sullenly on the front steps, poked around their new backyard, and finally turned her pale moon face up to my window, where she saw me standing and, after looking around to make sure no one was watching, slowly waved.

Her name was Liz, and she was a tomboy, pony blond and always into something. Aside from the day she moved in next door I never saw her wear anything but blue jeans. She smelled like hay and grape juice, and she had downy sunburned skin and long, thin limbs, and a habit of standing with her mouth open and dazedly blinking whenever she came across something that excited her. For reasons I'll never understand, she befriended me with a wide, sly smile one weekend afternoon just after they'd arrived. I was on my way to the corner mailbox with a stack of my father's letters, and she stopped me from the edge of her lawn, came down to the sidewalk, and asked me if I knew how to make a knot that no one could undo. When I said I didn't she sat me on the curb and showed me, using my own shoelaces and then laughing shamelessly as I struggled in vain to get them untied again. We finally had to cut them apart with a pair of sewing shears she borrowed from her mother.

For the weeks that followed we used to meet on the playground at school, sit side by side against the jungle gym, and eat lunch while she watched me with glittering eyes, then meet again at the end of the day to walk the few blocks home, where I'd leave her at the sidewalk and watch her as she dashed up the stairs to her front door. Then one winter's day she brought me into her house instead, and while her mother fixed dinner in the kitchen she led me down into her basement playroom, and under the matter-of-fact fluorescent light she simply disrobed and showed me, with perfect grace, in what besides her long hair our differences lay, as if she were the end paper of my favorite book come to life. I was silent through the entire event, I was so fascinated by that form, with its *trecento* shape and coloration, at once elegant, devout, and awkward. I still remember the soft, smooth texture and smell of her bare skin, already stippled with delicate goose pimples from the cold, the way it was gathered about her bones, the slight sharp taste of her breath on my face as she moved towards me and gently kissed my burning cheek. I couldn't have imagined that anything had the power to be so entirely naked, to be so present in its plainness: she was the first thing I'd ever encountered that depended upon nothing else to exist, either in itself or in my mind, and as the sun dwindled down at the horizon, unmoving, the afternoon stopped dead; and she suddenly grew serious, backed away, and said, OK, now it's your turn. When all at once I realized that she was looking at me as I was looking at her, I spooked and shook my head No, and when she tried to cajole me and reached her hand out towards a button I ran away, hightailing it up the stairs and through the kitchen, past her mother's astonished stare and out the back door. When I reached my own room, breathless and with my heart backfiring, I lay face down on my bed and dizzily replayed the moments I'd just passed, until my father came home from work and called me down to dinner.

What did you do today? he asked as we sat down at the table, and I, thinking he already knew somehow, lowered my head, reddened, and then to his astonishment blurted out everything. His awkward, nonplussed silence when I'd finished only confused me more: he shuffled the beans on his plate with a fork, cleared his throat, swallowed half a glass of water, and then changed the subject.

5

Liz drifted away on an uneasy tide, waving good-bye just once and half-heartedly from the foot of a long path that I invented and put in place of our own all too real driveway, just as, the week before, I'd removed our house from its neighborhood and put it in a green clearing in some dark, medieval woods. Afterwards she ignored me when I passed by her and her friends as they played hopscotch on the sidewalk in front of her house, and school, which for a few weeks had been almost a pleasure, again became a miserable duty, the more so since the princess had willingly gone to some unnameable dragon.

I remember very little of my teachers, with the exception of one young woman, fresh out of college and no match for me, who asked me to stand before the class and recite a patriotic poem we were all supposed to have memorized the night before. I refused at first, but she insisted, so I stood, stared at the ceiling, and repeated as much as I could remember, changing the word *country* to *monkey* throughout. The boys in the back row giggled, and her face as she scolded me remains clear to this day. Little monster, she said, and I left the room on a brief, imaginary trip to an island in the Mediterranean, where I quickly wrecked a passing ship.

The others have faded into a pale, multiform band, within which I can make out single features, a beetle brow, a bald spot, a chalk smudge, a hand holding a lesson plan, but not one complete person; they have become blurred into a dim audience, frowning at a failing act without seeing that failing was my act. See, the old books lie. Teaching Caliban to curse made him Caliban. And Huck is one part Tom, and Tom is two parts Becky, and we are all three parts runaway Jim. So I did a lot that others thought I'd do, and I did it because they thought I would; they were the spectators at my coming to be, and I was a master, a monster, of finding and finishing their expectations, the doctor's strange son, who seldom looked at a man directly, and never at a woman, who slouched and hid and whose voice was always quiet. As every local reviewer knows, the logic of character is so appealing.

Still, I suffered from the typical torment that children pay one another. My classmates' boos and catcalls were the never-ending music of my adolescence. It's so predictable that it hardly bears recounting; someone always gets it, and I was the one. Instead let me draw a picture of my own closing credit. It was the first example of my artistry, my way with nature and my powers.

It was a late spring day, sunny and breezy, and they were standing in a circle around me in the schoolyard during lunch hour, burying me with their usual insults. I was waiting expressionless at the center of the ring, and I was prepared to stand there and play the object of their scorn until recess ended, as I did each time some secret signal rang and they gathered around me. But on that day, as I stood and listened to the rising, hurdy-gurdy sound, a single syllable from a single voice – I don't know whose – suddenly appeared from out of the ring and, like a cold chisel, knocked at just the right spot to split my temper open, so that my fury spilled out: I opened my mouth and emanated ill will. I made fun of one's unkempt clothes, another's fat father, a third's disgusting lisp, and when I could think of nothing to holler at the next in line I simply invented a failing – and when the failings ran out I received a gift of tongues, and a flood of mean energy, and I began to rage and rave at their blank faces, cursing them with a might that grew inside me, stretching my skin until I was sky high, one thousand feet tall, bitter all the way up and so angry that the weather changed: the sky darkened and I shouted up a North wind; papers, notebooks, textbooks swirled at my feet, the trees bent almost to the ground, my hair whipped across my face; on the other side of the playground a line of bicycles in a rack collapsed with a soft clatter. Through my squinting eyes I could see a teacher coming out the back door of the school, with her skirt tearing across her legs. She stopped in her steps and watched on, transfixed by the impression I made, as the wind blew and I leaned back with my arms outstretched and howled commandments to the elements.

I don't think any one of them understood half of what I said, but they were so taken aback by what I'd done that one by one they backed away, as if in the face of a supernatural force. Only Liz stayed on: she was standing by the fence that separated the playground from the street, hanging on with one hand to a diamond-shaped link while her red jacket flapped in the storm and her blue eyes opened wide in a look of astonished, delighted admiration. When the rest turned and ran I was left alone with her, and I let the wind subside. I remember that it was very quiet afterwards.

Liz let go of the fence and gazed at me with solemn curiosity. – Then she began to clap her hands together, and as the girl's childish, single applause drifted across the pavement I raised my arms, called down a rainstorm, and walked all the way home in it. I wasn't bothered again.

6

Something mean hangs high over whatever law is made, whatever comfort a good man commands. To worst and best alike nature comes, in best and worst fashion. So I was made a sport, and my father was made with a weak blood vessel behind the wall of one temple.

One cold winter day it broke and he died. It was a Monday, and he'd gone home for lunch; a cancellation early in the afternoon left him free for an extra hour, and anyway he had left a file that he needed on the desk in his study. He was fixing himself a sandwich in the kitchen when all of a sudden he felt faint, his breath came short, and his ears rang, so he shuffled up the stairs to his bedroom, lay down on top of his bed, closed his eyes, and there and then he left.

I was brought out of civics class that afternoon by the school nurse, a usually chatty woman who silently monitored the passing tiles on the floor as we made our way to the principal's office. Am I in trouble? I asked. No, no, she said, and put her cool hand gently on the back of my neck. I'm sorry, child. She sniffled and sighed; I had no idea why.

I was ushered through the anteroom – they were all watching me – and into the principal's office, and he put aside his papers, took off his glasses, and told me that I'd been called home from school. Then he rose from behind his desk and walked me to the empty street outside, where a colleague of my father's named Cooper was waiting, dressed in the curiously old-fashioned manner that he preferred; under his coat he wore a white shirt, a string tie, and black pants. His ankle-high suede boots were wet with melted snow and streaked with grey from the street salt, and each had a shiny spot near the big toe where the leather had started to wear through. In one hand he held his hat; he put his other arm around my shoulder without speaking. I shrugged him off. As we walked to his car the snow squeaked under my shoes, and the wind was so sharp in my nostrils that I pulled the neck of my sweater up over my mouth and nose until I could smell my own sweet breath mixed in with the humid wool. Cooper's dark green sedan was in a cleaver-blade of sunlight at the edge of the parking lot, glinting against the muddy snow that had been piled up to the curb. We drove to the house in solemn silence, pulling gently into the driveway that my father and I had cleared the day before; I remember the sound of the engine ticking from the cold as we walked away from it, the dark house against the white edge of the rise in our backyard, the snow and blue sunlight. There were no shadows. I was fifteen years old. He was lying in his bed with his eyes closed, his rare soul having dissolved into the sky like the foggy vapors of my breath that afternoon. For a few minutes I was left alone with his body so that I could say good-bye, but I couldn't bring myself to utter anything at all to that wax effigy, and when the door opened again I was found sitting in a chair across the room, staring at the bed as if it were a macabre sideshow exhibition.

Cooper was assigned me for the next few years, and he was proud to have received my father's commission. He was a nice man, never married, a facile guardian: he gave me a room in his house to sleep in, and a meal or two a day, and after I'd rebuffed him a few times he stopped trying to draw me out of my obvious misery and left me alone. I was an easy charge, and since I intended to finish school and be gone as soon as I could, I never gave him a reason to try to be more. I wouldn't want to see him again.

My father had willed the house to me, and I insisted on leaving it more or less as it had been before he died, but I packed away his clothes and personal effects, and I donated the most useful of his medical things to a small, poor school nearby. The cutlery was worn, the silver dulled in spots from the years he held it, however gently, in his subtle hands, but he'd left a wish that I give it away. I put his books into storage and took his clothes to the Salvation Army; the furniture remained, along with the silent pictures on the walls and my own abandoned bedroom. I stopped by the house almost every day from then until the moment I left, although there was nothing for me to do there but sit in the living room and read the walls. On weekend nights when my classmates were at parties or cruising the main strip in their cars, at holidays when families gathered, on summer afternoons when girls went walking together and smiled at boys, I was alone in that dark house, too frightened to leave, waiting for my helpless youth to end.

One day during my last year of high school I decided it'd ended at last, and I walked out: that's all. That afternoon I visited Cooper in his office, stood before his desk, and told him I was gone. He fingered the frame of his glasses, nodded carefully, quizzically, and asked if there was anything he could do. I'd like for you to watch the house, I said. If you can, keep a little heat on to keep the pipes from freezing. He nodded again and promised me that he would. I dangled a set of silver keys over his papers, explained which fit where, and set them on the blotter before him, and he opened a side drawer and deposited them inside. There was nothing to say after that: he stood, shook my hand, and walked me to the door.

I left the next morning, wandering out into sky blue spacetime, footstep by footstep. Aside from the clothes on my back and in my suitcase, a day's food, and my toothbrush, I took only one thing when I left, a book of Daddy's, my favorite, the one Holiday had erased forever, the one in which I could make a couple appear and vanish again in neat, successive stages.

7

I've been a long time telling this, I know, but my name is not No One and I don't come from Nowhere, or Nod, or straight from a vague and perfunctory Nonage. I could have shouldered up a mountain and buried myself beneath it, or swum down to the Gulf, but I stayed in the Millers' garden, which was mine. You see, I thought I was supposed to be there. If not there, where? There was nowhere else in the world; I could see my future as clearly as saints see the heaven they covet, and for the same reason: I had read it from my past. So I moved in with them the next day.

It was a new day to them, an especially late part of the night before to me. On my hard knees, on my naked seat, open to the weather and soaked through my raw red skin, I'd shivered in a sleepless delirium and waited for the sun to rise, and then discovered that it doesn't; the grounds became as grey as a dove's wing, and then, as the sunlight burned off the folds of fog that appeared at the bottom of the garden, a morning blue gradually appeared, mixed with tinges of aching yellow reflected from the moisture at the edges of the leaves. But it was my bare and open eyes that finally made the world appear, that drew the forms of the mansion and its garden out of the darkness, and not a circling sun.

I waited through the endless early morning, drifting on the pale hours like a becalmed ship, and when they'd all left, Holiday to his office, Anne into town, and the girls off to school, I carefully crawled out from beneath a bush and sneaked towards the house, crouched down on my bare feet and shuffling across the pebbles in the driveway. There was a line of basement windows at my knees and I tested them all, but they were locked. So was the back door, and the ground-floor windows, in one of which I saw my own wild reflection, my arm rubbing my forehead for an idea like Aladdin rubbing his lamp. Next I scaled a tree to the second floor, but the window was out of reach, and in any case circumscribed by the silver tape of their alarm system; behind it was a cool, dark chamber with a soft bed and a delicate print of a riverside path among ancient yews on the wall. I searched the facade of the place for some way in that I might have missed, but it was sealed up tight. I'd been up all night and I was so tired, you know; I could barely get enough sense together to make a thought; it was like trying to strike something underwater. I sat there and stared at the impenetrable house, while around me the colors of the world drifted down like garments hung on a ghost.

A few dreamy wavering minutes passed. I scratched my abdomen. There was an air conditioner in a window above me, humming busily. It stopped suddenly as the thermostat sank past a switch, and the world stilled. I had just started to try to think again when I heard a noise at my feet, and before I could scramble up into the foliage a small, sharp-featured face appeared, gazing up from the basement to where I sat. Wilson? It was a second before I recognized the face, with its pale pink eyelids blinking in the sunlight. How are you? asked Jones. Why don't you come down here?

I slipped back down the trunk of the tree, chafing my thighs on the corrugated bark, and found him staring out from the basement, no smile on his face, no expression at all. He gestured with his hand. Come in, he said, and withdrew inside. The window slid shut, and I could see him through the dark glass, standing below me, staring up out of the darkness. In I went, crawling backwards over the casement and dropping down from the ledge onto the cool concrete floor. When my eyes adjusted I looked around, but my friend was gone; he wasn't behind the supporting post, or in the corner shadows, or hiding on the other side of the door, and I finally realized he'd left me again, and I let him go.

I'd come into a storage space lined with stacks of carefully labeled cardboard boxes. In the next room I found a boiler, and in the next a workspace lined with tools, with a staircase leading up to the kitchen. I chose the boiler room for my bed; it was already spring and I knew no one would be down to use it. I found an open box of musty blankets, and I stole a few and stuffed them behind the door until I needed them. Then I went looking for clothes and a little lunch. I was hungry and cold, and frightened, and I couldn't think.

Holiday was a fat man, where I was a skinny monster, not even fully grown yet, but I wanted his suit and went to find it. From the kitchen I wandered naked through the front hall, and naked up the carpeted stairs with the pile between my dirty toes. In the hall-way I paused, bounced once on the balls of my feet, and entered the old man's room. It was so tidy, with his bed made, the drawers closed on his clothing, his bureau top bare.

Under the shower in his bathroom I shampooed my matted hair. I dried myself with a soft white towel and buried it at the bottom of the laundry bin, and I was careful to open the window so that the steam would clear, and to brush away the talcum powder that had fallen to the floor, a little dusty pool within which, like obverse islands in an archipelago, lay the small oval giveaway prints of my toes. Then I walked bare-assed into his bedroom and rummaged through the full closets until I found a suit that I ad-mired; it was made of soft ash-grey wool, carefully tailored, beau-tifully cut and stitched; and when I thrust my hands in the pockets

I found a crumpled ten-dollar bill that the old man had forgotten, a prize slip of green paper. There was a blue-and black-striped tie hanging on a rack on the door, and a white cotton shirt in his drawer, still in the grey box from the dry cleaner and with its encircling paper band intact. As I stood uncovered in their bedroom I unwrapped it, shook out its soft folds, and buttoned it on; then I drew the suit off its hanger and shrugged it over my shoulders, and as I knotted the tie I sang this slow song:

> Oh, why don't you love me?
> Oh, why don't you care?
> Is it my clothes, dear?
> Is it my hair?
> Is it the way that I creep up the stairs?
> Oh, why don't you love me?
> Oh, why don't you care?

My new clothes billowed and bagged all over; the waist of the pants fell to my bony hips; the sleeves of the jacket hung over my hands. In the full-length mirror on the backside of their door I looked myself up and down and waved my arms like some giant, mad crow trying to fly. I gave myself a cheerful smile, I winked at myself, and then I wandered off.

In the kitchen I found some leftovers in a covered dish in the refrigerator, a sort of chicken stew. I quickly finished it, rinsed the bowl and put it in the dishwasher. I found a pale yellow cheese in a drawer, which I placed in my right-hand pocket, and a box of pale yellow crackers in a cabinet, which I placed in my left, and then with my suit bulging I made my way down the back stairs just as the sound of a motor came up the driveway.

For a moment I pondered my unlikely reversal; there I was, inside looking out on the driveway, waiting for Anne and her daughters to come home and fill the house with sound, to come to me. Instead a truck pulled to the side of the house, with a country song playing on the cab radio. As the engine died the music stopped mid-chorus, but one young, tuneless voice continued singing a few more words: Her old man, he never liked me, so me and her ran to Tennessee. Over the state line, we . . . umm . . . preacher said, Do you? and I said, I do.

I could hear them talking to each other as they put down the back of the pickup and began to take down their tools. I wonder what he's doing now, said Spot. Baker made a spitting sound. Off bothering someone else. That kind always finds someone to bother. Together they lifted down a lawnmower and dropped it with a bang and clatter on the pavement. Baker laughed. Now maybe we can, get some, settle back some. Jesus Christ. I mean — here he grunted as he lifted a bag of fertilizer onto his shoulder — I don't mind working, but that boy had us running all over the goddamn place. Put, put this here, plant that thing there, dig that up. He leaned back on the bed of the truck, wiped the sweat from his forehead, pulled a can of beer from his pocket, and laughed again: I thought I was going to take a swing at him one of these days. Spot said Amen and wiped his forehead on his shirttail.

Inside the house I hung my head and shook it slowly from side to side and then retreated back into the darkness.

8

Holiday went back to the gazebo every so often to make sure that I hadn't come back; I used to see him wandering down to the end of the garden, poking around the bottom of the frame. It was a useless precaution, no harm to me, no good to him. I simply made my way in and out of the basement window every night.

He had given instructions to the manager at Turner's; he wanted the place trimmed back, and from the first day Baker, Spot, and Willie had obediently tried to lessen it. Flowers were pulled up, plants pruned down, vines stripped off walls and lattices. But I knew that everything depended on making it beautiful and keeping it made against the old man; it was unthinkable that I should leave the grounds to the three careless hirelings. The house was at the center of the garden, and I was at the center of the house, drawing the great, growing circle of land to my chin like an enormous, bedecked quilt. In the quiet of night I moved about, my bare hands serving as hoe and clipper, rake and spade. Without the bitter taste of wage work I fattened myself on my free labor and kept on. I'd ordered my passions into a first paradise, and I wanted to populate the place with my own subjects, with dwarfs and hermits, a carnival of mystery rites and delirium, voices calling back and forth across the divide between myself and the world I'd made; I wanted to grow something that knew me, and people the place with little Wilsons.

The trees grew new branches for me overnight, silent, gesturing limbs, here beckoning, here shrugging, or stopping imaginary traffic, or raising hallelujah arms, or tossing off an obscenity. The flower beds crept across the paths until they formed a natural maze, a king's conceit with a dozen false turns and dead ends. A fat, high shaft of shrubbery changed, at its own command, into an antic natural topiary, with a bulbous top and a pair of protruding balls at its base. A small sea of white mushrooms popped up in the center of the lawn; their heads were mown down, but by the next morning they'd reappeared.

Turner's crew never did discover why all their efforts to turn my gorgeous garden into a polite little backyard failed. Holiday's contempt couldn't dissuade me, and his violence couldn't cow me. I still stripped off my clothes and wandered out onto the lawns; I still marched with my knees high among the hedges; I still splashed boldly in the fountain after they'd all gone to bed; I still ran through the paths and across the lawns as fast as I could, my parts flapping in the breeze, and then I stopped and crouched, buck wicked and berserk in the darkness: I was the royal better of the land, a usurper. For the first time I no longer felt watched by the world, under the great dome of its everpresent eye.

It was the garden of my America, the one I'd found, the one I'd made, a sky that faces a sky, with our boundless airs, our inventions and our atrocities written on it like vapor trails. No one had to tell me it was right. Here was my world, the world of my book, the book of my life; here was a country made for mooncalves, as if at any crossroads I might meet another like me, headed in another direction to make another backyard, and we'd tip our hats at each other politely, grin like drifters, and move on. Yes sir, I've always known that somewhere else some other boy is having his day, but there are plenty of places for us to invent our sudden trials, plenty of room for us all—though only one who wrote this song:

> I dug the ocean, I built the hills.
> Should have my face on dollar bills.
> I smoothed the Plains and planted grass,
> I made the devil kiss my ass.

I don't know what the house made of the home that surrounded them. Every night I listened for their praise, hiding behind the window onto the dining room with my ear turned to catch the flickers of their conversation.

. . . name was, said Anne.

Rocket. borrowed her shoes, said Marian.

window? said Anne.

After seven . . . , Holiday replied.

As the weather warmed they began to leave the windows open, and I know the sweet air charmed them; so I waited for a song back from the girls, though I wasn't sure what I was listening for. I knew if it were *my* house I would have hired an orchestra to sit in the windows and play music until midnight; but it wasn't my house, I was just a guest, and it was a strange house to me, with its lovely women and their fine manners, the walks they'd learned in dancing school (every Wednesday afternoon, in a smelly and haunted brick hall next to the hardware store downtown), the small, tasteful jewelry, seemingly painted on with a very fine brush (Olivia wore an antique silver and amethyst ring on her right hand, inter-

changeable earrings, and a tiny silver chain around her neck;
Marian wore a single pair of silver earrings, and Anne wore gold),
the rituals of borrowing and advising, and the fact, so curious and
impressive to me at the time, that they were never bored.

In time they became giddy. The girls would collapse into fits of
giggles at no point at all, laughing together until they snorted when
they tried to talk. One night they decided together that they
weren't going to speak for the rest of the night; instead they'd sing,
and soon even the most banal comments were couched in melo-
dies, which deteriorated to monotones as they grew bored. The
next day they chose to switch names: Olivia, lend me your grey
cardigan, Olivia said to Marian. Sure, Marian, said the older to
the younger, and they both went into the her bedroom, emerging
noisily a few minutes later: Olivia had a half dozen of her sister's
sweaters and was wearing them all. She banged into the door
frame and rebounded like a pinball, and Marian laughed so suddenly that she spit.

Later that week, while their parents were out to dinner, Marian
worked up a dance to a song on a record she'd bought and showed
it to Olivia. Come here, come here, come here, she said. Look at
this. I call it the Ass Dance.

Half-squatting on the floor, she waggled and swayed, and swiveled and humped, in circles around the kitchen table while the
song played loudly in the next room. She stopped and balanced
with her hands on the linoleum, then thrust her rear end into the
air, so that her hair fell in her reddened face and her shirt fell
down her front. Then she turned a short somersault, barely missing a trash can that was sitting on the floor at the end of the countertop, and ended up in a squat again. She got up to a crouch,
turned, pumped her arms like a chicken trying to fly, held her
hands out on her extended arms like an Indian dancer – and fell
into the table, knocking over an empty glass, which started rolling
towards the edge: Olivia lunged at it, lost her balance and fell,
bringing the whole thing halfway down with a huge crash. It

missed her sister by just a few inches, though a piece of wooden chair that had been shattered underneath did fly off and hit her arm. There was silence.

God, are you all right? said Olivia. I'm so sorry.

Marian was lying against the refrigerator. Oh, shit, she said, and laughed: they both laughed, and then Marian slapped the floor with the palms of her hands. Come on, Olive Oyl, let's go for a walk. We can clean this up later.

All right, but don't call me Olive Oyl.

Why not, Olive Oyl?

If you do I'll call you Marvin.

I don't care. Come on, Olive Oyl. She got up from her chair and started out the door.

Coming, Marvin.

Marian threw her shoulders back, took her sister by the arm, and started to march out of the room. We're the Miller sisters, she said. Marvin and Olive Oyl. Don't fuck with us — and at that moment the door shut behind them, and I didn't see them again until the next day, when they left the house together on their way into town.

If the girls were dizzy on sweet champagne, Anne warmed like a snifter of brandy in a taster's hands. She sang old songs as she went about the house. She switched to a brighter shade of lipstick. Her walk slowed and settled farther into her hips. One afternoon when the girls were out of earshot — Marian was out, and Olivia was playing *Jelly Roll* on the piano — I heard her make a lewd, affectionate suggestion to Holiday, who in return only furrowed his brow and frowned.

My house was gone: his house was mine. While they slept I reordered the books on bookshelves by color, by city of publication, to make long, absurd associations among their titles; one night I gently moved a bird's nest I'd found in a magnolia tree at the edge of their property to a spot under the eaves by Olivia's room, so that the singing would entertain her. I put mint leaves in their cof-

fee grinds and used lemon peels to sweeten the cistern. At midnight
I relit the house, divided it into pockets of shadows by changing
bulbs and bending lampnecks, until the places where they read
and relaxed were moved to where I could best cover them, and I
could hide where I wanted, and love and know.

Holiday and Anne began to bicker like a cartoon couple. I half
expected to find her in the kitchen doorway brandishing a rolling
pin; I thought he might come down one night in flannel pajamas
and a knitted nightcap to sleep on the couch. She teased him about
his overeating again, and anyway how was she supposed to get dinner on the table if he ransacked the refrigerator every night. He
couldn't find his favorite suit, the one he'd bought in New York,
and he was annoyed by the way she laughed at his absentminded-
ness. And she was spending too much money, he didn't know how,
and then she bounced a check that she couldn't even remember
writing. There were twigs and leaves all over the living room floor:
couldn't they keep the house clean? She didn't care. I heard her
purring to herself as she pruned an overgrown houseplant for the
third time in a week, her cheeks flushed, her eyes heavy-lidded.

That Saturday Holiday woke up early, dressed, and set off for
work, only to find his office closed. When he came home again he
blamed his wife for not stopping him, although she'd been fast asleep when he left. That Sunday at midnight I planted belladonna
among the flowers, whispering all the while:

> Sing oh! for a goblin's life
> Sing oh! for the life that's best
> Sing oh! for a goblin's wife
> And to hell with all the rest

You will scoff at how haphazard I was, as if I were some home-
grown Hamlet. His O was naught compared to mine. You'll think
me irresolute and dull, and you'll dismiss me. I don't care. Every
night as I returned to my bed I called the garden in, called it

closer. It did come. In time the house almost disappeared into the
foliage; they had trouble getting through the vines that hung down
over the doors. Low clusters of grapes hung over the back patio;
they jostled one another as they grew, until they shook free and
dropped from their own weight, spattering the flagstones with
blue juice. The rooms inside were as steamy as a hothouse, the air
was charged with oxygen, and the houseplants grew strong and
fertile, as if modeling the strength of the garden outside. Holiday's
mansion became a luxury liner lost at sea, and I became the sea.

9

I was everywhere in that house, an extra, unforseen
member of the family. I listened in on each conversation, spied on
each sleep. It became my avocation: if Olivia yawned, I saw. If she
sat down and then stood up again, I saw. If Anne took longer in the
bathroom in the morning, evaluating herself with her hands, if her
husband dialed a wrong number, if he changed his shirt before
dinner, if he muttered a name in his sleep, I knew. No gesture was
made without me, no midnight snack silently stolen from the refrigerator that my watchful eyes didn't mark. I knew where the
living room floorboards squeaked, knew the angles from the attic
windows.

It had been a while since the girls even bothered to say good-bye
when they left the house, but Holiday began to stop them as they
rushed towards the door, and he'd ask them where they were going, and with whom, and for how long; and if he wasn't happy he'd
keep them in. At the start Marian did as she was told; I remember,
in particular, an overnight birthday party that she missed because Holiday blocked the door. But after a week or two had
passed she began to ask him Why? with an expression of dismay
and offense. Then she started to argue with him, and once she sim-

ply waited until he and Anne had gone out to dinner, then left the house on foot, headed for a midnight picnic under the river bluff. When he came home and discovered her gone he decided to wait up for her, but she didn't return until early the next morning and by then he'd fallen asleep on the couch in the living room. When he awoke it was almost dawn and she was already in bed.

Apparently he went to her room and woke her, and there was some kind of terrible fight. I was in bed myself by then, fast asleep in the boiler room, and I didn't see it, but Olivia remembered waking up to her father's yelling and finding the lights on in the hallway, and pale-faced, dark-eyed Marian standing in her doorway in her underwear, staring defiantly at Holiday as he ranted. Anne tried to make light of it the next evening as she and Holiday were getting ready for bed, but he was still angry. Can't have this, he muttered.

Oh, leave the girl alone, she said, and touched her husband gently on his chest. She's just having some fun. But Holiday's dark stares at his eldest daughter continued for a week.

Olivia was more retiring than her sister, and as Holiday became more of a captor she became almost reclusive. Instead of going out at night she would go upstairs to read, or into the music room to practice the piano. Nonetheless, he began to watch her carefully, as if he were afraid she was planning to leave him forever, and then in anger at his own fear he became hard on her. He snapped at her when, in her sweet, thoughtless way, she forgot to close a window before a rainstorm, or knocked the dishes together while she was clearing the dinner table. He watched her from head to toe as she crossed a room, as if her very body were something she'd failed to get right – breasts on a girl like you? and where'd you get those hips? – until she became so self-conscious that she stumbled and blushed; he refused to kiss her goodnight anymore. Aren't you a little bit old for that? he said. She served the sentence quietly and without quite understanding, but she didn't let it disturb her powerful peace. I mean she was sugar.

10

Like sugar she began to melt and burn. She became sick with a sticky fever; it was with her when she woke up, opening her eyes amidst the smell of mud and sweet green garden fuses that had drifted under the window and into her room one warm spring morning. The girl hardly had enough energy to get out of bed. I watched from a crack in the basement door frame as she sat at the kitchen table, a plate of warm, gelatinous eggs before her. She stared at each forkful as if the food were ashes. Her face was pale.

Are you feeling OK? Marian asked, and her mother looked up and studied her, then leaned over and put the palm of her hand to Olivia's forehead. The girl shut her eyes and kept still. You're hot, Anne said. How do you feel?

Sick, Olivia answered. Tired. I'm not hungry.

Go back to bed. I'll call the school.

So Olivia went back up to her bedroom, pulled the shades, climbed under the covers, and slept for six more hours. The morning disappeared, and the afternoon was fading when she woke up again, went to the bathroom, and splashed water on her face. Her once clear eyes were cloudy with sleep, her nostrils pink around the edges. She was back in bed by nine that night.

When another day passed and Olivia wasn't better, Anne called the family doctor, who appeared solemnly at their door just before dinner and was led straight up to her room. He stayed there for a quarter of an hour; when he came out Anne was waiting in the hall, and I was waiting in the darkness at the top of the stairs to the attic. He shrugged and whispered.

It's probably just a bad case of flu, Anne said to Holiday in the living room. He said to wait a few days, and then call him again if it doesn't get better.

The next night Marian came home obviously drunk, her mouth slack, her walk uneven, and her clothes unkempt, covered with burrs and grass stains. She tried to slip past her father but she stumbled in the foyer and the noise alerted him. He came out of his study and stood in the door at the top of the stairs, waiting for her; when she raised her crazy eyes and saw him there she gave him a pained look and started to push past him; he took her forcefully by the arm. She tried to twist away; he squeezed and she yelped. You're going to wake your sister, he said, and then demanded loudly to know where she'd been. Swaying on her feet, staring at the ground for balance, she looked up at him slowly. I was out with some friends, she said, slurring her words a little.

No one wants you, he said suddenly, and then paused, embarrassed by the senselessness of his remark.

Marian looked up at him from under her brow, wearing an expression at once grievous and furious. A cumulus piled down into the hallway, thickening in an anvil shape above their heads. A mob ran past her into the rain—

Suck my dick, she said, then laughed a little and started to turn away; he tugged her back by her arm and hit at the side of her head with one open hand, slapping her awkwardly to the ground— suddenly she was lying on her side with her hand raised over her head to fend off another, her hair in her face, her hand to her cheek, hot tears falling through her helpless fingers. He stood above her, trembling.

Sobbing, with a shock that smothered her anger, she jerked her arm out of his grasp, and still on her hands and knees she pulled herself across the hall into her room, reached up for the handle, and pushed the door open. Before he could react she'd thrown herself inside, turned and twisted on her hip like a landed fish flopping on the floor of a boat, and slammed the door shut behind her.

A beat passed while Holiday stood in the hallway. Then he went to Marian's door, reached his knuckles up to rap, changed his mind, and let his hand drop again. Like the agents of a body's blood, the family began to move: Anne came to the threshold of their bedroom and watched silently as he turned and started downstairs. From Marian's room came the sound of something shattering against the door (it was a porcelain lamp base, a gift from her grandmother, and she would regret breaking it forever). A moment later Olivia's door opened and the girl came out. She stopped for a moment to rub the sleepy bewilderment from her eyes and then crossed the hall to her sister's room, where she knocked, spoke a word or two, and then, as the door opened just far enough for her to fit, slipped quickly inside. End of act umpteen.

11

Lights up on a circus ring. Midstage: monster. Feats of daring follow. One night, for example, I wrote an enormous O in bluegrass on the front lawn, homage to my unknown muse, a shade darker than the spears the firm had planted. It could hardly be seen from the ground, or even from the first-floor windows, but from the attic it was unmistakable, and in fact Holiday found it one weekend afternoon when he was up there searching for a box of papers, and had it pulled up the next day, though it took at least a week for the now-brown ring to disappear entirely. As they sat over coffee one evening later that same week, I slipped out into the dusk and made a planting of some phosphorescent algae in the fish pond so that at night it would shine with a greenish yellow cast. I'd found the rare and fragile stuff in a pet store in town, and while the light it eventually gave off was not the ghostly, electric glow that I'd hoped for – and had expected from the crude cartoon on the cover of the small white sack in which it came – I thought it was an interesting touch anyway.

12

In the garden, in the garden haze, I saw Marian walking briskly, wearing an expression so determined that I followed her, trotting slightly behind her and off to one side. Baker was in the front yard, clearing the grass catcher of a lawn mower. A moment later he started it up again, and the sound of its motor rose over the house and settled lazily down in the garden heat. Spot was on his hands and knees, pruning plants in the tomato patch, and as soon as Marian was within shouting distance she called to him without breaking her stride. Hey! she said, and he turned his head up and gave her a questioning look. Me? he mouthed, and gestured to his chest with a mud-spattered trowel. She didn't answer. Instead she stopped a few feet away from him, reached dramatically into the pocket of her jacket, pulled out a magazine, and began to brandish it at him. As soon as he recognized it he flinched, briefly looked to his right, as if hoping there were something there to carry him away, and then lowered his eyes. Is this yours? she demanded.

Where did you get that? he said, his eyes on a patch of grass just to the right of her right leg.

Is it yours?

Finally he looked at her, his face flushed and his eyes wet. That was in the truck, he said, softly.

The truck is in *my* driveway, she said, and shook the pages at him. What are you doing bringing something like this to my house?

I don't—

How dare you bring this around here. It's disgusting. She planted her feet and held the magazine by one corner so that it fell open in the sunlight, and I could see, even from a distance, the pale figure of a bare young woman on her back, her legs bent up as if she were balancing a large, invisible beach ball on the soles of her pink feet. There were two men bent over her. I had a sudden, absurd flush of worry for all three of them, buck naked and vulnerable as they were amid the branches and brambles of the garden.

Spot looked away. I thought if he got any redder he would burst like a piece of fruit, spattering the ground with seeds and bits of pulp. It's only . . . he said. Look, I'm sorry.

Marian closed the magazine and put it in her pocket again and then looked him up and down while he stood motionless, afraid to move. If you ever . . . she said, and spun on her heel. While she walked back to the house he went hastily back to his digging, though by the time she was at the back door the stubborn blows he made against the ground were utterly, ridiculously ineffectual.

She disappeared into her room, taking the magazine with her. She was locked away for the rest of the day, and no sound came from behind her door. Only very much later did I learn that she had been flipping through the pictures and thinking about herself, about boys and their incalculable want. She was bothered by the odd, too-sweet smell of the paper on which the photographs were printed; every time she turned a page it would come again. Occasionally she would pause and examine a spread; there was a secret somewhere, she knew, but nothing, no pose, no crevice or slope, seemed to hold a place for excitement to hide. She stripped her clothes off and compared herself frankly in the mirror on her closet door, posing herself in the afternoon sun as she thought a girl might, watching herself as she thought a boy might. She touched herself and caught, very briefly, a glimpse of the rude popularity she was looking for: her heart raced for a second: it was as if she'd turned her sex inside out like a glove and then tried to fit it back on her hand. The sensation passed, leaving her with a little touch of dizziness and a flush in her cheeks. She came down that evening to have dinner with her parents, and the look on her face was of perfect perplexity.

There were three of them at the table those days; Olivia was still ill, not getting better, not getting worse. Each evening her mother would bring her a tray of food and leave it for her to pick at. Each night they'd tiptoe past her room, afraid she'd wake if a floorboard creaked. After her meal on that evening Marian returned to her room, only to emerge again a minute later with the magazine hidden beneath her shirt. She entered her sister's room and shut the door behind her, and for the next hour they sat together and talked, a conversation of which I heard only one short part, the younger girl's sudden, loud giggling as Marian showed her the pictures.

13

As a rule Olivia started her homework at eight, though as the spring grew later she would sometimes wait until the sun had gone down. When she was ready she'd call a friend from a phone that her mother had brought her and placed by her bed, and would diligently write down in her notebook the work that her teachers had assigned, the exercises on pages 67-70 of *Second Year Algebra*, say; a chapter on Reconstruction in her social studies text (*The American Experience*); a poem by Poe for her advanced English class, with relentless feminine rhymes and a singsong meter that troubled her every night for a week as she tried to get to sleep. When at last she turned to her French lesson she pronounced the words out loud, *je veux, tu veux, il veut, vous voulez, nous voulons, ils voulent,* but softly, murmuring the unfamiliar phrases as if they were temptations to powers that she wasn't sure she wanted.

If she had favorites among the subjects they were hidden inside her head: her concentration caused her to frown over everything. The effort took its toll on the end of the only instrument she ever wrote with, a red-barreled fountain pen with a golden nib; it sat between her teeth as she thought, and she alternately chewed and sucked it as the words appeared and then vanished again. Out it came, the reversed cap still glistening from the sweet wetness of her mouth as she held it poised over the page, then crossed out a clause; in it went again, tipping up to her nose as she pursed her lips. Her handwriting was a girlish, eccentric half-script scribbled at a generous slant, within which fat loops appeared like loose threads in a seam, as if her thoughts were slightly unsure stitches in soft, deeply textured cloth. Upon finishing each night she'd turn to her diary for a while, and then, just before bed, hand the school papers over to her sister and say, Please don't read this, OK? Marian would deliver them to her teachers the following day, at the same time picking up the corrected pages of the day before. Her marks, I should say, were always high, and remained so until the school year ended. It ended – her indulgent mother let the girl go in on the last day, to cheer the coming summer with her friends – just a few days before Olivia and I met for the second time.

14

There was no reason for the hour I chose, though I would have liked to have had one. It was a Tuesday, and it was time, that's all. That night I lay on my back in bed as late as I could last and listened to the house make its midnight noises, the sudden cracks of the beams, the irregular pops of a window frame cooling, the rustling of a window sash above an air duct. A bright green parrot appeared from nowhere and perched in my thoughts. It pecked rapidly, silently, repeatedly at a wooden orange in a wooden bowl and then flew off again, dropping a single emerald feather that melted like a candy in my heated thoughts, leaving behind a slight sweet lime taste. I tried to ignore myself; instead, I imagined the lost pages of my father's book, posted the bones, felt the hard muscles and followed the veins, gave them nerves and wrapped the skin around them, savoring each addition as if I still held the pictures in my hands. When I was done it was still quiet, and I knew I couldn't wait any longer. I got up, smoothed my shirt, and began to tiptoe up the stairs.

When I came to Olivia's door I stopped. As I stood there, not moving, my seventeen years compressed into a minute that inflated like a soap bubble, with its reflected colors swimming and distorting on its expanding edge, a delicate sphere that soon detached and began to float slowly upwards on a current of warm air – and then burst when I finally touched her doorknob.

I was tender with the door; I closed it carefully behind me and stood at the foot of her hot bed, and my head filled with her unnameable scent, its specific gravity, the oil of her inflamed skin and her singular perfume. I was numb from the ache of sweet anticipation. There were strange electrons coursing through my nerves; my chest was a battery, heavy, warm and alive with artificial energy, and I thought the hum would wake her. It didn't: for a full five minutes I stood motionless in the darkness and watched her sleep under the moonbeams, so still, so quiet, a form under the bedclothes, slowly breathing, dreaming . . . A dark desk, a picture frame on the wall, its midnight glass reflecting my own uneven silhouette, a single shoe on the rug, a shelf of books and delicate mementos . . . I moved to the edge of her bed, and then sat slowly on one side and watched her until she woke up from the weight on her mattress, and –

She sat up suddenly and stared. Hello? Out came a soft, bare hand; when it met my wrist she dropped it gently back on the blanket.

Hello, I said. Her hair was matted and damp, and the bedclothes formed a second skin over her flesh. How are you?

Mmmm, don't know, she said, while her plump hands traced idle circles on the covers. She looked down from my face to her own covered body, blinking as if to see if she was still there. I touched a pair of fingertips to the side of her leg, drawing her eyes to my hand. I could feel the heat of her delirium escape through

the blanket. I was a mirage, a ghost shimmering in the headlights.
Who are you? she asked, not alarmed, curious. Her eyes opened
wide and then dropped half-closed again.

No one, I answered, and held up my threadbare arms as proof.
Don't worry. I bent to kiss her cheek; she offered it casually, made
a slight noise with her lips, smiled softly.

How did you get here? she asked.

I was made here.

No you weren't. How did you get here?

I live in the basement.

Why?

Back to sleep, I said.

No, she insisted. Talk to me; I can't sleep anymore.

Can't talk now, I said, and slipped away again.

15

You didn't think I'd hurt her, did you? Did you
think I could? From out of my years as a ghost? The stars would
have fallen from the sky, to die as glittering litter on their front
lawn. I'd never before wanted anything and I'd never again want
anything else, but I needed to be met in kind, or else the self that
made my wanting possible would vanish like an afterimage at the
edge of sight. I didn't know anything, I'd never known anything,
and my desires were like a film out of focus: for all their force, still
undescribed. I was out of time, out of place, like a pauper on stage
at the ballet, his hat in his hands, his eyes wide. I'm saying, I
didn't know about girls and their ways, I didn't know what was expected of me. I was counting on some atavism to prompt me. When
it failed to show I went into the garden, built a nest out of scavenged scraps of self-scorn, placed an egg inside, and waited for
something, anything, to break out.

16

Shhh. Holiday is by his daughter's bedside, his wide frame awkwardly hunched over in the girl-sized chair he's pulled over from her desk. It's late in the afternoon, but the shades are down over the windows and the room is dark and isolated. Not a word, not a footstep, not a sound.

How's my little girl? he asks. The family doctor was by this morning to take a few drops of her precious, sluggish blood. She hadn't flinched when the needle went in, but as soon as he was gone she peeled the bandage from the crook of her arm, and she spent most of the day with her forefinger absently resting over the tiny, blood-blue bump. Late this afternoon a tentative diagnosis of mononucleosis was phoned in to Anne. Plenty of rest, plenty of fluids, not to worry. She called Holiday at the office and he came home early, and now sits in her bedroom. We haven't spoken in a while, he says. You know I've been busy at work.

I know.

Your mother says you slept all afternoon.

I did, I'm sorry, she replies, and he, not even catching the absurdity of her apology, goes on to ask her – no, instruct her, to get well. She sighs and looks down at her hands.

Watch carefully, now: he is about to change everything. He hikes his cuffs up so he can cross his legs, leans forward in his seat, and frowns. Do you know, he asks his lonely daughter, his bored daughter, who sleeps too much and thinks too much and aches from both, who loves her sister, who believes that her father is to be admired, whom a boy like me wants the way a prisoner wants parole, Do you know why Marian is being so difficult? I know you know. You do. I want you to tell me if she's keeping something from me.

Olivia turned over in her bed and lay there silently until her father put his hands on his knees, sighed loudly, stood, and left the room.

17

That night while she slept I put a present on her dresser top, a large, clear marble with a blue glass coil suspended in it. The next night I stole in and left her a sprig of lilac I had grown, the night after a small blank book bound in dark green cloth, with a black ribbon to hold it shut. Each time I returned I noticed the previous item had been carefully worked into her room; the marble went into a cup on her shelves, the lilacs into a beveled crystal glass she'd stolen from beneath the sideboard in the living room, the book gone, presumably in a drawer. A small brass bell was next, then a new nib for her pen, then a map of the world. At last I left a small, impossibly ugly doll, a homunculus only a girl could love, with bulging eyes and wild hair, and a rubber belly, punctuated by the pock of its deep navel, that hung over its belt line—a troll, in fact, an effigy and a promise.

I waited to approach her again. I let her lie in bed, because I knew that even as I waited she was thinking; and with her thinking, she was changing. Had she heard her own voice back she might have wondered where those words had come from, but she'd never been angry before, and however long her temper had been in coming she was so unused to the sensation that she mistook it for a tension her sickness had described. To admit that her father had lost hold of her affections was like settling alone in a new town; but I knew and I was waiting to welcome her there. When the days had passed and she'd settled, I checked my trembling, came out of the basement, and headed straight up the stairs.

From the moment I crossed the threshold of her room I felt a kind of enchantment, as if I'd stepped into storybook chambers, outside of which was not a house but a child's bookshelf, so that upon opening the door again I'd find a raft of adventuring sailors on a dark blue sea, or a sultan's cave of shimmering riches. I locked the door from the inside so that we wouldn't be disturbed, and when I turned back I could see the shadows of her dresser, a faint grey image framed on the wall, her bed with its mysteries, her hillocks on the plains. There had been an electrical storm earlier in the night, and the air was thick with ozone. Olivia lay sound asleep with her blanket drawn up to her neck, her hands over her head, one set of fingers curled lightly around the post of the head-board, the other bent beside her ear.

I woke her by placing my left hand on her covered left hip until she stirred. She raised her head calmly, and her eyes were clear: Oh, hello again, she said, and sighed. A minute passed while the room filled with ancient, silent static, the noise of a phantom radio tuned to the spaces between the stars. You're the boy from our party, aren't you? she asked. I saw you in the garden last week. So sleepy. I nodded.

Did you leave me those things? I nodded again. That was sweet, she said, and then sighed: it sounded like the rustle a hand makes in a candy jar. My father's going to kill you.

He might, I said. How are you feeling? I brushed a strand of her hair from her cheek.

OK, she said. She frowned. Who are you?

18

Exterior of the dark house. Sound of crickets.

19

I said, It's true I'm an incubus, a disturbance, a rip-ple in your reverie. I said, Let me lie here and watch, seeing over you while you sleep there, selfless and unashamed, your face un-hidden, your body bare beneath your blanket. You've heard sto-ries, and they are true, of how the monkey got a monkey's face, how turtles sleep inside their shells, how worms eat dirt and birds eat worms. And at night fish swim slowly through your room, sculling silently in your dreams: there's a flash of silver skin, there's a hand upon your arm . . . Here, draw back the bedclothes, I said. Put down the shades.

You do talk, she said. But I know who you are, and I knew this would happen. And then without the slightest warning she tipped her head back and drew a breath, arched under my hand and parted her trembling limbs, exposing her tender, pale belly. Then she reached up for my shoulder and, brooking no denial or disbelief, pulled me down to her.

20

A first kiss is an element of supernature; there's no preparing for the shock of the lips first opening, of the slick tongue licking, of the taste of being tasted. There's the life of the beloved, the effortless, ongoing bellows of her body, her quickening eyes, the graceful shift of her limbs, her gulps and gasps, in a subtle breath that enters through her humid mouth, and leaves with particles of spent appetite. I bent over Olivia, but I couldn't see her eyes, only her warm, smeary lips as they opened to expose her mouth, a dark flash of her tongue, her sweet, hot breath as she sighed, and kissed me.

And then?

Puella. It's a long story.

Ring of Fire

1

When I awoke the following morning I was alone in her soft bed, with her yellow blanket pulled over my legs. There was sun under the window shades, and a bittersweet scent in the air. My skin was tender from the night before, my mouth still swollen and filled with an awkward taste. I could see my clothes in a small pile next to a pillow that had landed on the floor during the night, and her nightgown draped neatly over the back of the chair at her desk. Legs entangled in a shroud, a twisted sheet, I unraveled it and pressed it to my chest. It smelled slightly sour. The house was stalled, dead quiet, but I could hear a faint droning through the window from a tiny plane passing overhead, the dim white ceiling of her room, the sky.

I'd just resolved to sit up when the door opened and she came in, wearing a pair of navy blue sweatpants and a black, black-buttoned jersey. She crossed the floor and stopped at the foot of the bed, where she stood and watched me with a half-smile on her lips as I hastily pulled the bedclothes over my midriff. Down went her hand, and she grabbed the bottom of the blanket and pulled it away again, leaving me with only a sheet to cover myself, and still she watched me, still smiled.

Good morning, she said at last, in a voice like a country church bell. It's ten-thirty, you have to get up. It's a good thing I woke up early, or else my mother might have come in. She went to the window and jerked down on the shade, releasing it so that it flew up and flapped around the roll and a burst of sunlight leaped into the room. And I have to wash these sheets before she gets back. With that she reached down again, took hold of the top linen, and tore it off the bed, and as it hung to the floor from one hand she gestured towards a few sienna spots on the bottom sheet with the other. You see, she said. That's what happens. Now, come on.

She was all business for the next few minutes. She handed me my pants and turned away as I pulled them on, and she had the mattress stripped and was standing in the doorway before I'd buttoned my shirt. Everyone's gone out, she said matter-of-factly. I'll be back in a second, don't go anywhere.

But as soon as the door shut behind her I was gone: I ran to snowy Alaska, then sailed across the straits to Asia, wandered down through the steppes of Mongolia and crossed into vast, pale green China. There I hid in a farmhouse, drinking tea from a white porcelain bowl and passing pleasantries with the peasantry, until the door opened and glancing-eyed Olivia came in. She looked at the unmade bed, then at unmade me. She rubbed her nose with back of her hand, looked at the floor, looked at me, at the floor, out the window, at me. For a moment I thought that she'd forgotten everything, our numb introduction, the soft, sudden wrack of her body – and sleeping on her side afterwards, with her legs entwined with mine, her back against my chest and her backside pressed into my hips. Suddenly she laughed as if she had been tickled by a ghost and said, Marian . . . never mind. This is weird, it really is. I mean . . . you won't tell anyone, will you?

Me? I thought. I don't know anyone, here's to ten thousand miles of highway. No, I assured her out loud. She examined my face and then lowered her lashes. OK, she said. Well look, Wilson . . . I think you'd better go now.

At once I stood and started blindly into the hall, and she followed me out as far as the threshold of her room. When am I going to see you again? She asked as I reached the stairs.

Again is such a pretty word, a joining arc in a comforting circle of time. I turned around. Tonight, if you'd like, I said.

Come here. Taking me by both hands she stood up on her toes, quickly kissed my cheek, put her lips to my ear, and whispered. Then she backed through her door until our arms were outstretched like suspension cables on a bridge, slowly slid her damp fingers away, smiled briefly, and turned into her room. When she shut the door I was left alone in the hallway, with the heat from her hand melting on mine.

Exit, chased by a bear.

2

Her mind remained febrile through the following days, but I was there to distract her: I went to her every night, early if her parents were out at dinner or visiting friends, late if I had to. She would always be awake and waiting for me when I arrived, and she would always be relieved that I'd made it to her safely, always a little bit puzzled by my ability to move through the house without being felt, always excited that at last she had a secret worth keeping. They were a polite family, they knocked before coming into her room, and Olivia would ask them to wait a second. I was a character she had invented, a young boy dreamed by a young girl who was confined to her bedroom in her parents' house for too long, a lover she had conjured up to help her pass the hours.

The hours passed. I felt a wild english in my soul, and any moment that I couldn't be with her I grew dizzy with impatience and curiosity. While she was awake I entertained her with tales of my troubles and adventures, and she listened to them all with perfect peace, and told me her own as if they had been written in anticipation of my coming. When I sang her to sleep:

The lights go down, the music ends
Say goodnight to all your friends
Take my hand, and we'll get lost
To the tune of the Mississippi Waltz

she slept, for an hour, or an afternoon, or a week.

From here the time we had together looks like no time at all; however distended it may have been it had no duration, and nothing moved. We would not fall away. We were perpetual children in perpetual motion, and she smiled and smiled; I stole kisses from her now and then just to make sure she wouldn't mind, tentatively held the undercurve of her breast, bussed her shoulder while she smiled curiously. I danced like an ape at the foot of her bed, I was Olivia's fool, I could say anything, so long as it was either right, or wrong enough to make her laugh. Except – the first time I told her of my natural state, of my goblinhood, she frowned and dismissed the fact with one graceful wave of her pale hand. The second time she laughed uncomfortably. When I told her again she grew angry with me and told me harshly not to say anything about it again. So I put that letter down – anyway it was dying – shifted my weight, and lay my head in her lap so I could listen to her stories.

They wandered like an unfortunate sailor on the dips and swirls of her voice, its changing currents, the effort when it rose on a rock, the sounds on which her tongue caught and snarled like seaweed on a fishhook, weighing down the word. I memorized the manner of every note, how she burst words in exclamation, how she curled her mouth around a soft consonant, blotted one, ticked her tongue against another; some she allowed to drift into a smile; others she simply spoke with a wit that proved itself by hiding. You see, a woman and her body meet at a membrane, a thin, expressive film between her thoughts and the specific music her public knows: it is her voice. To this day I'd recognize Olivia's at the first word, the first vowel that her tongue produced, because I immediately loved her and loved to hear her.

It wasn't just her voice: I collected her habits as if they were

coins: she was afraid of heights; she would blush with embarrassment at the way her tongue slipped out of her mouth when she
laughed, then laugh at her embarrassment, grow embarrassed at
that laughter, and dissolve into ingrown red-faced giggles; she
would wriggle in response to the tip of my finger between two particular folds of skin . . .

I wondered at her body, how she softened into traces of fat
where her ribs collapsed, leaving gummy sections above her hip-
bones, mounted on her cambered spine and the hard, narrow
muscles of her lower back. I buried my blind mouth in the salty pit
of her throat, the coarse patch on the back of her elbows, the thin
line of sweat collected in the crease behind her knees, the private
lining of her thighs, the sudden, stiff black hairs and slick, darkened crevices, warm puddles and ponds. How damp she was, how
soaked with perspiration and saliva, hot tears in her eyes, balance
water in her inner ear, and just beneath soggy skin a flush of blood
and bile, sticky humors, sap, waste, lust and wetness. Kisses,
kisses. I couldn't touch her body anywhere without raising a
heavy, scented drop of molasses to my fingertip, or causing some
part of it to move, a limb to shift, her belly to tighten, the tone or
scent of her breath to change; I was fascinated by the resilience of
the cups and bowls of flesh that enveloped the tubules and crimson
gullies below, the numberless threads that attached them to her
thin spine and rigged splinters of bone; I could mold the porous
surface with my hands, and still each damp part would return to
its place, albeit reddened by a blush of blood that had risen to the
spot where the surface had been abraded, and which was all there
was to mark her with the suggestion that she hadn't been alone, a
fleeting sign of the contingency, the particularity of our engage-
ment.

When I was inside her I could feel the strength she drew on to
hold me, never leaving me, never faltering. I would give myself up
and brace myself to fall into her, hugely, half-terrified, out into
nothing, her powerful O. I didn't know, I always ended in her
arms, there was that familiar scent, familiar flesh against my

cheek; she was still there, beating beneath her breastbone, her hand on the base of my neck. I would nearly weep for sweet weakness and want of self.

I will now fold and seal this envelope, with its crumpled note and humid perfume, and carefully hide it away.

3

It was a clear Sunday afternoon, with a sky bluer than blue, and the air warm and just slightly damp. Holiday, Anne, and Marian were out on the back porch along with one of Anne's friends, a red-haired woman, in a blue dress who seemed to want to be elsewhere. I was in the attic, watching from the window. I wanted to hear them, so I pushed the glass up, raised the screen, and stuck my head out, but I was too far above them for the sounds of their conversation to reach me, and the angle from which I watched obscured their faces: I could read the motions of their bodies, but not enough to tell what kind of time they were keeping. Anne was brushing back a thin tree branch that had recently grown over the table, but each time she absently pushed it aside it would glide back before her face. Holiday was gesturing with one hand, and as he went on their guest leaned farther and farther back in her chair, like a timid swimmer trying to escape a giant wave. I could see her hands rise to her midriff in preparation for the blow.

It was not Holiday to whom she was responding: it was Marian, and he went on obliviously. Anne put her hand on her husband's for a moment, but he shook it off in the course of gesturing at his daughter, and then at the house. All at once Marian started to move; first she leaned forward, then she leaned back again, and I heard her voice as it rose to a hoarse shout. What's wrong with me! she yelled as she abruptly stood up from the table, spilling drinks into quickening laps. On her way into the house she halted and turned her head up towards me, squinting into the bright sky, and then dropped her eyes again and ran quickly into the house as I pulled my head into the attic and swore myself up and down for being careless.

4

Here, I have something for you.

For me?

You've been so nice about me being sick and all. It's just this little thing.

What is it?

It's just something I got. Open it. I'm not going to tell you.

She handed me a dark blue book-sized box. When I lifted the lid I found white tissue paper inside, folded over to cover the contents. With thumb and forefinger I delicately peeled back the translucent covers; beneath I discovered a dozen brown bulbs nestled together on a thin bed of white cotton. They were about the size of golf balls, and some had pale white tubules already poking through the surface. They gave off a faint odor of soil. I plucked one out and held it in the palm of my hand; it was as hard as a walnut from the compression of its patient cells. They're called orchid irises, Olivia said. The man in the store said they'd come up purple in the spring. I know you've been spending so much time with me that you haven't been able to work, so I wanted to give you something. If we plant them now, we can wait for them to come up. She nodded as she spoke, as if neither the words themselves nor her tone of voice, at once enthusiastic and questioning, were enough to convey her desire that we plant together, wait together, and then note what we had grown, and her confidence in the long association to which it testified. I replaced the bulb in the box, put the box on her night table, and then lay her down on her back on the freshly made bed, where I gave her a kiss as long as the Champs-Elysée.

My favorite thing from a book, ever, said Olivia as we were getting into bed later that evening, is that little man jumping up and down all by himself somewhere, when he thinks no one's looking, and singing, What a good thing it is, that no one knows, my name is Rumpelstiltskin.

5

The bulbs went into a secret corner of the garden later that night, away from the rest of the plants in a spot where I hoped they would form a secret patch of purple, unadmired by anyone but Olivia and me. Through the following days I tried to doctor the girl with attention, with a laugh late at night and a glass of water to wet her throat, with the drops of sweet love that I'd distilled over the day. In return she gave me a book, a kind of encyclopedia of occult arts and sciences, of which there existed only a single hand-written copy, bound in ocean blue. Together we leafed through its pages, randomly opening to one or another entry. In a chapter on botany we discovered a flower with large, fleshy petals that trembled and sweated at the merest hint of a stranger's approach. Under Sport we found a game for an unopposed team, to be played on a field abandoned after a summer rainstorm, when pond-like mud puddles appeared amid tufts of grass. Another entry described a kind of phenomenal origami for two, an art of topographic folds that made a stiffened nipple appear beside the rounded, covered plate of a kneecap, or the hanging drop of an earlobe press against an inner thigh. There were illustrations, too, of silver coins with tails on both sides, of the shy mouth of an upended bottle, of a fat lioness licking her belly lazily, or a fucked girl sighing thickly. Of other, less illuminated passages

I'll remain silent, except to say that she was a very curious, very adventurous girl, a girl given to fits of surprisingly coarse appetite, a beautiful, greedy girl; that she laughed a lot and winced a few times; and that as her store of achievements grew she began to shine like a mirror at which someone has aimed a lamp.

6

Aside from the planting I just mentioned the house and its garden were left alone, and although her senses were often stopped and I had only the sound of her sea-slow breathing for company, I left our hideout only when I had to, saving my foraging in the refrigerator for the latest possible hours. I sang:

> I got a girl, sweet sixteen
> Damnedest thing I've ever seen
> Sleeps all night, sleeps all day
> And what she dreams I couldn't say
>
> Well I got a girl, she treats me nice
> She loves me once and then she loves me twice
> And when again she falls asleep
> I give myself her soul to keep

I remember taking her arm in my hand and gazing at it, admiring its composition, the pallor produced by so many layers of fine translucence. I could see blue veins raised beneath, as if her blood had been replaced with warm saltwater. But I worried about what inner disability could have been rewritten into such outward beauty, so I used to try to wash away her sickness by opening the window to let in the cool, clear air, and then joining her in her hot bed again, where I would stroke her gently while she slept, as if to draw the illness out of her. I think of those first dreamy drops of morning, the fine grey cast out her window, Olivia waking within the compass of my unending and patient eye. I would forget the pointless movement of the clock, in those hours I spent patiently waiting for her to escape her oblivion, while the whole world, round as it was and surrounded by water, reveled in its roundness and gently revolved. So you can keep your money, and take my name, too; you can seat yourself at world's end and legislate like Solomon. I was seventeen, and knew neither the poet's lyric nor the schoolyard boast. She was sixteen and sick. But as long as I had Olivia I wouldn't have changed my lot with kings.

One night I came back from my dinner and found her in the bathroom, bending naked over the sink while she washed her face. She rose when I came in and smiled slightly at my reflection. I came up behind her and wrapped her in my arms. Her broad, naked hips hid mine, and her shoulderblades, still slightly clammy from her shower, pressed against my chest. Under the light I could see the inch-long scar on the front of her knee, the trace of an operation she'd had after falling from a horse a few years earlier (there was another, fishhook-shaped white line behind her ear, where her sister had hit her with a toy boat when they were children). She reached for a navy blue hand towel that sat amid the mess of her bath things on the counter before us, the English soap, an uncapped toothpaste tube with a blot of neon blue left extruding from the little nozzle at the end, a bottle of clear astringent, a red aerosol antiperspirant can. When she'd finished drying her face she looked up; I found my own image in the mirror, with hers before me, her head tilted slightly back to rest upon my shoulder, her spine curved until her shoulderblades pressed into my chest, her dark sweat-flattened curls framing her pale face. I put one arm around her waist, and with the other hand I gently cupped the dry closure towards which her hips tended. The light above the bathroom sink was on and it raked down across us; her skin was dull and pale from her illness, and the surface just beneath her eyes was drawn and damp, as if from lust. As I watched her face her gaze moved gently back and forth between us, so that sometimes I caught her looking at herself, and sometimes her indolent eyes met mine. Strangest of all was when, sensing her watching me as I watched myself, I felt brief jolts of belovedness. Then I could see myself, not a beast but loved, and with an uncommon, terrible, almost unbearable generosity. When she finally pulled away to fetch a towel my hand was damp with a spoonful of slick, mossy attar.

7

Here is a photograph of the two sisters as little girls. It was in a silver frame on Anne's bedroom dresser, a well-worn charm stamped with a trellis of serrated leaves, a precious and permanent border between the scene inside and the violence of passing days. Now it is in my memory.

I asked Olivia about it once. She frowned as if she were annoyed that I'd settle on such a thing, when there was so much that was more important to know. It was an heirloom, she said, passed on from her great-grandmother to her mother some years past. You get it next, I said. I suppose, she replied, and shrugged. Unless Marian does.

In the picture the two girls are sitting side by side on a short flight of marble stairs, while behind them looms the old oak door of a church, with a great brass ring doorknob and thick black hinges. Marian is about five, my Olivia perhaps three, and seems not so much a younger version of the girl I knew as a counterpart in some half-fictive metaphysical dimension. It's the afternoon of a cousin's wedding, and the two of them are flower girls; they're wearing white dresses trimmed with delicate lace and holding beribboned bouquets, and Marian has a small, crowning ring of white flowers in her hair. There are high-noon shadows on the stairs by their legs. Olivia is leaning so far over that she's sprawled onto her sister's lap, although she doesn't seem to notice; she's gazing obliquely down at something just beside Marian's shiny black shoes, her baby face wearing an expression of seriousness that borders on a pout. In contrast to her sweet absorption her sister seems positively theatrical: she looks out at the camera with a wide, gap-toothed grin, her elbows planted firmly on her knees, her small hands crossed under her sharp chin.

8

On the evening of the Fourth of July I went to visit my more majuscule O after dinner. The sun was just setting, and as the edge of the earth rose the clouds on the horizon turned into a red lipstick smear. It was going to be a hot night, the kind of night that cheated insidiously against screen doors and open windows, that made fat, bloody-wet babies born in April. Meet me by the pond in the backyard in twenty minutes, she said, and when I asked her why she put her hand to my mouth and then, as a joke, tucked the tip of one finger in upon my tongue. Just meet me.

I watched her as she sneaked out the back door and made her way across the lawn. She was wearing black jeans, a grey sweatshirt, and a pair of tan hiking shoes, and when she spotted me she hurried over, grabbed my hand, and pulled me across the grass towards the fence. Come on, she said breathlessly. If they know I'm gone . . . When we reached the fence she stopped for a second, and then climbed it awkwardly, casting her leg up to the highest strand and throwing herself half over until, with her hair down, laughing, she fell onto her feet on the other side. Come on, she said. I vaulted over to her side. Olivia, I said. Oh, shut up, she answered, and stuck her thick tongue out at me. Then she grabbed me by the hand again and led me running across the street and up the dark driveway of the neighbors behind. Shhhh! she said loudly. We skirted the side of the house and then crossed into the next yard. Watch out, she said as we came upon a patio with a swimming pool sunk in it, the moon dissolving into an ivory slick on its surface.

I was lost, running to keep up with her as the shadowy yards and fences passed, another road, a small copse of town trees, a road again, and then a chain link fence that she fell against breathlessly, causing the metal to rattle softly and distend inward. Behind it was a closely planted wood, so dense that it was impossible to see more than a few yards into the trees. She put one foot through a diamond in the fence, turned to me, and said, Help me, will you? Overhead a tower of high tension power lines buzzed softly. I could feel her feverish skin through her shirt as I steadied her.

The woods proved to be an illusion; a few quick blind steps brought us to the edge of a golf course, a fantastic landscape at that hour with its rolling, close-cropped fields and far tiers of trees, among which the blue dusk collected in darker, gauze-grey patches. Now, you've got to keep down, she said before she took off again. I followed in a crouch across a wide felt lawn, around a large pond, across another strip of grass, and then to the edge of a sand pit, which took both of us so completely by surprise that together we tumbled down into its soft, firm drifts. She let out a laugh and immediately began crawling clumsily back up towards the top, with me in pursuit. Look, she said as we arranged ourselves, side by side, with our heads just over the lip. Over there. She pointed to a building about a quarter of a mile away over the grass. I could see a line of cars parked in front of it, and a ragged line of dark figures gathered up to the edge of the green. This is where—

Oh! the sky blew open and an orb of red sparks rapidly expanded above us. Olivia ducked as another, green ball went off with a bang. I think we're—white flash—I thought! she yelled as a series of rockets swirled in a cloud of grey smoke that had collected in the illumination. I was afraid that if I reached my arm up I would lose it at the elbow. Oh my god. It began to rain bits of hot metal, and she rolled over to brush firelets out of her hair as a bright cobalt burst snapped open in the sky directly overhead, and then another. The noise grew, and she threw herself against me; I lost my balance and we fell, rolling in a rough tangle down the soft slope to the bottom of the sand trap again. There was a green shadow on her face, and a crackling sound in the sky. She grabbed my arm and pointed; above us there was nothing but the vault of the heavens outlined by the edge of the pit, and dying sapphire embers: then two more explosions, red rockets and sizzling white stars that intermingled with one another and the shadows of the dead sparks as they landed in the sand beside us – Another blue, unrelenting blue and emerald set of splashes, so low that they formed a triumphal ceiling over the pit, a dome of dumbstruck glory – and all at once the light grew and the percussion came faster and louder, lighting the air with fat flashes of white, and dense, symmetrical constellations suddenly expanding into soft motes and filaments of colored dashes. My ears began to ring painfully, my heart pounded in my chest, and my nostrils stung with the sharp smell of cordite. Olivia let out a squeal and rolled on top of me, shaking and clutching my shoulders with her soft hands. Then she began whispering hotly in my ear, frantically relating some long point that I couldn't quite hear; before she'd gotten the first word out a barrage of cannon shots and copper fire began that I thought would ignite the air. I could feel her stomach pressed against mine, her hips between my hands as if I were taking her down from a tree, her crotch pushing excitedly against mine as she spoke.

And then it was over, just as the last words – *rest of my life* – slipped from her mouth. Applause drifted from across the lawn, and then car horns. I asked her to tell me what she'd said, but she frowned at me and then scrambled up the side of the sand, and when I followed her I found her crouched down on the edge of the grass. Together we watched the headlights flash; and then the spectators congratulated each other, climbed slowly into their cars, and drove away. Olivia stood and dusted the granules of sand from her thighs. Oh, she said. I'm so sorry, and she laughed. Get up. I didn't know it'd be right here. I really thought we were going to die. Get up. She came to me, took my hand, and tugged me until I got to my feet. I could feel her pulse beating through the moist skin on her wrist, and I bent forward to kiss her. No, she said, and instead wrapped her arms around me, lay her head on my shoulder, and squeezed me as tightly as she could.

That night I heard her laughing in her sleep.

9

The heat at which the spring had hinted became full midway through the summer. Hardly a day went by in late July without a sunstorm interrupting the hours and enforcing an idleness that soon began to connect the month together, giving it a tone which a given afternoon might have lacked, but which, in retrospect, seems more real than any of our actions. I remember, for example, the idea of evenings that the day seemed to have exhaled more than I do any particular after-dinner stroll, and a blood-orange moon that sat motionless above the treetops for a week.

After everyone had gone to bed, I used to come down from Olivia's room or up from the basement and slip quietly through the dark house to the kitchen, where I would retrieve the day's newspaper from a pile of discards by the back door. One midnight I read that the captain of a barge on the river had fallen asleep at the helm the night before and had collided in the darkness with a motorboat. The latter sank, and the barge had cracked open so that its cargo – a shipment of sorghum, I think it was – spilled into the water.

Another night a windstorm tore off a large branch of a cherry tree in the front yard. It fell across the driveway, and Holiday had to wait the next morning until the gardeners arrived – forty-five minutes late. By cutting the limb into pieces with a loud chainsaw they managed to get him on the road by noon. When they were finished there were pale yellow drifts of sawdust on the blacktop.

A water pipe that ran behind the property burst one night later in the month, and the next morning the bottom half of the garden had become a silver reflection of the pale blue sky. Baker, Spot, and Willie were sent home.

Olivia sat in her room that afternoon, her skin dry and goose-pimply from her air-conditioning, and wrote a letter to her best friend, a classmate who'd moved off to Houston two years back. I snuck up to her as she was finishing it, and she folded it carefully in thirds and began to address an envelope as she described the girl to me. Her name was Susan, her mother was Mexican, her body was boyish, and her mind was wicked. She never left the house without taking along a camera and looking for a war.

— What do you want to be, anyway? she asked suddenly. The question was so unexpected that the first thought that came to me was, A rattlesnake. I said as much, and she opened her mouth in surprise and then laughed. No, be serious, she said.

Be serious? A vein of iron ore, a bass guitar.

Stop it . . .

A bucket of paint, a monkey's uncle, a pumpkin pie.

Shhh.

Why, what do you want to be? But by then she was mad at me and wouldn't answer; and the more I begged the more adamantly silent she was, until finally she said, Leave me alone! The batteries of the afternoon whirred down and went dead.

I raised the question again a week or so later, but instead of answering she stared at me as if I'd torn her clothing; I shrank, and she said, sarcastically, A potato bug. I never asked her again, so whatever distant occupation she'd imagined for herself — toy-maker? cardsharp? author? — was lost to me forever, evaporated in the summer sun like a poolside puddle.

Housebound and bothered by the hot, damp weather, the family became helplessly reliant on one another, and I was almost always hiding. There were not enough rooms. Holiday in particular

took the heat badly; if he'd thought he could stop it by sheer force
of will he would have tried, but it's not in a man to shed coolness.
His birthday fell at the end of the month; he would be fifty-eight.
Anne and Marian had planned a dinner out, but that evening he
came home, hung his coat in the hallway closet, and went to find
Anne.

I'd rather we stayed in tonight, he said. She was in their bathroom, putting on perfume. It's been a very long and tiring day.
I've already called the restaurant and canceled our reservations.

Anne gestured at her body to indicate the silk slip she was wearing, but he was already halfway out the door. She was left to blush
slightly, sigh heavily, and change her clothes again.

So there was a short, hastily fixed dinner at home (Olivia attended), followed by a brief, dry ceremony of presents, and then
he went for a drive alone, leaving his wife and daughters to clear
the table, watch a movie on TV, and reassure one another that, after all, he'd had a good time.

10

The king is in his counting house, counting out his
money. The queen and one princess watch television in the living
room, its bright chatter echoing through the house; and – quiet –
behind the door of her darkened bedroom the younger heir has a
secret audience with the jester. He shows her delightful tricks,
performs feats of magic (now you see it, now you don't!), impossible stunts for her hot laughter. In a moment of fast emotion she
said she loved me, and my heart inflated with rare motion at the
exclamation, so that I didn't answer. She smiled at my expression.

A little later we heard a knocking at the door, and the period
breached was so private that at first I thought someone was standing over her, asking permission to open her up like a Russian doll,
not knowing that I was in there. Within a moment I had slipped

out and scrambled into her bathroom, where I crouched behind her shower curtain, shivering and listening as he entered the room. What on earth are you doing in here? he asked, and I thought I heard him sniff the air slightly. Um, exercises, said Olivia breathlessly. The doctor said I should.

In the middle of the night? said Holiday. You can hear it out in the hallway.

Sorry, Olivia replied. I couldn't sleep. I'll try to make less noise.

. . . Later, I lay supine on the bed, and she sat like an outlaw astride my hips, her warm slick holding me; she cocked her head back gently to move her hair off her shoulder. Hush. Olivia was always trying to quiet me. She made a face from some effort inside her. Can you feel that? she whispered.

What?

I'm squeezing. She squinted again and something moved. There. Did you feel that?

A little, like a little grip.

I should work on that. Squeeze you. She rose up on her haunches slightly, bent over and put her hand over my mouth, and I could taste the invisible salt and sandpaper of her fingertips.

Later, the river quickened as it narrowed.

And later, she sat up against the headboard and began to tell me about her mother's family, a summer spent in a house by the beach with a dissolute uncle whom everyone but her aunt adored – but just as she'd started to describe the boat they took out into the Gulf she trailed off, turned her eyes away and mumbled, I'll never know what every one else knows. Her voice was so soft that I had to ask her to say it again. I'll never know. I'll always miss the glances, always stare stupidly at a joke that everyone else gets, and . . . everyone will always treat me like a child. Her eyes were glassy with tears. All these things happen, and I don't understand why, she said. I don't understand what everyone wants, I don't understand what I'm supposed to do, I don't understand, what, why do I . . . ?

She was shaking. I touched my hand to the back of her neck, high up under her falling hair, drew an encouraging breath, and began. Olivia, I said. Look at me: all I know is you. No one ever says anything. Come with me. Your grandmother, your mother had a father, but they left home. Your sister will go someday, and they'll be glad for her. You're no different; soon it'll be time for you, too. Please, you'll always be loved. Come with me.

She thought for a moment, with her head bowed until her chin rested on her chest and her hair fell over her face. I held my breath, held my hands still at my sides, held a blue-white pearl under my tongue. Her eyes slowly closed. Maybe, she said at last. Maybe.

11

She spent the next day in her bathrobe, reading in a chair in the living room. It was the second week in August, and even with the air-conditioning the heat seeped through the walls, and melted every bond. As the hours passed her pinned up hair came loose, until a long, curled lock reached the corner of her mouth, where she could blandly suck on it. By the time her mother came in from the kitchen with a glass of iced tea I'd darted off the patio and onto the grounds.

I was haunting a copse of trees just above the gazebo, and I decided to pay a visit to the place for the first time since I'd been cast out of it. It was like visiting a childhood home, ten years gone: once I had thought the Millers were on the far side of some impenetrable direction, like one's own back in a mirror, and I wanted to recapture that disproven perspective, so I started to cross the grass—but I heard a voice, and I had to turn back and crouch down beside the trunk. There, standing under the pitched roof, was the trio of workers, Baker, Spot, and Willie, leaning lazily against the balustrade.

They'd apparently been talking for a few minutes before I arrived; Baker's cigarette was burned down to the filter. They may have been planning for weeks before, but more likely it had occurred to them that morning. There's a window open into the basement, Spot was saying—he was referring to my way in and out. There's stairs up into the kitchen. All, the television, stereo and all are on the first floor.

Where are the bedrooms? Baker asked.

The parents sleep above the dining room, and the girls are above the kitchen. (Here pie-faced Willie giggled grotesquely and adjusted the fold in the front of his sagging pants.) But there are carpets on the floors. Besides, one girl is always sleeping, and the other one is never home. The old man has a study on the first floor, too, but he's usually in bed by eleven. So if we wait until, say, after one, we'll be OK....

Baker threw his cigarette butt out onto the lawn and spit after it. Wednesday?

Wednesday it was.

12

God is good and I'm a joker, a trickster, a comedian, a cartoon. Buster Keaton is my muse; I live in a slapstick world, with its happy props, its rubber masks, its breakaway bottles and bruised knees; I have a comic's love of sets and messes, and time and preposterous logic are my media. I waited for my foils on the night they'd named, made up with Olivia's gunk, my face slathered with fat dollops of her lipstick and mascara (she never used them: she said she'd bought them years ago). On my head I wore a bright red fright wig that I'd found in a charity store in town over the weekend. It was an overcast, inky black night, and at the crest of midnight I kissed my girlfriend on her cool, smooth forehead, went downstairs to the basement, and waited with my trouble in mind.

A calm, contemplative hour passed. I thought of Olivia, asleep upstairs, and began to whisper this song:

> If it's yellow, then it's clear,
> If it's clear, then there's sun,
> If there's sun, then there's beer,
> If there's not, then there's none.
>
> If it's blue, then it's grey,
> If it's grey, then it snows,
> If it snows, then he stays,
> If it doesn't, then he goes.

I'd just put the last words onto the second verse when I heard the bushes rustle outside. The boys were making their way past. The gravel on the driveway slipped beneath their feet. When the window opened I trembled: when the first foot hit the floor I sighed: when their flashlights came on and the beams began to swing across the dank room I waited until I could smell the reinforcement on Baker's breath, then grinned and backed up the stairs ahead of them. I knew my way, and they, for all their plotting, did not.

I was already in the kitchen, crouched down behind a counter, while they were fumbling through the boiler room. Finally they reached the stairs, and when the door opened and Spot poked his head out, glanced around, and slipped into the room, with Baker creeping behind him and lastly Willie . . . careful . . . quiet, –

Yaah! Yaah! I threw the light on and rose up from behind the counter with my hands open at my ears, waving my fingers, jumping up and down on my bare, slapping feet. Yaah! Yaah! my madcap hair flew up, my bruised red clown lips flapped in the light, and I pulled down a pair of saucepans that were hanging over the stove and began to bang them together until the whole kitchen seemed to crash down around them; and the three stopped and stood, shaking, and stared wide-eyed at my jack-o'-lantern smile as I heaved the dented metal at them. I heard a nice pop as one pot caught Spot square on the kneecap.

Baker started backwards as if a dog had leaped at his chest, and he slammed heavily into Willie, who was bringing up the rear, and who completed his short shadowy walk-on by falling backwards through the door he'd just passed through. His hand was still on the doorknob and the door shut behind him: I could hear a muffled thumping as he rolled down the stairs offstage, leaving my two friends to me – Yaah! They tried to push themselves through the wall and Spot dropped his flashlight, knocking it out. I turned off the light again, and the kitchen went black.

Jesus! Baker said in a high teary voice as I quietly slipped back. What the fuck was that? From his seat Spot made a mewling noise.

Arm in arm, they started hastily from the room, but the first door they found led to the pantry, and I heard the crash of shelving coming down upon their heads as they fumbled around. Out they came again, with a dozen boxes, noodles, sugar, cereal, rice, and two cans of soup preceding them across the moonlit floor before their feet. Spot was now in the lead, and he had the sense to head towards the basement door again.

They were going to get away, I knew; they were going to disappear back into the bottom of the house before I could bring them down for good. But just as Spot reached the door it flew open, and Willie stood there and stared – and looming up behind him I could see the dark flash of a familiar figure with his arms thrust out, his thin legs braced against the post of the bannister: it was Jones: he thrust his head forward in a strange motion, then there was a beating in the darkness, and Willie fell back into the shadows again and disappeared, though this time the sound of his impact after the door slammed shut was considerably louder.

At that exact moment Holiday's silhouette appeared at the kitchen door; and I ducked into the shadows and out the back door just as he turned on the merciless light again, revealing his

crimson-robed form, with a dull grey pistol in his right hand—
which he incontinently let fire, and simultaneous with the snap of
brass on burning gunpowder a blossom-filled bottle on the window
sill broke.

All right! All right! squealed Spot.

From the attic window I watched as two cherry-top police cars
appeared at the door a few minutes later. Spot and Baker were led
away, cuffed shadows on the front lawn while the whole family, father, mother, Marian and Olivia, stood in a row like ducks and
watched from the front porch. A moment later an ambulance arrived up the drive. As the corpsmen passed with their medical
things I heard the largest duck quack: the three burglars had told
some story about an enormous woman in the kitchen, just to rob
him of his single-handed glory.

One of them would have no telling left. When the gurney reappeared it bore a large figure, supine on the canvas and covered
with a plastic sheet: Willie had landed in the basement with such
force that he had broken his neck, and he was dead.

13

The excitement made Olivia uneasy. I knew why; I
could sense it on her thicker breath. What's more, I remembered
certain vivid symptoms from one of my father's books: she held
her arms protectively across her chest; and once pink flesh had
begun to darken as the pigment collected; and her appetite had
lost its shyness; and there was a powder-blue box that had gone
untouched in her bathroom for six weeks. I think Anne might have
suspected as well. She never asked, but she wouldn't leave the girl
alone, wouldn't leave her to me, alone. She stopped by twice in one
morning just before Labor Day weekend to check on Olivia; I was
in her bathroom, having left her when I heard her mother knocking, and I was standing by an open window, ready to slip out and

crawl silently down the side of the house. Do you need anything? Anne asked.

No, I'm OK. Soft, familiar voice.

How did you get this bruise here. She touched the purple flesh with the tips of two adjacent fingers.

I don't know, Olivia said. Where? She twisted her head to look at the shoulder that I had gently bitten the night before. I think, getting out of the shower.

Well, be careful. Oh – Mrs. Kelley stopped by this morning to see you, but you were still asleep. Kelley was her math teacher, an elderly woman I'd noticed only as she was leaving, and then just because she'd accidentally honked her horn. She says to say hello, and she hopes your whole summer isn't ruined.

No. That's nice.

I'm going to go into town. Are you sure you're all right?

Mmmm. Her mother stood up to leave. Mom, Olivia asked. Did Daddy come in to see me last night?

I don't know, her mother answered as she bent and stroked the girl's hair. She couldn't, since she and her husband had long since taken to different bedtimes; she went to sleep early so that she could be awake in the morning to see Marian off to school and make breakfast for Olivia, and he would stay up late, working in his study or watching television. They barely spoke, they had drifted into a sort of separation, and I was sure that her daughter's question wouldn't make it back to him.

It was well it wouldn't, because I couldn't let them have her, not an inch, not if I'd have gotten the world itself, and all its gardens and girlfriends, never, never, never. You see, she was precious to me, and she was carrying something precious. I watched her carefully, watched them, I should say, but I never said a word, she had decided, and we shared an unspoken, astounding secret. She kept it to herself until several weeks later, when her mother found her vomiting in the bathroom one morning and immediately knew why. Olivia had hoped no one would notice until it was too late for anything to be done, and that was why she hadn't told them: the child, curled like a comma inside an O, belonged to my bride and me, and she had chosen to keep it.

14

Is she?

Yes.

Is she?

Yes, she is.

Olivia. It can't be.

It is.

A child?

A baby. You will be a grandfather.

She is, then. And winter coming. I see now how it goes. The days grow short and cold, and she delivers snow.

15

A storm immediately broke in the house, her father's thundering in the living room, her mother's face at his shoulder, overcast with clouds, her sister's sudden flashes of protectiveness. Marian wouldn't stop moving around, circling around him, speaking out from a spot next to a floor lamp, then from the doorway, then from a position she had taken up behind the couch where Olivia sat, her feet planted on the floor defiantly, her hands in her thick lap. Finally Holiday ordered her to settle down, and she sat in a chair in a corner.

No father could be found: when they asked her Olivia simply shook her head and bit her bottom lip. Holiday was utterly unprepared, and his helplessness left his mouth as fury. Was it Henry Bell! he shouted. Was it that blond-haired boy, what was his name! In the hallway closet I recoiled at the possibility – unknown until that moment – that her eye might ever have landed on someone else. Bellness and blondness, boyness, blondboyness immediately entered my vocabulary, though I never had an occasion to say them. Olivia lowered her head and shook it again.

Well, this is fine, Holiday said suddenly.

Honey, why didn't you say something? Anne asked. You know we would have done everything we could to help.

Marian made a face that only Olivia and I saw. I thought of a cartoon cat and Olivia smiled despite herself.

This is funny? said Holiday. Marian started to laugh, Olivia laughed and looked away. The old man's face reddened: he made a noise like a racing engine and turned to his wife for help; her mouth was twisted, as if she were tasting lemon juice. No, she said, it isn't funny, really.

Holiday started to speak again, stopped, shook his head, and left the room. When he was gone the girls sighed and relaxed. I'm sorry, said Marian. I just, you know. I was nervous.

It's all right, said Anne. He's not going to get over this, you know. She was angry, although at whom I couldn't tell. She asked Marian to leave them alone for a few minutes, and when she was gone she took Olivia aside and pleaded, reasoned, reassured, but the girl wouldn't say, and finally she was allowed to return to her room, where she lay on her bed on top of the covers and – it was a scene she remembered from a movie – practiced breathing to relax. As the day closed her mother and her sister took turns visiting her, and it was impossible for me to see her, so I hid, hot-eared in the basement, until at last they retreated to bed, leaving her to me and my proud, pleased whispers.

I took her by the hand and brought her to the window onto the dark yard, and together we looked down at the long, wild paths and shoots, the bowers and glades; and as the trees shook in the wind, shadows slipped out from beneath the bushes to dance in the moonlight on the lawn, performing a wedding masque to faint, illegible strains of garden music. Now they spin in groups of two, now they bow and curtsy, now they dissolve into the darkness, only to appear at the edge of the pool of porch light to turn their faces up to where we stand and wish us well.

We went back to our bed and she lay on her back, her hands gently resting on her abdomen, as if she were coaxing the soft cells binding inside her. She said, Do you love me?

I said, So much. Do you love me?

You are perfect, she replied; then she suspired softly and turned onto her side, presenting me with her broad, moon-pale back, through which I could see her spine protruding like the skeleton of a snake. In a moment they were asleep.

16

I went to visit her father at his office one day soon after her pregnancy became a natural fact. I knew it was a dangerous thing to do, but I couldn't keep away; with his daughter's life now linked to mine by what we'd made together, the urgency of keeping her made me anxious to know as much as I could about his life and what he could do. So I called the number in Anne's phone book, and when his secretary answered I coolly told her that I was a local landlord looking for some legal advice. I gave my last name as Beech. How do you spell that? she asked. Like the tree, I said. There was a pause while she checked his appointments; I heard her inhale through her mouth. Well, Mr. Miller is very busy, she said at length. I won't be long, I replied.

That night I removed the page with my appointment on it from the leather-bound book he kept so that he'd be prepared for work each day, and the next morning I set off into town. It was a day so hot and bright that I could barely see, and the only life on the streets was a trio of black crows who followed me, circling and shouting comic insults. A half an hour earlier Olivia herself had left the house; out of her father's earshot her mother had taken her aside and, brushing her daughter's hair from her forehead with a quick stroke of her hand had said, I'm going to take you in to see my obstetrician today, OK? Olivia smiled shyly and nodded. Anne started the car and let the air-conditioning run for a few minutes before she returned to the house and retrieved the girl from her room.

Holiday's office was on the top two floors of a low office building near the courthouse in the center of town. I arrived at the proper hour, dressed in a new suit that I'd bought especially for the occasion. As I got off the elevator I noticed the firm's name painted on a pair of glass doors at the end of the corridor – Hunter, Tailor, Miller and Smith – as if her's was an ordinary sort of name and not the word I intended to change. In the reception area I found a black-haired woman with a thin, tense mouth who'd removed her shoes and sat with her tan-stockinged feet peeking out from beneath her desk. When I announced my name she invited me to take a seat and buzzed Holiday from the phone console before her. Beech, she said. No, Beech – like the tree. She looked down at the calendar on the desk before her and then glanced nervously up at me. He's here now, she said. (Pause.) Two-thirty. I have it right here. I heard a twittering from the receiver as his voice rose; she reddened in response, said Yes sir, and hung up the phone.

She ushered me into an empty conference room, handed me a cup of coffee, and left me to scan the shelves of law books. I quickly grew bored, and I'd picked up a coffee pot from the countertop that ringed the room and was idly peering into it – it was empty – when the door opened and the old man came in, puffed up, serious and sincere. At once I stared into his eyes to see if he started or some grimace took hold of him, but he barely saw me at all. He smiled; I smiled even more widely and got up from my seat to shake his hand. I'm sorry to keep you waiting, he said. He shook his head indulgently. My secretary is . . . His grasp was soft and formless, and I held his fingers a moment too long, so that a small ripple of discomfort passed over his face. Sit down, sit down, he said, doubling the greeting so that he had time to possess himself again. Do you want some more coffee? No, I said, and put the pot down again. He pulled a chair out from the head of the table and lowered himself into it; I sat at the opposite end.

He seemed to be intent on something at my chest, and I bent my head down to see what it might be, and then drew the ribbon of silk up with my hand and displayed it to him. He blinked. I'm sorry, he said. A nice tie you have there – and he unconsciously reached his hand up to straighten the knot in his own.

Thank you.

I have one just like it . . . somewhere, he said wistfully.

Oh? I said, and gazed down at it again, my mouth pulled down in an involuntary frown. I got it from my father-in-law.

Married?

More or less, I said.

There was a moment while he pondered what I might have meant. Yes, he finally said, to break his own absorption. From that moment on he was officious and patronizing. Well, what can I do for you? he asked. You're too young to be in much trouble, eh? He smiled.

No, no, I assured him. At least, I hope not. I was given your number by George Fowler (a name I'd lifted off a document in his office one morning before sunrise). I was, I said, a child landlord, thanks to a sizable trust that I hinted might be his to manage if he helped me. I was trying hard to be responsible. But I had a tenant left over from the last owner who was holed up in one of the best rooms in the building, and I was losing money on the little rent I was collecting from her. Did I make her an old woman? I may have, though if I did it I was taking things foolishly far. I was riding a bigger horse than I could handle, and I wanted to see how high he'd jump. When he landed I was still on his back, but that was luck.

Of course, said Holiday when I was done. He unbuttoned his

jacket, leaned back in his seat, smiled a fat yellow smile. This sort of thing happens all the time, you'll see. There's a lot . . . Well. Here's what we can do. For the next few minutes he outlined a system of shameless paper harassment. He said he'd be happy to execute it for me, named a ridiculous hourly fee, and gave me an estimate of his time.

Is there anything else? he asked.

No. Thank you, I answered – although at the words my tongue nearly shriveled and fell from my mouth like a dead leaf. I'll call, I said as he showed me to the door. His parting handshake was firm. When I left him I felt filthy, and my appetite had crumbled like a mudbank in a flood.

17

Stubborn Holiday kept on claiming Olivia, his daughter, my bride. He didn't know who his rival was, or even that he still had one, a force tearing her out of his mean gravity, an enemy so close that I could tell when he passed by a hiding place I'd taken by the sweet smell of his tobacco. He spoke to Anne one night about convincing the girl to abort her pregnancy – he wondered if there wasn't some way to force her – while I shook helplessly in the closet in the hallway outside their room. Don't you dare! said Anne, furiously, quickly. You just keep away from her! Her cheeks went splotch red; they offset the white around her eyes, making her look feverish with some admirable ethic. No one was going touch her daughter's body or what it contained without the girl's consent – and her daughter had no intention of giving it up.

The summer had come to a close, and she wouldn't be going back to school, not in her condition. By then my beautiful wife's belly had grown slightly round, as if filling with the time and life the year was letting out, until it became a gentle curve, with the skin stretched tight over our baby; and our baby beat it from inside with its little fists, already restless and angry, a fierce child, the precarious mixture of a pair of lovers. At night I lay awake next to Mother Olivia, locked safely in her room with my arms wrapped around the two of them, and gave in to my huge happiness. When I slept it was as if there never was harm in the world. It's true I was the monster under the bed, the monster in the midnight closet, the very figure of a child's sleepless fears, but I think she felt more secure knowing that I was always near her, that the only desire I had was to protect her. She took to talking aloud while I was hiding, telling me of the baby's movements, considering names, and shamelessly, wittily bragging about herself, her abilities, her body. I'm a mean machine, she whispered, and giggled redly. I'm the Queen of Sheba.

What about me?

You? You're just a . . . sperm thing. Could have been a turkey baster.

I made a hurt noise.

But you did very nicely. For a palace slave, and if you're good I'll let you live – if you service me. Write me a song, will you? She grasped my shoulder with both hands and rocked it. I want to hear it tomorrow.

By the next morning one was made. In it I fused the world as I knew it into a single word, which could be cracked open to reveal the world again, a menagerie, a republic: it could only be sung.

18

She began to talk to me even when I wasn't around, a change that made no difference to her parents, since they'd become accustomed to her speaking to creatures that they couldn't see: but it alarmed me. She believed that I was everywhere, and I tried to be. I would trail her as she went through the house, making eccentric, covert rings around her like a meteor making epicycles around a wandering planet, slipping into a hall closet, disguising myself as a coatrack, becoming a book on the shelf, crawling into a liquor bottle on the sideboard and watching her as she stood in the front hall and tried to decide whether to leave the house. Should I go out? she asked out loud, as if the house would fall down if she gave the wrong answer. What, honey? her mother answered from the living room, and in a moment she was no longer alone.

I knew she was uncomfortable, though she seldom complained. Night after night I felt her awake, rocking while I slept, a girl in a rowboat above a deep-sea diver. She would lie on her back and stare at the ceiling, her hands in fists at her side as she was moved by small, worrisome waves, waiting for a breeze and shifting restively from time to time. Just at dawn one day I awoke completely and rolled over to find her there. Hello, I whispered.

Hello.

You haven't slept all night.

Not really, no. She pulled herself up until she was leaning against the headboard.

How come?

I don't know.

Frightened?

Shhh. I don't know.

Would it be better if . . .

I don't know, she said patiently.

I lay my arm across her hips. Her skin was hot and moist.

I'm not frightened of, you know, no. It's just that I've been having these dreams. Last night, I mean the night before this one, I dreamt there were insects coming out of my mouth and my nose; the night before that my arms turned to legs, or they both, they were all like legs on a table. Before that I dreamt about a dog that spoke to me, but I don't know what it said. I knew in my dream, but when I woke up I couldn't remember. They make my days so slow and strange. She shook her head and slid back down onto the mattress, and when I said her name a minute later she didn't answer: she was asleep.

The next morning she was tired and temperamental. She burst into tears at any opportunity, and she made opportunities out of nothing. A fork dropped on the floor as she was fixing lunch was proof that the world was irreparably damaged: her mother found her sitting helplessly at the table a few minutes later, rocking back and forth and shaking, and when Olivia gestured to the fallen instrument she bent down, picked it up, put it in the dishwasher, and brought her another one – but by then she wasn't hungry.

At first I thought that she'd stumbled with the weight of her life and the one she carried, but as time passed and she grew worse instead of better, I began to be frightened for her; she seemed to be open to any influence, and it was impossible to tell what new fantasy might visit her next. She had a memory of me deep within her, but I think she couldn't quite believe what she'd done; through the haze of her doubt she could see herself in short perspective, the plane of her own cheek with the expression of her eye trapped in the corner, a glimpse of her pale, soft leg from her knee to her thigh, a patch of scrub black hair. I was reminded of a painting I'd seem in a high-school art appreciation class of a broken pitcher on a table and a girl with a stricken look who watched from the shadows. I didn't leave the house, and she didn't give me up, but she often avoided me, and when she did agree to stay with me she would quickly become bored, and then her face would fall and she'd leave again, as if I were nothing but a magic lantern slide projected on her bedroom wall, a wavering, unfocused image traced in pallid flesh and grey tones. In the morning I would hear her vomiting in the bathroom, but she wouldn't let me in to hold her, and she wouldn't look at me, or talk to me, when she was done.

19

It was four in the morning and I'd awakened suddenly to discover her standing by the window looking into the backyard, a parabolic figure in a white nightdress, overlaid with blue harlequin shadows. Wilson, she said without turning around. There's sap running down the bark on the trees, it's thick and sticky. Sweet. I don't know how it happens. When it dries it gets hard and clear. That's sex. If I could wedge myself open wider, I could hold the world, and be safe from everything that was safe in me. That's sex, too. I can't do it.

Olivia. She came over to the bed and sat on the edge; I wrapped my arms around her and rocked her to sleep with a lullaby:

> Sleep, my darling. Tears that burn
> In young girls' eyes will always dry
> With night's returning secrecy.
> So the wisest child learns.
>
> In my restful arms reserve
> Thoughts of your most splendid hour:
> Dreams that fix your passing powers,
> High on love's unbreaking wave.

So she slept, and for a single night peace was restored, but verses couldn't contain her worries.

She began to lie to me. There were times when I couldn't follow her as she went from room to room, wandering in and out of her father's study, the living room, the kitchen. If her mother came upon her she would ask if she were looking for something.

Nope, Olivia would answer. Just looking.

She'd grow annoyed with me and slip away, joining her sister in her bedroom or lying half-undressed on a white wicker chaise in the sun on the back porch. One evening she left the house in a tight sundress and peddled unsteadily off to town on her bicycle, sick as she was. I tried to follow her, but by the time I'd snuck out to the road she was long gone, and there was no way for me to find her. I stood there on the shoulder, a golem in a grown man's suit under the dusk and street lamps, and kicked vainly at nothing, like a coyote caught in a trap. In time I gave up and went back to the dusty attic, where I waited with my fists clenched by a window, counting the cars that passed by the house, the minutes, the number of times I involuntarily trembled. Were those her footsteps on the gravel? It was a raccoon. My consciousness was jarred by the sounds outside like a loose tooth suffering a kernel of uncooked corn. Every second brought another hour of waiting.

When she returned at last I asked her where she'd been, but she wouldn't say, and when I wheedled and worried her for an answer she finally burst out and said, I went into town. I went to the library to read. I didn't believe her, but there was nothing I could do: I couldn't leave her, and I couldn't stand for her to lie to me. I suspected her of everything, of harboring unfair intentions, of longing to betray me, of secretly hating me.

Who are you yelling at? her mother asked through her door.

No one, said Olivia, looking too deliberately at me — and I was gone. Instead of coming to bed that night she sat with Marian in the kitchen for an hour or two without me; I could see them at the table, under the light in the otherwise dark room, used tea things and a plate of cookies before them, making lazy talk, staring downwards.

20

She had always been an unselfconscious girl. I used sit on the edge of the bed and watch her get undressed each night. She took each piece of clothing off without moving from the spot where she stood: first she kicked off her shoes, then she bent like a crane to awkwardly remove her socks, then carelessly unbuttoned her jeans, pushing them roughly down her hips and stepping out of them. At last she pulled her shirt swiftly over her head and tossed it onto a chair. Then she would reach behind her, fingers twisting, remove her bra, and walk into the bathroom, bare but for the small cotton V curving down below the soft shelf of her abdomen. I loved to watch her go, swinging slightly on her footsteps. I admired her body's balance and obedience, the distribution of strengths to which it testified; it seemed to be carved out of a single generous piece of rose-white material, yielding nothing to its parts. Sometimes I would wonder what it would be like to live in it, and more than once I caught myself inadvertently imitating her proud walk, imagining breasts below my shoulders, a soft, short waist, a heaviness in my hips, the difference between my legs; and I would blush with curious excitement.

As she passed by me one night I noticed that she'd drawn on the flesh of her forearms with a marker, a mapway of arrows and circles and tiny symbols that she'd invented, using her body as if it were paper. I put my hand out and stopped her. Olivia? I asked. She didn't speak, but she sat down on the edge of the bed beside me and held her arms out, overturned so that the smooth flesh on the underside of her arms showed. The marks made sentences up to her bare shoulders. There's more, she said, and with that she lay gently back on the bed with her legs dangling off the mattress, and spread her knees as if she were opening the leaves of a rare book. On the skin of her pale thighs, just below her dark, silent mouth there were more marks, but I couldn't read them; whatever code they might have contained was as closed to me as a paragraph of Arabic. OK? she asked, and I shook my head. She frowned as if she were disappointed in me and went into the bathroom.

She decided that her medium was insufficient. By the next night the ink had been washed away. It was replaced by dried blood: she'd carved thin, painstaking cuts in her flesh, again on the tenderest lining of her arms and thighs. The ideograms were forgotten; the pink welts appeared in ragged and uneven rows, in one case a group of four intersected by a diagonal fifth, like a crude counting habit. When I asked her what she wanted to say she just showed the angry scars she'd inscribed and looked away. I took her wrists in my hands and searched her countenance for a reason, but I couldn't find one.

21

Strings snap on the blue guitar. Explorers fail to reach their mark and expire nowhere. Glamour ends its happy visit, and in the eyes of the one I loved I found a fish's lidless stare.

22

Late the next night I woke suddenly and found myself rafting alone in the darkness, the mattress empty beside me. The blanket was still warm from her body, still sweet from her perfume. The floor was covered with a cool, soft mist; it lapped silently at the edge of the bed. On her desk across the room I saw the luminous red glow of her alarm clock, and as I watched, wondering what the numbers meant, the last digit changed from eight to nine. I heard a movement in the bathroom, a kind of sigh. I heard it again. So I got up, shivering, to see. Olivia was sitting on the sink in her dark bathroom, with thin white shards of a light bulb scattered on the tile floor and a fragment of the glass between her fingers. When she heard me enter she looked up; I was yawning, I wasn't thinking of yawning. It was air into the manifold, and it propelled me across the tiles. I caught her soft sweaty hand in mine, yanking it to one side and prying it open until the glass fell: immediately she slapped my face with her other hand, pulled away, and pressed herself against the tiled wall in the far corner by the door. You took advantage of me, she said, her eyes filled with angry tears. You know you did. She opened her arms: And it hurts. My father is going to kill you. He's going to kill both of us. She panted for breath.

Every language has the worst five words, and everyone who has heard them was the first. Just then, as playground swings made silent arcs in the darkness, and waitresses held coffee pots above sleepless customers' cups, and traffic lights turned red on empty roads, she abruptly became calm and spoke them to me as if she were reporting bad economic news. Anyway, I don't love you anymore, she said. I wish you would leave.

I didn't ask her why, because I didn't believe her — it seemed like one of those sentences (all lovers are always liars) that couldn't possibly be true. She might as well have tried to convince me that I didn't exist, this best boy whom my love had made; it was like standing in front of a mirror and seeing nothing but the room reflected. I was suddenly very tired, exhausted really; my skin hung from my body as heavily as a wet robe. So I frowned, turned away, and went to my mattress in the basement, where I slept as innocently as a puppy. A few lost hours later I was awakened by Olivia herself. Wilson, Wilson, she said. There you are. I could feel her crawling in beside me. God, I looked all over. Don't listen to me when I talk like that, OK? she said as she put her arms around me from behind.

23

She wore long-sleeved shirts while she healed, but her mother discovered the fading scars on the skin of her arms one night when she came in to tuck the girl into bed. I listened through a wall as she told Holiday about it a few minutes later. He came in to see her afterwards but by then she was feigning sleep, and when he said her name from the threshold of her room she didn't answer. The next morning he stopped in on his way to work and tried again, but she was in the bathroom and wouldn't come out, and he couldn't bring himself to try once more.

That night there was a final summer storm, a full hour of thunder striking against the window, and clouds that dumped buckets of water onto the roof. Olivia slept through the night. I stood by the window and watched the wind bend the trees, turning the leaves into dark, violent spumes. Spouts of rain whirled through the grounds, casting themselves against the pane until it shook in its frame. A wicker chair that someone had forgotten to bring inside tumbled off the patio, came to a stop, underwent a crazy shiver, and then rolled end over end into the darkness. As I followed it my eyes landed on a faint form at the edge of the black into which it had disappeared.

He was standing in his torn coat, his hair hanging in wet mopstrings; I couldn't see his face, but I recognized his stance, and the quick, birdlike movements he made as he whipped the water up with his arms: it was Jones, come again to cure her. Suddenly the sky lowered to the eaves like the lid of a box; and the house, long since asleep, was engulfed by waves. There was the hiss of eddies foaming as they broke against the walls, and the casements began to rattle. The trees swayed like seaweed. I could see him swimming on the lawn, treading water as if he were slow-dancing in the downpour. After a few minutes he turned his back and started for the bottom of the garden.

A moment later I heard Holiday urgently calling his wife from the bottom of the stairs. Anne! he shouted. Anne! There was no answer. Olivia slept soundly, peacefully, her mouth slightly open, her fingers curled into a loose fist at her ear, as if she were holding a ladybug that she wanted neither to crush nor to let escape. Anne! I heard their bedroom door open and Anne's slow footsteps on the landing. Shhh! she said sleepily. What is it?

Call the police, right now.

What is it? she asked again. By then he was halfway up the stairs, and through a crack in the door I saw him holding his pistol loosely in his right hand, with its barrel pointed towards the ground. What are you doing? she said. He wore the look of a man who's just come, glassy-eyed, unthinking, and oddly helpless.

It happened again, he said quietly. I missed. Call the police, will you? Already? No, wait. I'd better call my office. What time is it?

It's two in the morning.

I'm all right, he said. But where's my phone book? I'd better call someone at home. There was, I shot at someone in the back yard. Anne started to put her hand up to her face, and then stopped, as if she were embarrassed by the gesture. She looked briefly at his gun-gripping hand as he reached the landing, and then looked away. For his part, he seemed to have forgotten about the weapon; he left it on a night table in the hallway as he passed into their bedroom to use the phone, though just before he shut the door he turned, waved at it shortly, and said, He ran away.

The police arrived some minutes later, and Holiday gave his story to them, in competition with their radios, which spat and called constantly. In time they left, taking the gun along with them to pass a perfunctory examination. It was returned to Holiday a few days later; it was legal and registered. The intruder was never found.

24

When Olivia awoke the next morning the sky was clear and bright, and gleamed like just washed glass. She looked at me with clear, bright eyes and right away I knew that she was better, that her brittle, unbearable panic had washed away. I wanted her to stay with me for a few minutes, but she hopped up from her bed, threw some clothes on, splashed water on her face, and left me with a longish, warm kiss. Smooch, she said, and then left the room.

It was a Saturday, and though it was late in the morning her parents were still home; Holiday was recovering in his study, and Anne was cooking in the kitchen. She went to the kitchen first, marching through the door the way a schoolgirl enters her favorite class. Mom, she said. I feel much better. Is it too late for breakfast? Her mother, who'd been facing the sink, nearly jumped out of her shoes. She turned around swiftly and stood with her back against the porcelain, unconsciously wiping her soapy hands on her apron as she stared intently in Olivia's eyes. Yes, it was true. She could see it in the girl's familiar posture, in her half smile, as if she were waiting for something funny to happen: in fact she laughed at her mother's surprised silence. Then, and still smiling, she walked over to the dishwasher, removed a clean glass, went to the refrigerator, and poured herself some orange juice, which she drank in two long, throat-pulsing gulps. The remains of her smile still showed in the corners of her mouth, and some of the juice spilled onto her chin. She wiped it away with the bottom of her T-shirt, pulling it up far enough to expose both her distended belly – her bloodless white navel protruded slightly – and the lower part of a black lace bra.

Olivia, her mother said, and then crossed the linoleum floor and stood before her with her hands on her shoulders as if to steady her before her eyes. Honey. I'm so glad to see you better. Are you really? The girl nodded confidently. I want to take you to the doctor this afternoon.

All right, Olivia replied. Can I have some breakfast first?

When she had finished eating Anne came and sat across the table from her and carefully explained what had happened the night before. I don't want you to worry, she said. Daddy will be just fine, and no one's going to get in here. When Olivia came back to her room I could see that she was trying to decide what to make of it – I'd never told her about Jones; I was afraid she would think I was crazy. She said nothing to me. Instead, she took a shower and changed her clothes, and then she returned to the living room to wait for her mother. Anne was taking her time dressing. Olivia started to walk onto the back porch, only to discover Holiday standing a few yards into the back lawn, staring at the bottom of the garden. She stopped, staggered, feinted once to her left as if she hoped to head around the corner before he spotted her, and then backed into the house again. At the sound of the door closing behind her he turned, blinking questioningly.

With a blank look she walked quickly through the house, opened the front door, stuck her head out, looked carefully around, and then sat down on the front steps. A few minutes later Anne found her: Oh, there you are, she said as she searched through her purse for her car keys. I was waiting for you inside. Sorry, said Olivia.

Through the windshield of the car I saw Anne turned as far around in her seat as she could as she steered the car backwards down the driveway and out onto the street. Her arm was cast out on the seat back behind Olivia's head; her daughter sat with her hands in her lap and looked straight ahead, unblinking, watching the receding, sunlit house.

Anne dropped her off later that afternoon and then left again, and Olivia virtually ran to her room as soon as she was through the door. I was waiting for her; she pulled the shades and sat down on the edge of her bed, her arms folded across her belly. The last sunlight was pushing weakly through the treetops: Olivia? Marian shouted from the bottom of the stairs. Do you want some of this cake I made?

No, thank you! to the door. The doctor says the baby is fine, to me, her eyes shining in the darkened room. Do I want to know if it's a boy or a girl?

Do we?

Oh, I don't know, she said. I don't think so.

No, I said. Let's not.

. . .

Olivia, are you really OK?

Of course, she said, looking away as she patted my knee with one hand. I'm just worried about a friend of mine. The remainder of the day was given to Marian, who dragged her sister out of the house and took her for a long, intimate walk, down the hill to the foot of the driveway, down to the end of the block, and then out of sight.

25

She managed to last an entire week without having to be alone with her father. She was at the dinner table every night, and he sat at the head, but she never looked at him, and he never spoke to her. Only once in the following week did he address her: he asked her what she was planning to do about school.

Marian immediately said, Nothing right now. Her gunmetal voice took Holiday by surprise, and he turned to face her angrily.

Who are you? he said to her.

She's not going to do anything, she doesn't have to worry about that right now.

Who are you? Marian didn't say anything. I'm talking to you, he said, and his voice grew louder.

Stop it, said Olivia, her eyes wide with supplication. The table immediately fell silent, and as if to take the attention off like a robe she got to her feet and began to clear the dishes. As she passed her father on her way to the kitchen he suddenly reached out and took hold of her shirt in his fist. He held her; his knuckles brushed her belly. She froze and stared at the stack of plates in her hands.

You are not my daughter, he said.

26

The music that I mentioned at the very start had already begun an unnerving melody, and it soon became martial.

Holiday chose one night that week to announce to Marian at the end of dinner that he'd been offered a new job with another firm in California. He and Anne had already discussed it, and he was considering it. The family, of course, would have to move. The tone of his voice suggested that he intended to make his decision based on what, by his own lights, would be best and most reasonable, and he seemed genuinely surprised at the pall that fell over the table when he'd finished. A wet magnolia sprig blew against the dining room window, the twig clicking against the glass before it fell rapidly out of sight.

What about school? Marian finally asked, her eyes wide in her suddenly bloodless face.

What about it? he answered.

I only have one year left—

There are schools there, you know, he said, as if, with a disappoinment so personal as to be almost unspeakable, he was telling her something that she didn't know.

Honey . . . said her mother.

But all my friends, said Marian.

You'll make new friends, said Holiday. Marian reddened, bent her head, and struggled with herself. Holiday waited patiently for her to cry. It was close. She picked up a fork in her fist and made two quick movements towards her plate. I expected her to lunge at him with it next. Her mother flinched. Anyway, Anne said hastily, it's not for certain.

But if it is . . . Holiday threatened.

Marian pushed her chair back and got up. We're not done with dinner, said Holiday. I am, she answered, and walked quickly from the room while he said her name like an order to her back. As she disappeared through the doorway he rose from his seat and started after her, only to stop again and call instead: Don't you dare say anything to Olivia.

As Marian's footsteps started up the stairs he returned to his seat at the head of the table. When he picked up his knife and fork again he had them in the wrong hands, and he spent a few seconds trying to exchange both of them at once — but his hands began to shake and he quickly gave up and set them down on his plate again.

That was nice, said Anne. He stared at her, and as he stared he grew elephantine, and leaned his big body over the table to trumpet. Why don't you decide, then? he said. You and Marian! Oh, and Olivia, why don't the three of you decide where I should work, and then tell me?

That's not the point, she said.

What is the point? What is the point? Florid, a flush-faced elephant, wallowing and thrashing around.

Anne became a stubborn bird, perched out of reach. She's upset that she might have to leave just when she was starting to get along . . .

Besides, it'll be better for Olivia to get away from here. And he pulled his head around, ears inertially flapping, and lumbered away.

27

From that night on my life with Olivia was losing her. It was like trying to watch a television with the vertical out of adjustment; it was always the first moment that she was drifting away, starting off again, starting again; but she was never gone. All her confidences went into her sister's pocket; as often as not a day spent in mutually secretive company — when they were together it was as if each one knew, even with her back turned, the precise location and attitude of the other — would end with her sleeping in the extra bed in Marian's room while I lay alone in the basement.

As her body continued to change, her ankles swelling, her hips thickening, her breasts becoming heavier, she became elusive; she went to some place where I couldn't find her, though I was the one who had put her there. When she saw me she treated me as if I were a friend who happened to stop by to see her. Oh, hello, she'd say, slightly surprised to find me in front of her; and then she'd be cheerful and friendly, in a somewhat distant way, until she'd abruptly mention that she had to go off and do something vaguely described, and she'd leave me again. If I tried to follow she would turn and stare at me as if she couldn't believe I would be so inconsiderate.

She disrupted the rhythm of my reason with the thousand decisions a frightened lover makes – Here I find her, after midnight, and she's asleep without me. Is it better to risk annoying her by waking her, or should I sit by the window, and painfully wonder what she dreams? If I confess with a hundred pleas and a hundred kisses, will she grow disgusted or ashamed and turn away? Every moment that she spends in the privacy of her senses is a moment away from me. She'll forget me, she doesn't care. I'll go crazy: I'll run to the river and throw myself in, and sink until the weeds wrap around my head.

She spent three consecutive nights in Marian's room. On the morning of the fourth day I waited for her in her room. When she came in she seemed slightly confused by my being there; she blinked a few times and unconsciously rubbed her upper arm, bunching her T-shirt up to her white, round shoulder. Sit down beside me, will you? I said. She frowned at the floor; she gently kicked her toe against the leg of the bed.

Listen, honey . . . she said. I stared at her. She wrapped her hands around the bedposts as if she were grasping the ropes of a swing, and swayed slightly over the mattress. Listen, things are getting all fucked up around here.

I heard, I said. I won't let them move.

I know, she said, leaning as far backwards as she could. But I don't want anything to happen. Can . . . ? I'm sorry. My heart began to hammer in my chest, and patches of my skin began to unstitch. Can you, I think it would be best if you went away for a while, because everything has to be normal around here, and—

Oh, honey, she said, as I shook my head to put out the sudden scraps of burning paper that had started to curl in the corners of my thoughts. They wouldn't die, so I rose to my feet and started for her bathroom; I couldn't find the door. She was standing at the foot of the bed watching me as I turned around again; she was actually wringing her hands. I've thought about this so much, she said. Please, just until the baby is born. Please?

I turned and said, No, Olivia. I can't leave now.

No? But you have to.

Why?

Because I want you to, she said firmly. Because you can't stay. I'm asking you, because I need you to go now.

Where can I go?

I don't know, go to Colorado, go to California, and when you come back you can tell me all about it. Save some money and when you get back everything will be fine, I promise. Please.

Her voice had taken on an excited tone, but I could tell she'd forced it for my benefit; it was theatrical and false. I'd never known her to turn a feeling into an effect, and I took it as a terrible sign, and shuddered inwardly at her tepid smile.

I want you to leave, she said. I could feel a cherub watching on over my shoulder, her roseate face downcast in grief; it was like a weight.

The baby, I said.

What about it.

I reached out my hand to her and she recoiled.

Don't! she said.

I took a step towards her. I just want—

Don't touch me! she said, and threw her arms up protectively, grimacing as if the thought of my putting my hands on her would cause her skin to shed like a snake's. You're crazy, and you have no right to hurt me. Go away!

She stared at me, terrified; I stared at her, shocked, and then began to shake uncontrollably; my legs trembled, my mouth trembled, I couldn't find a place to keep my hands. There was no one

154 / JIM LEWIS

else ever made but her, the rest were mechanical things in painted masks, but she was afraid of me. She backed to the door and my eyes dissolved, and when she turned around and ran from the room I began to sob, redly, brokenly, furiously, uncontrollably. At that moment I hated everything, and wanted to end the world, and everyone in it.

28

The next four months went by in a shallow succession of odd jobs, cold rooms, and unfriendly faces, overlaid in my mind like scenes on pallid acetate. I tended bar for a week in Shreveport, and rented a room in a cheap motel called the Regency, where I slept on a mattress no thicker than its blanket. In Tulsa I unloaded gunnysacks from trucks and slept in a shelter in the basement of a Baptist church. I was a waiter in a Wichita hotel – Heartbreak, said the manager when he hired me, gesturing across the lobby to the black-clad doorman and weeping bell-hop – and went home every night to my car, parked in an alley off Lonely Street.

You may remember that as a particularly cold winter; I remember it as a gradual fading of the countryside's color as I moved north, until some limit of blankness was reached, and then I met a succession of indistinguishable white days, a bareness as still and silent as an empty house, white lights, white walls, white sky, white freeze spread across the land. The sky was an idea of a sky, unbroken and impossible to compass; it was weather as the number zero.

And then as if from its very fragility the sky cracked one afternoon like the ice on a pond and the snow began, and the world became whiter still. I was trapped in my car in a storm on a highway outside Oklahoma City, peering through the windshield as I passed mile after mile of semis that had slipped off the road and fallen over into ditches, where they lay toppled and broken like great animals. There was no sound. I kept on and made it as far west as Colorado; for a week I stayed in a small town in the sky outside Denver, where with my last thirty dollars I rented a room and drank my dinner. In a bar late that night I watched intently as a man beside me drew a deep drag on his cigar, formed his mouth and locked down with his jaw, blowing a casual smoke ring across the room, a giant, soft O that wavered and expanded for a few full minutes, inescapable vowel, grey in the pale grey air.

A little bit later I was in the bathroom – then by the bright juke-box, with someone to my left in blue jeans and boots – then at the bar, looking for my room key, or my gloves, or my glasses, except I had no glasses – and trying to say something to somebody – then out the front door in the cold air, stars like white needles above the dark pines. Down below Tupelo, sang a song behind the door, and suddenly I was digging for it with my teeth, not fallen, I realized, but pushed – I heard something hit my head, and then I was on the ground in the parking lot, with gravel in my mouth and a dull grey lead billiard ball bouncing around inside my skull, and then some-one was kicking my back and my legs, over and over again. I woke up the next morning in my room, with blood on my pillow from the root of a lost tooth, a crack in my cheekbone with a swollen blood-purple bruise over it, and a limp that lasted a week and a half.

I sold the Ford for two hundred dollars so that I could afford to stay out of the weather. When the tracks cleared I went south by train to El Paso, sleeping in my seat as the wide ranches passed; then east again to the hills of Austin. There I tried to rob a car parts store south of the river; I waved a toy gun at the clerk and took one hundred dollars from the till, and I ran. I was standing in a shopping center parking lot ten minutes later when the police pulled up. The judge gave me six months in juvenile detention; I was told I would serve thirty days.

Locked up, I learned nothing, I saw no one. If I spoke more

than five words in a day it was because someone hadn't heard me
the first time. Every moment I had Olivia and my child in mind,
and this was the song that I sang to my bars and bunk:

> Long time!
> I hate it here
> Cold time!
> Get me out of here

I counted every day, at night I dreamed of bicycles and skating
rinks, volumes of rhyming verse and white bedrooms. I got out on
Christmas Eve. The New Year passed, and I knew the day of her
delivery was nearing; so I made my way slowly back to her again. I
was wondering all the while what I wanted, but I had been patient,
I had been good, and I was going to go home to find what was left
for me. I waltzed across Texas, alone, rolled through Louisiana
like a roulette wheel, stopped briefly at the bridge to take a gander
at the river and catch my breath, and then ran the rest of the way.
And so it was that on the evening of the fifth of February I found
myself at the cold side of their backyard.

29

The garden had long since gone into winter remis-
sion, but nothing else had changed. I don't know why I thought it
might, but I was a little surprised as I rounded the bend in the
road before the house and saw it come into familiar view. Like a
musician stepping back into a song after leaving the stage, I felt
oddly out of time, and I wondered if the music would still match.

It was dark in the amethyst light just after sundown; no lights
burned in the windows. The trees were leafless, so I had some
trouble finding a spot from which I could peer in through a window, but I chanced cover from a thick tangle of shrubbery outside

the kitchen. The room inside was empty and dark, but everything was in place; the pots were still hanging from their hooks, and there was a bottle of olive oil left out on a counter, and a few dishes washed and safely placed in the drying rack beside the sink. Through the open kitchen door I could see into the living room. On the far wall was a mirror, almost fifty feet away, and my own face stared back at double the distance, framed by the mirror's edges, the doorway, the window, looking emptily into the vacant house. As if for the first time – as nervously as the first time – I found my window and crawled in. The boiler was on, murmuring with hot water. Otherwise it was the same.

At ten that night I saw the headlights from their car sweep across the scrim of the curtains in the living room, making shadows swing prophetically inside the room. I was hiding in the darkness at the top of the stairs; I heard a pair of car doors shut and footsteps on the walk; then the front door of the house opened and Holiday and Anne came in. Under the foyer light their faces were drawn with fleshly shadows; they looked a full five years older, and they were alone. Olivia and her sister had gone to the movies, or out to meet with friends, or down to school for some evening event, a play, a cotillion, a basketball game.

Holiday removed his coat and hung it in the closet in the front hall; then, without a word, he started slowly up the stairs to bed. Anne went into the living room and turned on a light, sighed, and sat back on the couch without removing her outer things.

She'd just brushed her hair back wearily from her forehead for the tenth time when I heard a key in the lock, and my crouched breath began to quiver with excitement: I was home again, and soon I'd be reunited with Olivia. My mouth went dry, and my legs shook as the door opened.

Immediately, Marian came in and looked quickly into the living room, and I studied the darkness outside the door for the shadow of my wife, stared without blinking into the sliver of bright black framed by the white-painted pillars of the portico and swiftly diminishing under a contracting arc as the door found its way back into its frame. By the time I realized that Marian was alone she'd joined her mother in the living room. I heard them murmur to each other, daughter once, mother once, daughter again. Then the light in the living room went out and they started up the stairs to bed, and right away I knew that Olivia wasn't coming home, after all.

Sister

1

I spent three days trying to discover where she'd gone, but I learned nothing. It was a defeated house, the kind of house in which no voice is ever raised, and the corners of the rooms get uncommon scrutiny. Holiday and Anne would retire to the living room immediately after their silent dinner, where they'd sit before the television and slowly sip at benumbing drinks, he reclined in one corner of the couch, she upright in the other, in a room so mercilessly quiet that it was all I could do to keep from delivering my goddamns and bringing the roof down around them. When they'd had enough and rose from their positions at the end of the night neither of them would bother to bend down again to straighten the cushions that their weight had slightly dislodged: he walked slowly up the stairs, while she collected the glasses, took them into the kitchen, rinsed them halfheartedly, and left them in the drying rack, dawdling by the sink so that she could be sure he was in bed, with the lights out, before she reached the bedroom.

Marian ate her dinner alone in her room, and brought the dishes down to the kitchen by the back stairs when she knew her parents were settled in front of the television. Nearly everything else she did was a secret: her door was always shut; her book bag never left her side; phone calls to friends were whispered into the mouthpiece. Soon after dinner she would leave the house, and she wouldn't be back until late.

No one argued with her, and no one but me was ever awake when she came home. So I was the only one who noticed when, the night after I'd returned, she entered the house, hung her coat in the hall, and went into the kitchen. She took an apple from a lower drawer of the refrigerator and then sat at the table in the dark for ten minutes, chewing each mouthful deliberately. When she was done she threw the core away and headed to the dining room, from the dining room to the living room, from the living room to her father's office. She shut herself in, and a light silently appeared beneath the door. She was sequestered there for some time – the white moon rose an inch or two up the sky outside the window where I waited – but I couldn't tell if she'd found what she was looking for by the expression on her face when at last she emerged.

After she'd gone to sleep I let myself inside Olivia's door. Her furniture had not been touched, and each object had been left in place, but the room was as empty as any I had ever entered. As I passed by the foot of her bed I suddenly felt her hands on me, her palms on my back, her hips against my leg; the veins beneath my skin dilated, and I stopped and stretched my shoulders towards the feeling to make it last. It was a fool's memory, it was pyrite: she was long gone. A creak in the hallway made me start, and I quickly stood and headed for her bathroom, but it was just the house making tics as it slept, and when I was sure I was safe I went back and stood next to her bureau. The door to her closet was slightly ajar; there was a shoe protruding from the darkness, which had prevented it from closing completely. I nudged it back through the frame with my toe and pressed the door shut. Then I crossed the room and sat at her desk. Her red fountain pen was lying diagonally across the surface. The drawer was empty of everything but a pencil stub, a paper clip, and a two-page math exercise upon which a teacher had written a red *Very Good* next to a red 87. There was no note. I went through her closet, dividing the soft shirts on the hangers with my hands and peering into the corners; I dug through her dresser drawers, I checked the medicine cabinet in her bathroom, I looked under her bed. There was no clue.

I was careful to avoid her room from then on, though I was tempted to it like a drunk to a full tumbler; I could feel the flesh in my arms and legs dissolving, the string of my sinews coming undone; there was no relief for the numbness in my neck; and every surface that I touched was dull, was lifeless, loveless, and unpleasant, because nothing fit my hand and soothed the nerves there, and spread a flush throughout my body, as she had. I felt like a shadow casting a man. I would stop suddenly at a spot where I'd seen her, my only piece of the world, as she sat on the stairs the night of their party – or in the kitchen I'd find myself gazing endlessly at the tray upon which her dinner had been carried to her, now hung by one corner by a hook on the wall – or driven in by Anne on her way to the bathroom I would stand in the practice room by the flank of the grand piano she used to play, while the mocking sound of movie music drifted in from the living room.

From an upper window I watched as Holiday stood heavily in the dooryard one afternoon; I heard him mumbling to himself about the mess made of his grounds. Over there, he said to no one in particular, there was a yellow dogwood. Now there's . . . I don't know . . . I don't know what that is there. In fact it was all trash by then, fatuous litter. I could stir it with my hands and come up with nothing but debris. It wasn't just winter that had done it; no one had cared for it in months. Spring was coming, but no effort would be made to begin it again; it counted for nothing.

Everything counted for nothing, and I became convinced that the house without Olivia was actually empty, its characters cartoons, one step removed from the real, like insubstantial shades in hell. It was the latest of nights when I was reminded that it wasn't empty at all. I was reminded because I was found out, and I was found out because I was careless.

2

It was the third night after I'd come back; I think it was near dawn. I'd woken from my sleep to the hum of the basement and a darkness so deep and clear that it was like black water, and for a moment after my eyes opened I was uncertain that they had. But I could feel my heart beating in my chest, unaltered by the figures of dreams, so I decided that I was awake, and I sat up in my bed, allowing the covers to fall to my waist. I could hear the house breathing in around me, breathing out, counting the strikes of its architectural rhythm. I followed that breath with my own, a mirror of my mise-en-scene, and when I'd collected enough of myself I got up, pulled on my clothes, and slipped up the stairs to the kitchen, with the light from a far streetlight a faint illumination through the window; it was sufficient for me to glance down and see my hands, and remind myself that once I'd been determined to come into my agency.

I wanted breakfast so I went to the refrigerator, stuck my head in, and started to rummage through the dishes. Soon enough I found something in a plastic bowl, found a fork in a drawer, found a space by the sink, and I was standing in the darkness with my back against the countertop, picking at a casserole when my tongue suddenly went dead; it was as if my mouth were filled with sand and gravel. I couldn't hear, there were imaginary bells going off in the kitchen like a fire alarm: I couldn't feel the bowl in my hands: I couldn't make out a single word of my own thoughts through the din. But I could see, because the room was suddenly flooded with light.

She stood in the doorway with her legs planted and spread until her feet touched the corners of the frame; she wore a grey- and white-striped jersey, a blue-black skirt, and black leggings. One hand was propped up on the jamb while the other held her blue down jacket at her side. Her hair was swept back, exposing her wide, pale forehead. She was so utterly composed that it was as if some capricious sculptor had built her there years ago to hold the house up. She had a strange smile on her lips, but her eyes were dark and tired. She'd just come home.

It was a game to see who would speak first, and I was going to lose; I knew I was before the first few seconds were out, but I pushed my exclamations into my pocket. They started to escape: I pushed them back again, and held them down with my hand while they squirmed and struggled. Through it all she stood and watched me, just once raising a hand to her forehead to brush back a piece of hair that had fallen over her eyes. Oh, I finally said.

It wasn't enough to draw a response, so I said Oh again. My name is Wilson.

I know, said Marian. When did you get back?

The day before yesterday, I answered without thinking, though I caught myself quickly enough to clip the last vowel.

What will you do now that Olivia is gone?

I suppose my face might have fallen. I know I looked at the ground, trying to hide from her small, metallic gaze. I hoped that if I waited long enough she might simply dissolve through the kitchen door again, but she seemed perfectly unconcerned with my silence, as if she had her hand on me and had allowed me to hide behind my speechlessness only because she saw no need as yet to make me twitch or jump with words. She let a few long seconds pass that way. What are you going to do now? she asked again.

I don't know.

Nice suit, she said, as deadpan as a hanging judge. Reminds me of one of my dad's. She furrowed her brow. A little ragged though. What are you going to do?

I don't know, I said. Please, will you tell me what happened? Where is she? I'll go.

Go where?

I don't know.

She came out of the doorway, walked across the kitchen floor, and dropped her jacket on the table. Then she drew a chair out and sat backwards in it with her chest pressed against the wooden top. Casting her bare arms out on the table in front of her, she pulled a few crumbs along in a wide arc with the tip of one delicate finger and then brought it up and absently crushed them against her thumb. She looked up at me again. What are we going to do?

Do, I don't know. Where is she?

She's gone. She stared at me, and after a moment or two had passed she said, I suppose I have to tell you.

I'll go as soon as I know, I said. I promise.

She spoke quietly and with perfect calm, and I've forgotten almost every word she used. Within a minute I had lost her voice. But I didn't miss a motion of the story she told: I can still wring out every moment, and arrange them in a rude order of reasons.

3

Olivia had been well enough for a week or two after I left; Marian had watched her carefully to be sure. Still, she wouldn't talk to her father, or even look at him. She ate her dinner quickly, without glancing down to the end of the table, and when she was done she would cross her knife and fork on the plate, and wait patiently to be excused. Marian enfolded her in a circle of her own friends, and with her sister's help she was out of the house as often as possible. Once or twice Holiday knocked on the door of her bedroom late at night, but she knew it was him and she wouldn't answer.

Anne was unnerved by Olivia's silence and evasiveness. One evening after Holiday had retired to his office she tried to explain his behavior, but when Olivia went grey and silent and refused to look up she grew embarrassed and stopped. He wasn't mentioned anymore.

It had been some time since he'd stopped asking her for the name of the baby's father, but instead of letting it pass he began to conduct an investigation of his own. He tried to be quiet about it, but it was like trying to tiptoe through a flock of sitting swans; every move he made ended in an explosion of outraged cries. In response a tone of mixed deviousness and brutality attached to his efforts. He called her homeroom teacher from the year before and asked her to come by his office. There he asked questions for an hour, and when her teacher, who knew nothing, grew tired of knowing nothing and tried to leave, he suddenly lost his temper and began yelling at the bewildered woman. When Olivia found out, she cried to Marian, Marian went to her mother, and her mother told Holiday he should be ashamed.

The garden was dead, and worse, scarred by an incomplete effort that he'd made to reshape it in midwinter; a pile of desiccated rose bushes lay stacked against the foot of the house, and the herb garden was a shallow, angry hole that he had made with a spade. He went through her drawers one day when she'd gone to the doctor for her weekly checkup. He was looking for a letter, a name, an answer. He did find one extraordinary article, but it stole more meaning than it offered. He took it anyway.

When Olivia came home she noticed at once that her things had been moved; she confronted him in his study and begged him to leave her alone. He responded by yelling at her. Get out of here! he shouted. Get out of my house! Olivia ran from the room in tears just as Anne reached the door; Holiday turned his anger on his wife. It was Marian's fault anyway. Olivia must have gotten the idea somewhere, it must have been her sister. He knew something like this would happen, he announced. The girls could not be trusted.

She waited until he was done and then left the room without saying a word.

Then Holiday enlisted a doctor; Olivia wouldn't confess to him. He suggested a therapist, but she wouldn't go. Boarding school was mentioned; she refused to be threatened. Still she was coming apart. As she became convinced that her father hated her and wanted to hurt her she weakened, and for the first time she was frightened of the seriousness she faced.

She worried about love, and wondered where I was. She was angry with me. She had just one thing to remember me by, and it was huge and hurt.

Then she began to save things; it was strange. Her room became a reliquary for everything she used, no matter how disposable it was meant to be, everything, scraps of paper, peach pits, bottle caps, magazines, empty matchbooks, pennies, junk mail, coffee grinds, pencil stubs. She was trying to stop time from passing, to save the last moments of her childhood, because she knew it was over, that it had ended when she was looking somewhere else, and it was too soon. She would pull her chair by a window, look out on the garden, and clutch the armrests with her hands like a passenger convinced the plane is going down.

She wouldn't do her laundry, and her clothes gradually became dull and worn, like old coins. Finally Anne sent the girls out grocery shopping, and while they were gone she went into Olivia's room and gathered up the soiled garments, the shirts and jeans, the panties, the socks, and brought them down to the basement, where she stuffed them into the washer. When Olivia came home and found a pile of clean clothes on her freshly made bed, neatly folded and still warm from the dryer, she shook her head angrily, picked up the entire pile, and threw it on the filthy floor. After that she locked her door behind her whenever she left her room.

The doctor warned that if she became sick again it might hurt her. She became sick again; there was another sudden fever that attacked her, another day spent on her knees before the toilet in her bathroom, convulsed by dry heaves, and then a night of shaking in her bed.

She awoke the next day with cramps so terrible that she spent the morning lying on her back, wincing through her mother's gentle massage. By midmorning spots of blood had appeared. After lunch she felt a little bit better, and as three o'clock approached she decided she was well enough to wait in the living room for Marian to come home from school. Her water broke as she was walking gingerly down the stairs. It was several weeks early. Anne found her, legs drenched, sitting on the landing; she drove the girl to the hospital immediately, and Holiday met them there.

The baby was stillborn three hours later. Neither mother nor monster ever saw the child, an unnamed girl, a daughter; the small, flesh-soft corpse was removed before Olivia could shake off the first drops of the deep and dreamless sleep of her anaesthesia.

4

When she awoke and her mother explained, she turned her white face to the wall. Marian sat with her, holding her hand and gently stroking her arm, until a nurse asked her to leave and gave Olivia another needle to sleep by. A week later she was allowed to come home.

For three days in mid-February she hid in her room and grieved, and Marian stayed home from school and waited with her. On the first day she delivered arguments for her agony, charges that took hairpin turns, backed up in cul-de-sacs of tears, stopped, stuttered, and then started at the beginning again. On the second day she projected herself into an imaginary future, in which everyone was always staring at her. On the third day she just shook, as if her body had been inhabited by primitive devils, and as evening fell Marian swore she saw her sister levitate slightly above her bed, rising above the mattress by the force of a negative ecstasy.

That night she locked herself in her room immediately after dinner and didn't come out again until the next morning. Marian couldn't say how it happened, but Olivia came to some kind of agreement with herself during the night. At breakfast her voice was still unsteady, but she had weight again, as if she had just decided to give it to herself. If anyone asked how she was she would say, Fine, I'm fine. That afternoon she cleaned her room and began to put her things in boxes, which she carefully labeled and then carried to the attic.

A week passed. The last day was grey, and bitter cold. A grey day, and as cold as could be. Sometime in the evening Olivia used the telephone, but no one knew whom she called; Marian picked up the phone by accident and heard her say, Yes, tonight . . . Yes, I'll be waiting, but she apologized and hung up again before she heard another voice. Just before midnight she knocked softly on the girl's door and said, Olivia? It's me.

It's all right, said Olivia. You can come in. She was sitting on the edge of her bed, fully dressed except for her shoes, which sat on the floor by her feet. Next to them was a small suitcase, packed until it bulged. Her canvas book bag, also full and buckled tightly shut, was on the bed beside her. What's this? said Marian.

I'm . . . going to leave. I'm leaving tonight. Olivia nodded sharply, and her best earrings swayed violently, until one became entangled in a lock of hair. She turned her head slightly to the side, reached up, and straightened it with unconscious fingers.

Where are you going?

I can't really tell you. I don't really know. Someone's coming to take me away.

Who is it?

I can't tell you that either. No one. She shook her head. I don't mean to make this too mysterious. It's just that I shouldn't say.

Marian walked over and sat beside her on the bed and briefly stroked her hair. When are you leaving?

About half an hour.

What do I tell Mom and Dad?

Tell them whatever. You can tell them the truth. Olivia lowered her lashes and stared at her feet, which had begun swinging slightly above the floor like the pendulum of a novelty clock. And if Wilson comes back, tell him I said I was sorry about the baby. I mean, I'm sorry it happened.

. . . .

Marian, said Olivia. I love you, too. You're the best sister. After I'm gone I want you to take care of this house. You know what I mean.

I know, I will, said Marian. She put her arms around the sadly smiling girl and held her. Olivia touched her sister's chin with the soft tips of her fingers. Neither sister seemed to find the night quite real; certainly Marian never really believed for a moment that Olivia was on the verge of some mystery ride, in a mystery car, to nowhere in particular. If she had she might have tried to stop her, or tried to join her, but it all seemed so peculiar, so quick: there was Olivia, there were her bags, and there, across the room, was a large grey-white moth attached by its forelegs to the window screen, its sail-shaped wings beating softly as it wistfully studied the light inside.

Well, I'd better go down, Olivia said. She stood up from the bed, slipped her shoes on, and picked up her bags. Marian checked to make sure the house was asleep and then waved her sister forward. They headed down the stairs without looking around.

It was an overcast night, and the porch lights were off. Olivia set her bags down and then sat on the front stoop; Marian sat beside her, her feet pulled up beneath her, so that while one girl sat with her hands in her lap, the other hugged her knees. It was cold. What did you bring? Marian asked.

Some clothes, mostly. A few pictures. You know...

Do you have any money at all?

Olivia paused, embarrassed, and then briefly shook her head. Wait here. Marian went into the house; a minute later she was back with her hand clasped tightly around a small roll of bills, which she slipped into her sister's jacket pocket. Thank you, said Olivia. Marian nodded.

A little later a pair of headlights appeared at the bottom of the drive and started slowly up towards them, winking as they passed behind a row of trees. Marian glanced back at the house to make sure her parents hadn't woken; all the windows were dark. Olivia stood up and sighed deeply. Here we go, she said, her voice toneless from tension. The next moment the car was at the door.

The lights shone in Marian's eyes, blinding her so that she couldn't see the driver; but she could tell that it was a long black Cadillac, as big and dark as the night itself, befinned and broad-shouldered, with sleek chrome styling and Texas plates. Olivia's bright eyes were fixed on the windshield, thrilled; the engine throbbed quietly. Then the passenger door opened. She looked at her sister, kissed her cheek, and started towards the car. When she reached it she stopped, turned, waved, and then climbed inside and shut the door. The car started forward, and as it passed Marian saw her sister's profile through the window, and, across the seat, the small, sparrow-silhouette of the driver. In a moment they were gone.

5

I'm sorry, Marian said when she was done. I'm really so sorry. She paused for a moment and looked down at the table in deference to the expression I wore. I know, she said. It isn't fair. But the thing is, in the end Olivia decided she just didn't want to get too good at suffering. I heard the boiler in the basement start up, and the sound of hot water making its way into the radiators.

Where is she now? I asked.

I don't know. That was about a month ago, and no one knows. No phone calls, no postcards, radio silence. It was like a ship sailing off into the fog and disappearing. So my parents called the police, they called everyone they could think of, our congressman, everything, and they call again about once a week. But . . . she's gone.

There's got to be something.

What? she said. Aside from that? I mean, the girl just left. I'm sorry. She sighed. Her face was flushed with sympathy. I had a thousand thoughts; they swirled like tea leaves in boiling water. Seventeen years, it was impossible. At the end of days there lies a dump, where pigeons land and pick at scraps. I would appeal, send a letter, illustrated with hideous demons on every page, tear-stained and obscene with rage and regret. I would get going, as if to escape being pelted by the stones and clods of dirt that were being thrown by . . . who was it? Who was it? I saw the man.

You know I could help you, Marian said gently.

Help me? I said.

We could use each other, you know, she said, and I realized that there in the plain, bright kitchen she was petitioning me. Stay with me here, just for a little while. Let me tell you. . . . Olivia won't be coming back, but she left me with something to do. I was waiting for you, because she wanted us to help each other. Her voice became thin and strained as she spoke. Listen to me, she said. She was so frank that I wondered if it was possible that we were actually speaking, or if I weren't taking every one of her words wrong, as if in some preposterous lapse in language. I knew about you. I watched you talking to Olivia at our party. I knew. She told me the rest. She was my sister: she told me everything, she talked about you all the time – all the time. At first I thought it was part of her dreaming, or she was teasing me, but you know what? I thought I heard singing in the garden one night. That was a while before you two met. I wasn't sure – and then later when she said you made songs up all the time, I thought, maybe. She had so much to say that I started to believe her.

What did she say?

Marian bent her closed mouth up in a smile. Just listen for a second, will you? Also, I saw you one night, down by the gazebo, running around. She told me you once lived in it, and then you had to leave. I know why, too. You have no idea what he does. He told her she wasn't going to have that baby, and she didn't. She made an Oh! of utter frustration, dropped her fists onto the table and expelled a burst of pent breath through lips made pale by compression.

Olivia would –

Olivia had you, she said abruptly.

At that there was quiet in the kitchen. She was tired, her eyes fell, and she yawned. It seemed like the last breath of the night, like the only gallon of air left in the world, and I thought she would use it to swallow me whole, would actually consume me, so I braced myself. Instead she pushed herself back from the table, stood up, yawned again, and shook herself. Then she asked me to meet her the following night, in the garden, my own, my garden. I walked her to the foot of the stairs, where she turned, touched my cheek, and with an impossible smile said: You know I'm a monster.

6

She hadn't told me what time she would appear, or where I should wait, and I thought as I sat beneath the wet leaves of a big tree that she might have been kidding, or lying, or delaying, or dreaming, or plotting, or preparing to have me taken away. All that day I had been shaken by passing possibilia. They split my sentences like kindling, they splintered my thoughts. A wet smile, a bare leg, a loose bracelet. Those are verses that were her thighs.

It was a cold evening; there was a wind rushing through the yard on its way I don't where; it had started at the head of the river a thousand miles north, picking up notes from its travels and dropping them into the trees in their backyard, where they made a rustling in the leaves as they landed. I think it was a country's worth of labor left exhausted at the end of the day. I pondered what she'd told me the night before. It made such sense I was convinced it was true. Finally, I saw movement at the back of the house, an open door and spindles of light around Marian's thin legs and skirt, and then the light was extinguished. A moment later I found her shadow in the garden, moving among the trees, disappearing, and emerging again on the grass; I could see her head and shoulders in delicate silhouette against the final, fading azure of the winter sky, and I thought at once of pointing it out to Olivia, who was not there.

With a last measured guess at her loyalties I watched her walk towards me, moving confidently through my fiefdom like royalty paying a visit from a larger land. She strolled right past, wearing a grey jacket and a black scarf around her throat. When she'd gotten a few yards farther into the chilly darkness I softly spoke her name. She didn't jump. I thought she would. She turned back towards me, unerring in her direction, took a few steps towards my voice, and then stopped. So I stood up out of the darkness, rose up, and motioned to her. No, she said in a hushed voice, farther away from the house. Without any hesitation, without even a hint of presumption, she took my hand in hers and led me back to a bench by the flower beds.

That night was the first of her thousand and one, and it began with her telling a story she called Too Small to Count. On successive nights we met after dinner out on the road by the end of their driveway, and she took me into town in her mother's car; we'd sit in a coffee shop, or perch on the bars of the jungle gym in the elementary school playground, and once she made me spend an evening strolling among the moonlit stones of a cemetery. Every night she recited another chapter; they went back to her earliest childhood, an enormous catalogue, replete with frame tales and embeddings, that she'd collected like a mirror Scherezade, not to save her life but to end his. There was A Glass of Whiskey, and The Telephone Call That Never Was, and The Bathing Suit That Revealed Too Much, itself part of the much longer History of the Lost Vacation; and then there was an unhappy cycle of stories about boyfriends, begining with Johnny from Atlanta, through A Friend of a Friend, and ending with Mike Who Was Black. Olivia was a character in most of them, an implicit accomplice, a goad or a witness. I used to shiver whenever her name was mentioned, and

Marian, who never denied or downplayed my sentiments, would generously pat my knee, or cast a phrase or two for me to reach. I sat by her and followed her winding entertainment, and thought constantly of our Dunyazade, and how she would have listened, were it possible.

Marian had a theory of everything, tangled explanations of her father and mother, her sister and herself, which she recast and renewed every day. She was perpetually, finally understanding things, and the clauses and lemmas multiplied out into the farthest reaches of her researches, always ending just where my instincts ended, the equation balanced by subtracting Holiday. I listened to her and admired her for her resolve, for her cleverness and her ability to play in and out of her father's law; in comparison I was a crude and unpolished thing.

She took me for a state of nature, a force she could be friendly with and harness: water, wind, Wilson. So she studied me. She would propose a situation – a stolen bicycle, a town fair, the vice principal of the junior high school – and then ask me into it, to see what would happen. Most often what happened was madness, but a madness she understood: we were very different, Marian and I, but we had lessons for each other, and we wanted to learn; what's more we had a common object that gave our learning a foothold in the world, and we were close. There was a cast of relations, a page of *dramatis personae*, each wearing a little description like the tail on a mouse: the King, his wife, a soldier, a messenger, a monster. Marian and I were up for the same part, and had decided instead to split it.

So I came to know two girls, where once I hadn't known any. As I learned the second, of course, the first seemed to change – not to become lesser – she would never be less than the only girl – but she took on more edges and angles, like a ruby that has been rotated so that the cuts on its underside show. One day when she was in the sixth grade, for example, Olivia was late returning from school. When at last she showed up, just before dinner, she announced that she had been saved on her way home.

Saved? her mother asked. What happened? Are you all right?

I'm good, said Olivia. And now that I've accepted the Lord Jesus Christ into my heart...

Anne questioned her carefully and then called Holiday. The next day a group of fundamentalist Methodists that had set up in a storefront in town received a visit from an attorney for the city, and while Olivia cried for a few days, and worried over the fate of her parents' souls for a few more, it wasn't long before she gave up praying and threw away the pamphlets that she'd carried home in the pages of her social studies textbook. She refused to talk about the episode ever again, nor would she take any teasing about it.

On another occasion, Marian told me, her little sister had joined some friends in a kissing contest in a clearing in the town woods. She was about thirteen at the time, and she chose as her partner another girl, a tomboy named Liz, a Liz like mine. They kissed like lovers; they lasted an hour, and they won.

7

One Sunday evening a week before Easter Marian and I took a bench in a park overlooking the river. She seemed to be in a difficult mood—she scowled at me even before she sat down—and I asked her why. I don't feel great, she said. I feel soggy, and my tits hurt. OK? But when she spoke of her mother her hands beat rapidly in her lap, and she began to rock back and forth in her seat. You see how perfect she is, how well bred. I could squat and piss in the living room at a dinner party and all she'd do is apologize. Well...my mother's all right. She's just a little scared. She'll be much better off when he's gone.

She stared out at the river, her body bent over her legs for warmth. The wake from a passing barge, long since converted into small waves, broke quietly against the bank. Where does she come from, your mother? I asked.

I don't know, said Marian. Ha. Really, I don't know, I have no idea. I think my father invented her, made her out of colored paper and paste. Then she was silent, as if she were reflecting on the craft that went into the fashioning of her mother.

At length I said, Maybe we should go, and started to stand. Wait, wait, she said. I want—

She reached into her pants pocket and pulled out a penknife, fumbling with her cold fingers as she tried to open the small silver blade. At last she slid a thumbnail into the new moon-shaped groove at the thicker edge and managed to unfold it. Then she reached quickly for my hand, turned it face up, and took my index finger in her fist until a short, reddened inch protruded—and before I could say a word she'd stabbed down at it. I yelped in pain and pulled my hand away, staring at the red line of blood that had immediately welled up on my fingertip. As I watched, it began to dribble down the side like crimson syrup.

—Marian made a short squeak: I looked up to find involuntary tears in her eyes. She sucked her wet breath in. Hold out your hand, she said. She put her bloody fingertip on mine and squeezed them together until I could feel her hot pulse throbbing; warm drops of mixed blood dripped down to the leg of my pants, where they made small black spots. She stared at our hands as if she hoped they would fuse. My finger grew numb. Finally she relaxed her grip and wiped her hand roughly on her jeans. Now we're brother and sister, she said. All right?

Then she reached into her jacket and drew out a pair of books, one slightly smaller then the other, both anonymous in the darkness. I have something to give you, she said. I wasn't going to, but I figured I should. Just so you understand. She put the books in my lap, then stood up and started to walk away, but before she'd gotten ten feet into the night she stopped, turned her shadowed face to me, and said:

Now I'm in you and you're in me
I'm in you and you're in me
I'm in you and you're in me.

8

I've mentioned Olivia's diary before. She began it when she was a little girl, almost as soon as she had learned to write, and as the years passed she had collected the books as she filled them, placing them in a box which she hid on top of her closet. A few weeks after we met she finished the last page of one, added it to the treasury, and began writing in the volume I'd left her among my first gifts. She wrote in it almost every evening, and for the half hour or so that she spent sitting up at the head of her bed scribbling down the day's thoughts I used to distract myself by reading one of her books (I remember a strange substitution of concept for substance that occured one night when, while leafing through her dictionary, I came upon the word *gloaming* while the thing itself was waiting outside), or uselessly multiplying numbers on her calculator, or simply staring out the window until she would close the covers, put the book away in her desk, look up with a small, comely smile, and say, OK. Over here.

In it was every story she wanted to save – I remember her pausing in mid-anecdote to dig up an early volume, which she used to check a fact or a feeling – and from time to time I would remember that on a shelf behind her closet door there lay an image of herself, as she saw herself, a shroud of my girlfriend's writing. I was, of course, hugely curious about what she had said, and if I stopped myself from sneaking a look while she was out of the room, it was as much because I was afraid she would come in and catch me as because I felt honor-bound not to steal her reflection. It was just the sort of thing that would have made Olivia furious with me – so much so that it hadn't even occurred to me to look for them when I went through her room. I wouldn't have found them anyway; as soon as Olivia had driven off Marian went back into the house and took them before her father could find them.

I sat in my room in the basement later that night, with the earlier book in my hands and my hands in my lap, and tried to decide whether or not to read it. First I turned it over and gazed at the unbroken binding, and then I set it down on my thigh. I even opened the cover and found her name and a beginning date on the frontispiece, and the sight of her handwriting made my breath wet, because I loved it, but I shut the book again before I could read on. It wasn't that I wanted to preserve her privacy; still, the thing stayed closed on my lap and lay there mute for a few minutes, because I was terrified. When I'd worked up my courage I opened it again.

APRIL 16. In school today someone told me I was too nice. Another spring—Shit. What are you going to do, Olivia?—Be stronger, be smarter, waste less time, be more patient, eat better, try not to let it get to you, have a good summer.—But you have no friends, really, you don't know anyone. Why not? It wasn't made for you. Mom says I'm just fine, but she doesn't know.

MAY 7. No one is going to do anything to me that I don't want, because I won't let them. No one is going to do anything to me at all, because I won't let them. Today some girls were dancing in the cafeteria during lunch, dancing to the radio—I watched from the back and I was thinking, I wish I could do that. Freak.

MAY 20. There's something weird happening in the garden.—I think there's someone out there. Last night I couldn't sleep, so I went out onto the patio in the dark. I heard a boy's voice singing a song back by the pool, the pond. I want to know who it is. Everything's grown big and wild—it's wonderful. It makes me want to,—I don't know, I

like it. Mom's happy, Marian laughed at me because I tried to ride
my bicycle up to the front door, up the stairs.

JUNE 2. Sick in bed. So bored I could scream.

JUNE 12. He came into my room late last night while I was trying to
get to sleep again, or trying to stay awake, I can't tell anymore.
Whisper quiet, no birds. I looked up and he was sitting on the edge
of my bed, kind of staring. I remember him from our party. He
touched me, very gently, and I thought I would just about jump
straight up and hit the ceiling. I felt crazy right away. He said he
lived here, and then he left. I wasn't scared, I was so ready, and I
thought, What is wrong with you? You're very fucked up.—But I'm
feeling so fierce, I could just tear right into him, I want to sting him
like a bee. It makes me laugh.—Come back, come back. I'll give
you . . . presents
   pineapples
   parrots in silver cages.

JUNE 17.—Today there was a map of the world on my desk. I
unfolded it on my bed and thought about where to go. Paris, of
course, and Rome—But also Sri Lanka, to live in the tea fields,
New Guinea and all over Africa.

JUNE 19. Well it happened last night at last. It hurt a little, not a lot.
My own bed, late, late at night—he was there. I knew he would come
—I was calling him all day, thinking about him hard. He gave a little
speech, like he had to explain first. I just wanted to get on with it, so
I kind of grabbed him. Shameless. A little fumbling at first, but then
it was OK. I didn't realize it would go so far up.
   My stomach was making noise all night. I hope he didn't notice.

JUNE 30. He does love to talk. Sometimes I find myself saying
things without thinking, and then I stop and say to myself—Was

that you? So I feel like I can do anything.

He tells me stories, pulls me along with this voice he gets. I can't believe some of the things he says. I worry sometimes that I'm just going to go under in the dark, and I'll never come back up—so I get mad, and he doesn't understand.

JULY 2. He does this kind of—thing sometimes, it's like, suckling. Funny word. It's so nice I can't stand it. When he's inside it's like a circuit that's always open is suddenly closed, the power can jump across that gap; then the bulb starts to glow, the little clapper on the bell starts to quiver, getting ready to ring. I lean back and think, wherever you're going I'm going too—And then we go.

I like the way he smells.

JULY 10. When Daddy came home tonight he called me into his office, very serious about something—But then I thought about W.—We'd just finished doing it, in the middle of the day when the house was empty, really hard, so I was still aching from it—And I smiled, and when he looked at me I started laughing, I couldn't help it. He was mad. I wish I had a bigger bed.

JULY 18. Six days late. I feel heavier already, can feel it churning up and collecting like gelatin—It's scary. I knew right away, knew the night it happened, and I knew I was going to keep it, too.—It's ours, and if I don't tell anyone they can't take it away. Sooner or later W. can come out, maybe move in here for real. Hiding him is such a strain—But everything's going to change, it's all going to be better. Daddy won't like it, but he won't be able to do anything—It's a revolution in the petting zoo.

JULY 30. I think W. knows, but he hasn't said anything. I don't know what he thinks. He's paying a lot of attention to me, even though I got mad at him this morning—He got mad back but an hour later he was apologizing—But I didn't want to talk, I just wanted him to hold me for a while. I don't know what he's thinking, almost ever.—I don't know what to do.

AUGUST 4. Sunny day, sat on the back patio. W. very sweet today, snuck up and brought me flowers from the garden, with this look on his face that made me want to cry, or yell. He has no parents anymore, so he needs me. Don't blow it, you can do it.
—I feel like a jukebox, flashing lights and happy music.

AUGUST 17. Olivia Miller. Olivia Miller. Olivia Miller. Olivia Miller.

AUGUST 20. It was worse than I thought. How can Daddy yell at me now? I know what he's thinking, that I'm stupid, that I'll ruin my life. But W. showed me ghosts dancing in the backyard, and said everything was all right. I did see them, too.

SEPTEMBER 15. No control—Dreaming and dreaming, and floating—I can't feel myself anymore.

OCTOBER 2. Marian knows who it is, of course, and she says I have to send him away or else I'm just going to fall apart. Just tell him he has to go, he can come back later. If he loves me—no, she said, because he loves you. She said she'd take care of me. She said she'd tell him if I wanted but I said I'd better—I need just a few days more.

OCTOBER 6. I can't stand it—He left, I didn't give him any choice, I was scared. He hates me—Everyone does.

OCTOBER 20. So W. is gone, and now I don't know if he was ever here. I asked Marian and she said, Yes, of course. Did I think I was Mary? She gave me a long hug, said everything will be fine—I don't know that. I have to start classes at this school—Marian calls it Miss Andrews' School for Wayward Girls, and makes me laugh—But I'm falling behind and I have to go.

NOVEMBER 12. Another fit today, like I was six feet away from the world. No one saw. W. gone, Marian helps, as much as she can. There was a man standing at the bus stop today who looked at me, fat as I am, and said something so disgusting I can't even write it down. Argh. I wanted to go up to him and just pull my clothes off so he could see.

JANUARY 1. New Year. Watched it on TV with Marian, soon to be an aunt, she was sweet enough to stay home.

JANUARY 12. Daddy came into my room again this evening, so angry I thought he was going to hit me—he just stormed in without knocking, when Mom and Marian were out of the house. You cannot have that baby, he said—You will not—We'll send you away. Do you know what they do to girls with babies?—No school, no job, home forever. He said, when you were little we could take care of you, but you're a big girl now, and we're not going to help you with this, if you insist on going through with it. I said, It's too late anyway, I'm seven months in, and he just looked at me and said, This is my house, and you are my daughter. You will not have that baby.

JANUARY 17. I think my food is being poisoned, and I think I know who it is. The baby is kicking almost all the time. It wants to put its foot through my stomach and break out, like a cartoon chick out of a cartoon egg. No one ever wonders how the egg feels about it. I'm tired all the time but I can't sleep.

JANUARY 19. [There was nothing written here, but she had scrawled a crude picture of a big dog.]

JANUARY 20. There are dead animals in the yard. It's from Daddy—I think he's crazy—I think he hates me. The flesh comes off the bones, and the bones come off the marrow. I keep finding blood in my dreams. He's going to kill me.

F EBRUARY 4. I feel so sick.

It ended there, on that hard syllable; and I knew at once why bombers blow up banks, why tornadoes touch down in trailer parks, why the windows on a burning room weep.

9

There were eight empty glasses on the table. The jukebox was quiet for the first time in an hour. Marian's head was lowered over the table, her chin resting on her fists while she looked out blankly at a dime that was resting in a thin slick of fluid next to an ashtray. I can't stand it. I can't stand it, she said. It's so fucked up.

10

I took her down to the gazebo. We sat on the stairs, facing the house, and I drew an imaginary line with my forefinger, as if I were laying out the lines of a playing field. The house is his, but the garden is still mine, I said. From the edge of the patio to the bottom of the yard is a free zone. That's fair, isn't it?

Of course, she replied.

Marian, I want it proved, I said, and rose to my feet. So we're going to try him here tonight. OK? She put her gloved hands on her knees and then stood up by pushing down until she rose, like a toy girl with mechanical joints, and we walked hand in hand out onto the lawn. A few yards away there was a small hillock; I remembered having to strain to push a mower up it the spring before, and then suddenly leaning back to stop it from getting away from me as it rolled down the short slope at the other side. We

made our way to the top, turned, and faced the grounds. Marian
held her hands clasped before her. Can I begin? she asked, and
I gestured in deference. Ladies and gentlemen of the jury, she
said suddenly, addressing a row of hydrangea bushes that I had
planted the previous summer – Wait. She stopped and took a
breath to keep her voice from shaking. Ladies and gentlemen of
the jury. Your honor, she said, and looked respectfully towards a
rhododendron. My associate and I – she gestured towards me –
are here today to put a case against one Holiday Miller, who is my
father, and his . . . father-in-law. She stood with her back straight
and spoke sternly and precisely.

Mr. Miller is accused of being a bad man, she continued, emphasis on the penultimate word, which she dragged out until it
bleated. I suppressed a snort of laughter, and she smiled quickly.
There's so much evidence against him that I don't know where to
begin . . . She looked at me encouragingly, but I remained silent.
Something fluttered in a treetop a few yards away. All right, she
said. This is serious. To begin with, he drove my sister away.

A girl I loved, I said. The rhododendron nodded in a breeze.

Marian interrupted her advocate's pose and turned to me. Yes.
She loved you too. And I always approved of you. She'd never had
a boyfriend before, and I was so proud of her for having done
that, all on her own. In a few years she'd have been just another
one of his . . . Nothing. The judge and jury had become bushes
again; Marian's voice grew hard in premature defense of a com-
plaint. I'm sorry you had to leave. She was so scared of him she
didn't even know. Well. She turned back to address the jury
again, unconsciously smoothing her skirt with her hands. Then he
made her lose her baby.

My daughter, I said. The last syllable turned into a blue moth,
flew upwards out of my mouth, and got away.

That would be enough, Marian said. It would be more than
enough, but we're not done. Look at my mother – she was suddenly louder, her voice rising until it was almost shrill and I was
afraid that someone would hear her. How could she have married

him? She asked me as if she wanted to know and thought I could tell her. If she hadn't I would not have ever been born. I don't care. Look at me. I did, and I was surprised to find a girl my age standing there, thin and temperamental, her features narrowed by anger. Go on, she said sharply to me.

He burned me out of my garden, I said. But that's nothing, because Olivia . . .

That's right, said Marian firmly.

There was a nimbus around the moon, a magnified mist of white with a faint, ice-blue ring in it. I hadn't noticed it earlier. My colleague had paused to consult her notes. After a moment she spoke again: What is a bad man? she asked. A bully is a bad man. A boy might tilt up the world until it faced over him. A daughter might take a sword against him and prove her position. Say it, just say it.

While we waited we went back to the bench, and Marian picked up my hand and held it tightly. Open and shut, she said gaily. It won't be long. After a minute had passed I got up again, walked briskly over to the hydrangeas, and addressed the leftmost bush directly.

Have you reached a verdict? I paused. And what is your verdict? I reached down, plucked a single early bud from a branch, and brought it over to her. Out blew my nervous, enormous breath. All right. I peeled back the bright green carapace, and the petals below were small and tightly packed. Then I began to draw them off one by one, letting them drop to the ground at our feet until I reached a point where they were so tiny that I had nothing left to grasp. I split the remaining budlet with my thumbnail and glanced at the result: by the moonlight I could see a creeping black spot, a sort of signifying stain, in the deepest heart of the flower. I showed it to Marian. Guilty, she said matter-of-factly.

Guilty, I said.

OK – as if she'd just confirmed a law of nature. What's the sentence? She went over to the rhododendron. Her hands were clasped at her waist. She leaned over the bush and listened. After a few seconds had passed, she suddenly rose again and clapped her hands. Yes, she said excitedly. That's what we were hoping. She straightened up and turned back to me. Well, she said:

I can't say it but I know what it is
I can't say it but I know what it is
I know, I know, I know what it is

11

The verdict, you see, was mine, and it was a mere thing, but the sentence and all its meaning was hers. A boy can spend a year in school, in and out of class again, and no one will teach him: Violence has a way of its own, with rules of proportion, plot and design. That is violence. Vengeance is a perfect circle, as axiomatic and bold as any figure found in Euclid's abstract space. And that is vengeance. We make justice ourselves, like we make a house, with an eye to the distribution of our practical actions and the clearest view, and then we take our place in it and live. And that is justice. I hated Holiday and gave him every fault. He had thieved the one thing I had ever earned, and I would right the world by ruining him. My side was therefore chosen. But my jealousy and rage were incapable of anything; so the actions that followed were lessons Marian taught me in the arts of human agency, an education for which, in the end, I will always be grateful.

12

One paper-thin afternoon Anne went through Holiday's dresser drawers in search of a cotton shirt of her own that she thought she might have misfiled on laundry day. On the bottom of the bottom drawer, beneath a maroon sweater that he never wore, she found a magazine, a glossy, glaring thing that I'd already seen three times before. She wore a look of utter disgust as she carried it away, and for several days she came and went in the house without saying much to anyone, wearing an expression as if there were a very faint sound in her ears, a ringing that bothered her.

She knocked on Marian's door one night later that week and asked her if she wanted to go for a drive, and when Marian said Sure, she went downstairs and waited silently in the foyer for the girl to get dressed and find her jacket. Where are we going? Marian asked when she came down a few minutes later, stopping on the bottom stair to pat her pockets for her gloves. All her mother said was, You don't need gloves. Let's go.

According to the girl they never stopped, they just drove and drove, south on the highway for forty miles or so, then around home again on a county road. And her mother spoke only once, and then just as they'd gotten to the farthermost point of their trip and were turning back; she'd pulled off the highway onto a frontage road, and the car was stopped for the first time, caught at a red light that hung over the blacktop like the glowing eye of an irradiated insect. Some distance out into the darkness a shimmering green and white sign showed the road ahead splitting in two.

Boo, said Anne.

When Marian turned to look at her she found someone she did not recognize. The light turned green, and the car started forward again.

13

The next day, as Holiday sat in his study, Anne knocked on his door. She held something rolled up in her hand, and held her hand at her hip. Yes? he said, and she crossed in.

Holiday? He didn't look up, but his hand stopped writing.

Turn around, she said carefully. He swiveled his chair around with his feet; his hands grasped the armrests. He was in his shirt-sleeves, and his tie was undone, though it was still around his neck. All right. What is it? he asked impatiently.

What is this? She held the magazine up, but it was facing her, and he couldn't place it from the photograph on the back cover. He said, I – and then went silent and averted his eyes as he recognized it. I found this in one of your drawers, and I want to know why you have it, she said. She was on the verge of angry tears, and her voice quavered slightly, as if she was afraid.

I don't know.

You don't know?

I found it, he said.

You found it?

It was in Olivia's room. I found it after she left.

It was an answer so improbable and so apparently cowardly that at first she was at a loss for words. Oh, come on now, she said finally, with a disgust that he knew at once he couldn't answer. He stared at her through his glasses, reaching for an effect of clear, unblinking innocence that was somehow ruined by the bifocal line in his lenses. She turned around and left.

Out of the house, in a diner downtown, Marian and I ate ice cream and she remembered the magazine. Just as hard as a turtle's back, she said. It could have been all right, except that girl, with all that paint . . .

I described the look on her mother's face, her eyes held carefully on him, her skin insufficient to say, and asked her if it wasn't too much. She grimaced and shook her head. I . . . poor Mommy, I know. But she sat by and watched as all this happened. I don't blame her, but I do.

Will she be all right?

Best for all concerned, she replied brightly. Trust me: I know it looks bad, but think of what a mess my house is. Something has to change, or else my father will just take over again. See? And he will, you know. She bent over and spooned the last of the chocolate syrup into her mouth, then licked a blot of goo from her lips as she shook her head.

He can't be trusted with anything. They say – they, people in town – that my father had a partner once, years ago when Olivia and I were little. They set up a practice together, and then my father decided he didn't want him around, so he cheated him out of everything, cheated him bad, and he had to leave town. I don't know, all I remember is this strange little man who used to come by the house, bringing presents. He had these tiny little hands and feet. His name was ... something real plain, like Johnson, but that's not it. Something like that.

I asked her what she'd been looking for in Holiday's office that night, by then it seemed a year or more back, when another Marian, one I did not know, had let herself in after her parents had gone to bed and searched the place.

Magic books, she said, her eyes widening for effect. Spells and incantations, recipes, voodoo dolls, potions. My father is ...

Just then a friend stopped by the table, a girl with chopped blond hair and dark circles under her eyes. She placed her hand on the tabletop and said a weary Hey, Marian. How are you?

Just all right, said Marian as she looked up.

The girl looked at me curiously but we weren't introduced; she waited for a moment while Marian eyed her expectantly, but she didn't have any more to say and in a moment she had made her Good-bye and was gone. Under the guise of pretending to study the chalkboard menu above the counter Marian shot the briefest of disparaging glances at her retreating back, and then turned back to the table. She was a friend of Olivia's, she said. She's been spreading rumors all month, and she thinks I don't know. Maybe we should kill her too.

I was wondering how we might when Marian said, Jesus Christ, I was just kidding. Wilson? But by then I was watching the too bright sunlight out the window, watching the houses, the stores and churches dissolve in the midday like a fresh oil painting to which someone has taken a sponge soaked in turpentine, making a parti-colored smear on the far side of the glass, which, in my angry imagination, grew less and less substantial, until, at last, there was nothing left at all.

14

. . . on a bench by the brackish fish pond. She wore a pair of silver earrings and a bit of makeup. It was so cold that her breath steamed from her mouth, and she repeatedly lifted the side of an index finger to the tip of her nose to staunch an imaginary flow, a girlish gesture that made me think of the petals of invisible daisies. She was nervous and excited but she wouldn't say why, in any case not just yet. Instead she wriggled on her seat and said, Ask me something, go on.

Ask you what?

That's the point, I don't know.

I thought for a moment while she shivered impatiently, then sidestepped my lusterless imagination and gave her Olivia's question. What do you want to be?

An assassin, she said without hesitation, adding a short, violent nod for emphasis. I'm sorry, she went on, I just can't resist. Look what I got today. She dug deep into her coat pocket for something big and heavy – too big, in fact, to come out easily; it snagged on the lining, and for a few seconds she tugged and twisted, growing slightly frustrated, for her star actor had tripped over his entrance. At last a metal handle emerged in the grip of her small fingers, and then, with a final twist and pull, the long barrel of an enormous pistol appeared. She displayed it in her open hand, and I reached for it with one of those mechanical acts of taking that eight-year-old boys use to appropriate their friends' new toys. She gave it up, but her eyes remained fixed on the fat part of the casing as I held it heavily in my hand, raised it towards the house for a second, and then turned it towards the darkest part of the garden. Stick 'em up, I said softly. Across the lawn a boxwood reached for the sky. Bang. You're dead.

She smiled. Isn't it beautiful? I bought it from someone at school, she said. It was a lot.

It's big.

Yeah, I know. She seemed pleased with it. From her left pocket she withdrew a chocolate bar, already half-unwrapped. She broke off a chunk the size of her thumb and offered it to me. When I shook my head she shrugged and popped it quickly into her mouth. Shouldn't we use his? I asked.

We will, she said with some amusement, and took the pistol back. You will. It's a little too . . . symbolic? for me. I'll use this one.

15

Late that night, as I was lying restlessly on my pile of blankets in the basement, Olivia suddenly showed up in my mind, laughing at something I hadn't seen, holding her hands in fists at her waist. A little later in my sleep I was standing by a dresser in my room in Lincoln, and she came up to me, strong, naked, her skin vanilla, her lips and nipples pinkish red, flooding my dream-filled mouth with some sweet slippery substance. She had come to tell me she was leaving, and I begged her for one last hug, but her face fell, she frowned, and refused me sadly; someone was waiting for her. I watched her through the mirror above the dresser as she slipped out the door. When I woke the next morning I found a familiar throbbing halfway down the sheets, and a small breath-belaboring pebble in my throat.

16

There was a nut-brown bird singing in the bare branches of a tree, amid the stems of grey stalks and twigs that multiplied into the grey sky, splitting again and again like nerves stripped of their flesh, with no message to bring, no motion left upon which to insist. The bird sang, its chree-chree, its reet-reet, while Anne stood by a cold window and listened to the unbearable noise. The world was unreal and had always been so, and as the bird sang its last note and suddenly flew out of the branches in a flurrying, downward arc that sent it out of sight, she underwent a fit of fatidic panic; the house upended before her eyes, flipping over like the image in a *camera obscura*, while she hung down helplessly. She froze until, a few moments later, it had passed, and then backed away, leaving a patch of fog from her breath and prints from her sweating fingertips on the glass, where they lingered for a second or two before melting away.

17

You hate her sometimes. You don't know what happened, what to do. You want to yell at her, you want to kill her, you want to bring her back. It's OK . . . It's just you're angry. You want to touch her again, she could be doing anything, now. It's OK. I know all about it, it doesn't mean anything. You should have seen her when you left. It's OK.

18

Something unexpected was next. One night before bed Anne came down the stairs in her bathrobe and found Holiday in the living room, sitting with a book. She gently said his name and retied her robe. He didn't respond at all: he simply turned the page. She asked him to speak to her. He had his head cocked slightly back and turned to one side, while he stared down his nose at the page. He pushed his glasses up, he clamped his pipe in his teeth. She waited for a few moments and then asked again. His large head rose from the paper, his eyes fixed upon her, and he refused, the simple words – No, I will not – inducing a fit of unexpected temper that brought him out of his seat. She ran from the room; he sat down again. She was back through the door a moment later, and she supplicated him again, unaware that her robe had come half undone, revealing the sky-blue silk of her nightgown. She called him by a pet name as if the intimacy of invoking it would soften him. Instead he looked her up and down, made a harrumph, and pretended to go back to his reading, though of course the trembling page was filled with meaningless black ink spots.

She spent that night in the guest room. When morning came she went into her daughter's room and spoke to her for a few minutes while Holiday hid behind the door to his bedroom and I hid in the attic. Soon after, Marian came upstairs to find me. When I walked out from behind a cardboard box – the label said: Olivia/elementary school – she was standing by a shadeless floor lamp, with a look on her face as if she'd just seen a deer get hit by a truck. My mother is leaving, she said at once. It's really happening. She said she should have done it a long time ago, she said she was sorry. With a thin hand she tucked her hair behind her ear, and she smiled weakly. I'm supposed to stay until school is done. So you and I... She opened her arms for me. I went to her and she hugged me, rocking me gently, gently against her body for a few moments before she turned away and started for the door. Motes of golden dust that she'd kicked up when she'd come in streamed diagonally down in the currents of the attic air, infinitely fine grains endlessly pouring down into a pool before an unused wardrobe, like some magical wind-borne gift. I was still watching them when she walked out.

Anne's last scene with Holiday took place in the unlit wings,

amid flats and pulleys, and a suitcase full of brightly colored cos-
tumes. It began with memories and accusations, short lines played
fast, occasionally lapsing into unexpected rhyme – life with wife,
for example, and daughter with water. When she finished there
was music for a minute or two, cheap strings and a piano. Then
there was a noise like a man falling off a ladder – the set shook
slightly and the music stopped. The place was silent for a moment,
and then the queen's voice started up; it floated out over the
empty seats; she was delivering an unscripted soliloquy on the end
of majesty.

An hour or so later she left; Marian helped her take her bags
out, and I caught a glimpse of the two of them standing by the car.
The girl was looking at her mother, and her mother was staring at
the house, as if it were a tree that had strangled her hanging years.
Holiday was in his study trying not to listen, and he didn't come
out again until she was gone. Then he stood in the foyer and
peered through the window beside the front door at the empty
driveway, the bare sloping lawn, the line of trees shielding the
house from the road in front, the blue, blue sky. When he turned
back his face was pale and his hands shook at his sides.

Marian found me again soon after her mother left, and whispered hotly in my ear:

> Mom's in the car and the car's on the highway
> Mom's in the car and the car's on the highway
> Once it went his way, now it goes my way
> Mom's in the car and the car's on the highway

19

She had left the three of us, he to his empty days,
and Marian and me to him. Meticulous Holiday immediately be-

gan to set the house in order, as if he were preparing for some special event. He would stand in a room, looking over its arrangement carefully, and then fix it by moving a chair over to a precise place by a window, or clearing a coffee table of everything but an empty china bowl. He gave the impression that each adjustment was part of some elaborate recipe, and as it gradually became clear to him that Anne was not coming back he increased his efforts, and they became increasingly eccentric. Once I watched from the living room window as he went out into the garden and took a slow walk through the ravaged paths, the dry patches of burned grass, the fish pond, now covered with floating islands of bright green moss, the hard dirt where the herb garden had been, the scorch marks beside the gazebo where he had, in casting the stuff of my pared-down life into the flames, begun his end. He was collecting things here and there; from time to time he would stop, bend down, and examine a stone or a twig, and then, if it passed, place it carefully in his jacket pocket. Slowly and methodically he moved through the grounds, and when he was done he came back to the house and filled a glass jar with the fragments he had recovered, and then put the jar in the center of the kitchen table. He spent the next day cooking something foul-smelling, which he left in a pot in the refrigerator, and the day after that he went around the house and washed each window with warm water and vinegar, until the glass shined brightly, like silvery panes embedded in the walls.

As Holiday pursued his unlikely administration, Marian camped in the house like a loner beneath a highway overpass, gathering the few possessions she cared about around her and sleeping lightly. She did not allow her friends to call. Olivia's birthday was coming up, and we were waiting, restlessly, with little to do until then.

One night later that week I found myself distracted by a sudden clutching at my thoughts as I passed her room one night and helplessly remembered the motion she used to make as she locked her door, how the fingers of one hand lay softly on the knob while with the other she slowly turned the bolt, as if to prolong the delicious

sensation of enclosing herself with me inside. I stopped, and in my
faint reverie I failed to hear Holiday starting up the stairs, and
only awoke when the flicker of his shadow on the wall caught my
eye. I had to throw myself into the linen closet and shut the door
swiftly before me. I was sure he'd hear the noise, but he didn't; I
could see him through the slats, making his way up the last few
steps, his feet bare, his walk swaying, his face pressed down into
his open hands. I couldn't hear anything but the sound of my own
breath, I was so intent on controlling my gasps, but I watched him
as he turned and stared at his daughter's door, facing half-away.
His chest was heaving and his shoulders were shaking, and as I
looked he pulled his hands from his face, slowly, the way a child
will pull a bandage from a skinned knee; it was as if he were afraid
he would strip the skin from his features, and I saw the shiny glint
of tears melting on his wax-pale cheeks.

I said nothing to Marian about it. She and I intended to see to it
that he knew, but only at last. The force that countered him and
drew down such ill fortune had been hidden from him, a door
shutting at the far side of a room he'd just entered, a telephone
that stopped ringing as soon as he'd reached it; when the moment
came, we would lift the walls and reveal ourselves, as children, as
wild legislators.

20

Olivia's birthday fell on a Wednesday. She would
have been, would be, seventeen. Marian and I planned a little celebration, and that evening we met whispering in the basement, set
up an unsteady card table, lit a dozen and a half candles on a small
store-bought cake, and wished her many many happy returns.
Marian took her forefinger and dragged it through the white icing,
and then, with a look of exquisite suffering, sucked the dollop off.
With dim light below her face, eyes thick with thoughts.

All I ever wanted, she said. All I ever wanted was to have possession over All I ever wanted was to be, you know A charmed life Love, she said. Family My little sister and me, we were going to start a kind of tribe, just girls and boys. A nation of It was in the woods, and we were going to Make love, adventure. Little girls.

And that was me? I asked.

That was part of it, she replied.

21

Holiday went quietly to his room at around ten that night. Marian was sitting beside me at the top of the attic stairs, and when his door shut behind him she put her hands on my upper arm and squeezed. Soon afterwards the light beneath his door disappeared; she hit me gently on the side of my knee. We waited a long while, and then we rose up, tiptoed down the stairs, and entered Olivia's room. Well . . . Marian said. Here we go.

Her hands shook as she opened the door to the closet; she smiled quickly as she closed it upon herself. I heard a faint thud as she tripped over a box on the floor and fell backwards against the wall. OK! she whispered through the door. Go on! The room was pitch black. I held my breath, stood prepared for my accusation. My lungs were tight from frost. I climbed onto Olivia's bed, bed that we had broken in, and I began to bounce.

I had never shouted in that house. Hey! I shouted, and called him with a song that I sang out in long, slow measures:

> If I were a monster, and you were a man
> If I were a monster, and you were a man
> Would you let me take your daughter
> To the Sugartown dance?
> Yo-dee-o-lay-ee-hoo!

I've got a good reason, and my sister's got a plan
I've got a good reason, and my sister's got a plan
We didn't ask for ransom
We're going to kill a man
Yo-dee-o-lay-ee-hoo!

I could hear Marian punctuating my words with muffled exclamations from out of the closet, a door-dampened Yeah!, a distant
That's right! I was bouncing in a circle and I'd just come around to
face the door again when I noticed Holiday standing a step or two
into the room, holding a match up before his face and squinting
around it. I was so possessed by my bouncing and yodeling that I
hadn't heard him come in. The flame cast a small volume of ancient light around the room, a flickering field, not so much colored
as drawing out the colors and forms of the furniture, the base of
the wall, and a floor made round by shadows. He was barefoot,
dressed in the bottom half of a pair of pajamas, and above his
pale, puffy chest his features were smudgy and his dull eyes
stared. He was as calm as could be, and he watched me with pal-
pable exhaustion, standing so close that I heard his heart slowly
throbbing. The convex form of the room was reflected in his wet
eyes, and I could see myself represented there, my last face, a tiny
light. He was entirely alone.

The flame burned down the matchstick and bit his fingertips,
and he quickly shook it out and let it drop extinguished to the
floor. The room was dark again. I could sense Holiday standing
away from me, waiting for me to cease to be; I could hear his even
breathing, and I knew at once, I immediately knew, that my monster's amorous trials were ending as finally as the last few frames
of film flapping through a film projector.

Hm. He cleared his throat and hitched up his pants. At last he
spoke. Of course. You came by my office You were wearing my
tie. So it was you all along?

Yes.

Who are you? Fat Holiday, pursy Holiday, in his daughter's

room with his daughter's murder-minded boyfriend. I stared. Answer me. He turned on her desk lamp, and then stepped outside of its dim, diluted light. Where is Marian?

I'm right here, she said. She stood in the dark doorway of Olivia's closet with the big gun weighing down her soft small hand. He gazed at her, but he didn't seem to see what she carried. Or perhaps he was very brave, or very stupid, or very –

You hate me, he said, as if he was merely mentioning it.

You don't know, she answered.

Olivia – but before he could finish I'd winced my ears shut: Marian had shot a hole through the window. Not much of the glass had broken. The air was stiff with the sweet smell of gunpowder. Holiday was suddenly sitting on the edge of the bed. I'm sorry, he said. I was wrong

Marian stamped her foot and said, No.

He put his hands loosely on his knees, giving his shoulders a meaningless shrug. My daughters hate me. He looked up at me. Maybe you'll forgive me

Don't do that, said Marian. She was trying not to shake and she shook like a drunk; the barrel of her gun wobbled. My own wretched pistol had somehow found its way halfway into my front pocket, where it pressed against my hip. My hand was still on it, my forefinger resting against the trigger the way it would across my lips if I were trying to quiet him.

Instead he took a deep, storytelling breath. I tell you, he said, I made this place, and I wanted to keep it forever, like the pictures on Achilles' shield to keep the houses, the towns, the scenes in the square, the weather in the sky I would have liked to have died in a corner of my garden wrapped in a blanket and nodding in the sunlight. Well, I'm an old man, with thankless daughters and a joyless wife. I demanded a little love from them and they couldn't give it, because I demanded it. So I decided to unmake them He shook his head sadly on his chest. I'm sorry, he said again. Pause, while outside Olivia wandered. Pause

What am I supposed to do with that? you said.

I don't know. Defeated candidate, losing pitcher.

Your face contracted and you twisted on your hip, drew back the hand that held the gun and feinted with it. Then you swore a nameless syllable and threw it at him as hard as you could, with your head down and your eyes squeezed tightly shut. He jerked to cover himself and the piece glanced off his forearm, skittered across the floor towards a corner of the room, and abruptly disappeared.

You were leaning against the wall where a chest of drawers had been, softly crying. He rubbed the sore spot on his arm and looked up at me, as if he were seeing me for the first time. Well. Here he paused for a moment, and then spoke again. Are you going to murder me?

I said, No.

Will you be forgotten?

Yes, I said.

He stood up, and Olivia's bed evaporated, like perfume Why? he asked, as if it were a gentle sort of examination.

I have nothing left, I answered. There was a crowding within me, a slow drip of shame in my heart of hearts.

Give it here. He held out his hand for my gun, and I gave to him like a payment. I know you, he said. Olivia's curtains turned to mist and vanished. I know all about you and what you've done. It's been enough. So you would bind your abilities up in a chest and sink it in the sea He gestured with his hands to illustrate House, stick, trunk, strap, water You wanted to live with others as others live; but you can't, and you can't live alone I know you can't I tried myself long before you came. Boy, let go, he commanded, his voice echoing in the room, because the room was suddenly empty. It's too late, let go anyway.

Where will I go?

Anywhere, nowhere Just get away from here.

And then as if by some strange, uncommon force I felt my feet lift from the ground, and slowly I began to move across the floorboards, passing through the door, floating down the shallow, soft-

ening staircase, its flower-patterned wallpaper walls streaming up
and out of sight as I held onto a bannister like the railing on the
deck of a descending ship. I could hear Holiday roaring above me,
as a room went by from below, and then a string of rooms; they
were tilted and open like boxes, like balloons, reversing and re-
placing themselves, giving up long forgotten fragments of careful
speeches, stuck gestures, crayon drawings and clothes. In one I
saw a woman with your mother's features sitting in a chair, nursing an infant, the right side of her shirt raised to expose her breast
and the baby's mouth closed around its nipple. In a second a crystal decanter full of dark reddish liquor was floating a few feet
above the carpet, bobbing and turning gently. Jones was standing
in the middle of the next, neatly dressed and smiling broadly as he
held a red-barreled fountain pen out in his hand. There were
stray pages of music books, and telephone messages, and a souve-
nir fan from the state fair. With the sound of twenty years they all
rushed past me, pulling at my clothes like wind. Holiday, bellow-
ing and thrashing, had opened his bag and let them loose at last,
and in a minute they were gone.

When I next noticed my place I found my shoes were wet
through from the dew on the front lawn. You were standing beside
me, your face flushed; you were still sobbing, gulping, shedding
tears as you stared at the desolate house. I turned and followed
your gaze, to the front steps and closed door, the balustrades, the
sheltering trees towering above the eaves, the railings and the roof
pitched into the sky, and the window to Olivia's room, dimly lit
but forever empty of the girl we knew.

You had been holding my breath, and by the time I turned
around again you'd backed away and were gone with it, a small
figure in blue jeans and a black sweater, running down the yard
towards the bottom of the driveway, too quickly to say good-bye.

$\mathbf{M}$arian, I have no way of knowing where you are, with whom or in what mood, but you're the only one who might still care to have this told. Your father lives in an empty house, with his empty head full of sleep and forgetfulness, and your mother is steadfastly against the past. And Olivia . . .

When I lit out I went looking for her, and I looked for a long, long time. I stopped in every town I passed through, I peered into every car, I poked down every alley, and I talked until my tongue swelled up and choked my throat. I suspect at last that she does not exist. Or perhaps she does and simply wants to be left alone. In any case she does not exist, except as a product of our mutual recollection — just as the position of a point on the far bank of a river can be fixed as the junction of two observers' gazes on the opposite side. The river is not time, or love, or sympathy; it's just a river, maybe the Mississippi. I can't tell.

So we're the last ones left, and this book is between us. Last night I put the final fat period in place, put my pen aside, and stacked the pages neatly on the side of my desk. Today I will send the whole thing away, and we will see. I hope you'll come upon it one pale, pale blue afternoon when you're idly browsing in a local bookstore.

Sister, the world I wished for has become extinct, and despite these notes what we now remember will soon be lost forever in impermanence; no one will ever know that once, a long time ago and nowhere, there lived a boy (not any boy, but me) and a beautiful young girl (not any girl, but my Olivia), whom he loved, utterly and endlessly. Now every park is public, and every girl has taken her kisses and run away, and no one knows what another one wants. So what was the time? What was it like? This is my last and best testimony: there was a warm glance, a bed with the covers drawn, a bit of lingering weight, an allowance made.

Now tell me, where do young boys and girls get the sweet and terrible bravery that moves them?

About the Author

Jim Lewis was born in Ohio and raised in London and New York. He has degrees in philosophy from Brown University and Columbia University, and has served as an instructor in philosophy and literature at Columbia. His essays have appeared in *Artforum*, *Parkett*, and other art magazines, and he has contributed to exhibition catalogues for the Whitney Museum, the San Francisco Museum of Modern Art, and the Israel Museum. He is a contibuting editor to *Harper's Bazaar*, and a contributing editor and columnist for *Art Issues*.

His short stories have been published in the *Chicago Review*, *Fiction International*, *Columbia Poetry and Prose*, the *Quarterly*, and other publications. *Sister* is his first novel.